HUNGER

as a Factor in
Human Affairs

HUNGER
AS A FACTOR IN
HUMAN AFFAIRS

By PITIRIM A. SOROKIN

Translated and with a Prologue by
ELENA P. SOROKIN

Edited and with an Introduction by
T. LYNN SMITH

A UNIVERSITY OF FLORIDA BOOK

The University Presses of Florida
Gainesville

*Published with the assistance of the
Lilly Endowment, Incorporated
to whom acknowledgment is gratefully extended*

Library of Congress Cataloging in Publication Data

Sorokin, Pitirim Alexandrovitch, 1889–1968.
Hunger as a factor in human affairs.

"A University of Florida book."
Includes bibliographical references.
1. Famines. 2. Social history. I. Title.
HC79.F3S6713 1975 301.5′2 75–11850
ISBN 0–8130–0519–1

DESIGN BY GARY GORE

PRINTED BY KINGSPORT PRESS, INCORPORATED
KINGSPORT, TENNESSEE

In memory of

Pitirim Alexandrovitch Sorokin

ACKNOWLEDGMENTS

The history of *Hunger as a Factor in Human Affairs* is very special. It was written in Russia during the great famine of 1919–21. A prominent Russian publicist, Vityazev-Sedenko, managed to circumvent Communist censorship of this book and, with the cooperation of anti-Communist printers, published it in Leningrad in 1922. The censors nevertheless caught up with the book in its final stage of production and destroyed it. When Pitirim and I were banished from the USSR on September 23, 1922, we smuggled out the proofs of the book; but although the book was saved, it was to remain untouched for fifty years. On learning about these proofs, Professor Philip J. Allen of the University of Virginia asked me to translate them into English, and Professor T. Lynn Smith of the University of Florida graciously consented to take upon himself the tedious task of editing the translation. Thus the present edition came into being.

Mr. Eli Lilly, who organized financial support for the publication of this book through the Lilly Endowment, expressed his desire to dedicate the book to the memory of Pitirim Sorokin, his friend and my beloved husband. The publisher, the University Presses of Florida, gladly concurred.

To make the book more suited to this dedication, the publisher, the editor, and I decided to include illustrations that in some way related to Pitirim's life. When we left the USSR, I took away a few photographs of Pitirim, myself, and our families, taken in Russia between 1917 and 1922. Through exercise of photographic skill, our son Sergei restored these old photographs for publication and made copies of published illustrations of Leningrad showing scenes familiar to Pitirim and myself during our life there. The sources of these are mentioned at appropriate places in the List of Illustrations. Sergei and I added selections from the family album showing

vii

aspects of Pitirim's life in the United States between 1923 and 1968. Except where noted, these photographs were made by family members. We also include the Russian title page from the suppressed edition of this book and a page from a manuscript of Pitirim's dating from the same period.

In view of the memorial aspect of this edition, and also because I was a witness to life under conditions of famine and militant communism, it has seemed appropriate to present a few reminiscences of that time in an introductory essay, as well as additional biographical material in the descriptions of the figures. Accordingly, this has been done.

Elena Sorokin

CONTENTS

LIST OF ILLUSTRATIONS

1. Annissya Rimskikh, Pitirim's aunt and a Komi peasant woman. She was a loving mother to Pitirim after his own mother died when he was three years old. Her husband, Vassiliy, lived by hunting, trapping, and fishing in the vast forest lands of northern Russia, and they made their home in the village of Rymia. People in the area called Vassiliy *koldun* (wise man or shaman), partly in recognition of his ability to reduce swelling from dislocated joints. Both husband and wife exerted great influence on Pitirim during his early childhood.

2. Pitirim's younger brother, Prokopiy, bookkeeper in a peasant cooperative in the town of Velikiy Ustyug, and his daughter, Tamara, as they appeared on July 27, 1929. He described the yard of his house on the back of the picture: "A wicker basket is on the roof of the shed; the door behind leads to the hayloft. A door to the granary is to the left, and that to the barn is in the center." The words reflect the semirural quality of life in this small, ancient town. Prokopiy died in prison in the 1930s when the peasant cooperative movement was persecuted by the Soviet government.

3. Pitirim Sorokin in 1917 as secretary to Prime Minister Alexander Kerensky.

4. Elena Petrovna Baratinskaya-Sorokina in 1917, the year of her marriage.

5. Pitirim and Elena on a visit to Elena's family in Tambov, USSR, shortly before their banishment abroad in 1922. Left to right: Pitirim; Elena; her half-brother, Kolya, who was killed on the German front in 1941; Kolya's friend, Yura; Mme. Baratinsky; Dr. P. Baratinsky; and a medical colleague, who tripped the shutter.

14. The title page from the suppressed 1922 edition of this book. The Russian title reads "Golod kak Faktor."

15. A page from the manuscript of *The Sociology of Revolution*, written in 1923, when Sorokin was living in Czechoslovakia. That work represents an expansion of the materials discussed in chapter 10 of this book.

16. Pitirim lecturing to his class in Emerson Hall at Harvard University during the late 1930s. Photograph by Arthur Griffin (with his permission).

17. On vacation at our summer camp on Lake Memphremagog in southern Quebec. For two months each year Pitirim never wrote a line or read a serious book.

18. Our sons, Peter and Sergei, at the camp in 1948. Peter had just entered Harvard University and Sergei was a junior at Winchester High School.

19. A characteristic picture of Pitirim writing one of his scholarly books.

20. The family at home in Winchester, Massachusetts, in 1949. Left to right: Peter, Elena, Sergei, and Pitirim. The couch has been artificially lengthened one place in this composite made from two sequential photographs.

Illustrations follow page 120.

INTRODUCTION

As the reader will quickly discover, this is an extraordinary book. Its author was an extraordinary man. And it was written under extraordinary circumstances, circumstances about as difficult as it is possible to imagine, circumstances that always were grim, frequently gruesome, and often ghastly. Nevertheless, although it was written more than fifty years ago, it is eminently timely for mankind as it enters the last quarter of the twentieth century. In the 1970s, chronic, gnawing hunger is the daily lot of hundreds of millions of people. Malnutrition and actual starvation annually still afflict hundreds of millions of people. And as the English edition of this book goes to press, famine by no means is confined to sub-Sahara Africa and large portions of the Indian-Bangladesh sub-continent. It is not too irresponsible to predict that for many years to come this book will be read and studied by people in many lands long after most of the current works in anthropology, economics, geography, political science, and sociology are almost completely forgotten.

Pitirim Alexandrovitch Sorokin was born in the village of Turya, Yarensky County, Vologda Province, Russia, on January 21, 1889.[1] His father was Russian and his mother was of the Komi group of people. The Komi, as described by Sorokin himself, are "a tall, strong, and healthy people." Racially, they are a mixture of Nordic, Alpine, and some Asiatic stocks. Linguistically, their native tongue is related to the Ugro-Finnish, and almost all the Komi also spoke Russian, even when Sorokin was a child. This people, whose sociocultural world was the one in which his formative years were spent

1. The materials in this and the next three paragraphs have been taken from Pitirim A. Sorokin, *A Long Journey* (New Haven, Conn.: College and University Press, 1963), pp. 11–39.

and whom he idealized throughout his long lifetime, were among
the most literate in Russia. They had a rich heritage of folk music,
art, and religious ceremonies. They lived by farming, supplemented
by hunting, trapping, and lumbering. They were peasants, but they
had never been serfs. Sorokin's father was an itinerant artisan who
went about from village to village painting churches and embossing
and gilding the silver covers of the ikons, the so-called *rizy*.

Sorokin's earliest recollections were connected with the death of
his mother which occurred when he was about three years old. One
of his mother's sisters had a major part in his care when he was a
very small child, and he returned to her home periodically as long
as he remained in Russia. Very early, however, he accompanied his
father in the wanderings from village to village. After his wife's
death, Sorokin's father, who apparently was among the kindest and
most considerate of men when he was sober, frequently sought solace
in alcohol, and the influence of this turned him into a beast. During
one drunken spree, when Pitirim was eleven, his father attacked him
and his older brother, then aged fourteen, with a hammer, damaging
the older boy's arm and marring the younger one's lip so badly that
he carried the scar to his grave. This caused the two boys to leave
their father, whom they never saw again; on their own for two years,
they followed their father's occupation. Then, at age thirteen, Pitirim
gained admission to a "normal" school and began the formal part of
his education.

Early in life Sorokin personally became well acquainted with
hunger and starvation. As indicated in his autobiography, when the
distance between villages was great, they often had to spend the
night on the road with very little or no food. There were no public
eating establishments in the villages, and frequently they "could not
even buy food from the peasants." Their clothing was not at all adequate for the climate and often in the winter they were "half-frozen."
Their lodging generally was a "rented 'half' of a peasant home," and
they either prepared their food themselves or sometimes it was done
by a peasant woman. When times were good they had sufficient food,
but "during periods of unemployment we starved." He attributed the
fact of his somewhat "rickety legs" to malnutrition.

The child's early schooling was erratic, to say the least. In his
autobiography he states that he could not remember "how, when, or
where" he learned to read and write, and conjectures that he probably
picked up a knowledge of how to read, write, and make arithmetical

computations from his father and brother. In one way or another, however, he did learn the three Rs and he increased the elements of these by reading voraciously "all sorts of books obtainable in the Komi villages." According to his wife these books included inexpensive editions of all the great classics, volumes that were issued as supplements to the popular magazine *Niva*, which had a large circulation. "This rapacious reading" acquainted him with the works of Pushkin, Gogol, Tolstoi, Turgenev, and Dostoevskii, and through it he also came to know books such as Mark Twain's *The Prince and the Pauper*, some of the novels written by Charles Dickens, books dealing with the lives of the saints, some fairy tales, and various treatises on history and natural science. Village schoolteachers, clergymen, and peasants took interest in the boy and helped him by lending books, giving advice, and offering "food and warm clothes in the winter season." The religion of his people "was Russian Orthodox mixed with vestiges of the pre-Christian pagan beliefs," so that the two sets of rituals naturally became his own. Their influence was reinforced through his work in and around the churches, where he met and conversed with many priests and lay leaders. Some of these were learned men, and they greatly "influenced the early formation of my personality and values."

This is not the place to supply more details about the forces and events that shaped the life of one of the world's most creative and productive scholars.[2] Late in his career, however, he prepared a suc-

2. Moreover, rather extensive biographical materials in which his fruitful career is traced are fairly easy to consult. In addition to his autobiography, *A Long Journey*, cited above, Sorokin himself published a 310-page volume, *Leaves from a Russian Diary* (New York: E. P. Dutton & Company, 1924), material from the diary he kept between January 1917 and September 24, 1922, the day he and his wife crossed the frontier in banishment from their native land to which they never returned. This is drawn upon heavily in the pages that follow. Sorokin also summarized his life and work in a substantial contribution, "Sociology of My Mental Life," which appeared in Philip J. Allen, ed., *Pitirim A. Sorokin in Review* (Durham, N.C.: Duke University Press, 1963), pp. 1–36. Two small volumes by Carle C. Zimmerman, with whom he was associated during his years at Minnesota and Harvard, and with whom he collaborated in the production of two monumental books, *Principles of Rural-Urban Sociology* (New York: Henry Holt & Co., 1929) and *A Systematic Source Book in Rural Sociology*, 3 vols. (Minneapolis: University of Minnesota Press, 1930–32), also contain much important biographical information about Sorokin. These are *Sorokin—The World's Greatest Sociologist*

cinct summary of his life for use in *Twentieth Century Authors*,[3] and for present purposes it would be difficult to find a more germane summary. The materials in the following paragraphs are taken from it.

This sketch of his life opens with the generalization that "Eventfulness has possibly been the most significant feature of my life-adventure." Writing at the age of sixty-three, he indicated that he had already passed through several cultural "atmospheres," including the "pastoral-hunter's culture of the Komi," an agricultural one, the urban cultures of Russia and Europe, and, finally, "the megalopolitan technical culture of the United States." The child of a poor itinerant artisan and a peasant mother, in the course of his lifetime he was a farmhand, "an itinerant artisan, factory worker, clerk, teacher, conductor of a choir, revolutionary, political prisoner, journalist, student, editor of a metropolitan paper, member of Kerensky's cabinet, exile," a professor in Russian, Czech, and American universities, and an internationally known scholar. Other features of his life experience were no less eventful. He was imprisoned six times, "three under the Czarist and three under the Communist regimes." In one of these he had "the unforgettable experience of a man condemned to death and daily, during six weeks, expecting his execution by the Communist firing squad." He came to know what it meant to be both "damned and praised, to be banished," and to lose his brothers and friends in political struggles. He was convinced that these "life-experiences" had taught him more than all the books he had read and the lectures to which he had listened.

He was eleven years old before he saw even a small town. "Incidentally" he learned to read and write, and "incidentally" he came to study in a "normal school." With father and mother both dead, at the age of eleven he became "independent," that is penniless, but free to chart his own course in life. While earning his own living he "was a student of a teachers' college, arrested and imprisoned four months before graduation because of my political activities in 1906." Later as a starving, hunted revolutionary he studied at a night school, was

(Saskatoon: University of Saskatchewan, 1968) and *Sociological Theories of Pitirim A. Sorokin* (Bombay: Thacker & Co. Ltd., 1973). In addition Joseph B. Ford gives an important summary of Sorokin's life in his "Life and Work of Pitirim Alexandrovich Sorokin (1889–1968)," *Revue Internationale de Sociologie*, ser. 2, vol. 7, no. 2 (1971), pp. 820–37.

3. See S. J. Kunitz, ed., *Twentieth Century Authors: A Biographical Dictionary*, 1st supp. (New York: H. B. Wilson, 1955), pp. 936–37.

a student in the Psycho-Neurological Institute, and a student at the University of St. Petersburg. Through two more imprisonments he gained more first-hand experience in criminology and penology, the fields in which he did his graduate work and began his career as a university professor. While still in his junior year at the university he published his first book: *Crime and Punishment: Service and Reward* (1913). In 1916 he received the degree of Magister of Criminal Law, and in 1922 the degree of Doctor of Sociology from the University of St. Petersburg.

With the outburst of the Russian revolution he became one of the founders of the Russian Peasant Soviet (later dissolved and dispersed by the Communists), and the editor of *The Will of the People*, a metropolitan daily. In the revolutionary government, he was a member and executive secretary of the Council of the Russian Republic, in Prime Minister Kerensky's cabinet, and a leader in the Russian Constituent Assembly (also dispersed by the Communists).

From the beginning of the revolution he vigorously opposed Lenin, Trotsky, Kamanev, and the other Bolsheviki leaders, and for this reason, on January 3, 1918, he was arrested "and imprisoned for four months in the Russian Bastille, the Fortress of Peter and Paul." When he was released from this he resumed his struggle against the Communists, and "was one of the group which engineered the overthrow of the Communist Government in Archangel in 1918." In October of that same year he was arrested again and condemned to death by the Communist government of Vologda Province. "After six weeks of waiting to be shot, by Lenin's order" he was freed and returned to his academic work at the University of St. Petersburg. There he established courses in sociology, founded and headed a department of sociology, and before he was banished in 1922 "published five volumes in law and sociology."

To supplement what Sorokin himself has said about his role in revolutionary Russia, it is possible to add some important fragments from the materials supplied by Edgar Sisson, "Special Representative of President Wilson," relative to Sorokin's activities in late 1917. In his volume *One Hundred Red Days: A Personal Chronicle of the Bolshevik Revolution*,[4] Sisson dwells upon the efforts of the Americans in St. Petersburg during the upheaval. Among other things, "as a warning," a film made by an American firm entitled "The Ruin

4. New Haven: Yale University Press, 1931.

of a Nation" was shown in the cinemas of Petrograd. Just at this time "Pitirim Sorokin, who had proclaimed the ruin of the Russian nation in the Democratic Council, published in *Volia Naroda* [the organ of the Social Revolutionary Party]—N. 121, Oct. 17—an historical paper under the same title, 'The Ruin of a Nation' and this would-be 'Socialist' presented to the Russian readers the same prospects for Russia as were shown in the film." [5]

The Bolsheviks were quick to seize upon the identity of titles and to couple Sorokin's name with insinuations that he was a paid agent of foreign interests. Says Sisson:

> They were having cynical sport with the Americans and with poor Mme Breshkovskaya [leader of the Social Revolutionary Party, and "grandmother" of the Revolution], who did not emerge from hiding. The *Volia Naroda* on December 8, unable to communicate with her, printed, as translated, the following:
>
> ### Regarding an Unworthy Attack
>
> "In yesterday's issue of the *Znamia Truda*, the organ of the Socialist Revolutionary extremists, a Letter to the Editor has been published under the heading 'My Conscience Bids Me Speak Out.' In this letter, Mr. Bakrylov, former private secretary to Mme Breshkovskaya, the author of ultra-patriotic appeals to the soldiers, and of pamphlets on the war, the land, etc., suddenly turning to an extremist makes an unworthy attempt to dishonor Mme Breshkovskaya. He makes the basest insinuations in reference to financial means placed by her American friends at the disposal of the Grandmother and the committee for civil instruction. Mme Breshkovskaya is out of town for the present but we will do our utmost to enable her to give in one of the next issues of our newspaper her answer to the unworthy attack of Mr. Bakrylov. The Editors." [6]

Sisson never learned of any reply by her, and he says that the Bolsheviks undoubtedly knew "where she was, sneeringly but per-

5. Ibid., p. 45.
6. Ibid., p. 48.

haps not ungallantly protecting her, and winked to each other when she slipped past their guards."

With Sorokin, it was a different story.

> There was mettle in the man Sorokin, whom Bakrylov also attacked. In the *Volia Naroda* he came back fighting, thus: "Mr. Bakrylov, who has suddenly transformed himself into a radical from his previous shape of a patriot, devotes the following lines to me in his slovenly article, in which he is trying to discredit E. K. Breshko-Breshkovskaya. [Mr. Sorokin quoted the paragraph referring to himself in the Bakrylov letter.]
>
> "Anent this statement I consider it necessary to note the following: If Mr. Bakrylov imputes by his statement that I am in sympathy with the film 'The Loss of a Nation,' then I declare candidly that I consider this film very valuable and very useful, and would be extremely glad if someone could spread this and similar films all over Russia. Should, however, Mr. Bakrylov, by drawing a parallel between the film and my article which has nothing in common with the film except the title, insinuate something else, any commercial reasons in particular, then I would ask him to have the courage to formulate his thought clearly in order that I may bring him before a court of arbitration as a dirty liar."
>
> The challenge went unanswered. Besides, very soon, there were no courts of arbitration. Sorokin had a snappy last word in the newspaper controversy.[7]

Hunger as a Factor in Human Affairs is the second of Sorokin's major accomplishments during the second of the four rather distinct careers he had in the course of a long and highly productive life. This one began early in 1919, or very shortly after the Bolsheviki released him from prison, or even more importantly from the ordeal of expecting day and night that every hour might be his last. On several occasions during his imprisonment officials summarily executed some of his cellmates in the cells themselves; daily lists of the names of his fellows were read out, those designated were taken out, and almost immediately he heard the shots that put an end to

7. Ibid., pp. 48–49.

their lives. That his own life did not end then and there was due
to the personal intervention of Lenin, and Lenin's writings also are
the only documentation I have found for one of the most important
decisions Sorokin made during his lifetime. The materials themselves are in an article which appeared in *Pravda* on November 21,
1918, an article written by Lenin entitled "Valuable Admissions by
Pitirim Sorokin." Obviously it was written as an important feature
of Lenin's campaign to enlist the support of the "lower" and "middle"
peasants, and to this fact Sorokin owed his release from prison and
the lifting, temporarily, of the threat of execution. (In this connection it is important to note that Sorokin received more than three
million votes, most of them from the peasants, when he was elected
to the Constituent Assembly.) Fortunately, too, Lenin included the
information about Sorokin's resignation from his party (and politics)
and the Constituent Assembly.[8] The opening sentences in this article
are: " 'Pravda' today gives space to a remarkably interesting letter
by Pitirim Sorokin, to which the attention of all Communists should
be particularly drawn. In this letter, which was printed in the
Izvestia of the North Dvina Executive Committee, Pitirim Sorokin
announces his resignation from the Party of the Right Socialist-
Revolutionaries and his abjuration of the title of member of the Constituent Assembly. The motives of the author of the letter are that he
finds difficulty in providing effective political recipes, not only for
others, but even for himself, and that therefore he 'renounces all
politics.' Pitirim Sorokin writes: 'The past year has taught me one
truth: politicians may make mistakes, politics may be socially useful,
but also be socially harmful, whereas work in the sphere of science
and public education is always useful and is needed by the
people. . . .' The letter is signed: 'Lecturer in the Petrograd University and the Psycho-Neurological Institute, former member of the
Constituent Assembly and former Member of the Party of Socialist-
Revolutionaries, Pitirim Sorokin.' " [9]

Thus disillusioned with politics of any type, and very much alive
and active, late in 1918 Sorokin threw himself heart and soul into a
strenuous life of scientific work. The extremely behavioristic nature

8. See the translation of the article in A. Fineberg, ed., *V. I. Lenin,
Selected Works* (New York: International Publishers, n.d.), 8:144–53 and
the notes to it on pp. 409–11.
9. Ibid., p. 144.

of the frame of reference used in *Hunger as a Factor in Human Affairs*, his close association with Pavlov in the work at the Institute of the Brain, and the content of his *System of Sociology*, *Social Mobility*, *Sociology of Revolution*, and other books written between 1919 and 1930 are evidences of the dedication to pragmatic, empirical study which characterized the second of Sorokin's professional careers. He first wrote and published his systematic treatment of general sociology, and immediately thereafter produced the book now offered to the public in its English translation.

The conditions under which *Hunger as a Factor in Human Affairs* was written have been summarized by Sorokin himself under the caption "Life in Death—1919–22," in the abridgement of some chapters in his *Leaves from a Russian Diary*, which he used as chapter 9 of his autobiography, *A Long Journey;* and his wife, Elena Sorokin, herself an accomplished plant cytologist, gives us vivid details in her prologue to this volume. Even so it does not seem out of place to summarize here a few of the almost unbearable or intolerable features of the existence the Sorokins were leading while he was writing his *System of Sociology* and the book, now translated, which followed it immediately.[10] With the materials available this can best be done by quoting a few of the extracts from *Leaves from a Russian Diary.* His writing and the work at the University required the utmost dedication. He says that while writing,

> I sat with all my wraps on, gloves on my hands, and my feet rolled in rags. From time to time I got up and exercised to limber my half-frozen limbs. In the afternoons and evenings I went to my work, walking from one Institute to another, from eight to ten miles a day. Exhausted from these exertions and from constant hunger, I went early to bed—unless it was my turn to stand guard all night. . . .
>
> Depression overcame me everytime I went to the University. Entering the campus, you heard no more the sound of young voices and laughter. The place was dark except in the physics

10. The *System* as planned by Sorokin was intended as a three-volume work. However, after somehow managing to write and publish the first two volumes, Sorokin says "I postponed the writing of the third volume in order to study at first hand phenomena typical of the Revolution, [and I] began an investigation of the influence of hunger upon human behavior, social life and social organization" (*A Long Journey*, p. 188).

building where, by some miracle, Professor Khvolson managed
to get enough kerosene to keep his laboratory windows alight.
Lectures were given only in the evening, because all day the
students were struggling to get a living. As I walked through
the familiar [university corridor] I heard only the echo of my
own footsteps.

·   ·   ·   ·   ·

Passing the office of the University at the end of the main
building, I often read, by the flickering gleam of the "don't
breathe" lamp, the following announcement:

"By order of the Petrograd Soviet there will be, tomorrow
and the day after, compulsory work for professors, assistants,
instructors, clerks, and other University people. The work will
consist of transportation of timbers from one place to another.
Persons whose names begin with A to M must be at the
Admiralty Quay tomorrow morning at ten o'clock. Others must
be at the same place at the same hour on the following day.
Those who disobey this order will be arrested as counterrevolutionaries."

·   ·   ·   ·   ·

The faculty visited the University only for meetings and
conferences. In our reading-room, as everywhere, desolation
reigned. We had no new books or magazines, no scientific journals. Cut off from the whole world, we knew nothing of what
our colleagues abroad were doing. We were absolutely cut off
even from our colleagues in other Russian Universities. When
we met for dinner, the professors, standing in line with dishes
and spoons, which everyone had to bring from home, were like
the beggars' line at church doors in former times. After a half
hour wait these professors, many of them world-famous, sat
down to a dish of hot water with a little potatoes and cabbage
boiled in it. No bread, no salt, unless someone could contribute
a little from contraband stores. As we ate we talked, or tried to
talk, of ordinary topics of our work, but mostly the conversation
turned on who had been arrested that day, who had been executed, who had died. Sometimes our conversation was of a
timeliness rather ghastly. Professors Vvedensky and Swere enlightened us as to the number of calories in the food we ate, of

its chemical composition, and told us about how long human life could be supported on such a diet. Professor S. told of the dogs that had died of hunger in his laboratory and of their conditioned reflexes. Dr. L. gave us the chemical composition of the brains of twenty men and women who had died of want. Psychologists and psychiatrists gave us their studies of revolutionary psychoses and neuroses. We could not record very many of these discoveries because we had almost no paper, pens, or pencils. We had to give them to each other orally.

When we finished our dinner and our talk we went home. "Good-bye, I hope you will be alive tomorrow," was our usual parting. As the days went by fewer and fewer of us were left to say it (pp. 224, 227–28).

"What we had feared most of all for Russia in 1921 happened." With these words Sorokin began his gripping account of the stark realities of the great famine that decimated people by the millions in Russia that tragic year. "Looking over a map of the whole country, with provinces marked by harvests bad or totally lacking, we said: 'Twenty five million people, at least, are fated to die of starvation this winter unless the world comes to the aid.' We said this long before the government and Maxim Gorky issued their wild appeals to the nations of the earth to help the starving masses. . . . When the appalling famine of 1921 came, there was no remedy. No provinces had the necessary surplus of corn." [11]

This year of the great starvation also was the one, perhaps inevitably, in which Sorokin wrote the book that now is being offered to the English-speaking world. As mentioned, the constant preoccupation with food and hunger on his part, and all those with whom he was associated, caused him to postpone work on the third volume of his *System of Sociology*, and with his students and the close cooperation of his associates in the Institute of the Brain (Pavlov and Bekhterev) to investigate the influence of hunger upon human behavior, social life, and social organization. That fall, too, he had been forbidden to do any teaching. Accordingly "left with no work except research in the Institute of the Brain and in the Historical and Sociological Institute of the University, I felt myself comparatively free. I had studied city starvation, with myself as one of the subjects,

11. *Leaves from a Russian Diary*, pp. 282–83.

and now I had a very great laboratory in the starving villages of Russia. In the winter of 1921 I started out for the famine districts of Samara and Saratov provinces to make a scientific investigation of mass starvation." [12] The indescribable horror of mass starvation he encountered on this journey profoundly affected his life and work. If there had been any tendency on his part to deal in pure abstractions in his *System of Sociology*, a failure to ground his theory in the reality of actual, concrete, living societies (a malady by no means unknown among the sociologists of that day and of the present), this experience was of the greatest importance for the science of sociology. In any case, for the next ten years while he was producing the sociological treatises that brought him world renown and the invitation to found and head a department of sociology at Harvard University, the factual, empirical, pragmatic study of actual functioning societies fully occupied his time and attention. These facts alone should temper the judgment of failure which Sorokin made of these efforts: "I will acknowledge at once that in this intention I completely failed [the intention to do a scientific investigation of mass starvation]. No scientific study was I able to make, but I saw a famine; I now know what it means. What I learned in those awful provinces was far more than any scientific investigation could have given me. My nervous system, accustomed to many horrors in the years of the Revolution, broke down completely before the spectacle of the actual starvation of millions in my ravaged country. If I came out less an investigator, I do not think I came out less a man, less an enemy of any group of men capable of inflicting such suffering on the human race." [13]

The intense emotional crisis produced by this visit to the famine-stricken villages of Russia may well have portended the fourth of Sorokin's careers, that in which, following retirement at Harvard, he founded and carried on the work in his Harvard Research Center in Creative Altruism.[14] In any case, throughout life he carried deeply engraved impressions left upon his being by those horrible experiences. They must have been very potent indeed during the days he was writing *Hunger as a Factor in Human Affairs*.

12. Ibid., p. 284.
13. Ibid., pp. 284–85.
14. See, for example, Pitirim A. Sorokin, *The Ways and Power of Love: Types, Factors, and Techniques of Moral Transformation* (Boston: Beacon Press, 1954).

Little need be said about the actual editing of the text of the translation. The translator and the editor have worked together closely on every page of the manuscript. They both recognized that adequate translation is very difficult, perhaps impossible. They have been aided in this case by the fact that much writing on the subjects involved has been done in English by Sorokin himself, especially in *The Sociology of Revolution* (which is an expansion of chapter 10 of this work), *Leaves from a Russian Diary*, and *Social Mobility*. To the best of their ability they have attempted to present accurately the author's ideas as written in his own characteristic style.

T. Lynn Smith

PROLOGUE

The greater part of *Hunger as a Factor in Human Affairs* was written in Petrograd-Leningrad during the years 1918–19 and was completed in Tsarskoe Selo in 1922. During this time the Communist Government tried to create a truly communist society in a country that had been defeated in World War I and was devastated. This experiment was a complete failure; the communist society lasted only until the Kronstadt Rebellion of sailors which occurred in 1921. Thereafter Lenin introduced the New Economic Policy which permitted a limited degree of private ownership.

Since both Pitirim and myself were involuntary members of the communist society, we experienced all its deprivations, including nutritive deficiency, and from our own experiences could vouch for the material described in this book. This is how we lived at that time.

The University of Petrograd, the Academy of Science, and many other scientific and technical schools were located in Vasilievskii Ostrov, a section of Petrograd, which was not unlike many American cities in the arrangement of its streets; these were called "lines," they ran parallel to each other, and were designated by numbers. The houses along the streets were mostly apartment houses, closely adjoined and five to six stories high. Each had a separate inside yard accessible through an iron gate. The front entrance had an elevator, but the rear entrance had only stairs. During the time I am describing, however, the elevator did not work. There was no central heating. In the past the apartments had been heated by wood burned in famous Russian stoves that were constructed of brick and faced with glazed tiles. These stoves kept their heat very well even during the coldest weather. The wood had been furnished daily by the custodian (*dvornik*) who carried it on his back to all the floors of the apartment house. In this revolutionary period, however, there was no wood available for people to heat their apartments, and consequently the plumbing froze in practically all of the houses. Moreover, the electric power had been shut off in the apartment houses.

The winter of 1918–19 was exceptionally cold. At that time we lived in the fifth floor apartment of Mme Darmolatova, a dear friend of ours who asked us to move in, partly in order to prevent the intrusion of strangers, who could be quartered there by the ordinance of the District Soviets, who allotted a certain square yardage of living space per person. The house in which we lived had been confiscated from the previous owners and was now the property of the government. No rent was collected, but each house had a resident commissar whose duty was to register with the police the passports of the tenants, to watch the activities of the people, to report any suspicious doings, and to appoint representatives of each apartment for night duty at the gates of the yard. Since the front entrances of the apartment complex were permanently closed, the only way a person could enter his home was through the yard gates which after midnight were locked by heavy bolts and keys. As a result people usually did not venture outdoors at night, and thus a natural curfew came into existence. The only people to be seen out of doors after midnight were the detachments of the Special Commission (Cheka), who went about their general business of searching for counterrevolutionaries and speculators, and on some occasions had orders to arrest specified individuals. On one memorable occasion the husband of Madame D.'s daughter Nadya was on night duty at the gate when he saw the approaching patrol. Since the house commissar was not there, he rang the bell to our apartment in order to warn of the approaching search. Naturally, we immediately hid those few little treasures we still had and then were ready for the red guards. The electric power came on just as the undesirable visitors approached. This time they were searching for arms, hidden food, jewelry, but fortunately not for my husband.

With darkness arriving early in the day during January and December at the latitude of Petrograd, without electric power for lights, and with insufficient kerosene for the old-fashioned parlor lamps, human ingenuity created "*koptilka*," which means something that smokes. It was a simple device of a little jar with a wick drawn through the cork. It consumed very little kerosene and produced a very dim light. This was the illumination under which a considerable part of *Hunger as a Factor in Human Affairs* was written.

As I have mentioned, the plumbing system was completely frozen. We could use the sewer pipes, but water had to be carried by pail all five flights from the hydrant in the yard and therefore was used sparingly. In the morning we had to break the ice that had formed in the pail. Since the house was otherwise unheated, and because the winter temperature in Petrograd sometimes reached forty below zero, the people had to invent something to warm the house and cook some food. In consequence the famous *"burzhuika"* (feminine of bourgeois) was invented. It was a little sheet iron stove with a long extending pipe which fitted into a round hole cut in the window pane. Anything could be burned in this stove. But since there was no wood available, even the little needed for the small stove, books, furniture, fences, and wooden blocks of pavement were broken up and used as fuel (many streets in Petrograd used to be paved with octangular wooden blocks). Even this wood could be obtained only when the militia was not in sight.

On one occasion we received a notification that wood was to be distributed to citizens at the district Soviet. I took my sled and went there to obtain a slip letting me know where to get my quota of wood. On arrival at the spot indicated in my order, I found neither stored wood nor anybody to distribute it. As I turned to go back home, I noticed three sailors gaily approaching the place. They had the name "Avrora" written on their hats with the long streamers floating in the air. The cruiser *Avrora* had stormed the Winter Palace during the February Revolution and was one of the deciding factors in the downfall of the tsarist regime. Afterwards the sailors from the *Avrora* enjoyed a privileged position like the geese that saved Rome; Trotsky called them "the Beauty and Pride of the Russian Revolution." Noticing that these "beauties" had with them heavy tools and gear suitable for breaking things, I stopped and asked them, "Where do I get the wood according to this order?" They looked at me and said, "This house, you have to break it." In front of me was a beautiful wooden house, a so-called *"osobnyak"* (single house), which before the revolution obviously had belonged to some wealthy owner, or bourgeois—*"burzhui"* in the current terminology. Before I had time to ask why we should destroy such a fine building, the wreckers had torn a large gap in the middle. The sailors were very efficient and powerful in destruction. They gave me a door and a few planks, and I went back home wondering how I would be able to get this door up the stairs and then how we would saw it. My husband met me at the gate of the yard and easily carried the door up to the fifth floor. Late into the night the monotonous sound of our dull saw was heard. But at last we had enough fuel for our "*burzhuika*" to heat some water for bathing and to wash our underwear.

Officially we both were connected with the university, my husband as the founder of the chair and the first professor of sociology, and I as an "aspirant" in botany. Russian universities did not have graduate students. Requirements for graduation were much higher compared with American universities, and aspirants for advanced degrees had no further course work to complete. The duty of the "aspirant" was to study the selected subject, to write an original thesis, and after two or three years pass a rigorous examination on the thesis and the field to obtain a degree of Magister. Under normal conditions of life this was an excellent system in which the young scholar was not burdened by prescribed courses and by teaching undergraduates. He or she could dedicate full time to study, since there was an adequate stipend connected with the position. Nevertheless, during the times I am describing neither the salary of the professor nor the stipend of the aspirant was worth anything. It is true we received paper money, thousands of rubles, but at the black market it would hardly buy a loaf of bread.

The most important remuneration for work during this period was ration cards. There were three categories of ration cards. Manual workers received the first; intellectuals, artists, teachers, office workers, etc., received the second; and the parasites of society —housewives and old people, especially of bourgeois origin—received the third. I suppose that housewives were included in the third category because in their communist society everybody was expected to work. Children were placed in children's homes, and all meals were taken in the public dining halls, so that there was little for the housewife to do at home. The walls of the dining halls were decorated with the slogans "Who does not work, does not eat!" and "Proletarians of the world unite!" Those issued the first category of ration cards received about one pound of black bread per day, those of the second category a half a pound, and of the third a quarter of a pound. The bread had a large amount of additives, such as bran, which was good, and chaff, which was very bad. People also received monthly rations of two pounds of sugar, some vegetable oil, and frozen potatoes, but the main meals were served in dining halls (*stolovki*), where every person had to register his card beforehand. Most frequently the first course was soup made of water, a small amount of cabbage, and salted herring; the second course was millet cereal. In Eastern Europe millet is used as a food for man and fowls, but in the United States it is grown chiefly for fodder. Later on, the Soviet citizenry had so much millet gruel that, when a modernistic sculptor made a bust of Karl Marx with his beard protruding horizontally, somebody plastered the beard with cereal and inscribed the words "Eat it yourself!"

Even those holding first category cards could not live on the rations furnished; some obtained extra food as privileged Communist party members, while others received supplements at the factories where they worked, or else speculated on the black market. The middle-aged and elderly intellectuals suffered the most. Physically they were not strong enough to go through all the risks of obtaining food from the speculators, for detachments of the Cheka and the militia were busy all the time. Many of these people just died from hunger. Daily we saw mournful processions of people drawing toward the cemetery a sled with the coffin of their beloved one.

With the exception of the official trucks and automobiles, there was very little traffic on the streets. The streetcars were functioning and the ride was free. However, it was very difficult to get into the cars because they were packed to capacity, and many people hung on the steps, on the bumpers, and on other protrusions of the vehicle. Deserters from the front who did not go home to their villages sought opportunity in the city and meanwhile took pleasure rides on the streetcars. Later all these idle people were sent to their destinations, and rides once more became possible. The majority of the people, however, just walked along the snow-covered streets wearing their "*valenki*" (peasants' felt boots) which were warm and soft and well suited for that purpose. I once saw a ballerina perform a dance in those boots.

Our daily activities were conditioned by hunger and the necessity to get food. First thing in the morning we had to bring water from the hydrant in the yard and carry it to the fifth floor. Then we had to prepare on the "*burzhuika*" tea or coffee—so-called—from roasted wheat grains, after which we had to stand in a long line for the daily ration of bread. Furthermore, we had to walk about two miles to the university dining hall, where our cards were registered, to have dinner. The supper meal could be taken out to bring home. Since we had been for some time on a near starvation diet, and since the energy spent on all this walking and other activities had to be replenished, the thought of how to get more food was never out of my mind.

In the third chapter of this book, "Changes in Human Behavior during Starvation," my husband wrote of a considerable decline in his mental capacity during March and April of 1919, and attributed it to nutritional deficiency or deficiency starvation. In spite of this he remained a keen observer of human behavior and of current events, and continued to write and to carry out other intellectual activities. As for myself, I put aside my work on geobotany and ecology based on material that I had collected in expeditions along the Volga River during the previous three summers and devoted myself entirely to the illegal procurement of food.

For one thing there were the black markets, where barter trade flourished, but frequent raids by militia made this adventure hazardous. There were also speculators operating in their apartments. Friends gave you the addresses, which were changed frequently, but this operation had its own risk. The speculators were often caught and arrested. Then a special agent was usually left in the apartment to catch the unaware customer. Fortunately, I was not caught in any of my visits. At different times it was possible to obtain flour, butter, cereal, potatoes, or meat from the speculators. The trade took the form of barter for linens, rings, dresses, or any other goods that escaped seizure by the communists. The city speculators charged a very high price.

To obtain more profitable trade for your belongings, it was necessary to go to the villages. Once my friend and I devised such a plan. Because travel by railroad was free, requiring only an official permit or "*kommandirovka*" from one's place of work, we went to the commissar of the university, who was a young sailor replacing the most esteemed former president, and told him that we needed to travel to Novgorod province to get samples of wheat from different peasants in order to study the amount of weeds in the grain samples. Whether he believed us or not I do not know, but we got the permit and an official certificate with his signature. I prepared a number of small bags and labeled them with the names of fictitious peasants.

My friend, however, did not bother to do this and took just one big bag. We traveled by freight train. On the outside of the car was written, "forty people, or eight horses." There were no seats, so we just sat on the floor. After two or three hours of travel we arrived at the station we had in mind and proceeded to the homes of the peasants, whom we knew, and concluded our barter. I put the wheat into my prepared bags and carried them open in a basket. My friend became apprehensive that she did not have special bags and decided to hide her wheat in her coat, by pinning the bag to the front of her dress. No sooner had we arrived at the station to take the train home, then the red militiaman grabbed her by the chest and, with the word "wheat," led her to the commissar of the station. I followed her, and we awaited our turn to address the commissar, as there were many others ahead of us who had been caught. When it came I stepped forward, and, showing the commissar my permit, told him, "Tovarishch, I cannot understand what is the matter with tovarishch red militiaman; apparently he cannot read. Here is the official certificate from the university commissar testifying that we need this grain for our research, here is his official signature and the seal of the university." The station commissar replied, "Ignorance, ignorance, what can you do about it?" and let us go. So we came safely home and had wheat "*kasha*" for many days. Subsequently, we made several more trips, but they were uneventful.

Soon it became customary for scientific people to become attached to more than one institution, particularly to the agricultural academies, which had experimental farms and provided dividends in the form of produce and meat. Pitirim and I were both on the staff of the Institute of Agronomy. On one occasion we heard that meat would be distributed to the staff members and workers at a certain place. I took my sled and went to Kamennyi Ostrov, another part of Petrograd some miles away. On arrival I was told to go to the barn and help myself to meat. I opened the door of the barn, and to my great amazement saw carcasses of eight frozen horses lying on their backs with their feet extended in air. Soon people came apparently from the animal husbandry department and began to saw and dismember the horseflesh. I received for my portion a nice piece of rump, and when the man in charge told us that we could have parts of the heads and feet for extra pieces, I took some for my friends. For them it was the greatest of gifts.

The living conditions improved as spring approached. The pipes

in our house did not burst from freezing in winter, and so after the
thaw we had running water. The District Soviet announced that the
people were welcome to work in the communal kitchen gardens. The
work was remunerated by produce that was given out in proportion
to the amount of time spent at work. Here again the workers were
divided into categories, and the manual workers got the largest
share. We were both in the first category, Pitirim for his manual
labor in digging, and I as an agricultural expert because of my in-
structorship at the Institute of Agronomy.

During that summer I received a more substantial post at the
farm of the Institute in Tsarskoe Selo, which had been renamed
Detskoe Selo, in recognition of a great number of the children's
homes that had been moved from Petrograd. It was twenty-one kilometers from Petrograd, and the trains functioned efficiently. I was
in charge of the geobotanical experimental station. The Institute of
Agronomy received for its use the farm which before the revolution
supplied dairy products to the imperial court. Alexandrovskii Palace
(the actual residence of Tsar Nicholas II) was just half a mile
away. All the buildings surrounding the palace were given to the
institute to house its laboratories and to serve as living facilities for
students and faculty. I received a two-room apartment originally
occupied by guards of the Tsar's palace, sufficient wood to heat it,
some milk and produce from the farm, and a good plot of land to
raise potatoes and vegetables for the next winter. I was registered
at the institute under my maiden name, but had an official registra-
tion with the police in Petrograd under my married name. This was
done intentionally so that Cheka would not know where Pitirim
lived. Indeed, the Cheka came several times to the apartment of
Madame Darmolatova with the order to arrest Pitirim, but every time
they were given the same answer: "I do not know where he is." As
there were many whom they were seeking to arrest, they did not
pursue the search for Pitirim, and we continued to live in Tsarskoe
Selo until we were banished from Russia in 1922.

Elena P. Sorokin

PREFACE

This monograph emerges from one chapter of the third volume of my *System of Sociology*. Both the theoretical and the practical importance of the problem of nutrition as a factor caused the development of a single chapter into a whole volume. Strangely enough, up to the present time, we have no systematic, generalizing study of the social role of nutrition, particularly in a time of hunger. It is known that such a role exists, but it has not been systematically studied by sociologists. While dozens of monographs study less important factors, there is not a single solid sociological work devoted to the problem of hunger. This book is intended to fill that gap to a certain degree.

The aim and character of the investigation as well as the structure of the book are explained in the introduction.

The basic methodological principles which have guided me are described in the introduction to the first volume of my *System of Sociology*, so only additional points and methods related to this work are mentioned here. A more searching explanation will be found in the third volume of my *System*.

1. I attempt to verify every proposition by experimental data, by direct or indirect observations, by statistics, or by history, and not by mere "discussion." Contrary to the generally accepted approach, in order to explain the present by the past, I attempt to understand the past by analyzing the present, because the past is less accessible to exact study and observation than the present.

2. The statements which indicate the functional relationships between different phenomena have a "nomographic," rather than an "ideographic," significance. They are based upon two general propositions: "Under equal circumstances, similar causes produce similar results," and "Both the life of a man, which is generally nonrepeatable (in time and space) and a nonrepeatable historical process

consist mostly of repeatable (in time and space) elements." Provided that factual analysis of the phenomena is accurate, the second proposition allows for the possibility of discovering functional relationships in human behavior and social life, and also for the formulation of nomographic theorems (laws) in sociology.

The first proposition is unchallenged, but the second is debatable. It is said that history does not repeat itself, and therefore the search for nomographic laws in sociology is useless. I cannot agree. Truly, the history of mankind, like that of a nation, does not totally repeat itself. Nor does the history of the earth, the solar system, or the surrounding cosmos. However, does this prevent the occurrence of repeatable processes in this nonrepeatable world, such as gravity, the inverse ratio between gaseous bulk and pressure, the formation of water from hydrogen and oxygen, and other repeatable processes described in the laws of physics, chemistry, and biology? These repeatable processes also take place in the sphere of human behavior and cultural life. The multicolored fabric of human life and that of historical processes are woven from repeating phenomena. The tragedies and comedies of these processes are the same; only the actors, the costumes, the scenes, the times and places of action are different. The sociologist can and must disregard the differences and consider only the phenomena that are repeated. Furthermore, only the existence of such repetitions makes possible the formulation of real functional theorems or laws in sociology.

The latter are impossible without the former. The principal reason for the futility of most highly publicized "social laws" is that sociologists have ignored the sphere of repeatable phenomena in man's behavior and his cultural life. Disregarding the phenomena of repetition, they have attempted to find the problematical "laws of development," "historical tendencies," and "stages of evolution." Needless to say, such "laws" are worthless. I am deeply convinced that sociology will reap a heavy crop exactly in the "field of repetitions," and not in attempts to find problematical "laws of development" which depict the historical process as square dances in which different nations, coached by gracious ladies, dance figure after figure in an orderly way, crossing from "one stage to another" with the intention of graduating with "the class" to which "discoverers" of such "laws" gratuitously assign them. It is time to put an end to such notions.

3. Although the principal concern here is with objective facts available for observation by objective methods, psychological *experi-*

ences are not excluded from the field of study. Accordingly, I have attempted to relate the variations of the latter to one or more objective features of the process, or with their "independent variables."

4. The nature of the subject has forced me to treat very diverse topics. The amount of available evidence is immense and the inclusion of all of it would have increased the size of the volume enormously. Therefore I have limited to some extent the corroborating evidence and have referred the reader to further documents indicated in the footnotes.

5. Some of the topics touched on here only briefly will be discussed in the next volume of my *System*.

6. Finally, one more remark: "Too much biology," I expect to hear from some "ardent sociologists." "True," I reply calmly, "but there is very little unfounded fantasy." "Too much attention is given to man's behavior, and too little to the sociological processes," others will remark. "Without studying the former, it is impossible to know anything about the latter, because social life is ultimately created by the actions of people," I answer. "Can one apply the results of observations of the behavior of one individual to whole groups, and is it possible to start with the former for the explanation of social life?" will be the third question. It is possible and acceptable, because similar causes lead to similar results: that which happens with the behavior of single individuals under given circumstances may happen with a number of individuals found under the same conditions. True, there will be a slight variation (owing to inequality among individuals) and also additional phenomena factors may be present, but they will represent a direct consequence or a sort of integral of the differentials of the behavior of the individuals.

This book is dedicated to all those who are now saving the Russian people from death by starvation. This dedication is only a weak expression of the deep gratitude of one of the members of the great Russian nation to all the people and organizations performing this holy deed.

In conclusion I express my great indebtness for many valuable comments and other assistance during my work on this book to F. I. Vityazev-Sedenko, S. A. Zhebelev, N. I. Kareev, N. D. Kondratiev, A. V. Nemilov, I. P. Pavlov, E. V. Tarle, and many others.

P.S.

Tsarskoe Selo
June 1922

Part I

1

The Object of the Investigation

As any other organism, the human being represents a peculiar machine so complex that we still know neither its structure nor its action. As any other machine, the human organism requires energy for metabolism, just as a locomotive needs fuel. A human being cannot obtain energy from within itself; it is no perpetual motion machine. As any other organism, the human being transforms energy. Where does it get it? From without itself. In what way? In the form of food, drink, and air.

From this point of view human life represents a continuous process of metabolism in receiving energy, transforming it, and expending it in the form of excretions—urine, feces, sweat, and other processes of our animate existence in its concrete, explicit, and infinitely diversified forms.

Thus we represent a miraculous transformer, which changes the energy of a piece of meat or bread into Beethoven's *Eroica* Symphony, a Shakespearean tragedy, Newton's *Principia*, Michelangelo's *Moses*, a peasant's sown field, or a laborer's length of woolen cloth —in other words, into objects and events of culture in its innumerable manifestations, from the stone of primitive man to modern towns, buildings, libraries, museums, factories, and stores, and all the complicated, infinitely varied aspects of existence.

All these expressions of culture are specific forms of the universal energy and universal existence resulting from the transforma-

3

tion of the lower forms of energy by that miraculous machine called man.[1]

Because man's life activity consists of receiving, transforming, and expending energy, the behavior of the people depends to a great extent upon the type and quantity of energy received by the organism. Like the work of a machine, which depends upon the quality and the quantity of fuel, the work (behavior) of a man-machine depends directly or indirectly upon the quantity and quality of energy received from without. Deductively, it is possible to foresee that *the behavior of a human being represents to a certain degree "a function" of the quantity and of the quality of energy received, as an "independent variable." As long as every social process in the final result consists of the totality of human behavior-acts and the action of the people, it becomes obvious that social processes also are conditioned by this independent variable.*

Here is a sequence: The quantity and the quality of energy received by people (event A) condition their life activity (behavior, event B). The character of human behavior (B) determines surroundings (event C). Therefore, C (social processes) is in functional relationship with event A. This means that the variation and fluctuation of A must cause changes and variations in sphere B (human behavior), and through B also in sphere C (the area of social processes).

These facts explain why the process of human metabolism may and ought to receive attention not only from the biologist but also from the sociologist, i.e., from the investigator of human behavior and of social processes.

It is impossible to understand either the behavior of people or the mechanism of the regularity of social events without considering this "factor" or "determinant." A great many acts of man, and the variations in his behavior, as well as many social processes, depend upon the quantity and the quality of energy consumed by the human organism. This is obvious and requires no proof. Nevertheless, it is necessary to indicate here the complete lack of systematic investigations of the social role of this determinant. It was said long ago that "the whole history of mankind rotates around hunger (and love)." How this "hunger" (for food, water, and air) affects the be-

1. Here there is a reference to the works of A. V. Nemilov, M. Vervorn, S. D. Sherrington, and W. Roux.

havior of the people, what effects it produces in social life, what events are functionally connected with it, and finally which independent variables condition it—all this has received little systematic study. This work attempts to fill the gap to some extent. The first limitation is that absorption of energy by the human organism is considered here only in the form of food. The intakes of water and air are excluded from this investigation. Nonetheless, everything said here about the food metabolism is partially applicable to water, particularly "drinking water."

The second limitation consists of the exclusion of the forms of metabolism in which the intake of energy from food exceeds the output. *Attention in this investigation is concentrated mainly on those forms of food metabolism in which expenditure of energy by the organism is covered by its intake.* An excess of nutrition is referred to only when it is essential for the study of hunger. Such is the scope of the problem investigated. The next question is: from what point of view is this problem going to be studied?

From the preceding paragraph the answer is quite apparent. *The principal problem consists of the establishment of the functional relationship between a given determinant (starvation) and the effects it produces in the behavior of people, in the structure of population, in the organization of society, and in social processes.* In its developed form this task can be divided as follows. *First, I take this determinant of behavior and of social processes as a given "independent variable" out of the functional series, and I study three things: its constant "functions" in the behavior of people and in social events; how the latter varies with variations of the "argument," i.e., of the quality and quantity of food;* and *the events that occur in the behavior of people and in social life during the extraordinary fluctuations of this "independent variable."* After analyzing the corresponding events, when the determinant studied is taken as an "independent variable," I proceed further and consider it as a "function" of other "independent variables," and I study, second, *what are the basic "independent variables" that produce individual or mass starvation, and to what extent do the variations in the latter correspond with those in the former.* Third, after the problem has been studied from these points of view, in the concluding part I attend to the behavior of man and the social processes in their real surroundings. These surroundings depend upon or are found within "the field of influence" of forces, not only of a given determinant, but of many other determinants of

starvation. *Therefore, questions arise: What is the relationship be-*
tween the determinant studied and the others? What are its principal
forms? What are the results of this "duel"? On what do they depend?
What are the general theorems describing this relationship?

Essentially these are the problems confronting the sociologist who
is studying a given phenomenon. The program outlined here gives
an idea of the content of this book. In the study of these problems I
neither condemn nor do I approve anything, but merely describe
that which exists. *Je ne propose rien, je n'impose rien: j'expose.* The
reader is entitled to make his own conclusions.

Starvation and Its Forms
(An Objective Understanding of Hunger)

Let us define exactly the phenomena which we are going to consider
under the terms of starvation, as a determinant of the behavior of
people and of social processes.

Deficiency starvation belongs in first place. By this I mean all
the forms of metabolism in which the food absorbed by blood vessels
from the alimentary canal does not contain all of the elements in suf-
ficient quantities for proper functioning of the organism. Accordingly, this kind of starvation can be *absolute* or *relative. By the*
absolute-deficiency type of starvation is understood an inadequate in-
take of food by the organism. In this case the organism expends more
energy than it receives in the form of food. *The relative-deficiency*
kind of starvation is twofold: quantitative and qualitative. The first
includes the cases in which food absorbed by the organism contains
all the elements necessary for it to function properly, but only in
insufficient quantity. Here the intake of energy is less than the output
and this results in a deficit and a disturbance of the balance of metabolism. To the second type belong the cases in which certain essential nutritive elements are lacking in the food. If food is deficient
both in quantity and quality we have *quantitative-qualitative relative-*
deficiency starvation. The quantitative value of the food is measured
by calories, the qualitative by the presence of proteins, fats, carbohydrates, and supplementary substances such as salts, lipids, vitamins, and amino acids.

The caloric norms fluctuate according to sex, age, work, temperature, etc. For an adult male organism of normal weight and

stature the daily requirement of calories, according to some authors, is as follows:

Author	Light Work	Medium Work	Heavy Work	Very Heavy Work
Rubner	2,445	2,868	3,362	—
Atwater	2,450–3,050	3,400–3,800	4,150–5,300	7,355
Slovtzov	2,400–3,000	3,000–3,700	5,100	7,000–8,000
König	2,515	3,100	3,749	—
Gautier	2,450–2,860	3,300–3,800	4,000–5,000	—

These norms give approximately concrete measurements for testing the presence or absence of the quantitative-relative deficiency starvation. When the number of calories daily absorbed from food by the adult male is lower than the norms established, we have ground to suspect the presence of quantitative-deficiency starvation. Similarly, corresponding norms exist for women and children.

Obviously the problem is not limited by the purely quantitative measurement. The intake of 7,000–8,000 calories of carbohydrates does not eliminate deficiency starvation, because the organism must receive definite qualitative substances, and not merely a definite quantity of energy. The qualitative side of the problem is even more important than the quantitative, since the food which is taken in by the organism must contain a definite amount of proteins, fats, and carbohydrates, as well as several supplementary substances.

In the absence from food of one or more of these elements, or during their deficiency, we have either a qualitative- or a qualitative-quantitative-deficiency starvation. When, for example, feed given to animals is artificially deprived of salts, but contains sufficient quantities of all other nutritional elements, the animals become sick and die. In fact death occurs even faster than if they were to receive no food at all. All of the substances whose roles have been discovered comparatively recently have similar effects. These are the food ingredients called vitamins. They are either entirely lacking, or are found in insufficient quantities in non-essential proteins. The experiments of Funk, McCollum, Osborne, Mendel, Halliberton, Daniels, Nichols, and in Russia those of Palladin and Kol'tzov, have shown that without vitamins regular metabolism cannot take place, and the organism dies sooner or later.[2] All similar cases of the lack or deficiency of supplementary nutritional elements in food represent, accordingly, either qualitative- or qualitative-quantitative-deficiency starvation.

Such are the principal forms of starvation which I call deficiency starvation, and which represent the first and the basic category in the study of determinants of human behavior and of social processes.

However, *the range of the phenomena which are investigated here is not limited by the study of deficiency starvation.* The facts of substitution of a deficient nutrition for an adequate one not only influence the behavior of the people and through it the social processes, but the organism itself is also strongly affected by every strong and abrupt change in the quantity and quality of the food ingested. Rapid and abrupt change in the regularity of the intake of food disrupts the normal functions of the organism, which is accustomed to a regular diet, and which requires new forms of adaptation for the absorption of new food; in other words, it disturbs the digestive process. A simple verification of this is evident in the disarray of nutrition in the masses of Russian population during the change from the regime of religious fasting to normal eating and, conversely, from normal nutrition to the period of fasting, although in both cases nutrition was not deficient. Since every rapid change in the consumption of food affects the organism, it is possible to recognize the worsening of nutrition either as a result of decrease in the amount of intake, or of qualitative changes with respect to nutritiousness, ease of assimilation and absorption, taste, and diversity, even when in both cases the food is adequate. A man accustomed to delicate foods, such as caviar, oysters, fruits, truffles, etc., can hardly be indifferent to a change of this diet for one of *"tschi"* and *"kasha,"* [3] even though the latter contains all necessary ingredients of a normal diet. Similarly, although dried fish (*"vobla"*) contains 76.28 per cent proteins, while various meats have from 15 to 20.91 per cent, most people would sooner eat game, beef, mutton, veal, eggs, and milk (when they can afford them) than dried fish. If people are forced to change from a diet of meat to one of dried fish, their nutrition resulting from consumption

2. In these paragraphs the works of Kol'tzov, Slovtzov, Landois-Rosemann, and a number of other authors are cited.

3. A traditional meal of the Russian peasants consisting of cabbage or sauerkraut soup and buckwheat or barley cereal.

of food is worsened. The same can be said of all similar cases of the quantitative or qualitative deterioration of nutrition. The human being reacts differently to various foodstuffs even though they may be adequate from the nutritional point of view; a person likes or dislikes certain foods, and also he may not be able to assimilate some foods. One prefers a more diversified diet to the less varied, a more tasteful one to the tasteless, one easily absorbed to that more difficult to digest, etc. All these adequate diets form a gradation from a "higher" diet to a "lower" one, and if a change occurs it is considered by people as a deprivation, a worsening of nutrition, as something undesirable, but which, under the circumstances, may be inevitable. As soon as an opportunity presents itself to eat according to his taste, a person changes this adequate but "lower" diet for the "higher" one.[4] Such a preference has its own biological basis and may vary from one individual to another, and even from one country to another.

However, for European countries with a temperate climate, it is possible to indicate certain concrete forms of food that are preferred by the masses of population. We secure this information by comparing foods eaten by the more prosperous part of the population with those of the poorer classes. In contemporary society, prosperity is tantamount to the possibility of making a wider selection of food and of satisfying the appetite according to one's desire. Hence, foods eaten by the rich are "freely selected." [5] In comparison with the diet of the poorer classes, the food of more prosperous people is larger quantitatively, and it contains more meat. In his studies of the diets of different classes A. Grotjahn formulated a general principle: "the poorer the family, the greater the proportion of its food budget that is spent for vegetable products." This means that among expenditures for food by the lower classes, the percentage going for meats and fats is relatively small, whereas among prosperous families it is much larger. Furthermore, there is a change even in the use of the vegetable products: as prosperity increases, the relative consumption of white bread rises and of black decreases, and among the poorer

4. We find such a preference not only among human beings but also among animals. In the texts on the feeding of livestock the variety of foods and the taste are often emphasized next to the caloric and nutritional value. Similarly for cats and dogs we can observe a preference for diversified diets. (The work of O. Kel'ner is cited here.)

5. There is a reference here to the work of Grotjahn.

Sources of Calories among Peasants with Different Incomes
in the Province of Novgorod (per person)

Yearly Income (in rubles)	Plant Products		Animal Products		Total		Bread as a Component of Plant Products	
	Number	Per Cent	Number	Per Cent	Number	Per Cent	Number	Per Cent
Under 100	2,561	79.3	668	20.7	3,229	100	2,304	71.4
100–149	3,090	74.7	1,048	25.3	4,138	100	2,742	66.3
150–199	3,760	73.7	1,341	26.3	5,101	100	3,202	62.7
200 and over	4,039	70.1	1,721	29.9	5,760	100	3,521	61.1

Types and Amounts of Food Consumed Daily at Various Income Levels (per person)

Yearly Income (in rubles)	Proteins		Fats		Carbohydrates	
	Grams	Index	Grams	Index	Grams	Index
Under 100	77.1	100	43.6	100	375.9	100
100–149	104.0	135	65.6	151	454.9	121
150–199	126.6	164	84.5	194	547.7	146
200–299	148.0	192	100.8	210	568.1	151
300 and over	175.0	227	118.4	251	663.2	176

classes potatoes are substituted for bread as poverty becomes more acute.

Similar results were obtained by Klepikov,[6] who studied the nutrition of the Russian peasantry of different economic strata. He found that an increase in income of the peasants (i.e., the possibility of making better choices of food) results in an absolute and relative increase in consumption of products of animal origin. That is, as income rises, consumption of proteins and fats increases, and on a related basis, that of carbohydrates decreases. Still another table shows the change in consumption of various kinds of bread that takes place as income rises. We conclude from the data in these tables that as income rises the consumption of bread also increases, but that at the same time, a process of substitution takes place: there is

Changes in the Relative Importance of Different Kinds of Bread (in percentages of total consumption)

Yearly Income (in rubles)	Rye Flour	Wheat Flour	Flour and Legumes	Cereal	Total
Under 100	72.1	4.8	20.2	2.9	100
100–149	66.7	6.0	23.2	4.1	100
150–199	67.1	4.9	24.3	3.7	100
200 and over	61.2	9.2	24.4	5.2	100

6. There is a reference to the work of S. A. Klepikov.

some replacement of the heavier and less digestible products by foods which are lighter and more easily absorbed.[7]

The data indicate that human beings (or Europeans at least) prefer a diet of abundant and diversified foods to one lacking in variety; foods of animal origin to those secured from plants; white bread to black; etc. Thus, a distinct preference exists for one non-deficiency diet over another, which is also nondeficient, but which lacks some of the better qualities of the first. These cases are included here because their influence on the conduct and feelings of people are frequently similar to the results of deficiency starvation. *All such cases of qualitative and quantitative worsening of nutrition are denoted here as nondeficiency, or comparative, starvation.*

Whereas the range of deficiency starvation is rather short, the lower limit being absolute hunger and the upper the diet referred to above which in caloric values is close to the qualitative and quantitative norms, *the limits of comparative starvation are wider and more variable. Its lower limit corresponds to the upper limit of deficiency starvation* (because any lower limit would still be deficiency starvation); the upper limit of comparative starvation can be very high, since the "delicacy," "taste," and "pleasantness" of the food and its abundance, richness, and variety permit wide fluctuation and variation.[8] To determine more accurately the limits of comparative starvation, we subdivide it into *individual-comparative starvation* and *social-comparative starvation.* In the first are placed every deterioration in the quality and quantity of food of a given individual in comparison with the diet he used to have. *Hence, the upper limit of individual-comparative starvation is one's former diet.* The qualitative and the quantitative differences between the former better diet and the current poorer one (but still not deficient) are the indicators of the size of individual-comparative starvation. Hence, it is obvious that it varies from person to person. By social-comparative starvation I mean the difference between the diet which is near the upper limit of deficiency starvation and the most luxurious and refined diet which

7. Bibliographies in the works of Grotjahn and Klepikov are cited here.

8. According to Marshall, comparative starvation could be called elastic, and the desire for its satisfaction could be compared with the desire for objects of luxury. Unlike cases involving deficiency starvation, all of Marshall's speculations about objects of luxury and their curves of saturation are applicable to comparative starvation: Alfred Marshall, *Principles of Economics,* vol. 1 (London, 1891).

exists in a given society. *The upper limit of social-comparative starvation in this aggregate is the maximum food regime.* From this it follows that there are societies having a very satisfactory nutrition from the physiological point of view but in which there is extreme social inequality associated with a nutritional difference; those in the rich, aristocratic strata have the choicest foods whereas the members of the lower classes have a diet just above deficiency starvation, and the social-comparative starvation of the latter can be very substantial and acute. From this it follows that the magnitude of social-comparative starvation may increase in a society even when the general diet of the lower classes is improving; this may occur if the extravagances of the tables of the upper classes and the foods they eat improve more in quality and quantity than those of the masses. Conversely, social-comparative starvation may decline even when the general diet is deteriorating; this may take place during a rapid and substantial worsening of the nutritional level of the largest groups of the epicures.

The dimension of property differences in a society serves as a fairly accurate indicator of comparative social starvation. The increase of social inequality almost always serves as an indicator of a rise in comparative starvation. To the proletarian who has an adequate diet but who lives in a society of millionaires and billionaires (who, in turn, have a luxurious diet), social-comparative starvation may appear to be very great, and he would be highly motivated to achieve a better diet. In a society where differences in ownership of property are less and where there is less luxury and gluttony, comparative starvation will also be less, because the lower classes will have an adequate diet. However, if the diet were inadequate, we would have a case of comparative starvation plus deficiency starvation. *Thus, the greater and more intense the worsening of the diet of any individual, both qualitatively and quantitatively, provided it does not fall below the necessary nutritional norm, the greater the individual's comparative starvation. When this worsening passes the upper limit of deficiency starvation, growth of individual-comparative starvation plus deficiency starvation takes place. The greater the difference—in quality and quantity of food—between the essential norm of nutrition and the highest nutritional diet of the given society, or that enjoyed by the well-to-do strata of the economic and governmental aristocracy, the larger the social-comparative starvation of that society. When the diet of the poorest classes of a given society*

*is below the necessary physiological norm, this means that, con-
comitantly with great social-comparative starvation, deficiency starvation also occurs in that society.*

Such is the second range of the phenomena of comparative starvation which, together with deficiency starvation, is the subject of
this investigation. Both of these forms of starvation have distinct
effects on the behavior of individuals and of social groups, and therefore, they both are studied.

The relationships among different types of starvation are sche-
matically represented below.

Starvation

Deficiency		*Comparative (Nondeficiency)*	
Absolute	*Relative*	*Individual*	*Social*
	Quantitative *Qualitative*	*Individual-Social*	
	Qualitative-Quantitative		

Subjective Experience of Hunger ("Hunger-Appetite"), as a Function of an Objective Fact of Starvation: The Opposing Theory of L. J. Petrajitsky

The conception of starvation is established here quite objectively
without the help of a subjective experience of hunger. Figuratively
speaking starvation is limited here by an objective cessation, or decrease, or change in content and frequency of delivery of food to the
human mouth (or inadequate assimilation of food by the organism).
As our starting point we take this physical, observable, measurable
phenomenon as an "independent variable." Then, after having established this concept of starvation, we ask this question: *What are its
functions, its effects upon the structure, physiological processes, experiences, and behavior of human beings?* Still more precisely, consider a human organism which is either deprived of food for several
hours or even days, or is getting less food than required to cover its
expenditure of energy, or, still further, which is receiving some food
but in smaller quantity and poorer quality than previously. *What
changes occur in the physiological functions, psychological experi-*

ences, and behavior of this organism as a result of these concrete variations in the "independent variable"?

It is possible to conclude a priori that the effects of this "independent variable" are numerous and diverse. They are not restricted by one kind of phenomena, but form a very intricate and mutually overlapping complex.[9] Contemporary American behaviorists and objective psychologists have correctly formulated a thesis: "every stimulus, or a complex thereof to which an organism reacts, may be accompanied by more than one reaction," e.g., meeting a friend may cause a series of overt reactions (taking off the hat, shaking the hand), speech-reactions in the form of "How are you?," etc., or a series of "psychological reactions." [10]

Let us describe briefly some of the complexes. One of the consequences of the cessation of food intake by the human organism, or of its decrease in quality and quantity, is the change in the physical sensation which in our speech-reactions we call an "appetite" or "hunger" ("I am hungry," "I want something to eat," "I have a wolf's appetite," "I wish I had the food I used to have," etc.).[11] The main features of variations in these experiences will be discussed later. For the present, I regard *the subjective experience of hunger* ("psychological hunger-appetite," in the terminology of Petrajitsky) *as one of the sequences of an objective fact of a deficiency, and also in part of comparative starvation, i.e., of the cessation of, or an inadequate, intake of food by the organism, or cessation of its adequate assimilation.* The fluctuation of the latter, or the "independent variable," causes variations in the subjective experiences of the human being. For example, an abstention from food for a short period, or a decrease in the quality, compared with the previous diet, has its function in the subjective field by producing what is called "an appetite" (which is quite pleasant, if it is not complicated by some other conditions); further abstention from food causes "hunger" (a phenomenon which is different from an appetite and which gives some pain); still more abstention entirely changes this specific experience and begins to cause a general feeling of hurt, weakness, headache, dizzi-

9. Not only may the complicated determinants of behavior, such as starvation, produce various reactions, but even the simple determinants of behavior may do the same.

10. Works by A. Weiss, J. Watson, and M. Meyer are cited.

11. Works by L. J. Petrajitsky, E. Boring, and Marsh are cited.

ness, upset stomach, etc., which covers up the specific experience of hunger. The deficiency of various elements necessary for the organism (during relative-qualitative starvation) is usually accompanied by the experience of a specific starvation with concomitant speech reflexes: sometimes we wish to have "something sweet," or some "salted herring," or "meat," or "dill pickles." Specifically, there is a definite functional relationship between the "independent variable" studied and the corresponding subjective experiences.

This statement, which is considered self-evident by most investigators, has met with considerable criticism on the part of L. J. Petrajitsky. He separates distinctly "physiological" from "psychological" hunger, and insists on their independence from one another. "As far as the relationship of the hunger-appetite" (in the sense of a subjective experience) "to physiological hunger is concerned, they represent two entirely different categories of phenomena; they are neither related to one another in regard to uninterrupted contact nor through constant and absolute parallelism, an idea which is at the base of the current studies on hunger. The occurrence, the increase, the decrease and the disappearance of the hunger-appetite depend upon various factors which have nothing in common with physiological hunger." Conversely, in the presence of physiological hunger-appetite, the latter can be suppressed artificially by finding worms or insects in the food served, by the arousal of fear, surprise, anger, shame, etc., "which, of course, neither introduce into nor remove from the stomach the essential acids or other stimulants." Furthermore, physiological hunger must increase with abstention from food, while hunger-appetite forms a different curve: it appears at the time of the usual intake of food, such as dinner time, and disappears later even when there is no dinner. All these facts led L. J. Petrajitsky to indicate "the impossibility and hopelessness of any kind of attempts to establish a theory of hunger by means of finding, or inventing of physiological stimulants on the ground of insufficient nutrition and corresponding feelings." [12]

True, physiological or deficiency starvation, i.e., the lack of enough essential food to cover the expenditures of the organism, and psychological hunger, namely, the specific subjective experience of it, are as entirely different things as any other phenomena, e.g., the

12. L. J. Petrajitsky, *Introduction to the Theory of Law and Morality* (St. Petersburg, 1907), pp. 220–23 (in Russian).

prick of a pin and the corresponding subjective feeling of pain from the puncture. Nobody identifies them in this sense, and that is why I call the subjective experience of hunger a function (result) of an objective fact of starvation. But is it correct to assume that these two phenomena are "not related to each other in regard to the uninterrupted contact"? Is the following statement correct: "the attempts to construct a theory of hunger on the grounds of insufficient (or suddenly changed and worsened) nutrition is hopeless"? With all respect to the profound and forceful scientific postulations of L. J. Petrajitsky, I cannot concur with this thesis. The facts which he mentions are correct, but the conclusion and the interpretation are faulty.

That objective (in our sense) hunger and the subjective experience of hunger-appetite are connected, and that the latter is the function of the former, is self-evident. Any normal person (with the exception of a few rare cases) needs only to refrain from eating for several hours, or to decrease the food automatically, or to change abruptly to a poorer and less abundant diet, in order to make the hunger-appetite appear.[13] Everyday experiences of people in general and special experimental data provide sufficient evidence of this. On the other hand, it is interesting to know the bases, other than insufficient and worsened nutrition, on which it would have been possible to build a theory of deficiency and comparative starvation. This is the first argument.

Second, the facts which led L. J. Petrajitsky to his conclusions are correct; but they indicate not the absence of a relationship between objective and psychological hunger, but the presence of a more complex picture of this contact on one hand and, on the other, the intrusion of a whole series of supplementary conditions into the region of this contact. These change and deform the constant relationship between the independent variable (objective starvation) and "hunger-appetite," which is a function of the former in the region of subjective experiences. According to the principle of inertia, a moving body must retain forever its uniform rectilinear motion. But once it meets obstacles, friction, push, etc., it either stops or no longer

13. The citizen of the USSR can testify to this. During the starvation period in 1918–19 in Moscow and in Petrograd, the masses of starving people wanted to eat all the time. Their appetites were permanent. This was recorded in clinical observations. See Shervinsky, *Contemporary Nutrition* (Priroda, 1919), nos. 4–6, pp. 185–86 (in Russian).

moves uniformly and rectilinearly. This, however, does not mean that the principle of inertia is false. Similarly, when a person who has been starving physiologically for a protracted period of time is subjected to the action of a new determinant, such as an attack by an enemy or the stimulation of pain through pricking the skin, pulling the hair, etc., stimulating a whole series of new physiological processes that modify the whole structure of the organism, it becomes obvious that under these conditions "hunger-appetite" does not occur. This happens not because this appetite is not a function of deficiency or comparative starvation, but because this latter function was offset by the introduction of new conditions which in turn called forth a different series of objective reactions on the part of the organism. As a result of these, the usual subjective reaction of "hunger-appetite" in response to the determinant of lack of food may be canceled. Later we shall see that the same is applicable to the whole series of other functions of the given "independent variable."

Third, that which L. J. Petrajitsky calls a "physiological" theory of starvation represents something very primitive, which has little in common with the contemporary "physiological" theory of starvation. This simplified conception of L. J. Petrajitsky about the latter is one of the reasons for his erroneous attitude toward it. The facts brought forward by L. J. Petrajitsky can be explained by the contemporary "physiological" theory of hunger which was advanced by I. P. Pavlov and his school. From the point of view of this school there is no basis for assuming that the emotions of "hunger-appetite" represent a kind of "spirit" which miraculously governs the nutrition of the organism, which appears and disappears mysteriously, which links the psychic world with the world of objective action of humans but which at the same time is not connected with the outside world, i.e., not related to objective starvation and the physiological mechanism regulating nutrition. Not criticizing here psychologism in general, I must point out that all this theory represents is a refined "animism," as is true of most of the psychological theories in sociology.

An Objective Theory of Starvation and the Mechanism of Human Nutrition

1. Deficiency starvation, as we have seen, means insufficient intake (and assimilation) of food products by the organism, quantities which do not cover its expenditure of energy, thus threatening

the life of the organism. (For the time we leave aside comparative starvation.)

2. The importance of the nutritional function has, on the one hand, brought about the appearance in the organism of a complicated system of organs, destined to fulfill the functions of intake, absorption, and digestion of food products and, on the other, has introduced a whole series of mechanisms, which control automatically the nutrition of the organism. The mechanisms and the system of organs are both hereditary and independent of the "consciousness." The organs are the entire digestive system, through which the food is taken in and excreted, all the blood and lymphatic systems which nourish the organism, the pulmonary organs, in part, and the nervous system, which is the organ of contact with the outside world and the main controller ("analyzer and closure" apparatus) of all the activity of the organism.

3. From the physiological point of view the nutritional process is as follows. The mouth is the cavity for the intake of food. Here it is ground by the teeth and the tongue, wetted with saliva, and brought about to a form suitable for digestion. Through the esophagus the food is carried to the stomach where it acquires a mushy or liquid consistency and undergoes important chemical changes. The central digestive organ is the duodenum. Here and in the rest of the small intestine (partly also in the large intestine), the chemical compounds of the food are broken down into elemental components. From these indifferent fractions the intestinal wall can synthesize new nutritional material for all the cells of the organism. The residue which cannot be utilized by the intestines is excreted through the anus. The primary role in the whole digestive system belongs to the secretional function of glands located along the digestive tube.[14]

4. Thus, obviously the nutritional process is very complex. The system of organs is a complex laboratory, or factory, in which all the members perform definite functions, and all of them together carry on a very delicate and refined work. The teeth and tongue have one function, the esophagus another, the stomach and the intestines and the glands still others. The most remarkable fact is that all this is performed without our "consciousness of it." Most people have no idea about this work, but nonetheless their "food laboratories" work very well. Even a superficial survey of this factory and

14. Works of B. P. Babkin and E. London are cited.

its function causes amazement at the complexity of the work and the artistic adaptation of the system to the purposes of nutrition. This statement may be illustrated by two examples. The work of the salivary glands may be considered an example of a well-calculated adaptable function of the animal organism. In the mouth cavity the glands remain dormant when there are no stimuli. Nor do they react when the mouth cavity contains objects whose removal requires no saliva (water, ice, round pebbles). Conversely, in cases which require salivation, e.g., in the presence of corresponding stimuli, the saliva is produced quantitatively and qualitatively in full accordance with the requirements of the organism. Thus, the salivary glands produce either more viscous, or less viscid, saliva, in greater or smaller amounts, all in accordance with the degree of dryness of the food present in the mouth at a given moment. Because of the presence of mucin in such saliva, the food becomes slimy, and this facilitates swallowing and the passage of the food through the esophagus ("lubricating saliva"). A different, more liquid and watery saliva is produced to wash out the mouth cavity when injurious substances get into it ("liquifying or washing off saliva"). Finally, the quantity of saliva produced is determined by the degree (strength) of the stimulus.[15] The pancreas and the gastric glands have somewhat similar actions. According to I. P. Pavlov, "they appear, as if they have a brain. They secrete their juice which in quantity and quality is in accordance with the amount and the kind of food consumed, giving exactly that which is most profitable for the digestion of the given kind of food. . . . The fact of the purposefulness [of their work] is beyond question."[16] Similar results could be applied to work of the Brunner section of the duodenum. Here we see that: the glands do not work without a stimulus; every kind of food (meat, milk, and bread) stimulates specific amounts of the juices, each with its distinctive digestive value and acidity; and the amount of secretion is proportional to the quantity of food consumed.[17] These examples in-

15. A work by Babkin is cited.

16. I. P. Pavlov, "Lectures on the Work of Principal Digestive Glands," *Proceedings of the Society of Russian Physicians* (St. Petersburg, 1894–95) (in Russian). See also the limitations of this purposefulness in London's work.

17. Petrajitsky correctly calls the whole system of the regulation of nutrition "unconsciously genial" (p. 236). Babkin's work is cited.

dicate three things: the complexity and purposefulness of the activity of each organ in the human being's "food factory"; the complexity of the structure and activity of the digestive system in general; and the extent of the coordination of the work of its separate parts.

5. Therefore, this question arises: what is the mechanism by which all these problems are solved? *What "director" is at work, and how does it regulate the activity of each "working organ" of this food factory?* The earlier investigators were inclined to think that the whole nervous system performs the function of "control" of the food laboratory.[18] I. P. Pavlov has advanced a hypothesis according to which a special "nutrient" center in the brain controls the nutrition of the organism. This center is very complex, is not localized in any definite region of the brain, and contains a whole series of secondary nervous centers related to the digestion of food. It coordinates and regulates the work of every corresponding organ, which in turn is either stimulated to work or remains idle. For example, the salivary glands produce one kind of saliva under certain conditions, while a different kind appears under different circumstances.

The subjective experience of hunger is the result of a definite stimulus of the "nutrient center." When such stimulation is given, we experience "appetite-hunger." When such stimulation of the "nutrient center" ceases or when it is changed through the action of an inhibitor, the feeling of hunger disappears. Speaking objectively its activity is manifested in the form of a "reaction of motion directed toward the food object in order to reach it, retain it, and direct it towards the inside of the organism along the esophagus to the gastric glands in the upper section of the digestive tube." [19] Such is the nutrient center, which regulates the nutrition of an organism, and its relationship to "physiological starvation" and the "hunger-appetite." The whole procedure depends upon the definite stimulation of this "nutrient center."

6. *The next question is how does this stimulation occur. Under what conditions does it take place and how is it performed? Under what objective conditions do we experience subjective hunger-appetite?* The stimulation occurs in two different ways: automatically

18. Cf. Luigi Luciani, *Das Hungern* (Hamburg and Leipzig, 1890), p. 239.
19. Works by Babkin, Nemilov, and London are cited.

through the blood (the humoral mechanism), and by involuntary transmission along the afferent nerves. Prolonged abstention from food, a decrease in the quantity of food, eating food of a quality which the organism is not adapted to digest and assimilate quickly —all of these impoverish the blood and change its chemical composition. As long as the nutrient center is supplied with normal blood it remains "calm" and, therefore, we do not feel hungry. When the chemistry of the blood is changed, the nutrient center is stimulated, because the center and its receptors cease to receive normal blood. This stimulation is transmitted by the nerves to the stomach, the upper duodenum, and some other organs which are regulated by it, and, hence, we experience the "borborygmus" (noises in the stomach), etc. The occurrence of hunger-appetite is the subjective effect of this objective process, an experience which warns the organism of the approach of possible danger, and of the necessity to take in some food. Because the composition of the blood does not remain the same during starvation (during absolute starvation it is different from what it is during relative starvation, and it also changes in response to the duration of hunger, a lack of necessary elements in the food, etc.), and, further, because the composition of blood may vary in accordance with other physiological processes in the organism (e.g., pregnancy, typhus, etc.), the character of the stimulation of the nutrient center varies accordingly. Therefore, its function, which is our subjective experience of hunger-appetite, must also vary ("slight appetite," "hunger pains," a desire to eat something "sweet," "sour," or "salty," etc.). Such is the type of stimulation of the nutrient center through the blood, which is, as we see it, connected directly with the quantity and quality of food taken in by the organism. After food is taken in and absorbed, it penetrates the walls of the digestive tube and reaches the blood. This carries it to the glands and the apparatus of the nutrient center. Stimulated by this, the activity of the nutrient center directs the work (by stimulating or inhibiting) of all the other organs (glands, etc.) of the "food factory."

After the consumption of food restores the chemical composition of the blood, it ceases to stimulate the nutrient center and the glands; simultaneously the sensation of hunger disappears. Our subjective experiences of hunger-appetite and of its variations serve as functions of these complex physiological processes. These facts indicate a relationship between objective starvation and psychological hunger-appetite.[20]

The second way of stimulating the nutrient center is through reflexes, or by means of direct stimulation of the neuroreceptor apparatus with various food reagents. The stimulation, thus received, is transmitted along the conduction path and activates the nutrient center. This results in the emission of a series of "commands" from the center to subordinate organs to start their stimulation and thus bring into action the whole "food factory." The subjective effect of these processes is the well-known experience of "hunger-appetite." Let us illustrate: suppose we take a piece of beefsteak and put it into the mouth. The meat comes into direct contact with and stimulates the neuroreceptors of the mouth; the stimulus is transmitted to the appropriate section of the nutrient center, which in turn transmits it through the efferent nerves to the corresponding working organs (to the salivary glands, for example), causing them to emit saliva in quantity and quality called for by the given stimulatus, etc. The experience of hunger-appetite appears as the result of stimulation of the nutrient center. Thus, we have the expression "L'appetit vient en mangeant." [21] When the stomach becomes full, the peripheral neuroreceptors receive an impulse inhibiting stimulation of the nutrient center. This results in "abatement" of stimulation which is felt subjectively as a disappearance of appetite. Thus, *the appetite becomes weaker during eating*, and finally it disappears. Such, in brief, is the second, or the reflex-transmitted, stimulation of the nutrient center and of the corresponding organs in the digestive system.

All that is said above gives only a general understanding of the mechanism for stimulating the nutrient center and "hunger-appetite." For a complete understanding of the whole process, additional information, which would depict the whole process and its mechanism, is absolutely essential. Here are some of these conditions.

20. Works of Babkin, Nemilov, Tarasevich, L. Frederik, and E. Gley are cited.

21. I. P. Pavlov writes that he lost his appetite after a fever, and in order to stimulate it he took a glass of wine. "After the first swallow, I felt distinctly its motion along the esophagus and into the stomach, and immediately experienced a very strong appetite. The meaning of these observations is as follows: that the palpability of the stomach to the food received may serve as a push to stimulate the appetite, and also to increase it" ("Lectures," p. 133).

When reflexes are exciting the nutrient center, as mentioned, food objects stimulate receptors connected with this center. To accomplish this task the object must have some essential qualities. Not every object put into the mouth excites the nutrient center and the corresponding organs of the digestive system. The salivary glands, for example, are not activated in the cases when the mouth cavity contains objects which do not require saliva for their removal (water, ice, round pebbles).[22]

In order to activate the nutrient center, the receptors must possess certain qualities. The nature of these qualities is already predetermined by phylogenetic development, on one hand, during which occurs the selection of substances that are useful or harmful for nutrition, and, on the other, by previous experience of the organism. During the process of phylogenesis, and to a lesser degree that of individual development, a definite link is established *between certain substances, which activate the receptors of the nutrient center, and the character of the latter's response (and through it that of the whole organism) to the stimulation by these substances.*

Three categories of objects can be established, and accordingly there are three ways in which the nutrient center, the digestive organs, and the whole organism react to these substances.

One category of objects causes a positive excitation of the nutrient center, and through this the objects initiate the work of all the subordinated organs of digestion which are directed to absorption and assimilation of these objects by the organism. When such an object, for example a piece of nice, tasty beef, reaches the mouth, a positive excitation is transmitted to the nutrient center, which in turn emits "orders" for chewing, swallowing, gland secretion, all of which facilitate the passage of food into the stomach and further chemical reactions and absorption. The subjective function of the positive excitation is the experience of hunger-appetite, tastefulness, desirability, pleasure of eating, etc.

The next category of objects causes inhibitory or negative excitation of the nutrient center and thereby stimulates all of the digestive organs of the whole organism toward the elimination of such an object. If, for example, a piece of fecal matter or a dead mouse were placed in the mouth, it would excite the receptors of the nutrient center in a negative way. As a result of the negative excitation the

22. Works of Babkin are cited.

salivary glands are "ordered" to produce a thin saliva that washes and cleans the mouth cavity, and in cases where such objects are swallowed the "orders" direct the muscles to contract so as to produce vomiting and elimination of such objects from the organism. The subjective effects of this negative excitation are the repulsion of such objects, momentary loss of appetite that may have been present, nausea, and a series of very unpleasant experiences.[23]

A third category of objects apparently does not excite the nutrient center either positively or negatively. Small round pebbles are examples of these. Everything remains neutral during such excitation.

These are the three categories of objects and three forms of reaction to them by the nutrient center of the organism, and all of these were established during the process of phylogeny. *These relationships between the objects and the reactions of the organisms are inherited and absolute.* Normally they do not depend upon "consciousness." For human beings, as a rule, the objects which fall into each of these categories and the type of reactions they produce in the nutrient center and other organs of digestion are predetermined and become either positive, or negative, or neutral.[24] When babies suck milk, or when adults eat meat, fish, bread, eggs, butter, etc., on one hand, and do not eat (or spit them out if they get into the mouth) worms, caterpillars, feces, dirt, spoiled meat, etc., it is not because, through a conscious understanding of the chemical analysis and a knowledge of their nutritive values, they have come to a conclusion about the usefulness of the former and harmfulness of the latter. Rather it is because an unquestionable connection has been established during the process of phylogenesis, and because the nutrient center exists as a regulating mechanism, which decides "uncon-

23. Similar effects are found in animals. "The irritation of the mouth cavity of a dog by substances rejected by the animal (acid, mustard oil, pepper, etc.) produces thin saliva which washes out the mouth cavity, while the foods eaten by the dog elicit thick saliva." G. P. Zelenyi, *Study of the Auditory Reaction in the Dog*, dissertation, University of St. Petersburg, 1907 (in Russian).

24. Later we shall show that, due to certain specific circumstances, these relationships between the objects and the reactions may be perverted or destroyed, first through occurrence of variations and modifications, and second by intrusion of specific determinants. For example, Chinese may eat mice and rats, and Russians will not.

sciously genially" through one of the ways of stimulation described above what is useful for nutrition of the organism and what is not. The sensations of taste are mostly the results of this generic experience.[25]

The objects which cause unconscious and inherited positive or negative stimulation of a nutrient center may be designated as *positive or negative unconditioned stimulants*. The reactions which they initiate in the nutrient center, in the organs of digestion, and in the organism may be called *unconditioned reflexes*. The relationship between the unconditioned stimulus and the corresponding reaction is an *unconditioned hereditary relationship*. Such is the *mechanism of reflex stimulation of the nutrient center by unconditioned stimuli*.

The foregoing explains almost all the facts which L. J. Petrajitsky brought forward to prove the lack of connection between "physiological and psychological" starvation. Positive stimulation of the nutrient center by intensive, positive stimulants, such as taking tasty and favorite foods into the mouth, may occur even when the organism is satiated (since the amplitude of stimulation of the nutrient center, as well as of any other center, that of sex, for example, has fairly wide limits during artificial stimulation); therefore, under these circumstances, appearance of an appetite as a function of this stimulation may occur. A number of other conditions may serve also as stimuli. If a whole series of positive stimulants are working concomitantly, they may offset the excitation coming from the sated stomach, which tends to inhibit the nutrient center, even calling forth positive reaction by the latter, and causing appetite to appear. (This is similar to the case in which several forces are pushing a certain object in one direction and thereby are overcoming the resistance of a smaller force pushing in the opposite direction.)

Therefore, it becomes understandable why a wolfish appetite may suddenly disappear when, for example, along with soup, a worm or a cockroach or any other negative stimulant is taken into the mouth. The soup, being a positive stimulant, excites the nutrient center positively, and this results in the appearance of hunger-appetite. Conversely, the worm inhibits this excitation and causes a negative reaction in the nutrient center, and the latter condition is

25. See correct observations on the instinctive nature of our nutrition in Max Rubner, *Über Moderne Ernährungsreformen* (Leipzig, 1913).

accompanied by the decrease or disappearance of appetite and by reactions to eliminate the harmful agent from the organism.[26]

The sharpness of the feeling of hunger does not increase in exact proportion to physiological starvation. During the increase of the latter, the former may not mount, but increase in intensity only at regular mealtimes and then decrease later on, regardless of the fact that the person did not eat. Why is this? There are several reasons. First, because when feeding is regular "according to the clock," the periodic stimulation of the nutrient center occurs at a definite time. Similar to a good clock, the nutrient center gives timely signals of the need to eat. The subsequent disappearance of hunger-appetite may be explained by the presence of other stimuli, the nature of which is not always fully known, which inhibit the positive stimulation of the nutrient center. Second, it is also possible that the organism, not receiving food from the outside, may obtain it from "storage supplies" and thus "pacify the nutrient center." Third, in such cases the disappearance of hunger-appetite does not last; if food is not taken in, it quickly reappears. This again contradicts the theory of Petrajitsky. It is true that the specific experience of hunger weakens, and after two or three days of absolute starvation it seems to disappear. However, as we see further on, this disappearance of appetite signifies only that it is dispersed among other far stronger experiences which occur during prolonged starvation (general weakness, nausea, dizziness, headache, aches in the joints, etc.). The specific feeling of hunger sinks into the general set of acute sufferings and loses its specific features. Finally, rarely is there complete parallelism between the physiological process and subjective experience. This can be inferred from the following statement: the sensation does not increase absolutely parallel to the irritation (the "law" of Weber-Fechner, which is not true in the absolute sense, but which is correct in principle). (According to this "law," the sensation is equal to the logarithm of the irritation.) When a tooth is decaying, the process of destruction goes on incessantly if we do not take care of it, but the toothache does not follow absolutely parallel to this process: it fluctuates, now stronger, then weaker, although the process which

26. Such a victory of the negative stimulant over the positive is quite understandable and often purposeful from the general biological point of view of self-preservation of the organism. In most cases the temporary refusal of food is less harmful than the intake of poisonous substances.

causes the destruction and the pain is continuous. It would be difficult to prove, on this basis, that the psychological experience of a
toothache is not related to the physiological process of tooth decay
and to the irritation of the corresponding nerve.

The above discussion shows that all the facts indicated by Petrajitsky can be explained perfectly well from the point of view of the
"physiological" theory of hunger we have described.

The mechanism of the reflex stimulation of the nutrient center
(positive or negative-inhibitory), however, is not limited entirely by
the facts indicated so far. From general observation and from personal experience we know—and again these facts are correctly indicated by Petrajitsky—that the experience of "hunger-appetite" may
be stimulated or repressed by a whole series of conditions and irritants which are not unconditioned stimuli. As an example, the appetite may appear after hearing the clatter of plates in the dining
room, by smelling a favorite dish, by the sight of a well-spread
table, by reading descriptions of the Lucullan feasts, etc. Conversely,
it can be inhibited by means of stimulants, which are not the unconditioned ones, and which do not react directly upon the receptors of
the nutrient center. What is the explanation of such facts?

*Aside from the unconditioned stimuli which cause unconditioned
reflexes, there are also conditioned stimuli to which the organism's
conditioned reflexes may respond.* In the former group, as mentioned,
we place the hereditary reflexes, those in which stimulation of neuroreceptors produces a directly corresponding reflex of the working
organ without participation of the core of the large hemispheres of
the brain. Thus stimulation of the peripheral nerves of the mouth
cavity by a piece of meat is transmitted directly to the "salivary"
nutrient center and directly causes a corresponding reflex of the
salivary glands.

In these cases stimulation is not controlled by the decision of the
"higher instance" located in the core of the large hemispheres of the
brain. Local nerve centers decide such matters without reference to
the "superior power" of the brain.

The problem is different with conditioned stimuli and conditioned reflexes. If we were to consider a stimulant such as the light
of an electric bulb, the sound of a bell, or the sight of dinner plates,
it matters not how many times we would light the lamp, or ring the
bell, or look at the well-set table. All these stimuli would be unable
to stimulate the nutrient center and thereby to activate the salivary

and other glands of the digestive tracts, in the way that it is done by a piece of meat. Therefore, there is no hereditary, unconditioned relationship between them and the reactions of the organs of the digestive tract and the nutrient center. The latter does not react to them, and its stimulations are indifferent to them. However, under certain conditions an ineffectual stimulus may become active, may develop a relationship with the reactions of the digestive organs, and may force them to be stimulated positively or negatively. For example, it is possible to stimulate a nutrient center so that the salivary glands will secrete saliva in response to an electric light, to the ringing of a bell, or, in brief, to an indifferent stimulus. What is required for this? *It is essential for the actions of unconditioned and of ineffectual reflexes to coincide in time. After a series of repetitions of such coincidence* (the number of repetitions may vary in accordance with many circumstances), *the ineffectual stimulus, which previously caused no reaction, becomes a conditioned reflex.* In the examples given, a conditioned relationship is established between the once ineffectual stimulus and the nutrient center and the digestive organs, so that the latter begins to react to the action of the former. Thus, if we were to put a piece of meat (an unconditioned stimulant, which stimulates the nutrient center positively) into the mouth and at the same moment would light an electric lamp, or ring a bell, or observe a set table (indifferent stimuli), then after a series of repetitions of such coincidence, it would be sufficient to light a lamp, or hear the bell, or see a set table in order to stimulate the nutrient center and the "flow of saliva," and, as a result, to experience hunger-appetite.

When the ineffectual stimulus coincides in time with a negative unconditioned stimulation of the nutrient center, such as the ringing of a bell at the moment when feces or a rotten worm (unconditioned stimuli, which cause unconditioned negative reflexes) are introduced, the results are similar. Then, after a series of such coincidences, it would be sufficient to hear the ringing of the bell, or the action of any other once ineffectual stimuli in order to cause a negative stimulation of the nutrient center and of the corresponding reactions of the other digestive organs, and subjectively, to experience nausea, disgust, and the disappearance of hunger-appetite. Because of the repetition of the concomitant action of the unconditioned and the ineffectual stimuli, the latter cease being indifferent to the conditioned stimulants, and this produces the conditioned reflex.

Similar occurrences take place not only in the field of conditioned reflexes related to nutrition, but also in other fields. For example, after a series of concomitant actions of pricking the hand with a pin (an unconditioned stimulus, which causes reaction of pain, i.e., pulling away the hand) and lighting an electric lamp, it suffices to light a lamp in order to produce both the reflex of pulling away and a feeling of pain. Obviously, any ineffectual stimulus may become a conditioned stimulus. "Everything from the outside world may become a stimulant of the salivary gland. The principal condition for this is coincidence in time." [27]

The neural pathway for transmitting conditioned reflexes differs from that of the unconditioned. In the latter, the core of the cerebral hemispheres does not participate in the activity, while in the former it does, and the pathway of transmission itself is longer and more "circumscribed." The rattling of dinner plates (a conditioned stimulus) perceived by the ear is transmitted first to the corresponding center of the cerebral hemispheres. From there it is transmitted by means of nerve branches to the nerve center which is in charge of the given function, and only from the latter is it conducted to the muscles and glands, which produce corresponding conditioned reflexes. Figuratively speaking, it appears here as if the problem were relegated to the decision of the highest nerve instance—superior power—and follows from it to the lower instances, and, still further, to the executive organs. Thus, the "nerve system serves not only as a transmitting apparatus, but represents also a neuromuscular junction." [28]

Most diversified agents, once they become conditioned stimuli, may positively or negatively stimulate the nutrient center and the glands through this circumscribed pathway. (Accordingly, they may stimulate or inhibit the appetite.)

The agents may be *perceived by the organ of sight* (such as the sight of meat, a set table, a bottle, flowers, etc., and also by the vision of a cockroach in the soup, by the fingers of a servant in the dish to be served, or by the sight of an object which causes either a pleasant or repugnant association, by reading books describing delicious or unappetizing things, etc.); *by the organ of hearing* (such as

27. I. P. Pavlov, "Physiology and Psychology of Higher Nervous Activity in Animals," *Psikhiatricheskaya Gazeta* (Petrograd, 1917) (in Russian).
28. Ibid.

the rattling of plates, or, according to the experiment of Bogen, after forty repetitions, the sound of a pipe which becomes a conditioned stimulus, the sound made by jailors during distribution of food in a prison, pleasant and repugnant conversations, etc.); *by the organs of taste and smell* (such as the smell of fried meat, onions, flowers, foul objects, etc.). Any stimulation of the nutrient center and "secretion of gastric juice by sight, smell, etc., is a conditioned reflex." "The unconditioned reflex occurs after an irritation of the mouth cavity by the chemical, or perhaps by the physical qualities of the matter which the animal is consuming at the given moment. When eating the same matter, the conditioned reflexes are conducted toward the gastric glands from the perceiving surfaces of the eye, the nose, and possibly also of the mouth cavity." [29]

Whether the conditioned stimuli will cause a positive or a negative reaction by the nutrient center and by the organs of digestion depends upon positive or negative unconditioned stimuli with which they have become linked. In the complex conditions of life, different people may be found to react differently to somewhat similar circumstances: Ivan may have had the action of a positive, unconditioned stimulant coincide several times with one ineffectual condition, e.g., the music of the gramophone played constantly as dinner was being served, while Peter, on the other hand, associates dinner with the vision of flowers on the table. It is easily understood, therefore, that in some people a given object may cause a positive stimulation of the nutrient center and, accordingly, of appetite, while in others it may have no effect, and in still others it may give a negative stimulation. Thus, it is inevitable that we shall find great variations in these responses from one individual to another, from one population to another, and from one social class to another.

To conclude the discussion of the characterization of conditioned reflexes, I must indicate here that, in comparison with unconditioned reflexes, they are less stable and have the capacity to vanish. If we were to initiate a conditioned reflex several times by means of a conditioned stimulus without the participation of the unconditioned stimulus on which it is based (for example, to produce the secretion of saliva by lighting an electric lamp without substantiating it by giving food), then after a series of repetitions the conditioned stimulus becomes functionless and ceases to call forth the reflex, and the

29. A work by Babkin is cited.

latter vanishes. The organism ceases to react, as if convinced of a "deceit." To reinstall the vanished conditioned reflex it is necessary to repeat its concomitant action with the unconditioned reflex.

The conditioned reflex may be nourished not only upon the unconditioned but also upon an active conditioned reflex, which has not vanished.[30]

In brief, such is the general conception of conditioned reflexes and of the ways in which the nutrient center and the organs of digestion are stimulated by the conditioned reflex. Their significance in the nutrition of the organism is obvious.

The facts brought forward by Petrajitsky on stimulation and inhibition of hunger-appetite, in support of his theory of the independence of the latter from physiological hunger, can be explained perfectly by the "physiological" theory of hunger. They are not only explained, but in every case even can be predicted by it. The most capricious variations in "hunger-appetite" are well understood and coordinated after they are explained through the mechanism of conditioned reflexes. This leads to the formulation of a theorem: *The curve of the subjective experience of hunger is a function of the corresponding stimulation of the nutrient center, which depends upon the character of the conditioned and unconditioned, positive and negative stimuli acting upon it. This means that the subjective appetite-hunger is a function of objective deficiency and comparative starvation* (because we see that quality and quantity of food agents are not indifferent even in the lack of deficiency starvation). To understand any doubtful facts in this respect it is essential to consider: (1) the character of the stimuli which come from the blood and stimulate the nutrient center at a particular moment (the chemical composition of the blood); (2) the character of unconditioned and conditioned stimuli which influence the center simultaneously; and (3) the nature of other irritants, foreign to the nutrient center, which influence it directly or indirectly through the transmitter pathways. Our subjective experience of hunger-appetite is the equilibrium of these objectively given conditions, always concrete, difficult, and manifold. At any given moment the animal (as well as the man) is subjected to a whole series of influences, which impinge upon him

30. Works of I. P. Pavlov, G. P. Zelenyi, W. M. Bekhterev, K. S. Lashley, J. B. Watson, and P. A. Sorokin are cited. These references indicate the tremendous importance of the conditioned reflex not only for the present topic, but for human behavior in general.

from the surrounding environment; at a given moment any one or more of these stimuli may predominate. Thus, the organism is subjected either to one or another group of stimuli. But usually different stimulations are acting upon the organism simultaneously.[31] If this is so, if the organism and particularly the nutrient center are constantly subjected to the action of a whole series of stimuli, then, in this as in other reflexes, two principal cases can be distinguished. "During the correlation of concomitant reflexes only those which mutually complement one another unite into a harmonic group." Consider, for example, a healthy organism, hungry blood, clean air, stimulated by the taste of a piece of beefsteak, an appetizing smell of fried onions, a glass of wine, a well-set table, flowers, and pleasant music. All of this complex of positive conditioned and unconditioned reflexes, on one hand, and complete absence of the counterstimuli or inhibiting influences, on the other, result in a "wolf's appetite." These are the "alternating reflexes" which form a special reflex called an "alternating arc." [32]

31. A work of S. D. Sherrington is cited.

32. A work of Sherrington is cited. An excellent artistic illustration of this kind of reflex is found in Chekhov's story "The Siren." Here is a fragment of it. "We all want to eat now," says Zhilin, "because we are tired and it is already after three o'clock" [no food had been eaten for some time, hence the blood acts positively, and no inhibitive impulses come from the empty stomach]. "But, my dear, this is not a real appetite. The real wolf's appetite occurs after physical exertion, and after a hunt with the dogs, when one is so hungry, that it seems as if one could eat his own father" [the imagination plays also a great role (conditioned reflexes)]. "Suppose you come home from a hunt and want to arouse an appetite. It is necessary in such cases to think about the little carafe of vodka and the hors d'oeuvres. Once, on the way home I closed my eyes, and imagined a suckling pig with horseradish and became hysterical from the appetite. Furthermore, when you get to your yard, you should smell the aroma from the kitchen. After entering the house, the table should be nicely set. Then you sit down, take your napkin, place it carefully under your necktie and only then reach slowly for the carafe of vodka. You pour the delicious drink not into an ordinary glass, but into an old fashioned silver goblet, or in some other container with the inscription: 'The same is imbibed by monks' [all positive conditioned stimulants]. Then you drink it not at once, but first you sigh, rub your hands, look up at the ceiling, and then slowly bring the vodka to your lips [teasing and time are important for the work of the organs of secretion] and at that moment you will experience sparks throughout the whole body. Soon after you have had your drink you must have hors d'oeuvres [positive unconditioned stimulus]. Well, my dear, one must also know how to take a bite properly. Herring is the best thing as a snack," etc. (Anton Chekhov, *Complete Works* [Petrograd, 1918], 1:13–18). Everything

Similar cases of the concomitant action of negative, conditioned, and unconditioned stimuli (such as poor health, a full stomach, a piece of 'bad meat in the mouth, a cockroach in the soup, a soiled tablecloth, talk about corpses, etc.) may also affect the nutrient center. All these conditions taken together produce the same effect— negative stimulation of the nutrient center. It would be a miracle if the hunger-appetite were to appear under such circumstances. Such is the first type of concomitant action in which several conditioned stimuli react in the absence of the opposite, counteracting stimuli. In real life such situations rarely occur. More often, a series of conditions and stimuli, frequently quite opposite to one another, affect man and his nutrient center. According to Sherrington, there are antagonistic reflexes incompatible to each other. They not only fail to cooperate, but they inhibit each other.[33] As applied to the problem in which we are interested, this means *that one part of the stimuli with which the human being is surrounded stimulates the nutrient center positively and, therefore, produces hunger-appetite, while another part produces negative stimuli, which inhibit hunger-appetite. The two groups of stimuli are antagonistic to one another and tend to produce opposite reactions from the nutrient center, or in our subjective understanding they cause the opposite experiences.* In other words, there is a conflict of stimuli. The result of this conflict depends upon the comparative strength of the two antagonistic groups of stimuli. When these groups are unevenly matched, the victor dominates the nutrient center and calls forth corresponding reactions in the center and in the digestive organs. When the forces are equal, the antagonists annihilate each other, and until the conditions change, the nutrient center maintains *status quo ante*. This explains why we have no appetite after prolonged starvation, during illness, or in time of deep sorrow; why an appetite that was present

---

in this is correct. As a matter of fact it is so correct that by his descriptions of conditioned positive stimuli, Mr. Zhilin teased the appetites of his listeners (who had not had dinner yet) to such extent that they could no longer resist temptation and left the meeting to go to eat before finishing the purpose for which they had gathered. See the scientific verification of all this in Pavlov's lectures on "The Work of Principal Digestive Glands," *Proceedings of the Society of Russian Physicians* (St. Petersburg, 1894–95), p. 204 (in Russian).

33. Works of Sherrington, Zelenyi, M. F. Washburn, and S. B. Russel are cited.

disappears during fear, terror, etc.; why during intensive intellectual work, which inhibits the nutrient center, a good appetite is lacking, etc.[34] Conversely, under certain circumstances we experience the desire to eat even in the presence of inhibitory factors (for example, during distress, eating bad or little nutritious food which does not arouse an appetite, eating horse meat, dog meat, etc.) which in normal times would cause disgust. The former examples would indicate that the conflict has ended with the victory of the inhibitory stimuli, while the latter cases indicate the victory of the positive stimuli over the inhibitory.

The mechanism of the function of human nutrition has now been sufficiently outlined. We know its "director," its "working organs," the means by which its action is initiated, and the ways it regulates the work of the "food factory." The mechanism is very complex, very delicate, and very purposeful.[35] We also see that the principal part of its work occurs without the participation of the higher centers of consciousness (the humoral way of stimulation) and through the unconditioned reflexes.[36] We apprehend the complexity of all the conditions on which the work of the nutrient center and that of the whole food factory are dependent. The relationship between objective physiological processes and subjective experience of hunger-appetite, as well as their fluctuations, becomes obvious to us.

Therefore, for the explanation of the curve of hunger-appetite, it is not necessary to presume the existence of some other "independent variable." Hunger-appetite is adequately explained by the physiological processes consisting of objective, palpable stimulants which directly affect the nutrient center and the subordinated organs. The character of these stimuli conditions the character of the physiological

34. In the story by Chekhov cited above, Mr. Zhilin says: "When you wish to have a good dinner, never think about anything serious. Intelligence and learning always kill the appetite. You know yourself that philosophers and scientists are the last people, as far as food is concerned; even pigs, pardon me, eat better." A similar inhibitory factor occurs during intensive intellectual work: Pavlov, "Lectures," pp. 202–3.

35. Nemilov remarks correctly: "It is evident that nature does not trust the human mind to govern the necessity of the food intake. As soon as the body begins to feel the deficiency of fuel (food), it automatically starts the signals in the form of hunger."

36. Later it will be indicated that in man this mechanism may deteriorate considerably under the influence of some social conditions.

processes of nutrition, and, simultaneously with them, the character of the corresponding psychological experiences of fullness, pleasant appetite, weak hunger, or painful starvation. Thus, a bridge is formed between the outside-world and the subjective experiences. The quality and quantity of the food reagents taken in by the organism thus become the principal outside stimulants. The fluctuations of these independent variables (cases of deficiency and comparative starvation) call forth the fluctuations of physiological processes and corresponding variation of subjective experiences.

Once we have established the concepts of hunger, and of the mechanism of the "food factory," we shall begin the study of how those functions, through the variations in the frequency, the quality, and the quantity of food taken in by the organism, produce changes (1) in the organism itself, (2) in its physiological functions, (3) in its psychological processes, (4) in men's behavior, and (5) in the social organization and life of the population.

My immediate task is the elucidation of points four and five; but in the last analysis the social processes are a function of the behavior of members of the society, and the behavior of each member is a function of the structure of his organism, and its physical and psychological qualities. Therefore, without a brief elucidation of points one, two, and three, it is impossible to understand points four and five. Hence, it is necessary to consider the first three points. For detailed study the reader is referred to the courses in human anatomy and physiology, as well as to the special monographs. Points one, two, and three I shall discuss briefly, and only those aspects which are directly necessary for the understanding of my purpose, i.e., of the functions of hunger in the behavior of people and in the social processes.[37]

37. A number of arrogant defenders of "autonomy" in sociology and in some other disciplines may object to all the problems introduced here, and may consider the "introduction" to be superfluous. My answer to this is that they are essential, as a starting point. The autonomy of biology does not preclude basing its disciplines on the facts of physics and chemistry, and biologists find this not to be shameful, but on the contrary, promote it to the maximum. The same is true about the relationship between sociology and biology. By ignoring biology, the "autonomists" are obliged to base their theories on fantasy. I am not a believer in such procedures.

2

CHANGES IN THE STRUCTURE OF PHYSIOLOGICAL AND PSYCHOLOGICAL PROCESSES OF THE ORGANISM CONNECTED WITH VARIATIONS IN THE QUANTITY AND QUALITY OF FOOD CONSUMED (AND ABSORBED), PARTICULARLY DURING STARVATION

The character of the motion of any machine depends first of all upon its structure, and a change in structure causes a change in the movement. The same is applicable to man: if he loses a hand or a leg, the character of his motion and behavior inevitably is different. The same applies to any change in his organism, skeleton, muscles, organs of secretion, nervous system, etc.

Hence, we can conclude: *the structure of the organism is one of independent variables which determine the character of human behavior and, through it, the character of the social processes.* We may ask if the transformation of the organism depends upon the quantity and quality of food consumed, and if the variation in the latter produces change in the former. The answer to that is positive. This means that the variation in quantity and quality of food is one of the independent variables related to variation in the structure of the organism; the latter in turn produces variation in behavior and, in the case of mass variations, it becomes an independent variable influencing the social processes.

Changes in the Somatic Structure of Animals under the Influence of Changed Nutrition

It can be proved experimentally that by varying the quantity of food, the structure of the organism may be changed. In various species Darwin observed the relationship of nutrition to a whole series of morphological characteristics. Pikte "showed that strong modification of morphological forms occurs after caterpillars are given food to which they are not accustomed." According to De Fries "the variations depend completely upon the physiology of nutrition." Similar results were obtained by Jennings for the Protista.[1] Experiments with butterflies convinced Hoffman that the structure and coloration of the wings vary under the influence of changed nutrition, and that this feature is inherited. Pikte fed butterflies (*Ocneria dispar*) a special diet and produced hereditary changes in their coloration. In many zoological species parts of the alimentary canal show a great variety in structure in accordance with the type of food used by the organism.

Holmgren and A. Danilevsky proved experimentally the dependence of some morphological characteristics upon nutrition. By feeding pigeons exclusively with meat they succeeded in transforming them into birds of prey. The muscles of the stomach became atrophied, although they are well developed in grain-eating birds, the corneous mucosa became glandular, and, most interesting of all, the disposition of the birds changed; they became vicious, irritable, grabbed food eagerly, etc.[2] Furthermore, a whole series of experiments shows that changes in the structure of the organism, particularly in the organs of secretion, which are caused by nutrition may determine the sex of newborns. For example, *Daphnia*, which is generally parthenogenetic, produces females when food is plentiful, and males when it is scarce. Landois was convinced that good nutrition facilitates sex development while starvation results in underdevelopment of sex organs, i.e., the organs of reproduction. Many entomologists (Gentry, Treat) believe that malnutrition in caterpillars of butterflies results in formation of males only. Schults found that, with *Hydra*, starvation facilitates the early development of male

1. A work of R. Goldsmidt is cited.
2. A work of B. Koldaev is cited.

sex characteristics. Marshall found that, with Lepidoptera, malnutrition causes the early development of male sex characteristics and development of males in the next generation. But Young thinks that food of animal origin favors the production of females.[3] Experiments by Gedda and Thomson showed that whether the egg shall produce a queen bee or a sterile female worker depends upon the quantity of food. One hundred polliwogs produced 43 males to 57 females under normal nutrition, 22 males to 78 females when it was supplemented, and 8 males to 92 females when food was overabundant.[4] Many similar experiments have been carried out with mammals. Henseler worked with pigs, which were kept under similar environment but were fed with normal, supplemental, and deficient diets. After 199 days the starved and overfed pigs showed differences in structure and behavior. The overfed specimens gained from 17 to 140 kilograms in weight, while the starved ones gained from 12.4 to 23.5 kilograms. They also developed differences in the size and structure of their craniums. The overfed specimens had round, wide heads, while those of the starved pigs were long and narrow.[5]

The experiments of Osborne and Mendel, Halliberton and Drummond, Daniels and Nichols, and those of Palladin in Russia showed that in the absence of vitamins from food, or of the "factors of the growth," in Palladin's terminology, the growth of the animal decreases, and then ceases. Emma Kohmann experimented with rats and got the following results: growth of rats decreased when they were fed foods deficient in proteins (carrots), i.e., their weight fell 30–33 per cent in 9–10 weeks, and 46 per cent in 16 weeks; the tissues changed and edema occurred after 3 weeks, etc. The symptoms disappeared with the introduction into the diet of fully nutrient proteins.[6] Similar results were secured by B. I. Slovtsov. Addition of phosphoproteins (from milk) to food effects a particularly strong growth of teeth. In younger animals it may facilitate growth of the long tubular bones. Noticeable also is its effect on the blood-producing organs. The amount of ash increases in the long tubular bones. Calcification of bones is more intensive.[7]

3. A work of Lapinsky is cited.
4. A work of W. M. Bekhterev is cited.
5. A work of Henseler is cited.
6. Emma Kohmann, "The Experimental Production of Edema as Related to Protein Deficiency," *American Journal of Physiology* 51 (1920):378.
7. A work of B. I. Slovtsov is cited.

Similar facts are well known to animal breeders. Fodder produces profound changes in the organs of animals. Profuse and deficient feeding of young animals is a very important factor in the variability of animals, the real significance of which is not fully appreciated. A few experiments may be cited. One young goat was fed milk, and another given only vegetable fodder. The following changes were observed in the volume of different parts of the stomach, and in the length of the intestines. The kid fed vegetable fodder showed a volume of tripe and honeycomb bag of 6,910 cc and an intestine length of 22 m. The milk-fed kid had a volume of 3,150 cc and a length of 19.37 m.

The experiments of Chirvinsky with lambs (some fed adequately and others deficiently with a coarse fodder) gave after 15 months the following results. The overall length of the gastric tube was 44–51 times as long as the body in the animal with deficient nutrition; in well-fed lambs it was only 33–38 times as long. The difference in the volume of the stomach was still more significant. The first group had 270 cc of stomach volume per kilogram of body weight; the second group had 800–900 cc, or three times as large.[8]

Change may occur not only in the organs of digestion, but also in other organs. After intensive feeding of young animals, growth of bone is accelerated. Morphological changes may occur in the cranium and in various tissues. The experiments of Pashutin with dogs showed that before conception and during pregnancy, even a small decrease in food (from 1/10 to 1/3), and comparatively short periods of starvation, caused tissue changes in progeny. Tissues became edemic; the solids of the organism decreased from 23.4 to 18.5 per cent; fats also decreased.[9]

Thus, variations in the quantity and quality of food consumed by the organism cause structural changes in an animal. This occurs in all animal phyla, from the invertebrates to the mammals.

Changes in the Somatic Structure of Man under the Influence of Nutrition

The facts given about the changes in the structure of animal organisms with variations in nutrition suggest that a similar phenomenon

8. A work of Chirvinsky is cited.
9. A work of Pashutin is cited.

occurs in man. Numerous investigations and observations verify this proposition. Let us start with the digestive organs.

Changes in organs of nutrition.—When the ordinary food of a man, or of a whole group of people, is hard, coarse, and often eaten raw, then, according to our supposition, such a man or group, if they are not to perish, must have strongly developed jaws and teeth, which will permit them to chew and grind their food into a form in which it can be assimilated. Similar organs require no extraordinary development in groups of people who for generations eat light, less rough, and less coarse foods.

To compare from this point of view the development of these organs in "primitive," or so-called wild peoples, with those of "civilized" people, the priority goes to the former group. The food of the primitives is harder, rougher, coarser and less digestible. Herbert Spencer correctly pointed out that development of the jaws and teeth of primitive people is directly connected with the use of rough, hard, coarse and often raw food.[10]

A similar influence of the quantity, quality, and character of food is found directly, or indirectly, in the *structure of man's digestive system and particularly in the stomach and intestines.* Irregular eating by people, frequent shifts from starvation to gluttony and consumption of tremendous amounts of food (which partially facilitates survival), its low quality which necessitates large quantities, swelling of the digestive organs by gases from such food, etc., all must call forth strong development and great length and volume of these organs.[11] Indirect proofs apparently confirm this. Investigators of primitive people often observed that under such nutrition, the stomach is often protruding, pendulous, and swollen. The Bushmen, according to Barro, have very protruding stomachs; Schweinfurth speaks about the enormous swollen stomachs of the Akka tribe; and so on. Even if the protrusion and swelling of the stomach is partially explained by the development of gases during the digestion of rough food, we still could hardly be wrong in suggesting that the corresponding dietary regime of primitive people is the real cause of the increase in length and volume of the stomach and intestines.[12]

10. Works of Herbert Spencer and Theodor Waitz are cited.

11. Works of E. Westermarck and Waitz are cited.

12. It is a well-known fact that the digestive system of carnivorous animals is shorter than that of herbivorous animals which consume an enormous quantity of vegetable food.

Nutrition and stature.—The structure of the organs of nutrition
not only depends upon quantity and quality of food, but a whole series
of the somatic characteristics of the human organism is connected
with this factor. One of them is the stature, or *height*, of the organism. Because the dimension of stature depends upon the size of the
bones, the dependence of stature upon nutrition means a dependence
of the whole series of morphological characteristics of the organism
upon the same "independent variable." True, dimension of stature is
the function of not only one factor, nutrition, but of many others as
well. However, nutrition plays its role, and apparently a very significant one.

The above-mentioned experiments by Osborne, Mendel, Halliberton, Drummond, Palladin, etc., lead to the conclusion that lack of
"fatty factor A" (according to Palladin's terminology) in food which
otherwise is quite sufficient and of good quality hinders the growth
of mice, rats, and other animals. "Factor A" is not found in vegetable
oil, or in lard, but is plentiful in milk and butter. When the animals
were given food lacking "factor A," their growth stopped; when
this element was added, growth resumed and became normal.

With complete justification the authors apply this finding to man,
and connect it with the activity of the organs of internal secretion.
Growth and formation of bones depend on inner secretion, and this
activity depends upon the quality of the chemical elements received
by the organism in the form of food and drink. When necessary salts,
vitamins, lipids, and amino acids are absent, the organs of inner
secretion cease functioning normally; as a result the structure of the
bones, and of the organism, is deformed; and specifically growth
either stops or becomes very slow. Thus, as Lapinsky indicates, because of an abnormal chemical composition of drinking water, the
thyroid gland may be changed in the prenatal stage and this may
result in the abnormality of the skeleton (cranium and length of
bones) and of nerve centers, and may even produce idiocy (cretinism). Inhabitants of Eastern Siberia were victims of poor-quality
water and therefore exhibited abnormalities of the skeleton in the
form of shortening of the tubular bones. The symptoms of the ex-
ophthalmic goiter (Basedow's disease) and myxedema have somewhat similar origins.

From this point of view, it is easily understood that frequently
the food of a whole group of people may be unsatisfactory. During
periods of extreme starvation, like the present one [1922] in Russia,

food is deficient quantitatively and qualitatively and lacks sufficient amounts of vitamins, lipids, and factors of growth. The nutrition of poorer classes is even worse than that of the affluent.

If these suppositions are correct—that growth depends upon nutrition, and particularly upon the presence in food of the lipide factor of growth, and that the food of poorer classes is often deficient in this respect—it follows *that the average stature of the poor of a given race, sex, and age must be lower in comparison with the stature of rich people of the same race, sex, and age.*

The deficiencies in food mentioned occur frequently among primitive peoples who live in poverty-stricken countries and, therefore, their *stature must be very low.*

Finally, from this it follows *that with an increase in wealth of the population, and consequently with an improvement in nutrition, the average height of the people of one generation may increase in comparison with the average height of the previous generation which lived in a less favorable period.*

Such are the propositions arising out of discoveries in biology. Are they substantiated by adequate evidence? I think that they are. From masses of corresponding facts and measurements, I shall present here merely a sample, and for further information I refer the reader to the literature cited.

Consider first the stature of primitive people. The relationship between the extraordinary low stature of a number of primitive peoples, or even low stature of the poorest stratum of a given people, and their meager nutrition was observed long ago. "When we compare the differences in stature between the Polynesian chiefs and the lower orders within the same islands, or between the inhabitants of the fertile volcanic and low barren coral islands of the same ocean, or again between Fuegians on the eastern and western shores of their country, where the means of subsistence are very different, it is scarcely possible to avoid the conclusion that better food and greater comfort do influence stature." [13]

The low stature of several primitive tribes was noticed also by Herbert Spencer who indicated that the average height of Chukchis, Shoshones, Guiana Indians, Eskimos, Lapps, Kamchadals, Bushmen, etc., ranges from 4 to 5 feet, and rarely reaches 5½ feet.

13. Charles Darwin, *The Descent of Man* (London: John Murray, 1871), p. 46.

According to Spencer, this low stature is associated with scarcity of food and unfavorable climatic conditions. Inadequate nutrition is also considered by Waitz to be the cause of low stature. The height of Eskimos varies according to the relative prosperity of their habitats. The Yakuts living in the southern mountain valleys have good nutrition, range in height from 5'10" to 6'4", and are strong and well built. In contrast, the northern Yakuts are lower than average in stature, are weak, and have skin with an unhealthy color. The same contrast occurs between the deer-herding Chukchis and those living along the seashores. The former are in a better physical state. Similarly, the relationship between nutrition and height can be observed between different branches of Arabs: groups south of Damascus are shorter in stature and their nutrition is poorer, compared with the Fellah group.[14] O. Peschel indicates also that the average height of members of the ruling families of the Kaffirs is 110 mm higher than that of subordinate members of this society, and that the height of Bushmen living in a fertile region is considerably higher than that of the general population of the tribe, which is of low stature. The height of members of lower castes in India averages 1,634 mm, compared to the height of medium castes of the same race, which averages 1,646 mm (the sample includes about 3,000 individuals).[15]

Without further discussion, we conclude that our second proposition is confirmed.

Naturally, not all primitive people are of low stature, as not all of them are poorly fed, nor is food the only factor related to growth.[16] But biological experiments along with the facts indicated above, the number of which could be added to substantially, all sustain the probability of a relationship between nutrition and height of people.

Numerous measurements indicate that wealthy people and the better-fed of the same race, age, and sex are taller, on average, than

14. The work of Waitz is cited.

15. In this paragraph the works of Waitz, O. Peschel, and Crooke are cited. Among different strata of Indo-Aryans, e.g., the Rajput of Udaipur and the Chuhra of the Punjab, heights also differ; the former are taller, which reflects their better nutrition and other social conditions. See *The Imperial Gazetteer of India* (Oxford, 1907), 1:292–93.

16. Among Australian aboriginals, people of the Warramunga group are taller than the members of the Arunta, although the nutrition of the former is no better, and perhaps even worse, than that of the latter. [The works of Spencer and Gillen are cited.]

their fellows who are poorer and less well fed. Materials on heights of military recruits are numerous. They include data from France, Germany, Italy, Switzerland, the United States, and, to some extent, Russia; the general conclusion is that height decreases with a decrease in economic conditions of soldiers of the same race. Thus, according to Livi, average heights in centimeters of Italian recruits (in a sample of 256,166 soldiers) were as follows: students, 166.9; merchants, 165.0; peasants, artisans, and laborers, from 165 to 164.3. Longuet reported that heights of French recruits were as follows: students, 168.7; clerks, 167.4; merchants and shopkeepers, 165.1; laborers, 164.4. The heights of Spanish recruits, as given by Oloriz, were: liberal professions, 163.9; laborers, 159.8.[17]

Along with measurements of recruits and soldiers, there are numerous anthropometric measurements which were conducted for various purposes. Here it is enough to mention those made by Villermé and Kettlet, Roberts, Pagliani, Landsberger, Manouvrier, Collignon, Niceforo, Zampa, Gould, and Marty et al., and English, American and Italian official publications, to indicate that, in general, they all show that the stature of wealthy people is greater than that of poor people of the same age, sex, and race.

The authors mentioned have investigated the problem from different points of view. Some of them measured and compared heights of inhabitants of mountains, who have a poor diet and a low standard of living, with those of people living in valleys, who are more affluent and better fed; others compared inhabitants of more prosperous provinces with the populations of poorer regions; still others compared heights of residents of wealthy districts of a town with those in poor sections; a fourth group of investigators compared heights of those in various rich and poor professional and occupational groups. The more prosperous strata of a population are, as a rule, better fed. The greater height of their members is a function of many conditions, but the nature of the diet is a principal one. From numerous figures and data, I shall mention here only a few, and shall refer the reader to the literature for further details. Bertilion found in northeastern France two groups of people who differed in height, and he attributed this to a different degree of economic well-being. Manouvrier used the proportion of paupers' graves per 100 burials as an indicator of the poverty of population in different sec-

17. Works by Livi, Longuet, and Oloriz are cited.

tions of Paris. The lowest stature he found was in district XX, in which the percentage of paupers' graves was highest. There was a gradual decrease in stature (with a few exceptions) as one passed from the sections having the lowest to the highest percentage of paupers' graves. Niceforo studied the height of 3,147 children of Lausanne, and secured the following figures (in centimeters):[18]

Age (years)	Boys		Girls	
	Affluent	Poor	Affluent	Poor
7	120.0	116.1	—	—
8	126.2	122.5	123.3	119.5
9	129.9	123.9	129.6	124.4
10	134.2	128.9	135.2	129.7
11	135.2	134.2	137.4	134.1
12	140.5	138.8	142.9	140.1
13	144.4	140.5	148.2	146.5
14	150.1	146.2	152.6	146.4

The figures of Pagliani for the height of boys of Turin (in centimeters) are:[19]

Age (years)	Wealthy	Poor
11	133.6	128.5
12	137.0	132.5
13	142.5	138.6
14	150.6	140.0
15	157.2	148.6
16	163.8	151.2
17	164.0	151.4

The weights and heights of 72,000 school children were obtained in 1905–6 in Glasgow. The number of rooms in the parents' apart-

18. Alfredo Niceforo, *Les classes pauvres* (Paris, 1905), p. 21.
19. Luigi Pagliani, *Annales di Statistique* (1878), p. 228.

ment was used as a criterion of economic status, and the results are as follows:[20]

Number of rooms in apartment	Average height of boys (in inches)		
	5 years	9 years	13 years
1	39.0	46.5	53.4
2	39.9	47.6	54.1
3	40.7	48.2	55.1
more than 3	41.4	48.9	55.8
	Average height of girls		
1	38.9	46.2	53.0
2	39.8	46.9	54.8
3	40.2	47.7	55.5
more than 3	41.0	48.6	56.4

The average heights in centimeters of Englishmen aged 25–70 and of different professions, according to Roberts, are as follows: free affluent professions, 172.4; merchants and shopkeepers, 170.8; laborers working out of doors, 170.3; miners, 169.8; and laborers indoors, 169.6. His summary table of the heights of Englishmen is as follows:[21]

Age	Aristocrats and liberal professions	Town mechanics
20	175.46	168.91
21–24	174.80	169.03
25–29	175.61	169.72
30–34	176.81	169.29
35–39	176.81	170.38
40–49	176.22	169.67
50–59	176.53	168.78
60–69	175.51	168.91

20. Webb, *The New Dictionary of Statistics* (London, 1911), p. 47.
21. Charles Roberts, "The Physical Development of the Human Body," *Manual of Anthropology* (1878).

In all these measurements the greater height of the wealthy classes is not caused, of course, solely by better nutrition. But the latter is one of the main factors that produces this greater growth. Hence, we conclude that our second proposition is verified.

Finally, we can partially verify our third proposition, that the height of population born and living during economically favorable times is slightly greater than that of similar people living under unfavorable conditions (and this is particularly evident among children).[22]

Ammon noted greater height in German recruits in 1880–90 compared with similar groups in 1840–50, and he explained it by the better diet and greater affluency of the former.[23] Conversely, in Germany, when there were food shortages during the war years, the heights of school boys decreased about 2 centimeters. In France and Belgium during World War I, when nutrition was deficient, children lost in weight and in height.[24] In Petrograd the average height of children 7–13 years old was less during famine years than in more normal years. Table 1 gives measurements of the heights of boys and girls of Petrograd in 1920–21 and compares them with similar groups measured during previous years. The work was carried out at the Institute of P. F. Lesgaft by L. I. Chulitskaya, to whom I express my indebtedness.

The examination of the table suggests these things. (1) During starvation years the height of children is lower. The retardation is particularly noticeable among those aged seven to nine. (2) Children living in children's homes (intern) are of lower stature than those living outside (extern). The study also showed that there was a higher percentage of scurvy with deficient lymphatic system among the first group. This is indicative of poor nutrition, which is one of the causes of lower height. (3) The "externs" have a compensating growth at the age of ten years.

Furthermore, as shown by measurements of French army recruits during the 1890s, those who were conceived and born during the siege of Paris (and the great famine of 1870–71) were of very short stature. They even had a special name for them, *les enfants de*

22. A work of Anuchin is cited.
23. Otto Ammon, *Die natürliche Auslese beim Menschen* (Jena, 1893).
24. A work of Apert is cited.

Table 1
Average Heights of Petrograd Children in 1921–22 and Earlier Years (in centimeters)

Age	Data for 1921–22		Data of Bobrov	Data of Matveev	Data for Moscow
	Intern	Extern			
Boys					
7	105.9	112	118	115.8	113.1
8	112.8	115.8	118.5	120.5	116.32
9	117.4	122.5	122.9	123.3	121.04
10	121.8	126.5	126.8	127.0	125.91
11	126.0	129.5	130.4	128.9	129.56
12	131.8	134.5	132.01	134.2	134.05
Girls					
7	111.0	110.5	112.06	118.6	—
8	116.0	115.5	118.59	122.6	119.2
9	116.9	117.5	121.58	126.8	123.3
10	119.0	125.0	124.93	131.2	127.2
11	122.6	130.8	129.26	135.0	131.7
12	128.6	135.0	133.73	136.5	135.6

siège.[25] Religious fasting, even when not strictly adhered to, causes considerable starvation and some retardation in growth in stature of the young.[26]

In conclusion, I would like to quote the words of Topinard, which are quite appropriate: "The dimension of height can be regarded as a criterion of nutrition and of its effects, which are retained and accumulated by the organism." [27]

Character of nutrition and volume of the chest.—Experiments of biologists and animal breeders show that not only size and rapidity of growth of bones are influenced by nutrition, but that other parts of the skeleton, such as the cranium, also are changed by it. It is only

25. An article by Tarasevich on "Starvation," in *Grant's Encyclopedia*, is cited.
26. A work of B. Pashutin is cited.
27. P. Topinard, *L'anthropologie générale* (Paris, 1885), pp. 416, 428.

natural to assume that a similar change takes place among humans. Indeed a series of anthropometric measurements of volume of the chest (inhaled and exhaled) of wealthy and poor people of the same race, sex, and age showed that, on average, the first group has a larger chest volume. Here again I emphasize that this difference is not caused exclusively by difference in nutrition, but that the latter is one of the factors. For illustration here are some measurements of the perimeter of the chest (exhaled) of 3,147 boys from Lausanne and those from Turin. The indicators of the bigger chest volume of the wealthy boys show connection with better nutrition with one exception, for the 11-year-old boys.

	Lausanne: Chest Measurement in Centimeters [28]		Turin: Volume of Air Inhaled and Exhaled [29]	
	Wealthy	Poor	Wealthy	Poor
7	56.4	55.4	—	—
8	57.1	57.0	—	—
9	58.7	58.1	—	—
10	60.4	59.6	—	—
11	60.9	62.9	1717	1580
12	64.6	63.6	1868	1860
13	65.7	64.5	2022	1980
14	69.6	66.6	2875	2025
15	—	—	2870	2380
16	—	—	3060	2585

Nutrition and structure of the cranium.—Experiments with animals show that type of nutrition influences structure of the head and cranium.[30] A series of anthropometric measurements of heads of wealthy and poor people indicates that this observation is applicable to humans. These measurements show that circumference of the cranium, height of the forehead, and, apparently, weight of the brain

28. Niceforo, op. cit., p. 25.
29. Pagliani, op. cit. Cf. Lexis, "Anthropologie und Anthropometrie," *Handwörterbuch des Staatswissenschaft* (Conrad, 1908), Band F, pp. 535–36.
30. A work of Chirvinsky is cited.

of those belonging to wealthy classes are greater than the same measurements of the poor of the same race, sex, and age. According to Niceforo the corresponding figures are as follows:[31]

Age	Circumference of Head (millimeters)		Height of Forehead (millimeters)		Apparent Weight of Brain (grams)	
	Wealthy	Poor	Wealthy	Poor	Wealthy	Poor
10	528.0	523.3	52.3	50.4	1334.58	1326.75
11	533.0	524.8	53.7	50.8	1352.88	1335.45
12	535.5	524.9	56.2	52.9	1358.07	1335.45
13	536.4	528.4	55.3	53.1	1358.07	1335.45
14	541.8	528.4	56.9	54.8	1371.12	1337.19

According to Matiegka, average weights of the brain are as follows: workers, 1,410 grams; laborers and masons, 1,433 grams; merchants and musicians, 1,468 grams; doctors and professors, 1,500 grams.[32]

Similar results were obtained by many other investigators whose works are cited by Niceforo. If these results are general and reliable, they confirm directly results of experiments carried on with animals. Therefore, if we add to this the proved relationship between extreme deviations in structure of the cranium, e.g., of cretinism, and deficiency of normal thyroid secretion (and the action of the latter, as has been indicated, depends upon the character of the chemical elements taken in with food and drink), then, on the basis of these categories of facts, we conclude that deformation in structure of the head and the cranium may be caused by nutrition.

Nutrition and weight of the organism.—The relationship between nutrition and weight is quite obvious: good nutrition increases weight; poor nutrition diminishes it. During deficiency starvation the organism begins to digest itself, or to live by stored food and organs.

31. Niceforo, op. cit., pp. 33–37.
32. Matiegka, *Revue Scientifique* 1903 (cited in Niceforo, op. cit., pp. 37–38).

According to Foyt,[33] a cat which died from starvation lost from its earlier weight the following percentage of parts:

97.0 per cent of the fat	25.9 per cent of the kidneys
66.7 ” ” ” spleen	20.6 ” ” ” skin
53.7 ” ” ” liver	18.0 ” ” ” digestive system
40.0 ” ” ” sex organs	17.7 ” ” ” lungs
30.5 ” ” ” muscles	17.0 ” ” ” pancreas
27.0 ” ” ” blood	13.9 ” ” ” bones
3.2 ” ” ” nervous system	2.6 ” ” ” heart

Similar changes take place in human beings. Numerous observations on starving people are cited by Mulhall, H. D. Marsh, and others.[34] During the current years of deficiency starvation, many inhabitants of the USSR experienced first the loss of fat and other stored substances, then the loss of weight of the organs which are least important for the preservation of the life, and last of all, and also the smallest of all, decreases in the nervous system and the heart. However, the loss of weight during starvation was not always present because water often substituted for the weight lost by tissues.

Therefore, it is easy to conclude that the weights of people of the social classes that have good nutrition are higher on average than those of people (of the same race, sex, and age) who have poor nutrition. Existing anthropometric measurements confirm this observation. The following table of Niceforo gives weight figures in kilograms:[35]

Age (years)	Boys		Girls	
	Wealthy	Poor	Wealthy	Poor
7	23.0	21.1	—	—
8	24.2	23.0	24.0	22.5
9	26.5	24.7	26.1	24.2
10	28.5	26.9	28.7	26.4
11	29.6	29.4	30.8	29.1
12	32.3	32.3	33.3	33.6
13	35.3	33.5	38.1	37.5
14	40.5	37.8	44.9	41.7

33. A work by Landois-Rosemann is cited.
34. M. G. Mulhall, *Dictionary of Statistics* (London, New York: Routlege, 1884); H. D. Marsh, "Individual and Sex Differences Brought out by Fasting," *Psychological Review* 23 (1916):437–45.
35. Niceforo, op. cit., p. 22.

From this it follows that, *ceteris paribus*, the average weight of those in the wealthy strata of the population is greater than that of those in the poorer strata of the same race, and with an increase in prosperity and improvement in the nutrition of the people, their average weight increases—conversely, as starvation becomes more pronounced, it decreases.

Nutrition and composition of the organism.—Fluctuation of weight under the influence of nutrition indicates not only a morphological change in the organism, but a radical change in its composition. The following figures compiled by Gilbert give some idea of this:[36]

Animals	Nitrogen Compounds	Fat	Minerals	Dry Weight	Water
Lamb (lean)	14.8	18.7	3.2	36.7	57.3
Lamb (fat)	10.8	45.8	2.9	59.6	35.2
Pig (lean)	13.7	23.3	2.7	39.7	55.1
Pig (fat)	10.9	42.2	1.7	54.7	41.3

These animals were of the same breeds, but they were kept under different feeding conditions, and, as indicated by the data, they showed different constitutions. The same may be said of man. Intensified nutrition usually leads to obesity and to the increase of the "dry matter" as opposed to water. Conversely, starvation decreases fat and increases water content of the organism, and thus decreases the "dry matter." (Edema, due to starvation, was a common phenomenon of the inhabitants of the USSR's capital cities in 1919.) These phenomena, which are easily observed from the outside, are external manifestations of the complex internal, purely chemical processes of changes in the composition of the organism. Changes in the chemical composition of the brain during starvation serve here as an illustration. Previously, Chossat thought that although the composition of tissues and of other parts of the organism changed during starvation, the nervous system maintained its status quo. However, it appears that this system also changes. A. K. Lents studied the brains of eleven people who died from starvation in 1918. The weight of each brain was near to normal; even a small increase

36. A work in Russian by Kel'ner is given as the source of these data.

rather than a decrease could be detected occasionally; but in all cases the quantity of water in the brain was above normal, averaging about 2 per cent higher. The solid residue had diminished. The total quantity of proteins (nucleoproteids) had decreased. Particularly noticeable were the decline in neuroglobulins and the decrease in total amount of lipids. The general content of nitrogen and of phosphorus also decreased. In comparison with size of normal brains, the brains of starving people had lost 8.231 per cent in proteins, 11.48 per cent in lipids, 5.233 per cent in nitrogen, and 2.257 per cent in phosphorus. It is obvious that during starvation the brain loses its most important components and is destroyed in a way similar to other parts of the human organism.[37]

If such significant changes occur in the brain during starvation, the structures of other parts of the body must undergo even greater modifications. Changes of structure of the organism which occur as a result of changes in nutrition show that, in the end, *no part of the organism remains untouched* by sharp changes in nutrition. This means that all of our organs, or all parts of our body, show either internal or external variation in structure as a result of variation in nutrition. Taken as a whole, the indicated changes in the organism which occur as a result of starvation demonstrate beyond reasonable doubt the dependence of the structure of the organism upon the "independent variable" studied here.

To sum up, the following data from Niceforo depict the relationship between nutrition and physical characteristics of the inhabitants of northern and southern Italy:

	Northern Italians	Southern Italians
Physical characteristics:		
Average height (in centimeters)	165.5	162.8
Circumference of the cranium (in millimeters)	546	542
Calculated capacity of the cranium (in grams) (according to the method of Parchappe)	1,540	1,527
Cranium index	84.5	79.2
Chest perimeter (in centimeters)	87.5	86.2
Absolute weight (in kilograms)	65.2	63.9

37. Cited here from the author's resumé, which was kindly presented to me by A. K. Lents.

Nutrition (per person):					
Yearly consumption	of meat	(in kilograms)		17.9	7.7
"	"	of eggs	" "	4.3	2.1
"	"	of bread products	(in quintals)	2.1	1.6
"	"	of dried vegetables	(in kilograms)	9.3	7.0
Daily	"	of proteins (in grams)	" "	104	92
Income in francs				2,211	1,333

Conclusion: The human being is what he has eaten, particularly during the first years of his life, as well as what his parents ate during the time of conception and prenatal development. After this, it is not paradoxical to say that differences in nutrition, particularly during the periods of conception and development, may create anthropological types from persons of the same race. These types may be substantially different from each other, as are anthropological differences between those in poor and wealthy classes. This may even be independent of heredity. However, if we were to suggest that certain characteristics, obtained exclusively under the influence of nutrition, are inherited, then the difference solely in nutrition during several generations would have been capable of causing considerable variations among people of the same race. For this it would have been necessary that the nutrition of various groups of this race differ for several generations. In addition, we see that this factor has a direct and a very strong influence on the structure and the function of the organism, changing it "according to his own image and likeness."

Major changes in nutrition, starvation in particular, have their inevitable consequences. The organism's basic physiology is altered; this affects activity patterns which are summed up as the whole conduct of the organism. In turn, this results in deformation of mass behavior and leads toward modification of various social processes.

Nutrition and Physiological Processes

Fluctuations in the quantity and quality of food consumed, as well as in the time when it is eaten, cause variations both in physical appearance and in a number of physiological processes. The general mechanisms of stimulation and their variability have been described above. We saw that food and the phenomena connected with it (conditioned stimuli) stimulate the nutrient center of the organism (by means of humoral or reflex actions), and through it initiate the work of the organs of the food factory, which in turn changes its whole activity.

When the nutrient center is stimulated positively, the excitation is transmitted first of all to the working organs of nutrition, and later on is reflected in the whole constitution of the organism. The organism is an apparatus capable of performing quite diverse functions, first by the ability to perform two or more functions at the same time, second by alternating the functions; for example, at one time it is the reproductive function which is active, at others the nutritive, the protective, the creative (the transformation of lower forms of energy into the highest, i.e., creativity), etc. Either one or another group of the determinants of behavior takes possession of the organism, forcing it to react and to spread the reaction to still other groups of stimuli. During positive stimulation the nutrient center tends *to take complete possession of the organism as a "check payable to the bearer," and to convert it into an apparatus destined exclusively for the function of nutrition.* Accordingly, *in connection with this task, the whole life activity of the organism is rebuilt.* The organs which perform the function of nutrition (the muscles of the lips, tongue, cheeks, and pharynx, the glands, and the nervous system) exhibit at such times an intensified activity (in flow of blood, increase in size). The organs which are *outside the field of nutrition,* which do not facilitate this function, and often even inhibit it (for example, the sex organs) at such times become weakened and decrease their activity (exhibit flaccidity, decrease in size, and have an outflow of blood). The *essential* organs, those necessary for performance of all the functions of the organism and not just those of the nutritive functions (i.e., the heart, the respiratory system, etc.) may increase or decrease their activity in accordance with additional circumstances; but as a rule such changes are small and the degree of their fluctuation is limited. This briefly is the general scheme of fluctuation of the physiological processes of the organism during positive stimulation of the nutrient center.

Accordingly, at such times, the nutrient center "borrows" and "monopolizes" as its agents all the organs of the senses (sight, hearing, smell, taste, touch—briefly, all the receptive organs of the nervous system) and forces them to work intensively. They become the investigators, the controllers of the nutrient center, which detect, smell, touch, and find out what is suitable, good, and tasty for eating, and what is harmful. At such times "the nose" (i.e., the organ of smell) acts by itself to separate the appetizing from the unappetizing odors, the eyes survey the food, the hearing apparatus catches the conditioned food stimuli. At such times their "analytical capacity" becomes in some respects more acute and intense. As indicated later, these objective processes produce a series of subjective experiences in the form of "function" in the world of the subjective.

When this occurs, other working parts of the body, which have no relation to nutrition, serve as "agents" of the nutrient system. Thus, the arms stretch and bring food to the mouth; the feet carry the body to the place where food is to be found. In other words, a whole series of working parts that are not part of the system begins to assist in the function.

As to the organs of nutrition proper, they all begin to show an accelerated activity (the contraction of muscles of the mouth for seizing parcels of food, the work of teeth, tongue, gullet, stomach, intestines, secretory organs, etc.).

Under these circumstances, all of these physiological processes truly change the entire life activity of the organism. Because of this change, the behavior of the organism—i.e., the external and easily observed acts of motion—becomes different from the behavior when positive stimulation of the nutrient center is lacking (i.e., when the organism is fully satiated).

Such "transformations" or "deformations" of the physiological state of the organism occur daily in everyone because the rhythm of stimulation and deadening of the nutrient center alternate daily (hunger and satiation) in response to the conditioned and unconditioned reflexes which act upon it. Therefore, forms of behavior of man during the sated and hungry states alternate constantly, as a function of the physiological somatic deformations.

This rhythm of more or less regular intake of food, as we indicate later, causes daily repetition of people's activities, as well as daily repetition of the processes of social life.

It follows logically that deformation of the physiological state and of the total behavior of a man are particularly sharp when the intake and the absorption of food by the organism vary greatly. This occurs when intake of food ceases for a much longer period of time than is normal.

An organism which receives no food begins to live on its own energy. The nutrient center is stimulated by the impoverished blood and by a series of conditioned and unconditioned reflexes. This stimulation, however, is fruitless, because food energy is not taken in. After some time this stimulation occurs again, and again fades away. Later on, it sinks into the general abnormal state of the nervous system which results from prolonged absolute starvation.

Under such circumstances what happens with the fundamental processes of the organism? Studies of Pashutin, Luciani, Marsh, and others indicate that under prolonged starvation the temperature of the body and blood circulation undergo a series of changes. This is demonstrated by Marsh in Table 2, which depicts the results of starvation of the author and his wife over a period of three weeks. During the first week they gradually decreased intake of food, reaching zero at the end of the week; during the second week they ate no food at all, and drank only 500 to 750 cc of water; the third week they began to eat gradually, starting with insignificant portions of food and increasing the amounts daily.

The table shows the *fall of body temperature, weakening of activity of the heart*, and also the changes in morphological composi-

Table 2

	First Week		Second Week		Third Week	
	Male	Female	Male	Female	Male	Female
Outside T	85.3		82.7		83.3	
Pressure	29.81		29.85		29.95	
Blood pulse	69.3	66.9	71.4	61.9	75.6	69.3
Temperature	98.1	97.8	97.8	97.5	98.4	97.7
Pressure	30	36	14	18	33	40
Hemoglobin	90–100 for all the cases investigated					
Red cells	5,980 *	5,190 *	6,650 *	6,440 *	5,960 *	5,890 *
White cells	7,700	7,100	6,200	6,460	6,200	7,920
Polymorphonu- clear %	45.0	56.0	67.0	48.0	46.5	47.8
Lymphocytes %	44.0	36.0	26.0	41.0	41.0	43.9
Mononuclear %	3.5	3.0	5.0	9.0	1.0	1.0
Eosinophiles %	7.0	4.0	2.0	1.0	7.5	2.5
Basophiles %	0.5	1.0	0.0	1.0	1.5	0.3

* In thousands

tion of the blood. Particularly noticeable is the decrease in the number of white blood cells, which are protectors of the organism against bacteria (hence, during starvation, the decrease in immunity and rise of disease and of mortality).[38] Concomitantly, changes take place in respiration, which becomes weak and superficial. Similarly, other processes also change abruptly: salivary discharge and succiferous activity decrease, the mouth becomes dry and the saliva bitter, the mucous membranes desiccate, excretory processes change, urine becomes thick, and fecal matter decreases. Fat disappears, some muscles atrophy and their tonus decreases, sphincters of the urinary bladder and of the anus become weak so that the output of urine is not controlled and asthenia and cachexia follow.[39] In connection with changes of the composition of tissues and of the fundamental processes of the organism, there is a decrease in vitality; the strength of some muscles declines, and general fatigue increases. All these changes are augmented by prolonged starvation. The organism becomes more and more disorganized, its viability drops, and finally death results. The number of days of absolute starvation required for termination of life depends upon health, age, sex, and many other conditions. People have starved for 30 days (Sukki) and 40 days (Tanner), and even up to 80 days without the exhibition of any detrimental effects on the organism. These experiments were conducted, however, under laboratory conditions, with the supervision of medical specialists, and therefore can not be considered typical. Outside laboratory conditions, death occurs much sooner. The deficiency in vitamins in the diet may produce somewhat similar effects.[40]

Changes of physiological processes in the organism which are caused by starvation suggest the following proposition: *that a number of physiological functions may be essentially different in people and groups which have good diets and those who are ill nourished.*

If starvation decreases the physical power of the organism, then it is logical to assume that when other conditions are equal, *the*

38. According to Saatchian, "the number of red cells in the blood of USSR citizens decreased on the average to 3,700,000 per mm^3 during the three years of famine."

39. Waldman, "On the Problem of Clinical Starvation," in *Jubilee Collection in Honor of I. Grekov* (1921), p. 428 (in Russian).

40. A work by Kol'tsov is cited.

physical force of those in the well-fed strata of the population must be greater, on average, than of people of the same race, age, and sex in the strata that are ill fed. This proposition is confirmed by a series of experiments. Measurements with a dynamometer give higher indexes for people belonging to affluent classes of the same race. Consider the following data:[41]

Age	Force in kilograms			
(years)	Boys		Girls	
	Rich	Poor	Rich	Poor
7	10.0	8.6	—	—
8	11.8	10.8	9.8	9.5
9	14.5	12.3	12.0	11.3
10	15.7	14.6	14.2	12.2
11	16.7	16.6	14.8	13.9
12	19.0	18.8	18.2	17.2
13	21.5	20.0	20.3	19.7
14	24.8	23.3	22.0	21.8

The same can be said about the rapidity with which physical fatigue occurs. Figures received by means of repeated pressure of the dynamometer, and by some other methods, indicate that under similar external conditions, persons in classes that are poorly nourished fatigue more rapidly than well-fed people. The same is true with respect to psychological fatigue and force.

The difference in time of appearance of first menstruation in girls of the same race but of economically different classes has been considered by several authors as a function of nutrition. According to Raseri, in northern Italy menstruation appears earliest in girls from the affluent part of society. The richer girls experienced menstruation at 13 years 8 months, the peasant girls at 14 years 11 months, and the factory girls at 17 years 4 months. Similar results were reported also by Marro.[42]

A number of scholars (Raseri, Guy, et al.) found a difference in pulse (number of pulsations per minute) of rich and poor people.

The difference in vitality and immunity of the well-nourished

41. Niceforo, op. cit., p. 28.
42. Works by Raseri and Marro are cited.

and the deficiently nourished classes is well known. Statistics on disease and mortality support it.

Thus, comparing the well-nourished strata of the population with the poorly nourished classes, we find the same differences in their physiological processes which are observed in a single individual during periods of adequate and deficient nutrition. Concomitantly, with strong deformations of all the physiological processes, it is natural to expect occurrences of great changes in the behavior of human beings. The conduct of satiated people is never identical with that of hungry people.

Nutrition and the Subjective Experiences or Psychological Processes

We now consider those subjective phenomena which are a function of variation in quantity and quality of food in general, and of deficiency starvation in particular.

It has been shown already that a number of our subjective experiences are functions of corresponding objective processes of nutrition. Variation of the former has a diversified character which depends upon variations in the quantity and quality of food. If we put sugar or candy in the mouth, we have the experience of "sweet"; if we put in salt, the "psychological" function will be the experience of "salty"; other substances stimulate the experience of "sour" (vinegar), "bitter," etc. Furthermore, some foods stimulate the experience of "tasty," and others that of "not tasty," of "pleasant" and of "unpleasant."

A manifold complex of subjective experiences ranging from "satiation" to "hunger-appetite," with numerous quantitative and qualitative gradations, serves as a function of the objective fact of variation in quantity and quality, order and time in the consumption of food products.

The principal features of deformation of the psychological experiences, which are caused by different forms of starvation, are summarized in the following paragraphs.

Deformation in the region of self-consciousness and in the sphere of sensitive-emotional experiences.—The fundamental consequence of positive stimulation of the nervous center is the appearance of a peculiar experience called "appetite." This is a two-sided, passive-active experience, representing on one side a passive endurance, and on the other an active, impetuous ardor. When the experience of appetite is not complicated by other phenomena, it is rather pleasant (hence the expression, "bon appetit"). The complex of experiences indicated by this term is not uniform, and it is subdivided into a series of categories which differ quantitatively and qualitatively. *Quantitatively* we recognize different *degrees of appetite:* "wolf's," "a small appetite," or "I would not mind eating something," etc. *Qualitatively*, appetites in regard to meat dishes have a different character than those in regard to pastry, candy, etc.[43]

These quantitatively and qualitatively different shades of appetite may be considered as functions of stimulations of the nutrient center which differ in intensity and character. Qualitative ones, in particular, apparently represent the result of relatively qualitative starvation, i.e., deficiency or comparative lack of certain nutrient ingredients in the "household" of the organism. Also these various shades of appetite typically are experienced during the *first stages of starvation.*

The problem changes considerably as starvation is prolonged: the experience of appetite gradually is transformed into a different experience of hunger. The difference between the two consists of the fact that appetite represents a rather pleasant experience, whereas hunger, to the contrary, is a sensation of suffering. This difference is emphasized by many investigators.

"The appetite," according to Cannon and Washburn, "may exist independently from hunger, as, for example, when we eat delectable dainties merely to please the palate. Hunger, on the other hand, is a dull ache, or a gnawing sensation referred to the lower mid-chest region and the epigastrium. It may exist separate from appetite, as for example, when hunger forces the taking of food not only distasteful, but even nauseating. Besides the dull ache, however, lassitude and drowsiness may appear, or faintness, or headache, or irritability and restlessness such that continuous effort in ordinary affairs becomes increasingly difficult. That these states differ with individuals —headache in one, faintness in another—for example, indicates that they do not constitute the fact of hunger, but more or less inconstant accompaniment, for the present negligible. The dull, pressing sensation is the constant characteristic of hunger." The same difference between hunger and appetite is stressed, e.g., by Carlson and by Boring, who indicated that hunger is an ache. However, these au-

43. A work of Petrajitsky is cited.

thors differ in describing further characteristics of this difference.[44]

From an objective point of view, the experience of appetite usually appears only during the *first moments* of absolute- and relative-deficient starvation, while it is common during "comparative" starvation. Conversely, the experience of hunger rarely occurs during comparative starvation, and it is quite frequent during prolonged deficiency starvation, and particularly during absolute starvation. In other words, *the experience of appetite is mainly a function of comparative starvation, and of the first moments of the deficient kind, absolute and relative; the experience of hunger is mainly a function of prolonged absolute- and relative-deficient starvation.*[45] Such is the connection of these subjective occurrences with corresponding objective processes of variation in quantity and quality of food.

While indicating the differences between hunger and appetite, I must admit, however, that the limits between them are rather conditional. Appetite usually represents a rather pleasant experience, but if it appears under circumstances when there is no chance of satisfying it, when it is impossible to secure food, then fear for the future safety of life, fear of death from starvation, make it unpleasant and difficult to endure. Conversely, if a hungry person knows that within a few hours he will get a good dinner, that he is in no danger of dying from starvation, he will endure the hunger with no particular suffering and pain.

The experiences of appetite and hunger do not have a continuous but an intermittent character: once they occur, they may disappear, only to reappear and increase with greater intensity. The usual times for appearance and increases are those just before meals, such as breakfast and dinner.[46]

44. W. B. Cannon and A. L. Washburn, "An Explanation of Hunger," *American Journal of Physiology* 26 (1912):441; A. J. Carlson, "Contributions to the Physiology of Stomach," *American Journal of Physiology* 31 (1913):175-92; E. G. Boring, "Processes Referred to Alimentary and Urinary Tracts," *Psychological Review* 4 (1915):312.

45. A similar idea is expressed by Boring: hunger usually ceases as soon as food is taken. Appetite is more "ideational" and persists after food is taken. It is the desire for food, the opposite of aversion. Appetite probably constitutes the motive for eating dessert at any meal. Op. cit., p. 312.

46. In this connection the curve of the rise of "hunger" and of "appetite" is similar to that of some other experiences, such as "hunger for a smoke." When a person is trying to quit smoking, the desire to do so is very strong in

When absolute starvation lasts more than two or three days, or when the prolonged relative-deficiency starvation is indeed very deficient, *then after two to three days, subjective experiences acquire new characteristics.* The specific experience of hunger disappears, or, more correctly, dissipates in the general mass of painful experiences which give a new impulse to life activity. This impulse consists of a combination of experiences: weakness; dull pains in the head, the joints, or the whole body; a feeling of emptiness; an absence of emotions; sleepiness, nausea, and dizziness. All of these produce in the organism a general state of apathy or indifference, which may be interrupted from time to time by irritation and anger, the latter disappearing quickly in a general sea of apathy.[47] With continuation of starvation, delusions begin to appear in a number of cases, the clarity of consciousness becomes obscured, and hunger psychosis develops. In a word, mental life becomes disorganized.

Such is the schematic representation of the general feeling of self, and of its ramifications during different forms and stages of starvation. This schema allows for a number of individual variations, but seems to be correct in principle. Partially to illustrate the schema, and partly for its verification, I give here a few descriptions of mental experiences reported by starving people who experimented upon themselves.

This is the way Marsh described his feelings after 11–12 days of starvation. (During the first week the intake of food was gradually decreased, reaching zero at the end of the week; during the second week there was absolutely no intake of food.) "The heart was beating very strongly, and more or less constantly, especially when the stomach was empty; the heart beats fast and apprehensively during

---

the morning after coffee or tea, after dinner, and during intensive mental work, i.e., during the usual times of heavy smoking.

47. Irritation and sudden anger have been described often by starving people who observed themselves, and by other observers. "The neurosis of exhaustion in children during the years of famine in the USSR consists of deep depression, an inclination to tears, and an overwhelming irritability. Many children are in a state of pathological expression of anger and rage." (A work in Russian by Aronovich is cited.) Leshkoff says that during the famine of 1840 in Russia, a sinister indignation increased among people. Husbands beat their wives for no reason at all, old men abused the children and their daughters-in-law, everybody blamed others for lack of bread and wished harm to each other. We have observed a similar increase in anger and irritability during the present years of starvation.

mounting of stairs. Unable to work in the afternoon and in the evening. Great faintness, headache and discomfort of a general nature. The throat is dry, but no desire to drink water. Pains in the head, eyes, in the back and in the legs—when lying, sitting or standing. There is no nausea, but some uneasiness of the stomach is obvious. The feeling of sympathy, joy and respect etc.—became colorless and lifeless in fact." His wife, who was starving along with him, wrote, "swimming does not give pleasure. During mental experiments and in the afternoon I felt like bursting out crying. I get startled from the sudden noise. The feeling of starvation was present only at the beginning of the experiment. At night I dream of fried cucumbers and chopped olives. It takes great effort to undertake something and when in a hurry I run like an old woman. After a number of days of stupor passed, the emotions returned again." Both of them added, "The typical symptoms of hunger appeared during several days at the same time as that of the usual meals and in woman were accompanied by heartburn, nausea, and vomiting. The feelings, which were sharp during the first days of starvation, became later numb, and apathetic." [48]

Some other experimenters who starved for research purposes characterized their experiences in a similar way. Nine American scholars (six men and three women who had advanced degrees in psychology) noticed the sensation of dull pressure, dull ache, pain, strong gnawing pressure, etc. *These fluctuated, alternated in succession, were not localized in any specific part of the body, but occurred most sharply in the region of the stomach.* For instance, after 20 hours of absolute starvation, the experimenter wrote: "What I feel now is a general bodily weakness. I do not feel like doing anything, even to get up." Furthermore, they emphasized the *sensation of emptiness* as a characteristic feature of the starving self-feeling. Self-experimenter A wrote, "I am empty, but not hungry"; similarly, scholars X and Y added that they had *feelings of emptiness.* [49] In his novel "Hunger" Knut Hamsun describes similar features, particularly the emptiness. As is well known, Hamsun starved for two months. He says, "My head was empty, I could not write anything. As soon as I made attempts to write, my head immediately became empty. Nothing came out, although I was very diligent." Mikkelsen has

48. Marsh, op. cit.
49. Boring, op. cit.

Table 3
Summarized Results of Fasting Tests *

[The larger the number the less the ability]

Activities Tested	Descending M.	Descending F.	Fasting M.	Fasting F.	Ascending M.	Ascending F.	Group Names and Results (Estimated)
Food Intake	4.5	4.5	8.5	8.5	3.5	3.5	
Weight loss	7.3	7.2	7.9	7.0	3.9	4.0	
Lung capac.	5.3	2.8	6.8	7.5	2.8	4.5	
Grip—right	2.3	5.7	6.1	6.9	6.8	5.1	A. Vitality
Grip—left	4.0	5.7	7.7	5.7	7.5	5.1	
Fatigue	7.3	4.3	8.2	8.4	1.3	3.7	
	5.2	5.1	7.3	7.1	4.5	4.5	Fasting loss
Association time	4.3	5.2	7.3	5.0	4.2	3.3	
Naming time	4.1	6.0	3.6	6.7	1.8	3.6	
Addition time	6.3	6.0	6.0	6.9	4.5	2.8	B. Rapidity
Subtraction time	7.5	8.7	5.4	5.1	3.4	3.3	
Multiplication time	8.7	8.8	6.3	6.0	2.5	1.8	
	6.2	6.9	5.7	5.9	3.3	3.0	Practice loss
Touch	6.4	5.7	5.1	6.2	4.8	3.9	
Pain	4.0	6.5	6.0	5.0	5.5	6.8	
Sight	6.3	6.6	3.8	4.7	5.5	3.5	
Steadiness time—R	6.5	4.8	2.7	4.0	5.3	5.7	C. Passivity
" " —L	4.0	4.0	5.5	4.6	5.2	6.2	
" space—R	6.3	5.0	3.6	5.4	3.2	3.5	
" " —L	7.3	7.3	4.6	4.4	2.7	2.5	
	5.8	5.7	4.5	4.9	4.6	4.6	Practice gain
Association errors	6.5	5.5	7.0	7.0	4.7	6.0	
Naming errors	5.5	6.1	4.1	1.8	2.9	3.3	
Addition errors	4.0	6.0	2.5	4.0	3.5	1.0	D. Accuracy
Subtraction errors	8.3	7.8	3.5	3.3	4.5	3.8	
Multiplication errors	5.3	7.2	5.1	6.0	5.7	5.5	
	5.9	6.5	4.4	4.4	4.2	3.9	Fasting gain

Memorization	4.0	4.7	8.1	2.7	4.8	6.5	E. Memory
Reproduction	5.0	4.7	8.5	4.2	5.0	8.1	
	4.5	4.7	8.3	3.5	4.9	7.3	M., loss, F., gain
Total	5.6	5.8	5.7	5.3	4.2	4.1	

* Marsh, op. cit., p. 442.

described his experiences of hunger during the polar expedition: "Hour follows hour and a growing sensation of emptiness in the stomach increases. It appears as if all the other organs have disappeared, and only the stomach is left which calls: eat, eat! How terrible is hunger, the real hunger when one wants to shout." [50] My own experiences during two and a half days of absolute starvation were approximately the same: after one day the appetite turned into hunger with its typical features; on the third day hunger disappeared in a general mass of painful sensations.

As a general rule, the sated state of the organism encourages joy and gladness, while hunger, particularly under real conditions and not in a laboratory experiment, induces somber, depressed feelings. All other conditions being equal, the former mood is the function of satiety, the latter that of hunger. The fluctuation in quantity and quality of food calls forth corresponding fluctuations in mental disposition. This occurs particularly in cases when deficiency starvation occurs frequently. Such, for example, were the conditions described by several polar explorers. Reading the diaries of Nansen, Mikkelsen, Perry, and Scott, we find constant fluctuations in their moods in response to nutrition. The days of hunger and even of deficient nutrition were for them also days of somber moods, depression, and pessimism. However, as soon as they happened to kill a bird, a bear, a musk ox, or to reach caches of food, their depression and somberness vanished and exuberant joy appeared. All the world began to look joyous and gay, and jokes, laughter, and songs were heard. In other words the mood had changed entirely. The opposite conditions were observed with the recurrence of hunger.

In general such is the deformation of self-feeling, which is called

50. The Russian edition of Mikkelsen's *On the Track of the Victims of the Polar Desert* is cited.

forth by variation of nutrition, and particularly by starvation. The above facts indicate a connection between fluctuation in intake of food by the organism and its psychological experiences.

Deformation in the area of cognition.—Now let us consider briefly the deformation of separate psychological processes which occur as a result of starvation. In Table 3, Marsh summarizes briefly the character of this deformation in a number of cognitive psychological processes which he and his wife observed during a three-week period of fasting. The bigger the number in the table, the stronger the decrease of corresponding ability. The first column, indicated in the table as "descending," gives an average of results of numerous experiments of the first week, with the exception of the first day; the second column, "fasting," gives the results of the second week, plus the first day of the third week; the third column, "ascending," is the result of the last six days of the third week.[51]

To interpret this table correctly, it is necessary to keep in mind the influence of practice. The frequent exercise of an ability, repeating an exercise several times a day for three weeks, leads to its perfection. If there had been no fasting during these three weeks, then all the abilities investigated would have increased. The fasting prevented this and acted in the opposite direction. The last column gives exactly the idea about results of this duel between fasting and practice. The ability to work (A) falls sharply from hunger. In group (B) the summary says, "practice is losing," which means that due to fasting, the successes, which are due to practice, are decreasing and are considerably lower than would have been the case had there been no fasting.

The capacities of group (C) lose little from fasting: the "practice gains." Group (D), all in all, gains from fasting: where improvements of corresponding abilities are attributed to lack of food. Finally, in group (E) hunger inhibits ability to remember and to repeat in men, but acts in the reverse way in women.

Such are the results shown by this table. It indicates that some of the abilities change little, others decrease considerably, and still others improve. In certain cases the differences between men and women are obvious. Similar results were obtained by Luciani in his studies of Sukki, who fasted for thirty days. The general result of the influence of fasting on the psychological state of Sukki, Luciani

51. Marsh, op. cit., p. 442.

characterized as follows: "We did not find that the fasting destroyed, decreased, or increased his mental ability in any way. Only at the beginning of fasting he showed some irritation against the assistants of Luciani, but apologized for this later on. During the long period of fasting he was in good spirits, was quite talkative, did not quarrel with the personnel, nor with the investigator and was occupied almost exclusively with his financial interests." [52]

On the basis of these data, can we conclude that starvation does not destroy our mental capacities, and that it has little effect upon intellectual processes? Taking into account these data, and also considering certain historical examples of fasting (such starving ascetics as Mahomet and Loyola, whose starvation did not destroy their psychological functions), it seems that we could conclude that starvation has little effect on the cognitive processes of our mental life. Luciani and some of the other investigators apparently think it does. [53] This conclusion was based on the supposition that our nervous system does not change during starvation.

I think that this opinion is absolutely wrong. Why? First, because the Marsh data and those of Luciani indicate the deformation during fasting of the simplest psychological processes, but not of the preservation of the status quo. Second, this deformation is positive in some cases and negative in others. Third, it is necessary to consider that the figures refer to the simplest psychological processes, and not to the more complicated ones; as we see presently, the latter are least affected by starvation. Fourth, the laboratory conditions of fasting are themselves quite different from forced starvation. The former can be interrupted any time; it occurs under the supervision of physicians, it does not threaten life, there is no fear of death from hunger, the starving person is isolated from many ordinary irritations, and he does not spend energy in the ordinary routines of life. The conditions are quite different during forced starvation, when the fear of death from hunger, anxiety, expenditure of energy, suffering for near relatives, are ever present.

Furthermore, the fast by Sukki, that of Marsh, and other laboratory starvations were performed for definite purposes, either scien-

52. Luciani, *Das Hungern*, pp. 67–68.

53. Tarasevich, "Starvation," p. 14, writes: "if the lack of food is the only injurious factor, the organism can cope with it in order to put the nervous system in more or less favorable conditions."

tific or practical, and both purposes are psychologically different from enforced starvation. Sukki was not irritated by anything during his starvation. In a quiet laboratory, under pleasant surroundings one can keep busy by adding, subtracting, and multiplying. In real life, as the example of Hamsun indicates, it is difficult to do direct things while starving. In this connection L. Tarasevich is right, saying, "if other injurious elements, such as cold, fear of death, suffering, etc., are added to starvation, the nervous system quickly reaches the state of unbalanced equilibrium and a number of acute neuro-psychological symptoms develop." [54]

From this point of view laboratory fasting gives results that are entirely different, in many respects, from starvation which occurs outside the laboratory in real life. The latter is important for our study, whereas the first is rather exceptional.

Fifth, and perhaps most important, is the fact that there is much evidence showing that definite acute deformation of the cognitive psychological process results from starvation.

Hunger deforms the functioning of the mental processes, the substance of consciousness (ideas, representations, conviction, theories, etc.), and the intellectually cognitive sphere of the psyche.

In the region of sensation and perception, starvation has a tendency to cause corresponding direction of attention, i.e., psychophysical accommodation, toward catching and perceiving impressions, which are related to the function of nutrition.[55] We have seen already that under positive stimulation of the nutrient center, the sense organs begin to exhibit increased activity in a definite direction. All of the sensory organs become fixed on nutritive phenomena and become particularly sensitive toward them. Conversely, phenomena which are not connected with nutrition cease to stimulate them and they become insensitive. Various phenomena connected with food activity "strike the eyes" and hypnotize them. The ear catches appropriate sounds, and the olfactory organs pick up smells, etc. All this is performed without volition or conscious desire.

This means that during starvation our analytical apparatus becomes particularly sensitive to stimulations which have to do with nutrition, and quite unresponsive to other stimulations. The latter do not enter the field of consciousness, evoke no sensations, and are

54. Ibid., p. 14.
55. A work by Petrajitsky is cited.

vanishing, as far as the world of psychological experiences is concerned. The former stimuli produce more internal reactions when the organism is in a state of hunger than when it is sated.

Next to this deformation, there exists still another. Not only does hunger sharpen the sensitivity of the sense organs in this or that direction, but at the same time *it directs our attention toward objects and phenomena connected with food. During starvation the attention of the man, willingly or unwillingly, is fixed in the direction of everything which concerns food, and neglects, or passes by, everything unrelated to nutrition.* This may be clearly demonstrated by a dog. Take a piece of meat or bread, and show it to a hungry dog. By this you attract the dog's attention to the hand with the bread, much as a piece of iron is attracted to a magnet. Swing the hand either right or left, and the head of the dog will turn in the same direction. All his attention will be fixed upon the object and he becomes oblivious to everything else, so that even slapping or pushing will not distract the dog's attention from the food. I have noticed similar behavior in a cat; even just the sound of the container in which the milk is kept can become sufficient to attract the animal, who has become indifferent to everything except food.

"The cooking of food during the polar exploration," Mikkelsen relates, "engaged the attention [of the dog] to such extent that it became blind and deaf to anything else. Neither our caresses, nor kindly words distracted its silent vigil from the kettle with cooking food. Only the tongue was in motion and the saliva was drivelling from the corners of the mouth." [56] In a more complicated form, similar behavior may occur in man. Good illustrations of this are seen in literature, e.g., in de Maupassant's story "Vagabonds" and in Hamsun's *Hunger.*

Hunger definitely orients the attention of man toward the phenomena which have relation to nutrition. As with the dog, man's attention is riveted upon food, and he neglects everything else. Whether this attention is intentional or involuntary makes no difference. Most often it occurs irrespective of our volition and conscious activities. But even if conscious intentions arrive post factum, the picture remains almost the same, with one difference. In such cases the whole intellect is turned to means of satisfying hunger and attention is intentionally fixed upon the phenomena having to do with satisfaction

56. Mikkelsen, op. cit., p. 135.

of hunger. A massive verification of this may be found in the behavior of children and adults in the USSR during the present famine.
According to the observations of teachers, pupils are apathetic with
respect to everything except food. In children's homes, asylums, and
colonies the constant topics of conversation are those concerned with
food which entirely occupied the consciousness of children of both
preschool and school ages. Talk about food is the only approach to
them. To all other topics they react with extreme irritability or
negativism.[57] The adults are inattentive to and poorly informed about
many things, but in regard to rations, giving away provisions, distribution of food, and other similar things, they are extremely atten-
tive. They have information about when to receive the ration cards,
and do not miss any distribution of provisions on these cards; in other
words, in this respect *they give their maximum attention.*

Finally, during very prolonged starvation the world of sensation
and perception undergoes a third deformation, *consisting of stupor
of organs of feeling and perception in general. All perceptions become less vivid and less acute.* During the first stages of starvation
our perceptive apparatus works better, and it analyzes the medium
and its irritations more exactly and sharply. With very long and deficient starvation this sharpening of perception is replaced with
apathy, which is expressed subjectively by complete indifference to
everything, and by the lack of colorful experiences and strong feelings. "The feelings, which are very sharp during the first days of
starvation, later on became very apathetic for the time," wrote Marsh
with reference to his fasting.

During starvation, as death comes near, apparently all the analytical nervous apparatus is disorganized. Accordingly, it begins to
notice and perceive very poorly everything that happens in the surrounding medium; its signals of feelings and perception become incorrect and faint, and it ceases to notice, or to outline only faintly
and weakly, many things. Men cease to react even to electric stimuli.
Rosenbakh says that the excitability of the brain by an electric
irritation decreases or disappears entirely as a result of starvation.
The effect of starvation on the excitability of the brain was demonstrated by changes in motor response to strong currents. Some animals did not react at all by twitching their limbs; others reacted
only very faintly.[58]

57. A work by Aronovich is cited.
58. A work by Rosenbakh is cited.

The distortion and the impoverishment of the world of sensation and perception are functions of anatomical-physiological changes of the nervous system. This phenomenon of lowering the irritability during starvation was confirmed by Rosenthal and Frolov. "Starvation causes decreased irritability of the nervous system and develops sleepy conditions, which decrease the whole activity of the large hemispheres." [59]

Starvation produces various deformations in the area of beliefs and in the course of ideas. As a result of starvation, formerly associated sequences of ideas (or chains of thoughts) are interrupted and new ones emerge. Notions or thoughts, in their sequences or chains, are no longer connected as they once were but become associated with, or logically bound to, nutrition and food. [60]

Under the influence of hunger the whole field of consciousness comes to be filled with notions and ideas, and their complexes, which are directly or indirectly associated with food. They intrude into the field of consciousness, unexpected and uncalled for, and displace other notions and ideas, crowding them out of the mind, regardless of our will and even contrary to it. During the most acute starvation, the force of ideas associated with food becomes so intense that the strongest effort of our volition often is helpless to resist them. Furthermore, as Petrajitsky indicates, with the increase in the intensity of spells of hunger-appetite, corresponding notions become so vivid and clear that they come to resemble perceptions, and finally they acquire a hallucinatory character. This is the beginning of an abnormal action of the intellect, known as hunger delirium. The dreams of hungry persons often have various foods as their object.

I personally experienced acute starvation during two months of my life, in the forests of northern Russia. It was a strong relative-deficiency starvation, both quantitative and qualitative. After a week of such life it was very difficult for me to concentrate for any length of time on anything but food. For short periods, by forcing myself, I was able to chase away the "thoughts of hunger" from my consciousness, but they invariably returned and took possession of it.

The same was observed by the American psychologists mentioned who experimented upon themselves. When they experienced thirst, as well as hunger, the thoughts of water and food became obsessive. After 23 hours of thirst, A wrote: "I am working and

59. Works by I. Rosenthal and N. Frolov are cited.
60. Petrajitsky's work cited again.

come to a break in the work; automatically I start to get up and move in the direction of the faucet. Before I have taken a step, I get a kinesthetic shock, or check and remember the experiment." Later on, "a vague visual image of a glass for water, the shape of the carafe, or some other container became common and unconsciously I began to reach for them, but remembering in time about the experiment, I usually returned to my work." The other participants in this experiment had similar experiences with both thirst and hunger. Boring summarizes the experiment thus: "The ideation of food is no doubt a usual concomitant, and presumably it often constitutes a desire for food. . . . There can be no question that this desire may also often be unconsciously carried and may become manifested automatically in the movement of going for a water drink." [61]

"For a very long time it was difficult for us to talk about anything but food," said polar explorer Mikkelsen of his experiences during his travels in Greenland. "Of course, it was pleasant to chat about this subject, and it did not tire us out until the chance to eat presented itself; only then one was liberated from the perennial topic of food and it became possible to converse about something else. All thoughts depend on the stomach." That day the explorers had had a good meal and could talk about something other than food. [62]

Of his trip across the Andes, Tschudi said, "the thirst became more intolerable from minute to minute. I had different hallucinations: either I saw a lake, or heard the splashing of water quite near me." The sailors from *Medusa* experienced hallucinations of seeing shores with plenty of fruit; as a result of this, they plunged into the sea. [63]

A clear representation of the intrusion of "hungry ideas" into the field of consciousness is found in a number of literary writings. Several such examples are given in Flaubert's *Temptations of St. Anthony*. While St. Anthony was meditating about the decline of righteousness and about the proceedings of the Nicene Council, suddenly some thoughts flashed into his field of consciousness: " 'It is because I have fasted too long; my strength is leaving me. If I could eat—only once more a piece of meat. . . .' He closes his eyes with languor. 'Ah! some red flesh . . . a bunch of grapes to bite into!

61. Boring, op. cit., pp. 307–15.
62. Ejnar Mikkelsen, *Lost in the Arctic* (New York, 1913).
63. A work by Pashutin is cited.

curdled milk that trembles on the plate! But what has come upon me? What is the matter with me?' Later we see the picture of the delirium of hunger. St. Anthony begins to visualize pictures of tables full of food, meat, roast wild boar, ragout with cream, etc. Realizing that this is the temptation, he says: 'Ah! Go away, go away!' But the temptation was very strong." [64] Many similar pictures are found in accounts of the lives of ascetics and Christian saints.

The people of the USSR during years of famine represent another verification of the deformation under consideration. The principal topics of conversation at that time were rations, bread, and food in general. Irrespective of where you went and regardless of the initial topic of conversation, the talk turned eventually to the problems of food, ration cards, black markets, the costs of edibles, and the ways of procuring them.[65] The constant conversation of preschool and school children also was concerned with food. Aronovich says that the persevering topics of hunger became fixed ideas. Further evidence to prove the validity of the point under discussion is hardly needed.

The character of the deformation as described means that *during starvation the realm of notions and ideas of human beings is greatly impoverished*—both qualitatively and quantitatively—when these notions and ideas *do not deal with nutrition, but it is enriched in regard to ideas and notions relating to food.* The latter begin to multiply abundantly in the consciousness, and they acquire a diversity and unprecedented vivacity often reaching the stage of hallucinations. The former meanwhile fade from the field of consciousness, become very vague and uninteresting. One who is starving does not want to think about them, and their free play and exchange vanish.

Such is the deformation of these mental processes caused by starvation.

In connection with the changes in sensations, perceptions, and notions which are the result of starvation, there is also a deformation of *memory and the ability to recall in general.* From the preceding pages it is easy to foresee what direction this deformation takes. In this respect the experiments by Marsh are rather indefinite: during

64. Gustave Flaubert, *The Temptations of St. Anthony* (New York: The Modern Library).

65. Illegal black markets were common where people could exchange their clothing for the grain brought in by peasants from the villages. E.S.

starvation both of these abilities decreased in the man and increased in the woman. I presume that a decrease of the ability should be considered more typical than an increase. During starvation the organs of senses become very "sensitive" to nutritional ideas, and quite oblivious to other conceptions. The latter are forced from the field of consciousness and fade away in favor of nutritional conceptions and associations. Hence the mind easily retains and remembers processes and objects connected with nutrition, and becomes quite weak in remembering phenomena and objects having no connection with it. In respect to the former, memory will increase and become quite firm and exact; in respect to the latter, it will weaken. Similar effects could be registered with respect to the ability of recall. The processes, facts, and objects relating to nutrition are reproduced clearly, exactly, and vividly because they were fixed more strongly in the consciousness and perceived intensively; contrarily, the phenomena, occurrences, and facts unrelated to nutrition, which have hardly reached the consciousness and which were weakly perceived, will be recalled with great difficulties and with considerably less vivacity and exactness.

It is not surprising, therefore, that when we are starving we perceive and remember some things easily and sharply, and that we also recollect and recall exactly the phenomena, facts, and objects directly or indirectly connected with nutrition. During the first stages of starvation both of these abilities may increase. However, both perception and recall definitely decrease in regard to other phenomena. Therefore, it would be a serious mistake to conclude that during starvation there is a general increase in ability to remember and recall based solely upon facts in the first category. Furthermore, if we were to consider not just the supposed increase and decrease in memory and the ability to recall in respect to "nutrient" and "nonnutrient" objects and phenomena, but their increase or decrease in general, then there would be grounds to suppose that during starvation, particularly prolonged starvation, memory decreases in comparison with memory during satiety. Such is the second feature of this deformation. In this respect I questioned a number of scholars in Petrograd in 1918–21. Almost everybody complained about a decrease in the ability to remember.

Professor A told me that his "memory had weakened considerably." Two of the scholars pointed out that, to their complete embarrassment, they could not recall names and dates during lectures. At the end of the two months of my relative starvation in the forest of northern Russia, I also observed a decrease in my ability to remember. Various clinical observations mention similar facts. Waldman's clinical studies indicated that a condition of mixed-up psyche and loss of memory occurs during strong forms of emaciation. The patient forgets his name, does not know where he is, and does not remember where he used to live.

Pashutin says that quite frequently simple words are forgotten. Thus X told him that he had forgotten entirely the word "ax," and Z could not remember the word "birch." The memories of sailors from the *Medusa* suffered considerably during their starvation after the shipwreck. The problem discussed here is far more complicated and is not limited to the examples mentioned.

Deformation in the realm of desires, vigor, and volition.—During the early stages of starvation the perturbation in the realm of psychological experience consists of weakening and suppression of all desires and vigor which prevent the satisfaction of hunger, or are antagonistic to it, and, contrarily, in excitation, and strengthening of the desires and intentions which are leading to satisfaction of hunger. The world of human desires is changed during starvation. All the cravings and longings which occupied a central position in a satiated stage are relegated during starvation to a secondary place because they are antagonistic to the satisfaction of hunger. The craving for a "lentil porridge" is entirely lacking in a well-fed man, but becomes of vital concern when one is starving. Below we give adequate verification of these statements.

The processes of volition also undergo a comparable change. Many psychologists place volition in opposition to desire and aggressiveness, but I consider it to be a complex of them. The volitional act which is directed against the satisfaction of hunger meets an opponent in that sensation, which tries to subdue, suppress, or weaken it. In such cases volition has to overcome the resistance of hunger, and this rarely occurs. The volitional act which is fostering the satisfaction of hunger, on the other side, finds hunger to be a mighty ally, which increases its power and, so to say, "carries the volition on its mighty shoulders." Correspondingly, with the sharp variation in satiety and hunger, there is also a sharp variation in the relative forces of different processes of volition and the whole volitional sphere of mental life. Still another phenomenon occurs (in addition to the changes mentioned). With the changes in mental experiences

that take place under the influence of hunger, our own volitional "I"
also changes. The entire mental picture of the man becomes sharply
deformed, and before our eyes there emerges an entirely new "I" in
the old, but somewhat modified body. Accordingly, as long as volition is a unity, it is intimately connected with "I," and with the
change of the latter, it also changes.

During prolonged and hard starvation the "I"—the unity and
the wholeness of mental life—gradually deteriorates and falls into
uncoordinated pieces so that the total comes to resemble a broken
mosaic picture, held together only by the frame. Volition also falls
into pieces. It ceases to be uniform and whole, and fragments into
separate, uncoordinated streams which flow in the frame of the disturbed human organism. Will power becomes weak, soft, and loose.
Apathy and a dull indifference occupy the place of the will during a
period of long starvation.

Deformation of character and of temperament.—Although direct
proof does not exist, there is a series of statistical data suggesting
the existence of a relationship between nutrition and what is called
the "character" or the "temperament" of a man. Above we have
seen that pigeons became birds of prey after they were fed meat,
and that changes in the character of bears, pigs, and dogs are produced by switching them from vegetarian diets: the meat diet makes
them disobedient and vicious.[66] On this basis, it is possible to expect
similar results to take place in humans. Furthermore, it is now
established that the qualities of "temperament" and "character" are
connected to inner secretions, and that the latter depend to a large
degree upon the quantity and quality of the food from which the
glands secure their secretions. This is a second indication of the
existence of the relationship postulated. Finally, there are facts which
prove this directly. It was noted that people, particularly primitive
ones, who live predominantly on meat are rapacious, energetic, and
aggressive. Pivion connects the large number of murders in England with meat diets. Conversely, many vegetarian peoples and
groups are mostly peaceful and not predatory. Pointing out that several people express strong disapproval of a meat diet because it leads
towards rapaciousness, Pashutin concludes that it must be admitted
that in all these condemnations there exists sound truth, and not
mere sentimentality.

66. A work of Pashutin is cited.

Although this problem has been studied very little, the considerations mentioned suggest that the proposition is not completely absurd. The placid character of the Russian population in general, and during the years of famine in particular, may serve as a partial verification of it. In comparison with the populations of most European nations, and in particular with the Anglo-Saxons, the Russian peasant always ate and is still eating comparatively little meat. He is far more placid than the masses of other peoples. Perhaps because of the almost exclusively vegetarian diet of the population of Russia during these years of starvation, they became excessively passive, placid, and lacking in volition. If this is so, then those rulers who wish to dominate their people should eat meat and keep the population on a vegetarian diet.

Deformation in the totality of mental life and of personality.— Thus, under the influence of starvation, abrupt changes occur in all the specific "elements" of our mental life, as well as in elemental psychological processes. Our sensations, emotions, self-feelings, and outlook on life all change. Our perceptions, attentions, understandings, ideas (their quantity, quality, and sequence), as well as the remembrance and arousal of desires and will power, all become deformed. With the change of specific elements of our mental life also come changes in their totality or of our entire mental life (or of all the contents of our consciousness) which is composed of these elements. Thus *starvation (or, on the other hand, satiety) deforms strongly our entire mental personality, all "the intellectual baggage" of our personal "I." From the point of view of the contents of this "baggage" it changes the ideas, convictions, beliefs, tastes, desires, longings, evaluations of the senses, and emotions, and of the whole outlook on life. From the point of view of the mechanism of change in these elements, it also alters the "baggage" of the mental processes.* Starvation forces some of these elements out of our field of consciousness, and replaces them with others; it depresses and weakens some of the ideas, convictions, beliefs, tastes, desires, and emotions, and reinforces and strengthens others of them. The role of variation of quantity and quality of food absorbed by the organism is similar to that of a change of directors of an institution: each change at the top leads to others among the subordinates of that institution, to the promotion of some workers and the demotion of others. As a result, there is change in the whole make-up of the officers and employees of an institution. The change from satiety to starvation (a result of

variation in quantity and quality of food) produces similar transformation in the "compositions" of the elements (ideas, convictions,
desires, etc.) of our "institutional" consciousness. The policies of the
institution and the mechanism of the work usually change concurrently with the change in directorship and the regrouping of personnel. Similar modifications occur in the whole mechanism of intellectual life during the change from satiety to starvation and vice
versa. The machine of mental life works differently in each case.
Changes in contents of our intellectual baggage are discussed below.
At present I shall indicate certain features of the deformation of the
mechanism of our whole mental life during starvation.

*Prolonged deficiency and, to some extent, comparative starvation,
which cause sharp changes in our nervous system and in the brain,
disrupt the whole mechanism of our mental life by upsetting its unity,
completeness, and coordination of its parts.* This is manifest first of
all in the *weakening of the oneness of the personal "I."* During extreme starvation its completeness begins to dissipate, to fall apart, to
become divided. Different I's emerge and begin to fight one another.
The main ruler of our consciousness, which governs the whole psychological machinery, disappears, and a number of smaller rulers
emerge. The whole mechanism becomes uncoordinated, full of fric-
tions and interruptions. We have corroboration of this statement in
a series of experimental self-observations. During the starvation experiments of the Marshes described above, Mrs. Marsh was trying
to do some mathematical computations: "I have a feeling of impa-
tience: as though one part of me were having to wait for another
part; and it is almost as if the impatient part were saying: stop trying and let me do your work; I can do it faster and better than you;
and when I do stop trying this unseen part puts down the answers
with such great ease and speed that I marvel at its achievements.
This dual-personality experience was present a number of times and
the side of it which felt like 'doing things' often produced results
just the opposite." [67]

Very characteristic experiences of this kind are described by
Hamsun in *Hunger.* There is the following scene: the hungry hero
decided to go to the police station because he had no lodgings. After
he was led to a cell and the light was extinguished, "the dark had
captured my brain and gave me not an instant of peace. What if I
myself become dissolved into the dark, turned into it? My nervous

67. Marsh, op. cit., pp. 444–45.

condition had completely taken over, and no amount of struggle against it helped. I sat there, a prey to the weirdest fantasies, gurgling to myself, humming lullabies, sweating in my effort to be calm." In such a condition the hero performed a series of manipulations. "All at once I snapped my fingers a couple of times and laughed. Hellfire and damnation! I suddenly imagined I had discovered a new word! I sat up in bed, and said: it is not in the language, I have discovered it—Kuboaa.

"The word stood out clearly in front of me in the dark.

"I sat with wide eyes astonished at my discovery, laughing with joy. Then I fell to whimpering: they could very well be spying on me, and I must act so as to keep my invention secret. I had arrived at the joyful insanity of hunger." Later he tried to decipher the meaning of the word, and here the dualism and the splitting of the oneness of "I" appeared particularly sharp. He debated the different meanings which Kuboaa could have: God, the Tivoli Gardens, a cattle show, padlock, sunrise, and emigration. He argued with himself, suffered, and finally decided that Kuboaa meant something spiritual. "And I thought and thought to find something spiritual. It occurred to me that someone was talking, butting into my chat, and I answered angrily: 'I beg your pardon? For an idiot, you are all alone in the field! *Yarn?* Go to hell!' Why should I be obligated to let it mean *yarn* when I had a special aversion to its meaning *yarn?* I had discovered the word myself, and I was perfectly within my rights to let it mean whatever I wanted it to, for that matter. So far as I knew, I had not yet committed myself. But my brain sank deeper and deeper in chaos." The unruly chain of the association continued; he saw the policeman, the harbor, ships, dark monsters, floating clouds, himself falling down, and finally: "I said to myself, now I will die! Then I sat up in bed and asked intensely, Who said that I will die? Haven't I found the word myself, and haven't I the right to decide what it is going to mean? *I heard myself* raving, could hear it while I was still talking. My madness was a delirium from faintness and exhaustion, but I still had my wits. Then a thought shot through my brain—I had become insane." This dualism of "I," and the argumentations of the one "I" with the other, continue throughout the novel.[68]

68. Knut Hamsun, *Hunger*, trans. R. Bly (New York: Farrar, Straus & Giroux, 1967), pp. 77–81. (The original quotations were from a Russian translation. E.S.)

Delirium, complete derangement of consciousness, and the dissipation of the unity of personality occur when death from starvation is near. The basic component which controls the center falls out from the consciousness, as in the picture presented, and it becomes the prey of unusual and accidental fantasies! The field of consciousness becomes a mere area of irregular, unregulated circling and twisting of conceptions, ideas, senses, and emotions not at all connected with one another. Man comes to resemble a ship which has lost its captain and rudder and becomes a toy of accidental volitions and irritations.

According to Waldman, famine psychoses, either impulsive or hallucinatory, and unconscious deliriums are induced during the extreme stages of emaciation.

Rosenbakh indicates that lack of food often leads to a specific form of mental disorder, called inanition's delirium. Emaciation may be endured for a long time without any psychotic symptoms, but when it reaches the extreme stage, disruption of the consciousness begins. The association of ideas ceases, the restricting influence of consciousness is weakened, and thoughts flow fast and with no relation to one another. Multiple hallucinations of vision and sound appear and intrude into the consciousness, where they produce absurd ideas, mostly connected with persecution but sometimes with glorification. These ideas do not remain in the consciousness, but they change as fast as the hallucinations. The patient, weakened to an extreme, becomes excited, gesticulates, and mumbles words incoherently.

The weakening and decline in thinking capacity in general are usually considered to be a result of disruption of the integrity of our "I." The process of thinking requires the concentration of attention, a logical train of ideas, and subordination of lesser processes to the principal one. In other words, it requires autonomy to tie together ideas and notions, and to separate them from accidental influences of stimuli, which may be present in the medium at a given time. Only when the field of consciousness is free from accidental associations, when it is sheltered from the extraneous complexes of sensations, and when the "I" is the dominant center of a restricted field is productive thinking possible. In the absence of this condition a sequence of incoherent ideas may occur, and they will follow each other in no logical plan.

Prolonged starvation leads to a similar state. Since the unity and completeness of "I" are weakened by starvation, because the "host" disappears from the consciousness, and because a capricious dance of emotions takes place, it would be miraculous if the work of the intellect were not weakened during starvation. This weakening is expressed in four ways: in a peculiar emptiness of thought; in increased difficulty in concentrating attention upon a given object; in a growing reliance of the process of thinking upon external influences, accompanied by a decrease in the autonomous, self-regulating sequence; and in mental disorders, that is, increased disorganization and the lack of any system in the thoughts. Absolute starvation and prolonged relative starvation—taken together, as well as the deformations described above—lead, directly or indirectly, gradually or suddenly, to a decrease in mental ability.

This conclusion may be illustrated further. After a period of prolonged starvation the hero of the novel *Hunger* tried to earn a few krones by writing an essay. "The head was empty," he relates. "Now I could not write anything, my head becomes empty immediately after I attempt to occupy myself." "Nothing came out anymore, although I was very diligent. My brain became bankrupt." These passages are quoted here not only because the book is a literary classic, but also because it is a sincere human document. Similar occurrences were recorded by the starving American psychologists. "I am empty," wrote one. "I am weak and have a feeling of emptiness," stated another.[69]

Concurrently with emptiness of thought, other forms of its decline are also observed. They include the difficulty of concentration on anything except nutrition, and the lack of any system in thoughts. The hero of Hamsun's story could not figure out the cost of $3\frac{5}{16}$ pounds of cheese at 16 cents per pound. "After trying to compute these figures for two minutes, I began to feel that everything was dancing in my head, I became completely mixed up. . . . Excessive perspiration appeared. I tried with all my force to think about these mysterious figures and pensively blinked my eyes. It appeared as if something was cracked in my brain." Cannon and Washburn emphasize that as a result of starvation, "anxiety appears which makes it very difficult to perform the ordinary tasks."[70]

I experienced a considerable decline in my mental capacity in March and April of 1919, the cumulative result of severe starvation

69. Boring, op. cit., p. 312.
70. Cannon and Washburn, op. cit., p. 441.

during the last quarter of 1918, and relative deficiency starvation during the first part of 1919. During 1918–21, I had an opportunity to discuss this problem with a number of professors and intellectual workers in Petrograd and almost all complained about the decrease of their mental energy and capacity to work. Objectively, the majority of them produced far less than in years of normal nutrition. These years showed a smaller number not only of printed works but even of the unpublished ones. The number of books and periodicals published during these years is considerably smaller than for 1917, when 367 periodicals and 4,690 titles were published in Moscow. In 1920, these numbers had decreased to 165 and 919, respectively. The number of students who graduated from colleges in 1917 was 2,379, and in 1919 only 315, although the total number of the students had increased considerably and the requirements for graduation had been lowered.[71] The same is seen in the region of more simple mental work. During these years the general productivity of labor decreased everywhere in the USSR, particularly in the centers where famine prevailed. This was true not only for the physical laborers, but also for the semi-intellectual occupations (printers, clerks, accountants, etc.). The attention, exactness, speed, energy, etc., once prevailing all disappeared.

The decline in mental capacity of children was observed by many educators. "On the intellectual side we notice the decrease in attention and mental capacity. Hence follow the failure and poor achievements."[72] I realize fully that a whole series of conditions other than hunger may produce a weakening of mental ability, but starvation plays a very important and perhaps even the dominant role in it.

The higher and the most complex forms of mental processes are the first to be afflicted and the ones most affected by starvation. The experiments of Frolov with dogs showed that during starvation the formation of new conditioned reflexes was almost impossible, and that those formed were very unstable: the artificial conditioned reflexes were the first to disappear, and only later were the natural, unconditioned reflexes affected. "The sequence of the disappearance of the reflexes before death is in a reverse relationship to the order of their appearance during the early period of life."[73] Apparently something similar takes place among human beings.

71. *Krasnaya Moskva* is cited.
72. Aronovich, op. cit., p. 31.
73. N. Frolov, op. cit., pp. 169–70.

Finally, the growth of mental illnesses among the population of Russia during recent years, and spread of these diseases in the provinces where famine prevailed, indicate the disorganization of mental life as result of starvation. Mental illnesses among the population of Petrograd increased in 1918–20 and are still increasing; a number of investigators have indicated correctly that the main factor responsible for this growth is the famine.[74]

The daily press tells of cases of mass mental disorders in the provinces where famine has been particularly severe. "The cases of insanity increased during starvation in the village Ol'khovka." "In the village Molchanovka three cases of madness were registered today." "Many people become insane. During a dark night a disheveled peasant rang the church bells with all his might. He rang the bells and danced, he imagined that one must ring louder and stronger. There are whole villages where not a single person remained normal. Everybody had hunger psychosis." [75] Such news was an everyday occurrence.

The disorganized brain apparatus is incapable of working normally and purposefully. All of its connections disintegrate, so that the oneness of the "I" is split. Some of the particulars of the developments are as follows.

I do not deny the possibility of temporary emotional outbursts of mental energy during the early stages of starvation. But these are temporary and they soon disappear.

Neither do I deny the possibility of feverishly one-sided outbursts of mental work during starvation. These outbursts produce, along with absurd deliriums, such works as the "Spiritual Exercises" of Loyola, the founding of Mohammedanism, the bases of some ascetical theories, fakirism (in the Islamic religious orders), and the other products of paroxysm of the brain. But the one-sidedness and semidelirious character of such creations (the social roles of which are important, be they negative or positive) testify in the first place to the abnormal work of the brain. In the second place, just what causes originality and depth of certain creations of this kind is still a matter of dispute. Is it starvation, or some other factor which counteracts starvation and which has annulled the injurious effects of hunger? The human being and its life activity are the

74. A work by Gorovoi-Shaltan is cited.
75. The quotations are from *Izvestia*, February 12, 1922; *Petrogradskaya Pravda*, March 10, 1922; and *Krasnaya Gazeta*, January 31, 1922.

function of many determinants of behavior and not of starvation alone. Concomitant influences may offset the effects of various other factors, and specifically those of starvation.

The abstemious life and the temptations of the ascetics, Christ, Mahomet, Buddha, the fakirs, Loyola, and other representatives of the elites, developed peculiar expressions of the psyche during fasting and prayer, which could condition the originality and depth of their mental processes. Such facts do not contradict the conclusions described above.

Such, in brief, are the fundamental forms of the deformation of the psyche induced by starvation. We see that variations in the psychological experiences are in direct and close relationship with variations in the quantity and quality of food.

Therefore, the hypothesis that differences in nutrition of various social strata of the population and of professional groups may influence the mental development and psychological processes of the members of these groups is not an absurdity. Indeed, a series of investigations proves this point.

The sensibility of tactile perception was studied, for example, in respect to pain, taste, light, chromatics, hearing, muscle, etc., in the wealthy groups and professions who had the best nourishment, and in the poorer groups who were less well fed. The result was "that almost all forms of sensibility were less developed in the second group, in comparison with the first." [76]

Similar investigations of psychological ability in general, and of mental development in particular, of such groups were carried on by a number of investigators, usually by the method of Binet-Simon, modified in the United States by Jerks.[77]

To sum up: there is a high correlation between the levels of mental and professional development (in the children of the same age and school). The children from the affluent classes are about two years more mature than those of the poorer classes.

Similarly, Dr. Voronov noted a difference between richer and poorer peasants in the occurrence of mental disorders:[78]

76. Niceforo, op. cit., p. 104. Other investigations are mentioned by him.
77. See the summary of their materials, statistics, and diagrams in I. W. Bridges and L. E. Coler, "The Relation of Intelligence to Social Status," *Psychological Review* 24 (1917):1–31.
78. The citation is to a work by Gorovoi-Shaltan. [No group 10–14 desyatin is given.]

Size of the allotment in desyatin (one desyatin is approximately one acre)	Mental disorders per 1,000 patients
No allotment	3.18
Under 5 desyatin	1.56
5–9 desyatin	1.30
15–24 desyatin	1.05
25 or more desyatin	0.91

To seek the cause of this difference solely in diet would seem to be naïve. But to exclude entirely the diet from the list of factors which cause retardation and lesser mental ability of the groups of poorly fed also would be incorrect. The above description of the mental effects of starvation and of inadequate nutrition gives a basis for stating (and at the same time, it is indirectly substantiated by this difference) that the food regime has played and continues to play a role, along with the conditions which have initiated this phenomenon.

Therefore, we see that variations of the independent variable we have used, i.e., the form of quantity and quality of food, cause changes in man's somatic structure and in his physiological and psychological processes. Man as a whole is changed. *In all these respects, and in a considerable measure, he is what he has eaten and is eating (particularly in the period of his prenatal life, and the first years of it), how he absorbs his food, and what and how his parents and forefathers have eaten.*

Since man as a whole is changed, it is natural that his behavior also is changed, i.e., all the reactions of motion in the performance of which the whole organism participates, directly or indirectly, and the totality of which constitute his behavior.

3

CHANGES IN HUMAN BEHAVIOR
DURING STARVATION

It is impossible to consider all the concrete changes in the behavior of man which are caused by deficiency or comparative types of starvation: they are simply innumerable. To conserve effort, we shall identify here the central phenomenon in the sphere of man's behavior which occurs as a result of this general transformation in the course of starvation. The numerous modifications of the forms of behavior which are initiated by our "independent variable," and which vary further in accordance with additional conditions, are all developed out of and explained by this central factor.

The Concept and the Forms of Food Taxis and of the Activities Initiated by It

This central factor I identify as the phenomenon of food tropism, or food taxis, which is the special form of chemotropism, or chemotaxis. Concretely, I define this factor as the attraction of the human being to foods when he is starving (deficiency or relative), or to objects such as money which make it possible to obtain food, with a conscious or unconscious purpose of securing and consuming food to satisfy his hunger. Every part of man's behavior which is directly or indirectly stimulated by hunger, and which is for the purpose of procuring, possessing, and consuming foods or their equivalents (such as money) which make it possible to obtain food, is designated as "the behavior stimulated by food taxis."

88

All the acts which fall into this category I call food taxis acts. As indicated, I am not concerned with whether or not these acts are conscious or unconscious. As soon as the obstacles are overcome, in either case, the final result is the same: the assimilation of food.

According to the forms of starvation, it is necessary to distinguish, first of all, the food taxis acts which are caused by deficiency and comparative starvation, respectively, or which are stimulated by objects which satisfy either of them. Not only does a hungry man attempt to satisfy his appetite, but one who is adequately fed also is attracted, both quantitatively and qualitatively, by foods of better quality. We call the former acts *deficiency food taxis*, and the latter ones *comparative food taxis*.

Each of these kinds of acts is further divided into *pure* and *mixed*. In the first of these categories come food taxis acts which are called forth exclusively by deficiency or relative starvation; in the second are placed all acts stimulated concomitantly by starvation and some other determinants of behavior.

When an individual A travels from Petrograd to Pskov and is stimulated exclusively by the "nutritional" determinants, the whole chain of his activity represents an expression of pure food taxis. However, when a journalist writes a paper because he needs money for bread, but also because he wants to settle a score with his opponent, acquire glory, be a man of note, etc., we have a case of a mixed food taxis act.

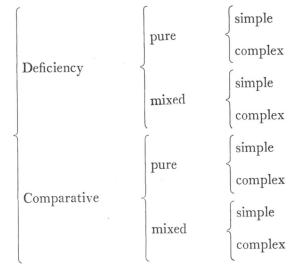

*The Multiformity of the Food Taxis Acts and Their Role
in the Total Budget of Man's Activities*

Observation of the complex food taxis acts indicates that *their concrete forms can be very diverse. Aside from the specific acts of eating*
(taking food into the mouth, chewing, swallowing, etc.), *there is no
direct connection between stimulation by hunger and the concrete
form of the food taxis acts which are produced by it.*

Depending upon the quantity and quality of obstacles in the way
of satisfying hunger or procuring an adequate diet, the food tropism
acts may assume very diversified forms, and superficially these may
seem to be unrelated to nutrition. Relative to nutrition the social life
of a human being resembles the labyrinth or maze used by scientists
who investigate animal behavior, with an intricate combination of passages in which it is difficult to find one's way out or to reach the exit.

At the first glance it appears strange to consider acts such as
typing, writing a newspaper editorial, performing a religious service,
singing an aria from Faust, stoking the furnace, etc., as functions of
hunger or as examples of food taxis acts. Nonetheless, in the contemporary system the labyrinth they represent is in most cases nothing
but a complex form, if not of pure, at least of mixed food taxis, which
force the human being to obtain food in a "circuitous way." "One
must eat," and a man tills the earth. "One must eat," and another
works several hours on the factory. "One must eat," and others type
and file in an office, dance and sing on a stage, give lectures, write
articles, preach sermons, so that each one and his family can have
their "daily bread." By this I do not exclude the possibility that similar acts may be caused by some other determinants (e.g., by the sex
determinant, self-preservation determinant, or by a number of conditioned determinants, religious, legal, esthetic, etc., which are not
connected with starvation). But I do say that all these diversified acts
can consist either of pure food taxis, or of those concomitants of starvation together with other determinants of behavior.

The next question is *what is the proportion of food taxis acts in
the totality of the human behavior.*

Obviously, in different people and groups there is variation in
the proportion of food taxis acts. Furthermore, it may vary in the
same individual during different periods of his life.

Either leaving aside all other conditions, or considering them as being equal, we are going to formulate the basic theorem, which postulates that the proportion of the food taxis acts, in the sum total of all human acts, depends upon the size of the obstacles encountered in efforts to obtain food. *This theoretical proposition, which emerges from the preceding, is as follows: other conditions being equal, and particularly during the equal intensity of food taxis, the more obstacles there are in the way of obtaining similar foods in general, or better foods, the more complex a man's pure and mixed food taxis acts become, and the greater proportion they constitute of his total activity. In other words, the more time, energy and activity he must spend in procuring food, the less becomes the proportion of his other acts which are stimulated by other determinants. In brief, the percentage of the food taxis acts (pure and mixed) in the total sum of human activity is directly proportionate to the size of the obstacles which are found in the way of obtaining the means of nutrition.*

If we were to put some food at the beginning of the complex passages of the labyrinth, the rat would take it at once upon entering the experimental apparatus. If, however, a piece of fat were put at the end of the maze, the animal would have to run a complex pathway, overcome a whole series of obstacles, spend more energy and time before it would reach the food magnet.

Similar events occur in the behavior of the man. When the food is under his nose, he takes it and eats it. In this case food taxis acts constitute an insignificant part of his behavior; they require a minimum of time and energy. The rest of his time and energy, in such cases, may be used in other tasks or forms of activity.

Quite different is the behavior of a man, who is equally as hungry as the first, but who has to overcome a number of obstacles in order to obtain food. The life of such a man represents complete pure or mixed food taxis: in the case of deficiency starvation he will be completely absorbed with filling his stomach, and in that of comparative starvation he will be concerned with improvement of his diet. The remaining requirements will be satisfied only as long as they enter the realm of mixed food taxis acts, which encourage him to have fun while also eating well, or speaking in the vernacular, to kill two or three birds with the same stone. The study of budgeting of time, when it can be applied, and of budgeting of income and expenses may serve as a verification of the above statement. Let us consider a few facts.

In respect to nutrition most primitive peoples are in far worse conditions than the peoples of the countries with more developed cultures: they must overcome considerably more obstacles obtaining food than the latter. We observe that *throughout their lives almost all the time of the primitives* who live in poor and unfavorable conditions with respect to the procurement of food is spent in this task.

K. Bücher writes that during the perennial migratory life of the primitive man, the search for food occupied him completely. He could not even develop feelings that we consider most natural. Bücher states that if we were to take away from the lives of the Bushmen or the Veddas of Ceylon the use of fire, of bows and arrows (although the preparation of the latter is also a food taxis act), an individual's entire life would consist of his search for food. The need for food is most urgent, and is at first the only requirement which forces man to search ceaselessly until this requirement is satisfied.

Caesar said that the Suevi, who lived by hunting and animal breeding, spent a great deal of time in hunting. *Agriculturae non student maiorique pars eorum victus in lacte, caseo, carne consistit. Neque multum frumento, sed maximam partem lacte atque pecore vivunt, multumque sunt in venationibus.*[1]

"During their early life (up to the age 14), the children of the Australian tribes spend their time mostly in the search for food in the bush country."[2] The same applies even to a greater extent to the adults.

P. Piri reported that the Eskimos of Smith's Gulf had no government, no religion, no money, no property, wore clothing made from skins of animals, and ate meat, blood, and fat, and that, having no concern except for food and clothing, they were entirely occupied with ways of procuring these objects. He said they had only one occupation, hunting, and preparing the objects with which to hunt.

"Man is naturally inclined to idleness," concludes Westermarck after summarizing certain facts,[3] "not because he is averse to muscular activity as such, but because he dislikes the monotony of regular labor, and the mental exertion it implies. In general he is induced to work only by some special motive which makes him think the trouble

1. Caesar, *De bello Gallico*, Libro VI, p. 22.

2. W. B. Spencer and F. J. Gillen, *The Northern Tribes of Central Australia* (London, 1904), chap. 10.

3. E. A. Westermarck, *The Origin and Development of Moral Ideas* (1908), 1:268–69.

worth his while. Among savages, who have little care for the morrow, who have few comforts of life to provide for, and whose property is often of such kind as to prevent any great accumulation of it,
almost the sole inducement to industry is either necessity or compulsion. Men are either lazy or industrious according as the necessaries
of life are easy or difficult to procure." [4] "While a severer clime and a
ruder soil are favorable to industry, foresight, and a hardy temperament," [5] according to Yate, "the natives of New Zealand are industrious: and compared with their more northern brethren they are a
hard-working race, while the Polynesians on the Island of Tonga,
who live in a very lush environment, are lazy and spend little time in
procuring their food." [6] The natives of Sumatra, those of many places
in Africa, the Negroes of the Gold Coast, etc., who live in places
where food is easily obtained, are lazy and carefree, while the Green-
landers, Eskimos, etc., who live in severe climates, are diligent,
energetic, and constantly at work. The Samoans, the Tahitians, the
Sandwich Islanders, the natives of New Zealand, the Nukuhivans,
etc., work only when there is no food and spend time in some other
activities when food is plentiful.[7]

From these facts, the number of which could be increased considerably, we see that: (1) hunger is a force which pushes the individual to obtain the means of existence; (2) in the life of the
natives the time spent and the proportion of food taxis acts increase
proportionally to the difficulties in obtaining food; (3) these acts
vary directly with the increase or the decrease of these obstacles.

Similar causes give rise to similar consequences. We see the
same phenomena in the behavior of more cultured peoples when the
obstacles in the way of obtaining food increase. Indeed, if one opens
the pages describing the lives of explorers (e.g., Stanley, Prźhevalsky,
or any of the pioneers who visit regions where food is difficult to obtain), he sees that the coefficient of time (and energy) spent in procuring the means of existence rises so high in the general "budget of
time" that, on a daily basis, it may occupy the entire twenty-four
hours, or at least all of the hours the people are awake. As the ob-

4. Ibid.
5. Horatio Hale, *Ethnology and Philology: U.S. Exploring Expedition*
(Philadelphia, 1846), p. 17.
6. William Yate, *An Account of New Zealand* (London, 1835), pp.
105–6.
7. Westermarck, op. cit., pp. 269–71.

stacles decrease, the coefficient falls. As an example I cite the diary of Mikkelsen, who explored the uninhabited islands of Greenland in 1910–12. "We are tramping in the valley some 12–14 hours, we are not tired, but we have no success. . . . The time goes slowly when walking hour after hour without seeing any game. What only don't we do? We are lying down by the holes in the ice and are luring the seals." After four days of constant walking they succeeded in killing only a few partridges. This was repeated several times. "The more hungry we are, the nearer is the day when nothing shall be left from our supplies, the more we exhibit energy for obtaining food by hunting, and the more we are sneaking back and forth among the ice crevices of the gulf." [8]

Still more colorful in this respect is the budget of time and the behavior of J. Nowells, who, on October 4, 1913, went into a forest with no clothing and no implements for procuring food, in order to determine whether contemporary man can survive "in the bosom of nature" without any objects of culture. Regardless of the very favorable surroundings, the first days of his life were spent almost entirely in procuring food. The first day and night he was not hungry. "After awaking I felt for the first time a painful paroxysm of hunger. I crossed the pond along the beaver dam and kept my eyes on the shallow water, where I thought I could get a trout. Then I picked blueberries until I was satiated, but I returned to the pond in the anticipation of getting a trout." In other words, most of his time and energy during the first two weeks of this experiment, which lasted for about two months, were spent in procuring food. [9]

Finally, we can confirm the correctness of these theorems by the behavior of the people of Russia during the years 1917–22. The division of labor almost disappeared during these years—we all came to be encyclopedists—and the obstacles in the way of obtaining food increased tremendously. *The part of time (and energy) which was spent in procuring food grew disproportionately.* It included getting ration cards, standing in all sort of food lines, traveling to villages to exchange domestic articles for food, going to distant markets in search of food speculators, performing a series of tasks exclusively to obtain additional rations, going to the communal dining halls for meals, preparing and cooking food, working kitchen gardens, etc. *The part*

8. Mikkelsen, *Lost in the Arctic*, pp. 257–64 and passim.
9. J. Nowells, "Two Months in the Forest," *Prometei*, pp. 20–28 (in Russian).

of time spent in other activities decreased correspondingly. Certain activities ceased entirely, such as visiting friends, going to the theater, viewing exhibits, and walking for pleasure; others were restricted to a minimum, such as scientific work which promised no immediate reward in the form of a pound of butter or meat; still others were performed because they were bread-winning lectures in Communist cultural organizations.

This means that *with an increase in the obstacles in the way of obtaining food, the pure and the mixed food taxis acts increased while other activities decreased.* These statements are corroborated by facts concerning individuals, as well as those for the masses of the population.

The study of budgeting income and expenditures of human beings still further confirms it. In contemporary society the size of income is, *ceteris paribus,* an indicator of the number of obstacles in the way of obtaining food objects: the higher the income, the easier it is to obtain them, or the fewer obstacles there are, and vice versa.

A man's poverty is an indicator of many obstacles in the way of attaining the food magnet. Thus the yardstick of budgeting income and expenditures may indicate (1) that in the limited budgets, those barely sufficient to maintain life, nutrition plays the role of forcing a man to perform certain acts; (2) which groups of requirements are displacing others precisely as the budget is being limited, i.e., during an increase of obstacles to secure the essentials needed for satisfaction of most needs; (3) the proportion of changes in the food taxis acts to those of other acts during the fluctuation of the budget, i.e., during variations of the obstacles in the way of satisfaction of hunger.

We find complete substantiation of this statement in the following: (1) when income is very small, the proportion of it expended for food is tremendous, i.e., where obstacles to satiation are great; (2) as income and expenditures decrease, the proportion going for food increases; (3) this increase takes place on account of expenses for satisfaction of wants not connected with food; and (4) as the total budget increases, the percentage going for food decreases. When food is easily available, man is liberated from the burden of food taxis.

Here are some of the data. Various investigations have shown that in the budgets of laborers and peasants—the most limited budgets of peoples in Europe and America—expenses for food fluctuate from about 40 to 80 per cent, and the percentage of total income or expenditures going for food decreases as the budget of the same type increases. The higher the income-expenditures, the smaller the proportion of the expenditures used for nutrition (Engel's Law with Laspeyrer's correction). Consequently, a greater proportion remains for use in satisfaction of other wants, and vice versa.

D'Avenel reports that four-fifths of the families of France spend three-fifths of their income on nutrition. As their incomes increase, the percentage spent on nutrition decreases. Among those having yearly incomes of about 10,000 francs, from 35 to 40 per cent of it is spent for nutrition; when it is 20,000 to 50,000 francs, the corresponding percentage for the food is 15 to 25 per cent.[10] In the study of the budgets of the laborers in France in 1907–8, this relationship is represented in the following figures:

Weekly income	Percentage of income spent for food
Under 20 shillings	62.7
20–24 shillings	60.8
25–29 shillings	58.6
30–34 shillings	57.9
35–39 shillings	56.1
40 or more shillings	52.8

In England (1,944 budgets of laborers):

Under 25 shillings	67.0
25–29 shillings	66.2
30–34 shillings	65.0
35–39 shillings	61.0
40 or more shillings	57.0

In Germany (1906–7):

Under 25 shillings	65.0
25–29 shillings	62.3
30–34 shillings	59.2
35–39 shillings	57.7
40 or more shillings	56.3

10. Georges D'Avenel, *Le mécanisme de la vie moderne*, 5th ed., 1st ser., pp. 154–55.

In the United States (11,156 budgets in 1901): [11]

Under 16 shillings	50.85
16–23 shillings	47.33
24–31 shillings	46.99
32–39 shillings	46.88
40–47 shillings	46.16
48–55 shillings	43.48
56–63 shillings	41.44
64–71 shillings	41.37
72–79 shillings	39.90
80–87 shillings	38.79
88–95 shillings	37.68
96 or more shillings	36.45

In Russia (the budgets of laborers from Kiev): [12]

Yearly income	Percentage spent for food in relation to the total expense
100–200 rubles	71.95
200–300 rubles	56.70
300–400 rubles	52.45
400–500 rubles	54.30
500–600 rubles	52.40
600–700 rubles	49.8
700–800 rubles	44.5

Similar figures are found in studies of peasants. For example, in the province of Vologda, among those having the smallest incomes (less than 2 desyatin), the expense for food represented 70.8 per cent of total income. As income gradually increases, the corresponding percentage falls to 67.6, 61.9, and 60.7 for the richest group.[13]

From these figures we see, first, in budgets of a similar type,

11. Figures for France, England, and the United States in A. Webb, *The New Dictionary of Statistics*, pp. 156–65.

12. Pervushin, "Consumption," in Grant's *Encyclopedia*, 33:168 (in Russian).

13. Ibid., pp. 167–69.

and, second, in budgets in general, that as the total budget increases, the proportion of it spent for food decreases; as the former decreases, the latter increases. If the nutrition of a rich man were similar to that of a poor person, then in his budget of acts the food taxis acts, which are as indicated by the percentage of his expenditures going for food, would be very insignificant. But even with his better diet (due to comparative food taxis) the percentage of his budget spent for food would be lower than that of a poor person.

When the income falls to an insignificant amount, expenditures for nutrition take almost 100 per cent of it, or often even more, thereby producing a deficit in the budget. In such cases the amounts spent for other needs become zero.

The people of many Russian towns in 1918–21, and first of all those of Moscow and Petrograd, serve as a massive example of similar budgets and behavior. To satisfy their hunger many people consumed not only what they earned, but sold everything they possessed. Their activities unrelated to food fell to an insignificant level. Whatever they did in order to find satisfaction had to be in the form of mixed food taxis acts. Whoever could not afford to do otherwise faced a life which was nothing but a mere chase after food. During these years expenditures for clothing, shoes, clean and comfortable dwellings, lighting and heating, cultural requirements (books, lectures, theaters, the church, etc.) all fell to the vanishing point. This can be seen from a comparison of the budgets of individual workers in Moscow in 1918 and in prewar times, when the food was easy to get.[14] The table indicates that as obstacles to obtaining food increased, the proportion of corresponding expenditures for food increased, and that in so doing they greatly diminished the proportion for other requirements. All activities (artisanship, the writing of books and articles, lecturing, painting pictures, employment, etc.) became mere means of obtaining food during these years. The activities which did not pay in this way (lecturing, writing of the articles, and other work which was not remunerated with food rations) gradually decreased and were replaced by the "acts which brought rations." Furthermore, as we shall see later, the food taxis related to this produced far more important changes; it "reversed" and "changed" the entire "soul" of the people, forcing them to "burn everything that they admired."

14. *Red Moscow* (1918), pp. 185–86.

Requirements	Expenditures (in percentages)	
	Before the war	In 1918
Food	37.3	75.7
Housing and household expenses	12.0	3.8
Clothing	12.8	7.8
Hygiene	4.2	3.0
Cultural requirements	2.6	2.2
Remittances to home village	27.6	2.2
Others	6.3	5.3

Such is the concept of food taxis, and of its different forms and roles in the behavior of people.

Preliminary Remarks on the Mutual Relationship between Hunger and Other Determinants

Because of the concept of a food taxis, as the main function of starvation, from the moment of its appearance this determinant of starvation tends to dominate completely our organism like a "check payable to the bearer"; and it tends to turn the organism completely into an apparatus at the service of nutrition. If it were not for the other determinants of behavior, at such times a man would be like a ball pushed exclusively by hunger and subjected exclusively to food taxis. Such "check to the bearer" then would be a personal check belonging exclusively to "Mr. Hunger."

Such a supposition, of course, is not correct; aside from hunger there are numerous other determinants of behavior. The human organism possesses a highly sensitive network of receptors of the nervous system and resembles a complex radio receiver which receives "waves of stimuli" every minute, not only from the "hunger station" but from many other stations as well. This means that the organism is always subjected to the requirements of numerous determinants in the sphere of influence in which a person is situated.

The human being must react to all these stimuli, and, therefore, the behavior of a man is a "function" not merely of one, but of many "independent variables." At each given moment he is situated in the "field of action" not of a single force—quantity and quality of food—

but of many others. Human behavior serves as an equating force for all these independent variables.

The relationships between hunger as a determinant and all other determinants of behavior may be characterized as follows: (1) complementary, i.e., when all the determinants are mutually beneficial, and when they are "pushing" the human being toward the performance of certain actions at the same time; (2) antagonistic, i.e., when the hunger factor and other determinants are incompatible in time, thus forcing the organism to react in opposite directions; (3) neutral, when these forces are compatible, but are not always pushing in the same direction. However, the third type of relationship is comparatively rare. In most cases, either the first or the second type predominates.

The hunger determinant attempts to seize a man and to convert his behavior into a complete food taxis under two conditions: in the complete absence of antagonistic determinants, and when other determinants are weak and inhibited.

The cases when a determinant (namely, hunger) acts in the complete absence of other antagonistic determinants are comparatively rare; in real life we are for the most part in the field of action of multiple determinants. In other words, we usually are in a situation of conflict between hunger and other antagonistic determinants. Once there is a conflict the inevitable struggle results. When there is struggle, three alternatives may exist: a victory of hunger over the antagonists (resulting in the predominance of the food taxis acts over the others); a victory of the antagonists over hunger (producing a predominance of non-food taxis acts over food taxis acts); and mutual annihilation and the rise of something intermediate between the other two.

Such are the main conclusions about food taxis. Every occurrence and growth of food taxis acts is possible only after the victory of the determinants of hunger over the antagonistic determinants or in their complete absence.

In the next chapters of this book I consider in detail the problem of interrelationships between hunger and the other determinants, as well as the results of the competition between them. At present, however, I introduce some facts which show the suppression or weakening through hunger of the other antagonistic determinants of behavior. These facts indicate that, in the duel, hunger is often the victor. (The opposite cases are discussed later on.) All actions of the individual which show that under the influence of starvation he ceases to react toward a series of other determinants, to which previously he did react, are the manifestations of such victory. And, vice versa, hunger may induce human beings to perform acts which would not take place in the absence of starvation. To the first category of "suppressed" acts and determinants belong all acts and determinants incompatible with food taxis, which hinder the satisfaction of hunger, and to the second category, all acts encouraging the obtaining of food.

We proceed now to a consideration of corresponding facts.

The Suppression and Weakening through Hunger of the Individual's Self-Preservation and of Corresponding Life-Saving Reflexes

Among the stimuli affecting the human being are a considerable number of dangerous ones which either threaten the life of or cause very heavy injury to the health of the organism. These may be very diversified, such as, for example, homicidal actions of other people (shooting, stabbing, beating, etc.); attacks by wild animals; poisons produced by pathogenic microorganisms (of typhus, plague, cholera, etc.); extreme variations in temperature; being struck by heavy falling objects, etc.

Similarly, in this or other forms, harmful stimulants are frequently encountered by us. To lessen these dangers man has developed a whole series of counteracting devices, which permit him either to avoid such dangerous stimulants (acts such as running away from a dangerous animal, man, fire, flood, or automobile horn; abstaining from poisonous food or polluted water, and so on), or to attack in various ways their injurious consequences through defensive actions against the animal, human beings, microbes, climate, extremes of temperature, and other natural catastrophes. These defensive actions consist of taking antitoxic drugs, putting on warm clothing during cold weather, closing the eyes to an uplifted fist, disinfecting to control microbes, etc. He may also seek to prevent the occurrence of such dangerous consequences (hygienic measures, provisions for sanitation, etc.). From this it follows that these defensive reflexes—partially conscious, partially unconscious—are numerous and diversified. Man's life span would be considerably shorter, were it not for them.

The totality of these defensive reactions constitutes the group of reflexes of self-preservation, and the stimuli causing these reflexes make up a special group of determinants of human behavior which may be called determinants of individual self-preservation.

The observation of human behavior (and also that of animals) shows that determinants of hunger, and all the reflexes caused by it, sometimes conflict with determinants of individual self-preservation. All the phenomena in which satisfaction of hunger forces the human being to perform acts which endanger his life and health belong to this category. The determinants of self-preservation tend to inhibit such actions and lead the organism in a different direction. Thus, in time the corresponding reflexes become incompatible and begin to conflict with one another. Hunger is often the victor in such conflicts and succeeds in inhibiting or repressing reflexes of self-preservation.

The numerous examples of the victory of hunger over the self-preservation determinant may be divided into two categories: in the first, hunger conquers its opponent by a "frontal attack," in an "open struggle"; in the second, it overcomes the opponent by a "slow siege," by diminishing gradually the vital forces of the organism and weakening the energy which is necessary for the successful performance of protective reactions. Examples of the first kind are found abundantly in the behavior of soldiers under siege in fortresses after their food supply is exhausted. The besieged men find themselves in such cases "between two fires," between influences of the forces of hunger and those of determinants of individual and group self-preservation. As influenced by hunger the soldiers may forage, or break the siege, or surrender unconditionally. The determinant of individual self-preservation tends to inhibit any acts which threaten the men either by immediate danger to all of the besieged, or to a considerable proportion of them.

The histories of the wars of the primitive peoples to secure salt, the wars of ancient Egypt, Assyria, Babylonia, Persia, Greece, Rome, and the Hebrews, the wars of the Middle Ages, and those of our times often record the capitulation of people suffering from starvation. They also tell of desperate forays, attempts to break sieges, and of many who perished in the end. Such behavior indicates that hunger had overpowered the determinant of self-preservation and forced people to perform acts which were detrimental to their health and life. Had it not been for hunger, such acts never would have been performed. Thus, the method of conquering by a "hunger siege" has long been known and practiced in war. When an enemy does not have the capability of overcoming an opponent directly, he tries to shut off supplies of food for the fortress, town, camp, etc., thus putting the latter into the "field of influence" of hunger and repressing the reflexes of self-preservation.

Further confirmation of similar problems may be found when, in order to obtain the necessary "daily bread," a man performs a series of acts detrimental to his health and even dangerous to his life. Such acts, indeed, are very numerous and quite diversified. People desperate from starvation steal to get bread, or to get money to obtain bread, even if strong resistance is expected and the robbery may be severely punished. During the years of starvation in Petrograd (1919–20) theft of vegetables from the communal kitchen gardens became quite prevalent, and it took place despite the declaration by the government that such offenders would be shot to death. At this time hunger also induced bandits, deserters, and political fugitives to report voluntarily to prison authorities, or to surrender for prosecution, respectively.[15] During the years of famine the inhabitants of Petrograd frequently traveled by railroad into adjacent provinces to exchange their meager domestic possessions for grain, flour, or bread. These journeys were extremely dangerous because, first, there was the possibility of contracting typhus, and second, there was danger of being shot by the "zagradilovka" (special guards).

Hunger also induces individuals to eat food which is known to be poisonous. Likewise, during the epidemics of cholera in Petrograd and Moscow, many starving people did not hesitate to eat raw food in order to satisfy their hunger. The mass migration of people from regions of deficient food supplies to those with more abundant food is another expression of the same problem. This occurs even when the latter location is very unstable and hazardous. Furthermore, regardless of the protection of supply trains and other vehicles by armed guards, the starving people attacked them, thus endangering themselves, and even perishing as a result. The sale of the last pair of

15. My friend [A.V.T.] and I [P.S.] happened to be in a similar situation in 1918. While we were living in the forest as political fugitives, after we exhausted our food supplies, hunger forced us to leave our hiding place and to go to a village for some food, even though there was a great possibility of being caught and shot to death on the spot or after a little delay. Fully realizing this, we made the attempt nevertheless. Due to the extraordinary efforts of my friend (who spent the night barefoot in a frozen swamp, almost without clothing, and afterwards swam across a big river), the expedition was successful.

shoes and the last clothing in order to get bread also occurred, despite the danger of pneumonia, etc. All of these facts, and thousands of similar cases in the past, as well in our own times, indicate the conflict between the hunger determinant and that of self-preservation, and the suppression of the latter by the former by means of "a direct attack."

The suicides resulting from starvation depict a similar picture. The statistics have even included a special category of suicides as a result of that cause. According to Wagner, in a total of 100 suicides, 12.9 per cent were caused by poverty (mainly starvation); according to Block, in France in 1851–52 there was an equal proportion, 12.3 per cent; in 1855, 12.5 per cent; and in 1866, 11 per cent. According to the Prussian statistics the corresponding percentage in 1860 was 11, and in Saxony, 7.3.[16] A similar relationship between suicide and poverty (hunger) among English farmers was expressed in another form, shown in the table below.[17] These figures indicate that a "frontal attack" by hunger annuls all protective reflexes and destroys the will to live.

Years	Number of suicides	Number ruined
1878	71	626
1879	112	1,196
1880	104	1,097
1881	69	918
1882	74	533
1883	58	422

Therefore, it is not surprising to find that during periods of great starvation, similar to that which occurred in Russia, the curve of suicides rises. It would have risen still higher had it not been for two counterinfluences: an extremely high general mortality rate (from hunger, typhus, etc.), and the fact of the existence of revolution, which reinforces social ties between people in periods of popular upheavals, and so, according to Durkheim, lowers the rate of suicide.[18]

16. A. Oettingen, *Die Moralstatistik* (1882), pp. 780–84, table 110.
17. William Ogle, "On Suicides in England and Wales," *Journal of the Royal Statistical Society* 49 (1886):113–14.
18. Émile Durkheim, *Le Suicide* (Paris, 1887).

This explains why, during the years 1918–21, the curve of suicides did not rise. The years 1921 and 1922 signified the end of the revolution. With the decrease of the mentioned counterinfluences, the role of hunger in suicide became quite apparent in the provinces of Russia. Newspapers of the period are filled with information about suicides, but exact statistics are still lacking.[19] However, in the province of Saratov, medical statistics indicate "the increasing growth of suicides of adults and children which is connected with starvation." Entire families ended their lives by monoxide poisoning, by infecting themselves with spotted typhus fever, by hanging themselves, by drowning, etc.[20]

Starvation causes a decrease in and elimination of reflexes of self-preservation in still another way. With continued starvation, absolute or relative, the vital forces of the organism, which otherwise repelled, prevented, or overcame the dangerous effects of the threatening stimuli, are weakened. The decrease of purposefulness of the protective reactions, which occurs as a consequence of prolonged absolute or relative starvation, leads to the same final result. The work of the higher centers of consciousness is weakened and the individual begins to record conditions and influences of the surrounding environment in a less exact manner. His reactions, therefore, become less and less favorable, so that his adaptation to the medium becomes less successful. Under these circumstances man ceases to realize the danger of many events, he does not find means to repel them, etc. The mind becomes obscured; apathy, semi-delirium, inertia, indifference to everything else occur. The "will for life," "the desire to live" diminish, and as a final result man perishes, often without any rebellion or protest.

In this case we have a chain of events: (1) starvation; (2) a weakening of the physical and psychological forces of the organism; (3) a diminution of "instinct of life" and of self-preservation, i.e., the weakening and depressing of the determinant of the reflexes of self-preservation; and (4) death of the organism.

The following examples substantiate the above proposition. (1) There is an inevitable decrease of the vitality of an organism during

19. It should be remembered that this was written in 1922. E.S.
20. Vasilevskyi, "The Sinister Chronicle of the Famine," *Ufa* (1922) (in Russian). See also *Krasnaya Gazeta*, no. 172, 1922; *Izvestia*, February 12, 1922.

starvation. The experiments of Canalis, Morpugne, Castellino, Féré, Proust, et al., proved the decrease of immunity during starvation. Hence, it is easy to understand why various epidemics and a rise in the death rate occur as inevitable concomitants of mass starvation. This topic is discussed in detail later in this book. (2) The occurrence of apathy and indifference and a weakening of the "will to live" seize the population after long, severe starvation. In the early stages of starvation, hunger leads the individual to an energetic search for food. But as soon as the peak of intensity is passed, when the reserves of the organism are exhausted, when starvation has lasted for a long time, the energy of the organism falls sharply, and, concomitantly, the "struggle for life" and the "will to live" are weakened. "Dull and hopeless apathy was the principal mood of the population during the years of famine in the Middle Ages," writes a historian.[21] The mood of the masses was quite similar in India after prolonged starvation.[22]

In Russia during our years of famine we observed many similar events. The people died like flies from starvation. They were falling down in the streets and dying in homes, like extinct candles. They expressed neither damning condemnations nor feverish attempts to save their lives. Hunger had dried the sources of their "will to live" and extinguished all of their protective reflexes. In the provinces where famine prevailed, the masses of population exhibited similar attitudes. "Indifference and apathy" were reported by observers in the provinces along the Volga River. This "dull and hopeless apathy" occurs as a result of long and severe deficiency starvation.[23] It is a manifestation of the indirect, basic weakening by hunger of the contractual and, concomitantly, protective reflexes of the organism.

In summary: (1) The determinants of hunger and the food taxis acts caused by it frequently come into conflict with the determinant of individual self-preservation and the protective acts called forth by it. (2) The contest between these two determinants frequently ends with victory by hunger, and this is followed by repression of the determinant, and of the reflexes of individual self-preservation. (3) This goal is achieved by hunger in two main ways, namely by "direct

21. F. Curschmann, *Hungersnöte im Mittelalter* (Leipzig, 1910), p. 53.
22. W. Digby, *The Famine Campaign in Southern India* (1878), vols. 1 and 2.
23. I emphasize here the long duration and the deficiency of starvation, since hunger of short duration and not very deficient in nature causes no abrupt weakening of the organism, and may even stimulate its activity.

frontal attack" or by "prolonged siege." (4) Other conditions which influence the results of this contest are considered in the chapter on the relationship between hunger and other determinants.

The Repression and Weakening by Hunger of the Determinant of Group Self-Preservation and of Corresponding Reflexes

The reflexes of group self-preservation exist side by side with the determinants and reflexes of individual self-preservation. To this category belong all the acts which are concerned with the preservation of life and of the unity of the social group. The stimuli which call them forth are those of close kinship: members of the family, friends, people of the same tribe, persons of the same faith, those of the same party, fellow citizens, etc., namely, the persons in the groups most congenial to us, related to us, and closest and most dear to us. The reflexes of human behavior which they stimulate and which are, either consciously or unconsciously, for the preservation of the life, unity, and survival of the group differ sharply from the reflexes of individual self-preservation. The latter may be either congenial with or antagonistic to the former. In some cases the self-preservation of the individual requires inflicting harm on the group; vice versa, the interests of the group (family, church, party, government, circle of friends, nationality, etc.) may require the sacrifice of the individual. For example, he may have to perish in a struggle in the interests of his family, government, or other groups.

The comparative history of behavior—genetic sociology—may indicate the occurrence of group self-preservation in the animal world. Such are all the acts concerned with the preservation of the species, and not that of the individual. They are very diversified. The most typical of them are "parental" and "herd" reflexes.

Parental reflexes begin with the acts of nursing, incubating, guarding the offspring, and end with the acts of direct sacrifice to save the young (e.g., the act of the monkey that subjects itself to be shot by the hunter to save its offspring). The "herd" reflex is also expressed in collective defense, or the attack upon an enemy by a group of animals.

Among human beings the reflexes of group self-preservation represent a more complex form of acts than those of animals. They are manifest among us partially in a conscious and partially in an unconscious way. The principal forms of the reflexes of group self-preservation are in reality a complex set of reflexes, in which the basic, purely biological reflexes of self-preservation are augmented by many kinds of conditioned reflexes, which are complementary with and are enforced by them. Such are the patriotic, religious, political, and other sacrificial acts in the name of "duty" to family, party, church, etc. The unconscious forms of reflexes of group self-preservation are more simple in content and are closer to the purely biological prototype found among animals. This distinction between these two forms, which is important in many ways, is unimportant for my purpose here. We shall consider both forms together, because repression by hunger of many conditioned reflexes of group self-preservation would only indicate the fact that hunger may suppress not only pure reflexes of that type, but also those which are accelerated by a series of conditioned reflexes (i.e., those that are acquired, not hereditary).

Disregarding this difference for the time being, we may say that by reflexes of group self-preservation, we understand all acts which tend to safeguard the interests of life, safety, and well-being of one's intimates. They begin with the parents' acts in caring for their children and end with acts of self-sacrifice for the sake of family, tribe, government, or church.

Observation shows that the hunger determinant and the acts called forth by it frequently are antagonistic to the acts called forth by the group self-preservation determinant. Thus they become irreconcilable. We find everywhere cases in which satisfaction of hunger requires acts that inflict injury to preservation of the life, unity, and well-being of the "intimates," and, vice versa, those in which the determinant of group self-preservation requires acts which interfere with the satisfaction of hunger. Observation also indicates that hunger often is the victor in this confrontation, i.e., it suppresses the antagonist, so that food taxis acts inhibit or weaken the reflexes of group self-preservation, including those which are most deeply rooted among human beings. A series of facts exists which proves this proposition beyond question.

Endocannibalism.—Among these acts the first place is occupied by cannibalism, and especially by endocannibalism (eating other members of the group), when such acts are caused by hunger and would not have taken place under normal conditions. If we were to indicate hunger by a and cannibalism by b, then using the simplified method of the confluent changes and methods of differentials, we may state that in many cases b is a function of a [$b = f(a)$], so that if there were no a, there would have been no b. This means that in such cases hunger had suppressed one of the most fundamental forms of the reflexes of group self-preservation—abstaining from the eating of "intimates," which often is an unconditioned reflex not only among humans, but among animals as well.[24]

The fact is that cannibalism frequently occurs as a result of a lack of or insufficiency of food of animal origin. According to Ellis, in the South Sea Islands the torments of hunger often lead to this act. During an extreme emergency in the tribe of Nukuhivans, women and children were killed and eaten. Among the tribes of northern and western Australia, during acute lack of food, parents sometimes ate their own children. Similar events occurred among the Indian tribes north of Lake Superior. Among the Eskimos of the Hudson Bay, "There were cases when during extreme starvation of the family, and after having eaten all the dogs, the skins and other leather objects, the people began to be cannibals." [25] Hooper, Codrington, Hahn, Sceman, and others indicate that among a number of primitive tribes, old persons are killed and eaten during periods of starvation.[26]

In the Bible, and in some other ancient codices, there are indications of cannibalism during periods of need. "And you shall eat the offspring of your own body, the flesh of your sons and daughters, whom the Lord your God has given you, in the siege and in the distress with which your enemies shall distress you." [27]

Endocannibalism also took place in the history of Japan, China, Rome, Greece, and other nations. During the famous famine of A.D. 1200–1201 in Egypt, cannibalism acquired mass proportions.[28] During periods of starvation in the Middle Ages in Europe, cannibalism was a fairly common occurrence. "The worst result of starvation—is cannibalism. It was known to take place in the years 793, 868–69,

24. R. Steinmetz is not right in saying that primitive man was a habitual cannibal, i.e., that he had no reflex of self-abstention (*Endokannibalismus* [Vienna, 1896], pp. 25–34).

25. E. Westermarck, op. cit., 2:555.

26. Ibid., 1:390.

27. Deuteronomy 28:53.

28. According to St. Jerome, "During the siege of Rome the women returned their offspring back into their own bodies from which they had just emerged" (i.e., they ate their own babies). Stasyulevich, *History of the Middle Ages* (St. Petersburg, 1913), 1:139, 2:887–89 (in Russian).

896, 1005, 1032, 1085, 1146, 1233, 1241–42, 1277, 1280–82, 1315, 1317 A.D."[29] There are numerous facts recorded by the historians; one of them thus cites: "Anno Domini 1317 et 18 et 19 tanta fuit caristia et fames in Polonia et Silesia, ita quod pluribus in locis parentes filies et filii parentes necantes deveraverunt, plures etiam carnes de suspensis cadaveribus comederunt."[30] "In France during the famine of 1030–32 one man was executed because he killed and ate 48 people, and in Hungary one man confessed that he ate 30 children and 8 adults."[31] In Germany during the famine of 897, people dug out and ate the corpses from the new graves; parents killed their children, and children killed their parents.[32] In Burgundy in 1031–33 "fresh human meat was sold on the market, and children were led into woods to be killed and eaten."[33] During the rebellion of Dolchino in 1307, the besieged patarenos reached such a stage that they ate the flesh of those who died from sickness and deprivation.[34] The contemporaries of the famine in France during the reign of Louis XIV (in 1661–62, 1663–64, 1699, 1709) also told of cases of cannibalism.[35] "In China [in time of famine] mothers ate their children, and young men ate the older ones."[36]

Cannibalism occurred several times in Russia during periods of famine. The old chroniclers (called letopisets in Russian) recorded that during the famine of 1230–31 "some killed children and living men, others ate the meat of the cadavers."[37] During the famine of 1601–2 "men became worse than animals; not only did they rob and kill for a piece of bread, but they devoured each other." "Fathers and

29. Curschmann, *Hungersnöte im Mittelalter*, pp. 59–60.

30. Ibid., p. 217. Further citations are found in the same work on pp. 90–91, 98–99, and 112–14, for the years of famine in 793, 868, and 1032.

31. Tsitovich, *On Famines in Western Europe and Russia* (Kiev, 1892), p. 2 (in Russian).

32. J. von Hazzi, *Betrachtungen über Theuerung und Noth der Gegenwart und Vergangenheit* (Munich, 1818), p. 11.

33. Dobiash-Rozhdestvenskaya, *The Epoch of Crusades*, vol. 2 (1918) (in Russian).

34. Kautsky, *From Plato to the Anabaptists* (St. Petersburg, 1907) (in Russian).

35. Eugèn Bonnemère, *Histoire des paysans* (Paris, 1856), 2:86.

36. A. Issaev, *Crop Failure and Starvation* (St. Petersburg, 1892), pp. 5–6 (in Russian).

37. Karamzin, *The History of the Russian Empire*, vol. 11 (1853) (in Russian).

mothers ate their children, and children their parents; hosts ate their guests, human flesh was sold as meat on the markets, and travelers were afraid to stop at the inns." The chronicle records that the people ate things which are "indecent even to mention." [38] The same occurred again in the eighteenth and nineteenth centuries.

Similar causes produce similar results. When the inhibiting determinants of contemporary man become as weak as those of the cannibal, and when hunger is very great, suppression of the reflexes of group self-preservation leads some people to cannibalism even in modern times. The behavior of people who have been shipwrecked provides some examples of cannibalism. In order to save their lives, a number of them, even belonging to civilized nations, ate the bodies of their comrades.[39]

The famous case of the vessel *Mignonette* (1884) serves as an example. The three sailors who saved themselves in a boat killed and ate a boy. After four days at sea, they were rescued by a passing vessel. They were tried and condemned to death, but later the verdict was changed to six months in prison. Somewhat similar was the Holmes case in America in 1842. Similar things took place also during the shipwreck of *Medusa* in 1816.[40] In the province of Kansu, China, during the famine of 1909, people are known to have eaten human cadavers.[41]

Cases of murder and cannibalism also have taken place in our times in Russia. In Moscow in 1920 a starving husband killed his wife, made soup from some of her body, roasted other parts, and made jelly loaf out of her feet. A similar case was recorded in 1919 in the province of Minsk, where two children killed and gradually ate a third. In the village Esipovka, Buzuluk County, one peasant woman cut up the body of her seven-year-old daughter and used it as food. In the village of Andreevka starving people ate the body of a woman.

---

38. Soloviev, *History of Russia*, 3d ed. (Petrograd), 2:740–42 (in Russian). See also "Golod" (Famine), *Encyclopedia Brokhaus-Efron*, 17:102–4 (in Russian); and Leontovich, "Famines in Russia," *Severnyi Vestnik*, April 1892 (in Russian).

39. Westermarck, op. cit., 2:570.

40. F. Oetker, "Notwehr und Notstand," *Vergleichende Darstellung*, 2:328; Westermarck, op. cit., 1:285–86; Pashutin, *Experimental Pathology* (St. Petersburg, 1902) (in Russian); Edgar Allen Poe, *The Narrative of Arthur Gordon-Pym*.

41. *Russkii Vrach* (1909), p. 935 (in Russian).

Bodies were stolen from the barns, and cadavers in graves were dug up and stolen at night.[42] In the district of Tagaurov in Bashkir S.S.R., a native Bashkir Ishbulda and his wife killed and ate their ten-year-old daughter. After a short time their second child also disappeared.[43] In the provinces along the Volga River in 1921–22, cemeteries had to be patrolled because cadavers were stolen for food. Reports of murder of people for food became so frequent that it was impossible to record them all.[44] Indeed, similar causes do call forth similar consequences. (And still people say that "history does not repeat itself"!)

No further facts need be mentioned here. The citations already are quite extensive. They show clearly that at the base of many horrible actions lies the simple quantity of calories of food required by the organism. At the same time they signify beyond doubt the fact that hunger suppresses the reflexes of group self-preservation, even when they are augmented by a series of other conditioned reflexes.

The murder of parents, children, spouses, and "close kin" as a result of starvation.—The next series of evidence indicates suppression and weakening by hunger of reflexes of group self-preservation. To this belong the murders of close relatives which are done as a result of starvation, and which would not have taken place under normal conditions.

Consider some of the facts. The murders of parents are quite common among the nomadic tribes and are called forth by the severity of life, and particularly by hunger. It is beneficial for the total membership of the group that the old and useless members perish during periods of starvation, in preference to the strong young members.[45] Hahn reports that the Hottentots often abandon their aged parents because of their poverty and lack of food for all. Various other peoples have similar practices. In ancient Latium there was a custom of killing old people in order to have plenty of food for the rest of the tribe, "ut reliquis cibaria sufficerent." [46] Similar behavior was observed during famines in later periods of history. Along with the killing of parents and old people, hunger also often leads to the killing of chil-

42. *Krasnaya Gazeta*, December 31, 1921 (in Russian).

43. *Peterburgskaya Pravda*, January 5, 1922.

44. For example, see references in *Peterburgskaya Pravda* of February 10 and March 26 and *Izvestia* of January 29 and March 12, 1922.

45. Westermarck, op. cit., 1:387–92.

46. N. Leshkoff, *The Russian People and the State* (Moscow, 1858), p. 454 (in Russian).

dren and young people. It was one of the principal causes of the frequent killing of children by primitive peoples. There is no doubt that the murder of the children among the primitives is caused principally by difficulties of life. The child hinders the mother in following her mate in the search for food. Severely suffering from starvation, primitive people frequently have to make the choice between killing their burden, the children, or facing death from starvation. They frequently practice the murder of children as the means to save their lives. In certain tribes the children are not only killed, but also consumed.[47] The same phenomenon occurred sometimes among semi-civilized peoples. Because of poverty, in the poorest districts of China baby girls often were killed at birth by the parents.[48]

During the seasons of the year when hunger is greatest, similar killings have taken place among the Arabs,[49] in some cases among Hindus, [50] and in ancient Mexico, where to relieve their poverty the needy parents could dispose of one of their sons.[51] Similar phenomena occurred in Russia during starvation. Thus, Leshkoff says that in 1230–31, abandoned children were devoured by dogs, brother would take no pity on brother, father and mother became indifferent to the fate of their children, and a neighbor would not give bread to his neighbor.[52] During the famine of 1726 one woman threw her starving daughter into water to drown.[53] In Prussia during the famine, parents killed their children, and children murdered their parents.[54]

Similar facts were observed somewhat recently during famines in India. In Bombay, in 1876 "a father was brought to court on accusation that he smashed by stone the crania of his two children. In his defense he pointed out the difficulties of feeding the children during the hunger." [55] In Madras during the famine of 1876, "great unhumanity was shown on the part of mothers towards their chil-

47. Westermarck, op. cit., 1:399–401; Herbert Spencer, *The Foundation of Sociology* (St. Petersburg, 1898), 2:92, passim (in Russian).

48. Gutzlaff, *Sketch of Chinese History* (1834), 1:59; Douglas, *Society in China* (1894), p. 354, passim.

49. W. Robertson Smith, *Kinship and Marriage in Early Arabia* (London, 1903), p. 293.

50. Westermarck, op. cit., 1:407–8.

51. Clavigero, *History of Mexico* (1807), 1:360.

52. Leshkoff, op. cit., pp. 455–56.

53. Soloviev, op. cit., 2:876–77.

54. Curschmann, op. cit.; Tsitovich, op. cit.

55. Digby, op. cit., 1:195, 349.

dren." [56] Numerous killings of children occurred in Russia during the famine of our time. In Samara, in the museum, "are collections of pictures of children suffocated by the hands of demented mothers." [57]

Aside from outright murders, hunger even more frequently causes indirect killing of children by abandoning or selling them, on one hand, or by causing wounds, suffering, and deprivations, all of which indicate weakening and suppression of parental reflexes. "Adzhigarta dying from starvation was ready to sell his son in order to buy food" (Laws of Manu).[58] In Nicaragua, in extreme cases, a father could sell his children for food.[59] During the hunger of the eighties in China, women and children were sold for minimum amounts of food, and, for the sake of a few grains of rice, fights and murders were committed.[60] During the Middle Ages dire need very often caused parents to sell their children.[61] During the famine of 1032 in Byzantium, inhabitants sold their children.[62]

The murders of fellow men and co-workers which were caused by hunger, and which otherwise would not have taken place, serve as further demonstration of weakening by hunger of reflexes of group self-preservation. Not only acts of murder, robbery, theft, maltreatment, and crimes against fellow citizens occur during periods of starvation, but the conduct of people sometimes becomes bestial, particularly among children. Brutal people are ready to see anyone as the cause of their hunger, and to seek salvation by all possible means. Hence, the beating and killing of shopkeepers appear first during a famine. Thereafter follow a series of tragic ways of sacrificing intimates in order to keep from dying from hunger, further demonstrating the fact of the weakening by starvation of reflexes of group self-preservation.

56. Ibid., 1:13–14, 149–59.

57. *Peterburgskaya Pravda*, no. 215, 1921; *Krasnaya Gazeta*, November 11, 1921; Kudelli writes in *Derevenskaya Pravda*, no. 162, 1921: "In the Tatar Republic many are killing their children because there is no other way out." Later, in 1922, the phenomenon occurred *very* often and was reported almost daily in newspapers.

58. Issaev, op. cit., p. 6.

59. Westermarck, op. cit., 1:607.

60. A work by Nemilov is cited.

61. G. Roscher, *Traité d'économie politique rurale* (Paris, 1888), p. 60.

62. Scabalanovich, *Byzantine State and Church* (1884), p. 250 (in Russian).

Human sacrifices often represent means of bringing devastating starvation to an end. Similar actions took place among ancient Greeks and Phoenicians, and in Sweden, where King Domaldi was sacrificed. This happened also during the seven-year famine in China which occurred during the invasion of Tang and in lower Bengal in 1865–66 where children were sacrificed to Shiva; similar cases were known to exist in Peru at the beginning of unfavorable weather, and in Great Benin during torrential rains which threatened the crops.[63] The same has occurred in Russia. In the province of Orell in 1840, in the belief that a candle made from human fat would prevent hunger, some peasants killed Kozhien.[64]

The weakening of social reflexes by starvation is even more pronounced among children and simple people. The following facts, selected from many in the history of our famines, serve as illustrations. In one village in the province of Orell during the famine of 1840 when almost all of the adult population were away begging for food, two little girls age thirteen were left at home. The girls were given a few crusts of bread and a bundle of twigs to heat the house a little. The girls spent several days hungry and very cold, and then one of them brought in a sheep belonging to someone else. As they started to kill the sheep, the son of its owner arrived and threatened to tell his father, whereupon one of the girls invited the boy into the house and killed him. Then in the same stove they began to cook the meat and at the same time burn the body of the boy they had killed. But there was not enough fuel, and the murder was discovered.[65]

During the present famine similar facts are recorded. Through the kindness of P. G. Belsky, I received on July 25, 1918, a brief, No. 1143 (2104), of the Commission on Minors Accused of Dangerous Actions. The accused were N. G. Yakovlev (age eleven) and A. G. Yakovleva (age eight). They had killed their twin brothers (age one year, eight months). They were starving. Their mother was working in the hospital as a dishwasher, and their father was dead. One of their mother's friends had said that if it were not for the younger brothers, Nicholai and Anna would have had better food. As

63. Westermarck, op. cit., 1:442–44.

64. N. S. Leskov in *Udol, Complete Works* (Marx Publisher), 33:39–44 (in Russian).

65. Ibid., pp. 39–52.

a result their weak inhibitions were overcome, and the children were killed.

Violation of allegiance to one's group as a result of hunger.— Similar states of depression are manifest in hundreds of other milder events. Cases of this are turncoating, or the violation of allegiance to one's group and going to the other side because of hunger; the mass shift of soldiers from the "white" army to the "red" and vice versa; engaging in espionage for payments in bread and money; entering into the service of Ch-Ka and other "ration-giving organizations"; denouncing friends and entering, for the "ration's sake," punitive expeditions to kill one's fellow villagers and associates; the behavior of some "specialists," which obviously is against their own convictions and perilous to their country just for the sake of a ration of food; taking away children's share of the food; all sorts of strikebreaking among the workers for the sake of half a pound of bread, or a ruble; and thousands of other similar facts. In all of those cases, starvation has depressed and weakened the conscious reflexes of group self-preservation, and has forced a person, directly or indirectly, to cause harm to his own state, class, family, corporation, party, etc. All this is further evidence that in a series of cases, hunger is the determinant that depresses the reflexes of group self-preservation which are in conflict with it. The same is seen in even more acute form in the behavior of children. During recent years in Russia's asylums, and also in families, a pathological greediness toward food was often observed in children. They became affectionate, emotional, irritable during the distribution of the rations just for the sake of a warm place near the stove. They took food away from each other, they searched the cupboards in the dormitories, they stole food from storage rooms, and the personnel took away the allotments of the weaker children. The older children lied, deceived, i.e., they performed a whole series of acts indicative of the breakdown of the social and legal reflexes.[66]

Similar and even more bestial acts are found in abundance. The same occurs not only in respect to human beings, but in connection with favored animals. Read, for example, the accounts of travels in polar regions by Piri, Nansen, Mikkelsen, and Mulius. When experiencing dire hunger and there was nothing else to eat, they killed

66. Aronovich, "On Starvation and Defectiveness in Children," *Viaticka Medical Journal*, Department of Public Health, vol. 2, pt. 2, pp. 3–4.

and ate their favorite animals, which normally they would not have done.

From the evidence given, we may conclude that the above thesis is proven. We consider next the reverse results of this contest between hunger and the reflexes of self-preservation and of their causes.

Depression and Weakening by Starvation of the Sex Determinant and of Sexual Reflexes

The sex determinant is one of the major determinants of human behavior. By means of certain stimuli, it causes a series of diverse experiences, beginning with "falling in love," looking for dates, rendezvous with the object of "love," and ending with the experience of sexual passion (libido sexuali), acts of coition. The acts caused by this determinant may be very diversified. They may force the one in love to seek the affections of and woo the beloved, to engage in a tournament, to kill from jealousy, to engage in crimes, and to perform noble deeds. They also make the lascivious person enter a house of prostitution, or may force the unfortunate lover to commit suicide. In other words, sex reflexes, pure and mixed, simple and complex, occupy a considerable proportion of the general budgets of human acts, similar to the food taxis acts.

The mechanism of stimulation of the pure sex impulse, as a subjective experience, and of the pure sex reflexes occurs apparently as a result of stimulation of the "sex nervous center" (analogous to the food center). Like the latter, it is stimulated (1) through the blood by the sex hormones, which are secreted by the sex glands (the blood, rich with the hormones, stimulates positively the nerve center as it surrounds it); (2) by means of reflexes, through the peripheral parts of the nerve center: unconditioned reflex, e.g., by a slight mechanical irritation of the sex organs, and conditioned reflex, perceived by means of sense organs (such as enticing pictures, photographs, observing the naked body, the objects of the toilet of the other sex, reading tempting novels, listening to exciting conversation, songs, emotional music, or smelling the perfume of the beloved person, all of which are received by the sense organs).[67]

67. Works by Nemilov and Landois-Rosemann are cited; Sechenov, *The Physiology of the Organs of Senses* (1867), pp. 5 ff. (in Russian).

Thus, a whole series of the most diverse objects and occurrences may serve as unconditioned or conditioned stimuli of the unconditioned or conditioned sex reflexes—simple and complex, pure and mixed. The adult organism is almost always under the influence of such stimuli and, were it not for various inhibiting stimuli, which offset the stimulation of the sex center, and, concomitantly, the sex reflexes, the organism would be constantly stimulated.[68]

The sex determinant and the sex reflexes which are caused by it frequently are antagonistic to the determinant and reflexes of hunger. The two are incompatible in time. Hunger forces the organism to perform certain acts, and the sex impulse impels it to do the opposite. Conflict and struggle between the determinants ensue, and in the end one of them must be inhibited. Observations and experiments show that hunger often is the victor in these duels. Its victory is manifest by the following. (1) The sexual reflexes are not performed, which would not have been the case in the absence of hunger. (2) Some sexual acts are performed mechanically without the sexual impulse "for the sake of daily bread," i.e., they become a form of food taxis acts, which again would not have happened were it not for the direct or indirect influence of hunger. (3) Under the direct or the indirect influence of hunger, the sex reflex becomes perverted and assumes an unnatural form, a perversion that would not have taken place had it not been for hunger.

The problem is not limited to these conditions because, through them, hunger influences the consequences of sexual life and thereby affects the curve of fertility and births, and the viability of the progeny conceived and born during the period when the parents are starving. Such are the phenomena of depression of the sex determinant by hunger.

There are two ways in which hunger may produce these effects: by "frontal attack," directly inhibiting sexual appetite and sexual reflexes, and by a "slow siege," or the slow deterioration of the organism exhibited in changes in the secretorial action of the sex glands, changes in the blood, and a gradual weakening of sexual appetite and

68. Freud's theory, which posits that a multitude of sexual reflexes exist in the human being, almost from the moment of birth, can hardly be considered valid, because it requires an enlargement of the concept of the sexualism (autoerotism and narcissism) to include the child, and by doing so, the sexual concept is lost.

the physiological processes of sex. Some confirmation of the expressed postulates are as follows.

The possibility of conflict between food taxis acts and sexual reflexes is indicated, first of all, by the fact that the systems of the sex organs and of the organs of nutrition are quite different and that they compete with one another. The performances of the sexual reflexes tend to change the whole organism into a sexual apparatus, to concentrate, so to say, all its energy on the organs and acts of reproduction. The goal of satisfying hunger is to change the whole organism into an apparatus of nutrition, and to direct its energy and function exclusively to this task. Each of these determinants tends to change the organism similarly to changing a "check payable to the bearer" to one payable to a specific person. L. J. Petrajitsky [69] remarks correctly that sexual stimulation (stimulation of the sex nerve center) directs the supplies of blood, and generally the life energy, in a direction opposite to the one stimulated by hunger. Organs which are quite "unfamiliar" with activities connected with hunger acquire the role of special organs of mobile stimulation, and become the locale of extensive inflow of blood. Contrarily, the salivary glands, which are extremely important in the field of nutrition, become unimportant, particularly during strong sexual stimulation (which is manifest in drying of the throat and lips, and hoarseness resulting from the abnormally dry condition of the vocal cords).

Thus, within the organism competition arises between the two contenders, and this results in a struggle between the two whereby one of them must be inhibited or excluded. Subjectively, this incompatibility is expressed in the inability of the organism to experience simultaneously strong impulses of both hunger and sex.

General observation and self-observation show that hunger frequently overcomes the opponent. From the moment of the occurrence of the intense symptoms of hunger (i.e., the stimulation of the nutrient center), the sex stimuli are inhibited. The customary stimuli of the sex appetite begin to have less and less effect. "The tempting desires" fade away or disappear. Hunger inhibits sex experiences and reflexes by a "frontal attack." When absolute, or strong deficiency, starvation lasts longer, its repressive actions become even stronger; in these cases sex impulses and reflexes are inhibited even more and may be

69. L. J. Petrajitsky, *Introduction to the Theory of Law and Morality*, pp. 241–42 (in Russian).

eliminated. Actually the process is not this simple, because the curve of variations in intensity of sexual impulse follows a more complex course. At the beginning of starvation it rises sharply, and thereafter follows a highly irregular course.

Such are the conclusions of Rudolsky from his experiments with rabbits, which did not show a lowering of their sex appetite during a first period of starvation. On this basis Pashutin [70] is inclined to admit an increase of the sex reflexes during starvation, at least in males. As additional evidence he cites increased sex appetite among tubercular patients. However, we cannot agree with this opinion because: (1) from the description of the experiments by Rudolsky (cited by Pashutin), it is obvious that there is neither an increase nor a decrease of sex reflexes; (2) during further starvation he noted a complete loss of sexual ability; (3) the experiments of Ugryumov (also cited by Pashutin) mention that during intense starvation the males were not capable of fertilization or even of coitus and were indifferent to females. After they had lost 20 per cent in weight, the males were ineffective as sires.[71]

From this we conclude that increase of sexual appetite is possible only during the first and easy stages of starvation when the animal under laboratory conditions is not required to seek food, and is not afraid of death from starvation.

In general as deficiency of food increases and duration of starvation lengthens, the curve of intensity of sexual impulse falls until it reaches zero. Some confirmations of this are as follows.

1. The mechanism through which the sexual nerve center is stimulated explains this statement. The nerve centers are stimulated by hormones which are secreted by the sex glands; these, in turn, receive energy from the blood, which it obtains from food. When food is not received by the organism the blood changes, and it ceases to deliver energy to the sexual organs, which, in turn, stop producing hormones. It is true that during the early stages of starvation the sexual gland may borrow energy from other tissues of the organism, as is exemplified by the Rhineland salmon. This source is limited and sooner or later it is exhausted and the fading away of sexual reflexes takes place. The stimulation of the nerve center by hunger apparently

70. Pashutin, op. cit., pp. 55–56.
71. Ibid., p. 1604.

Pitirim's brother Prokopiy.

Pitirim's aunt Arissya Rimskikh.

Pitirim in 1917.

Elena in 1917.

With Elena's family in Tambov.

Embankment of the Neva River.

The Fortress of St. Peter and St. Paul.

During the white nights of springtime.

The University of Leningrad.

Its famous corridor.

Autographed work by Ivan Pavlov.

Camping near Monarch Pass, Colorado.

Sociological picnic in Minnesota.

ПИТИРИМ СОРОКИН

ГОЛОД КАК ФАКТОР

ВЛИЯНИЕ ГОЛОДА НА ПОВЕДЕНИЕ
ЛЮДЕЙ, СОЦИАЛЬНУЮ ОРГАНИЗА-
ЦИЮ И ОБЩЕСТВЕННУЮ ЖИЗНЬ

ПЕТРОГРАД
„КОЛОС"
1922

Original title page of this work.

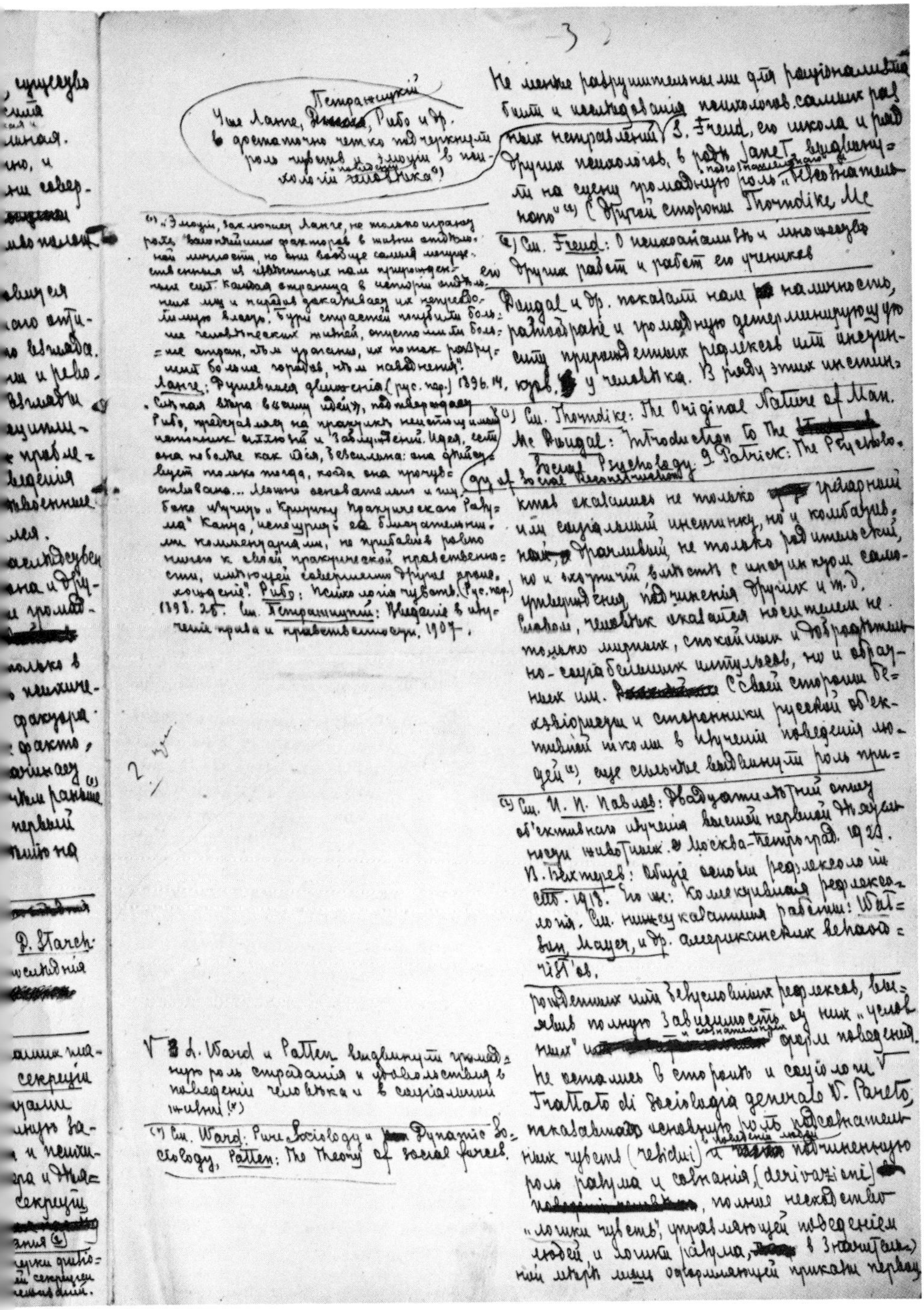

A handwritten manuscript by Pitirim, 1923.

Lecturing at Harvard University.

Vacationing on Lake Memphremagog, Canada.

Our sons Peter and Sergei.

Pitirim at work.

The family assembled.

inhibits reflex stimulation of the sexual center; impoverished blood is a very poor stimulator. Inevitably, diminishing of sexual reflexes, and even increased difficulty of coitus, follow.

2. A series of other experiments and investigations on the conditions of the sexual organs during starvation also confirm the proposition. Poyarkov's experiments with two dogs show that after three months of starvation one dog lost fifteen pounds and the other eleven pounds in weight. The amount of semen secured by masturbation was equal to two drops after the dogs had been starved, compared with ten drops before. Post-experimental feeding restored the normal quantity of semen from the same dogs. Through starvation the number of sperm decreased from 1.5 billion to a few hundreds of thousands, and the sperm after starvation were less viable, less developed, and more defective. On this basis the author suggests the possibility of castration of dogs through starvation.[72]

Similar results were obtained by Morgulis who experimented with *Tiemyctulus viridescens* in which the ovaries and eggs were reduced in size by starvation.[73] In the experiments by Stoppenbrink with *Planaria* and *Dendrocoelum*, "the processes of degeneration of the sex organs, up to their complete disappearance, was observed during starvation."[74] After twenty-six days of starvation the spermatogenesis disappeared completely in a dog.[75] Similar results were obtained with pigeons by Grandis. Degeneration of sex organs, cessation of the spermatogenesis, etc., indicate the destructive influence of starvation on sexual reflexes. These experimental data can easily be applied to human beings.

3. A number of everyday occurrences indicate similar influences of quantity and quality of food on human beings. Long ago it was observed that a meat diet stimulates sexual appetite more than a vegetable diet, and that alcohol stimulates sex impulses. In Italy even a

72. I. Poyarkov, "L'influence du jeûne sur le travail des glandes sexuelles du chien," *Comptes Rendus Société Biologique* 74 (1913):141–43.

73. S. Morgulis, "Studies on inanition and its bearing upon the problem of growth," *Archiv fur Entwicklungsmechanik der Organismen*, vol. 32 and vol. 34, p. 179.

74. Stoppenbrink, "Der Einflus der Ernährung, etc.," *Zeitschrift. Wiss. Zool.* 79:543.

75. Loisel, "Influence du jeûne sur la spermatogénèse," *Comptes Rendus Société Biologique* 53:836.

special dish of shrimp is used as an aphrodisiac. The richness of food in such components, on one hand, or its lack of them, on the other, influences the increase or decrease of sexual reflexes accordingly.

4. There were similar clinical observations on behavior of people during the famine of 1918–19 in Russia. Thus, V. Shervinsky records: "it is necessary to indicate here certain deviations from normal behavior in the field of sex caused by prolonged starvation. The men have a decreased sexual appetite, which is oftentimes considerable; the women frequently develop amenorrhea during two or three months." All this is connected with the changes in activity of the glands of inner secretion. The disappearance of menses results from the depressed activity of the ovaries, and the decrease of libidinis occurs because of the decreased function of the seminal gland.[76]

On the other hand, it has been established that sexual maturity (first menses) occurs earliest among the best nourished individuals of a given race. In Russia, beginning in September 1917, the number of cases of amenorrhea increased and it reached 2.5 per cent by the first of September 1918. (In 1915 it was only 0.4 per cent.) But the increase continued until it reached 6 per cent in September 1919. The main reason for this increase was starvation accompanied by heavy physical labor.[77]

5. Certain social practices which had been used for a long time, and are still in vogue now, indicate that human beings long have understood that hunger depresses the sexual reflexes. I understand here, first of all, the practice of ascetics to combat sexual sin. A maxim often adopted as expressing guiding principles said: "Fatigue your flesh by fasting and prayer" and "abstain from meat, wine, and everything which causes the sex relationship"; this has been known from the time of Pythagoras. "The first Christians recommended the abstention from wine and meat, partly for the sake of confession, but particularly as inhibiting the stimuli which lead to bodily sin." [78]

According to Cassianus, first place in the list of seven mortal sins

76. V. Shervinsky, "Contemporary nutrition," p. 194 (in Russian). Nilsson, who studied amenorrhea during the war in Stockholm, indicates that the increased number of cases corresponded to the changes in the character of nutrition.

77. Okinchits, "The influence of the war and revolution on the sexual sphere of women," *Vrachebnaya Gazeta*, no. 1, 1922.

78. Pareto, *Trattato di sociologia generale* (Rome, 1916), 1:696–97; see also pp. 595–624, 693–753.

is occupied by gluttony and the second by bodily sin. Seraphic teachings say that these phenomena form a causal chain, in which an excess of gluttony induces bodily sin. "The fornication occurs as a result of the excess of food. The stomach which is filled with all kind of food causes lust . . . relates Cassianus. . . . The fast is the means to avoid it. Fast conquers the passions. Fast saves from bodily sin and impurities." [79] The same practice was recommended by Augustine, Tertullian, and other Church fathers.[80] Fasting was also recommended by a number of ancient non-Christian peoples and ascetics. "Fasting was recommended on various occasions." "One occasion was the desire to prevent a bodily sin and pollution." "Fasting is the beginning of cleanness." [81]

Such practices are not accidental and not senseless, as is well known. They are exercised even now. They represent additional evidence of the existence of a relationship between hunger and sexual desires.

6. During the years 1919–20, questionnaires answered by a number of people, as well as their personal observations, all indicate the weakening of sexual appetite and sex reflexes during a prolonged period of deficiency starvation. This is also reflected in literature.[82]

7. The opposite conditions point out a similar relationship between hunger and sexual desire. Namely, among the primitive Koroborri, a massive orgy begins after a plentiful feast. The natives accompany every feasting by debauchery and irregular sexual relationships. Excited by dancing, they indulge to excess in massive sexuality every time that a successful hunt, a victory over a neighboring tribe, etc., provides them food in abundance.[83]

Many literary classics indicate that similar actions have taken

79. J. O. Hannay, *The Spirit and Origin of Christian Monasticism* (London, 1903), pp. 136–41.

80. See St. Augustine, *Enarratio in psalmum XLII. 8. Migne, Patrologiae cursus* (Parisiis, 1845–49), 36:482; Tertullian, *De. Jejuniis De ressurrectione carnis, 8. Opera omnia, Migne, Patrol. cursus, 1844,* 2:806. See Manzoni, *Osservazioni sulla morale cattolica, 1887* (Florence), p. 175.

81. Westermarck, op. cit., 2:292–95. See ibid., chapters on Restrictions in Diet, Ascetism, and Celibacy.

82. "At the present I have absolutely no desire," says the hero of Hamsun's *Hunger*, refusing the invitation of a street walker to go with her. "The girls became like men to me: because my misfortune dried me up."

83. Kharuzin, *Etnografia: Family and Clan*, p. 55 (in Russian).

place throughout history. For example, in *A Thousand and One Nights*, *The Iliad*, *The Odyssey*, and *The Mahabharata*, various myths and fairy tales often depict the heroes as first satisfying their hunger, and only after that going to bed with their spouses or beloveds. Modern literature also provides numerous examples. In Russian villages the most intensive moments of sexual life occur during festivities in celebration of the Day of the Patron Saint of the church, when during the feast which follows enormous amounts of food and alcohol are consumed.

These facts have long been observed by many, particularly by the physiologists. Sexual passion reaches its maximum and induces sexual acts during times of greatest satiety, i.e., the correlation between the intake and the expenditure of energy is most favorable.[84] Leuckart concluded from this that animals come into heat and mate during spring and summer—the time most favorable for procuring food. This statement, however, needs some modification, as was shown by Westermarck.[85] The mating seasons of animals vary from species to species and domestic animals are capable of going into heat and mating during the whole year because of the regularity and improvement of nutrition. However, the most urgent sexual attraction—the time of the highest heat intensity—occurs in spring and fall (March–June, September–November).[86]

In both agricultural and industrial countries contemporary human beings mate at all seasons of the year because there are no physiological handicaps, and the means of obtaining food for themselves and their progeny depend not upon seasons but upon many other factors. However, this fact does not contradict the hypothesis, stated and verified by Westermarck, that: (1) "The time of mating of our remote human and half-human ancestors, similar to that of the animals, was restricted by definite seasons." (It is more correct to say that their mating more frequently occurred during certain seasons. Other than this, it is hardly valid to speak about "limitation" of human mating

84. See Leuckart's article in Wagner, *Handwörterbuch der Physiologie*, 4:862.

85. E. Westermarck, *Geschichte der menschlichen Ehe* (Berlin, 1902), pp. 19–32.

86. Gageman, *Physiology of Domestic Animals* (St. Petersburg, 1908), pp. 232–33 (in Russian).

by seasons.) (2) We may still observe the survival of this among primitive people, those who live in the "bosom of nature," and who have had little contact with civilization.[87] Indeed, such periods may be recognized among certain natives. Oldfield states that "Like the animals the primitive people have definite mating seasons." Such periods were observed and reported for the Watshandies, Tasmanians, a number of mountain Indian tribes, Santals, Pundschas, Kotars, Hottentots, ancient Romans, New Caledonians, and Australian Negritos.[88]

Documents prove the existence of such events in the histories of contemporary European peoples. Ancient holidays, such as Yarilin's Day, Ivana Kupala, or Kolyady in Russia, and similar festivities in Germany, England, Estonia, and other countries, were times of sexual excesses.[89] Periods of intensive mating of primitive people most generally coincide with seasons of the blossoming of nature and the greatest security in obtaining food. In addition, before the beginning of such festivities, natives usually accumulate a plentiful supply of food. Mass mating occurs after great quantities of food and drink have been consumed and after dances and religious ceremonies, and these happenings are not accidental.

"About the middle of the spring, when the *Jamswurzel* is in the fullest strength, when the animals have their offsprings in abundance, when there are many eggs and other foods, then the Watshandi begin to perform their great semi-religious festival of Saa-Cho which precedes the obligation to reproduce the clan." [90] The festivities of reproduction among the Tasmanians occur about the same time.[91]

87. Westermarck, *Geschichte*, pp. 21–22; Oldfield, "On the Aborigines of Australia," *Transactions of the Ethnological Society of London*, n.s., 3 (1865):230.

88. Kharuzin, op. cit., p. 50, passim; Westermarck, *Geschichte*, p. 23, passim; Spencer and Gillen, *The Northern Tribes of Central Australia*, pp. 20 ff. In Russia, as seen from the documents of the thirteenth and fourteenth centuries, such periods also occurred in June on the Day of St. John the Baptist (Ivana Kupala) and Christmas Eve. (Quotations from old documentaries follow. They are in old Slavic language which I have not translated. E.S.)

89. Mannhardt, *Wald und Feldkultur* (Berlin, 1875), vol. 1, chap. 5.

90. Oldfield, op. cit., p. 230.

91. James Bonwick, *Daily Life and Origin of the Tasmanians* (London, 1870), p. 198.

Among the Hus—Indians of the mountain tribes—such a festival occurs in January when their barns are full of grain, and the people, as
they themselves say, are "full of deviltry." [92] Among Australian tribes,
studied by Spencer and Gillen, such saturnalia, called koroborri,
again coincide with the blossoming of nature, following the rains,
when plants grow vigorously and animal food is plentiful.[93] Thus,
among a number of primitive peoples, periods of intensive mass mat-
ings coincide with periods of the year in which food is most abundant.

Among contemporary peoples such regularity does not exist, of
course, because their nutrition is more or less equal throughout the
year. But even here certain facts and coincidences point to the dependence of the sexual appetite upon a full stomach. Some statistical data
indicate that the moments of overabundant nutrition induce an increase of sexual appetite, and that fasting tends to decrease it. This is
confirmed by the statistics of marriages and births which I shall present later. Only limited materials are given here.

The relationship is indicated, in the first place, by the extent of
participation in sexual crimes on the part of rich and poor classes,
respectively. "Regardless of the fact that for the lewdness of the rich
a number of quite secret disreputable places are prepared, in which
coarse, unnatural, criminal fornication may take place, nonetheless,
criminal statistics depict the filth of the sexual life of the well-to-do
classes. In Germany sexual crimes are at the top of the list among
officials and persons of liberal professions, while among laborers and
daily workers they rank seventh." [94] The same is also shown by statistics of legitimate and illegitimate conceptions, calculated by time
and number of births. These may depend upon many factors, but one
of them, according to Oettingen, is that "The price of edible produce
has its significance." In European countries, statistics show the highest number of conceptions come in December (holidays when people
eat abundantly) and also in April–May (Easter holidays). In March
there is definite scarcity of conceptions (due to fasting). Thus, May
and December are most fruitful months for conceptions. In Christian
countries they are also the months of overindulgence in food. In

92. Westermarck, *Geschichte*, p. 23.
93. Spencer and Gillen, op. cit. See their description of the koroborri,
marriage ceremonies, and other customs.
94. Gernet, *Crime and the Fight against It* (Publisher Mir), p. 392 (in
Russian).

March the number of conceptions falls to a minimum, although the climatic conditions remain favorable.[95]

8. Other studies of correlation between the variation in marriages and births and fluctuations in nutrition indicate somewhat similar results. After the facts indicated are taken into consideration, we may consider the thesis of depression of sexual reflexes by hunger to be proved.[96]

The next category of factors showing the influence of hunger on sexual reflexes concerns women, i.e., *the facts of performing sexual reflexes purely "mechanically," without inner impulse or appetite.* In such cases, sexual reflexes become one of the forms of the food taxis acts, or the means of procuring food, i.e., they are subordinated to the determinant of hunger, and are conquered by it. If it were not for hunger, many of these acts would not take place.

Hunger forces their performance similarly to the way in which the mixed complex food taxis act compels a person to write an article, give a lecture, cut wood, cultivate kitchen gardens, or enter service in order to gain daily bread. "One must eat," and in return for a ration or a pound of bread, the women, often disgustedly, sell themselves, enter brothels, become "sovkomshi," etc. Such sale of self by women and girls has been observed during almost all major famines.[97]

Other examples may be cited. Leshkoff in his recollections of the famine of 1840 in the province of Orell in Russia says: To men who were buying cats for fur (koshkodraly) women and girls were selling

---

95. Oettingen, op. cit., pp. 303, 307; Emile P. Levasseur, *La Population française* (Paris, 1891), 2:21–22.

96. Certain facts may appear to contradict the thesis expressed here. One of these is the occurrence of sexual lasciviousness among the city and even the village population of the USSR during recent years. Another is the fact that fertility of rich classes is lower than that of poor. As far as lasciviousness is concerned, it was principally manifest in the part of the population who did not starve (the commissars, the sailors, the speculators, and the highly remunerated specialists [spetz], etc.). As far as women are concerned, the increased sexual activity usually meant prostitution for the sake of "a piece of bread," a "ration," or some other food necessities. The lessening of inhibiting reflexes of religion, law, morality, public opinion, family honor, and everything considered as "social prejudice" played a considerable role in disguising the process.

97. Even the ancient codes of law mention prostitution as a result of starvation and call it blameless in some cases. See, e.g., *The Laws of Hammurabi*, and the *Laws of Manu*. Cf. Curschmann, op. cit., p. 213.

"their maiden's beauty," i.e., their hair and very often their honor, the price of which fell so low that the girls were offering themselves in "addition to the cat." More energetic women used to go to the well at night to catch merchants and other people and there in the darkness of the night repeated the famous event of by-gone days at the well of Laban. And all this was done just to keep from "dropping dead from hunger." [98]

Similar things happened during the famines of 1906, 1918, 1919, and 1920 among the populations of afflicted towns and villages. A whole class of women appeared, the so-called "sovkomshi," and "sovbary" who openly lived with their providers—the commissars. Finally, study of causes which induce development of prostitution testify to the same. Parent-Duchatelet studied 5,183 prostitutes.[99] Out of this number, 1,441 were registered as prostitutes because of poverty and need, 1,225 were orphans who took the fatal decision when in a state of complete destitution, 37 for the purpose of feeding their parents, 24 in order to provide means of subsistence to younger relatives, 23 to feed and educate their own children, and 1,425 were abandoned by their lovers and had been deprived of everything. Other authors confirm these conclusions.[100]

Under similar conditions, similar causes produce similar results. When famine is very severe, inhibiting factors are weak and buyers of women's flesh are always present. For the sake of a piece of bread women have become prostitutes in the past; they do so in the present, and they shall do so in the future.

Finally, the important role of starvation in affecting sexual reflexes is sometimes manifest in an indirect way. The change, modification, and deformation of many sexual reflexes may occur under the influence of limitation in nutrition for the individual himself and for his relatives. By this I mean such phenomena as a conscious postponement or refusal of marriage or of sexual relationship, unnatural satisfaction of the sexual appetite in order to avoid pregnancy, and other forms of abnormal sexual acts, which are not so much forms of sexual promiscuity as they are of conscious or unconscious neo-

98. Leshkoff, op. cit., pp. 52–55.

99. Parent-Duchatelet, *De la prostitution dans la ville de Paris* (1857), 1:10, 2:78.

100. Elistratov, *The Fight against Prostitution* (1910) (in Russian).

Malthusianism which is caused by insecurity and by the abundance of mouths to be fed.

From the above we can deduce that the absolute and prolonged deficiency-relative starvation, *ceteris paribus* depressing sexual reflexes, must also lower the level of fertility of the starving population, and that deficiency starvation of parents during periods of conception and pregnancy weakens the viability of progeny.

The Depression by Hunger of Reflexes of "Freedom" of Behavior

Ivan P. Pavlov has discovered the existence of special reflexes of "freedom." Under this somewhat figurative expression, it is understood that the reflex of an animal is directed toward its liberation from those obstacles which limit its natural movements, or its "freedom." An animal that is tied up, for example, tries to break the ropes or chains. A bird placed in a cage, or a tiger or a sheep confined within a small pen, attempts to get out, particularly at the beginning of confinement. Thus, even though the term "reflex of freedom" is inadequate, the existence of reflexes, denoted by it, is not to be doubted. Their biological significance is obvious. The animals' freedom of motion plays a tremendous role in their interest in preservation of life, and lack of that freedom often threatens danger and death. To prevent the latter a number of reflexes had to be developed philogenetically. From this it follows that the strength and the richness of these reflexes must be different in various groups of animals: the predatory animals (tigers, lions), which lead independent individual lives, must have them in abundance; and the animals that feed, or travel in herds, possess them in lesser degree. Wild animals have them to a greater extent than those that have been domesticated.

Needless to say, such reflexes of "freedom" also exist in human beings. A man who has been bound by ropes obviously tries to liberate himself, and one who is confined in a room attempts to get out. A person who is limited in his actions in one way or other, even including his speech reflexes ("freedom" of speech, press, religion, personality, etc.), endeavors to overcome such obstacles and submits to them only under extreme pressure of powerful determinants. Together with the conditioned reflexes and super-reflexes of "freedom" which are developed on the bases of the unconditioned reflexes, such "reactions of freedom" occupy a considerable place in the total number of reflexes which make up the life and behavior of the human being. Pavlov's experiments with dogs indicate that different dogs show unequal development of reflexes of freedom. Among them are found "specimens with highly developed reflexes of freedom," and others which are "slaves." The situation among people is similar. One individual can't stand restrictions, fights against them irrespective of what they are, is independent, and loves freedom. Another is a slave by nature, submitting easily to restrictions and not fighting against them. He reminds one of Pavlov's dog "Umnitsa" who wagged its tail before anyone, lay on its back, moved its feet, and surrendered entirely to the victor. Similar differences may be observed in groups of people. Consider for example, the Anglo-Saxons with their highly developed reflexes of freedom, compared with a number of Eastern nations (Kalmyk, Kirghiz, etc.), or even our Russian people, who easily submit to every hard-striking stick, and the difference appears quite clear. All this is clearly reflected in the histories of these countries. The part of this that should be relegated to the unconditioned and the part attributed to the conditioned reflexes is not determined here. It suffices to indicate that both heredity and historical conditioning play roles.

These reflexes of "freedom" often conflict with the reflexes of hunger, and frequently are conquered by the latter. Pavlov's experiment with a dog which was endowed with freedom reflexes, and which refused to eat when confined in a certain way, showed that after seven days of starvation the reflex of freedom was broken down, and the dog began to eat even in confinement.[101]

During the training of wild birds and animals, many people have observed, unquestionably, that at first they refuse their food, and only after the lapse of some time do they begin to eat. On a massive scale the same phenomenon may happen to human beings. A hungry person may agree to perform various things for bread, or "upkeep," which he would not do without this determinant. A well-known practice of many criminals, who as a rule have strong "reflexes of freedom," is to surrender voluntarily and go to prison in winter. They sacrifice their freedom for free "room and board" in prison. During our years of deprivation we observed repeatedly suppression

101. Personal communication of I. P. Pavlov to P.S., for which the author expresses gratitude.

of reflexes of freedom in a multitude of individuals (professionals, laborers, peasants, intellectuals, etc.). For the sake of a food ration they gave up their usual forms of behavior and thinking, and accepted the burden of subordination to brutal force. As we shall see, this phenomenon is the base on which well-fed people enslave the hungry during years of famine; it has served and is still serving now as a source of slavery, serfdom, colonialism, and other forms of compulsory dependence of a human being, or of a group, upon another group.[102]

Starvation's Role in Depressing, Weakening, and Eroding the Conditioned Determinants of Behavior, and of the Conditioned Reflexes Called Forth by Them (Religious, Legal, Moral, and Aesthetic Acts and Forms of Social Behavior)

In the preceding sections I have described the depressing influence of hunger on a number of determinants and on corresponding groups of reflexes, the nucleus of which consist of unconditioned reflexes, i.e., such as are received hereditarily and are not acquired by an individual during his lifetime. A number of protective reflexes of self-preservation, as well as those of group self-preservation, are determined by heredity. (These include a mother's "instinctive" acts, some of the sexual reflexes, jerking the hand away from a pricking object or something that burns, etc.) Although this "nucleus" of unconditioned reflexes in man is covered by layers of conditioned reflexes (the stimulation of the sexual reflexes by looking at suggestive pictures, reading "spicy" novels, seeing naked bodies of beautiful people of the opposite sex, etc.), nonetheless, the "nucleus" of unconditioned reflexes lies at the foundation of all these complexes.

In man's behavior there is a multitude of purely conditioned reflexes, those which are not inherited but are acquired by him during life with his fellows. Spencer indicated that a constant preservation of a certain equilibrium and an incessant adaptation of inner conditions to surroundings are absolutely essential for the preservation of the life of an organism. Each of us is in the "sphere of influence" of

102. Comments such as this probably led the Communists to burn this book. E.S.

hundreds and thousands of different stimuli, in which the central place is occupied by other men and women and the products of their activities, as well as those of preceding generations (a complex of conductors, or all material culture including buildings, roads, domestic implements, instruments, arms, books, etc.). From the day of birth to the time of death all these determinants impinge upon us, and require us to make corresponding adaptations. The forms of these responsive reactions are not determined by heredity. For example, heredity does not prescribe that a man must react by nodding his head, or taking off his hat when he meets a friend, that he must cross himself when he hears the sound of church bells, or that a soldier must salute an officer, etc. These kinds of reactions to the stimuli mentioned are acquired by people in the course of their lifetimes, and are not received hereditarily. They may have one form in a given social medium and a quite different one in another. They can be induced in or stripped from an individual. They are like a social costume: it is possible to dress a man in one costume of social-conditioned reflexes, and it is possible to remove them (sometimes with difficulties) and to replace them with other "costumes." The tailor who decides the style of these costumes of conditioned reflexes for all of us is the totality of these conditioned determinants, in whose spheres of influence we happen to be. Among these, first of all, are the people who surround us—living or dead—and the material culture which was created by past and present generations. During his life, everyone establishes definite connections between conditioned stimuli, or complexes of them, and definite ways of reacting to them. This may be accomplished in a dozen different ways, i.e., by "education," by one's "bringing up," "conscious suggestions," "unconscious imitations," punishments or rewards, personal experiences which teach us to know successful and unsuccessful reactions to various stimuli, by applying physical force to other persons, etc. This connection is as follows: during the action of a certain stimulus, or the complex thereof, man reacts in a certain way. For example, when one meets a friend, he takes off his hat; when a soldier sees a general, he salutes; when one is given an order by his father or his superior, he obeys; when a person is standing in a church he causes no disorder, crosses himself, and drops on his knees; when one hears the bell of the telephone he goes to the apparatus, lifts the receiver, and answers the call; and when he goes to a ball he observes the rules of the social etiquette, he dances, etc. In all cases he does all that he would not have done in the sphere of influence of other stimuli. In various cases he uses different words, i.e., he performs different speech reactions.

To dwell on the methods by which such connections are accomplished is superfluous here. It is sufficient to say that a part of the conditioned reflexes are induced on the bases of the unconditioned, a part of them on primary conditioned reflexes (conditioned reflexes of the second order), a part of the latter on reflexes of the third order, etc. The degrees of their complexity and also of their stability may vary; and they can be of various orders, up to the nth.[103]

Obviously every person has such conditional reflexes or patterns of behavior; but various individuals and groups react differently to the same stimulus. For example, the reaction of an aristocratic lady to blowing the nose with the fingers is different from that of a peasant woman; at the sight of a church, an orthodox believer crosses himself, and not so the unbeliever, or the member of another church; the conditioned reflexes of Australian Negritos do not resemble the patterns of behavior of Europeans. The same can be said about different forms of conditioned-social behavior of bourgeois and laborer, of rich and poor, etc.[104]

People's definite convictions about the rules of proper behavior (which may be designated as "legal," "moral," "religious," "aesthetic," "norms," "rules," "good taste," "social conduct," "decency," "rules of honor," etc.), which indicate proper, moral, decent, honest, legal, beautiful, noble, and gentlemanly behavior under certain circumstances, are the subjective component of these objective phenomena.

These convictions vary from person to person and group to group, but in one form or another they exist in everyone. The rules "thou shall not kill," "thou shall not commit adultery," "honor thy father and thy mother," "thou shall not bear false witness," "help your neighbor," "do not lie," "do not blow your nose into the curtains," "give your seat to an old lady," "kill the enemy," "pay your taxes," "pay

103. A. K. Lents, "Methods and region of application of conditioned reflexes in the study of higher nervous (psychical) activity," *Journal of Psychiatry and Neurology* 1 (1922):38–51. Ivanov Smolenskii, "Conditioned Reflexes and Psychiatry," ibid., pp. 80–89. See other works of those of Pavlov's school, and those of American behaviorists.

104. The system of social coordinates, i.e., of the elementary and cumulative groups to which a given individual belongs, are the basic general conditions which determine the character of his conditioned reflexes: P. Sorokin, *The System of Sociology*, vol. 2 (in Russian).

your debts," "obey the authorities," "if insulted demand a duel," "dress for dinner," "do not eat with your knife," "be honest," "beat the bourgeois," "say prayers," "love your country," etc., and hundreds of other norms represent patterns indicating the proper groups of reflexes or the models of behavior under various circumstances.

Objectively, similar convictions and corresponding norms of behavior represent a subjective reflection of the described conditioned patterns of behavior, or reflexes, which are inculcated into man during his lifetime. Once the connection of determinant a (e.g., somebody's belonging) and the complex of reflexes b (acts with respect to the object) is established, then in the presence of a, man responds to it with acts b, or he acts "according to his convictions."

In the absence of obstacles people always react according to their "convictions," i.e., according to the conditioned reflexes or patterns of behavior established during their lifetimes. And they consider such behavior as being "free," "entirely according to their volition," not forced, restricted, or restrained by any "outside foreign forces."

However, the conditioned determinants and their reflexes sometimes are contradictory, and they may offset each other (e.g., the religious reflexes of many Communists offset the anti-religious actions which are called for by their party determinants, and vice versa). They also may be antagonistic to and offset by some of the unconditioned stimulants and their reflexes. It is not surprising, therefore, that the "convictions" of one and the same man are not fully coordinated; they often conflict with one another, and the human being is not always logical.[105]

It also is not surprising that under the pressure of opposing stimuli people often act against their own convictions. For example, under one set of stimuli man proves that a equals b (prohibition against killing, war, and the death penalty; professions of the sanctity of property, the undeniable rights of man, freedom of speech and press, etc.). After some time has elapsed, however, the same man may seek to prove just as strongly that a does not equal b. For example, he may state, "I am against killing, war, or the death penalty in principle, but taking into consideration conditions x, y, and z, I consider that I have a sacred duty to hang the killers, to carry on this patriotic or revolutionary war, to annihilate the enemy, or in the

105. Pareto, *Trattato di sociologia generale*, vols. 1 and 2. Also the chapter "Líazione son logieho."

name of the king (or the general, the bourgeoisie, the proletariat), to shoot and kill the hosts of those who oppose me and whom I consider to be prejudicing all of the rights of freedom, etc." Such behavior is not exceptional. In one form or another, in various degrees, it occurs in almost all people, because all are under the influence of many contradictory determinants.

The determinants of hunger and its reflexes often are found in conflict with a number of conditioned determinants and their reflexes, which, under existing conditions, hinder satisfaction of hunger. Accordingly, the hunger determinants tend to suppress the offsetting behavior, to depress their reflexes, and, thus, to open the way for the food taxis acts. Observation shows that this task often is very successful. We shall cite here some facts taken from different areas of the "conditioned reflexes," and show that hunger suppresses, often in different ways, a number of these reflexes, which are commonly called "religious," "legal," "moral," "esthetic," "professional," "honest," or "decent," when under the prevailing conditions they prevent satisfaction of hunger. Under such circumstances the man resembles a ball which, when pushed by the food taxis acts, severs the hundreds of ropes and ties (the conditioned reflexes) which prevent its motion toward the food magnets, i.e., the satisfaction of his hunger.

Depression by hunger of the "religious" reflexes of behavior.— There are a number of conditioned reflexes, designated as religious acts, which often are antagonistic to the food taxis. Some religions prohibit certain foods in general (totemic animals and plants, prohibition of "unclean food" by a number of religions, etc.), or prohibit eating it during definite periods of time, or by people of a certain class. There is a great variety of such prohibitions. One religion or another has prohibitions against eating reptiles, certain kinds of birds, eggs, milk, swine, oxen, certain plants, etc.[106] These prohibitions are sometimes abolished under the impulse of hunger, when the possibility of satisfying it by eating them presents itself. In this case the corresponding reflexes of abstention from the forbidden foods are depressed and hunger "leads to sin," i.e., it suppresses the religion determinants.

There are numerous examples of this kind. In 1917–21 in Russia, religious fasting was almost entirely abolished. Believers ate

106. Westermarck, *The Origin and Development of Moral Ideas*, vol. 2, chap. 38.

everything available including horse meat, dog flesh, and other "unclean foods." Thus, hunger had depressed the established religious reflexes. Similar behavior had been known much earlier. During famines in the Middle Ages, people were forced to eat "unclean" animals, because, obviously, the clean animals had all been devoured. Then they ate dogs, cats, donkeys, horses, even wolves, frogs, snakes, and, in extreme cases, even carrion.[107] In Russia's ancient chronicles (A.D. 1213) it is recorded that during the great famine in Pskov people ate horse meat, a fact which particularly enraged the chronicler.[108] They ate other people and their cadavers. Numerous facts are mentioned above. Cannibalism was the most disgusting occurrence during the famines of the Middle Ages. It is mentioned in many sources. In some instances it is known that people sold cooked human flesh in the market.[109]

In our recent famine, cannibalism was "an ordinary occurrence." Cannibalism, which occurs during periods of extreme starvation, indicates that hunger depresses not only the religious determinant and its reflexes, but also moral, legal, and aesthetic determinants and even those related to group self-preservation. They testify that here, hunger succeeds in "overthrowing" simultaneously all these determinants, in annihilating their combined forces. They are indeed direct victims of the mighty power of this "unmerciful Tsar."

This victory of hunger over religious, moral, and legal reflexes is demonstrated by the fact that religious norms and their makers are obliged to abandon legally their prohibitions during famines. During one famine, for example, the bishop of Paris permitted the eating of meat on fast days. In the laws of the ancient world, in those of the Middle Ages, and even in our times, a number of non-European nations have a statute of "extreme emergency" in which hunger is always included. Acts performed in a state of hunger (breaking moral and religious rules) are excused and considered as unpunishable and not illegal following the canonical principle "necessity knows no law, it makes laws itself."[110]

107. Curschmann, op. cit., pp. 56–57.
108. Soloviev, *History of Russia*, vol. 1 (in Russian).
109. Curschmann, op. cit., pp. 57–59.
110. Ibid., pp. 6–7; cf. Rosin, *On Dire Necessity* (St. Petersburg, 1899), chap. on Canonical Law (in Russian).

Various religions prohibit burial without corresponding religious rites. During years of famine the breaking of this prohibition is quite common. Bodies found on the streets are collected, and buried without any rites. Under normal conditions such behavior would have been scandalous, forbidden, and sacrilegious.

In this case hunger makes a norm of abnormality and the sacrilege becomes a tolerable and permissible act. Since this "sacrilege" would prevent satisfaction of hunger, starvation mercilessly rips off the "social" garments from man and shows him as a naked animal, on the naked earth. We all know numerous cases of religious degeneration "in the name of mammon and the voice of the stomach." Only the blind fail to see how in our times (in Russia) many believers, in the state of starvation, become communists who forget for the sake of a ration of food their faith and old traditions. "There is no time anymore for all this," because it is necessary to cultivate kitchen gardens, to stand in line for rations, to travel out into the country to procure food, etc.

The observing person can collect a vast store of material of similar nature. In our days Russian society is a free laboratory. Just look, and do not think much!

Depression by hunger of legal, moral, and conventional determinants and their reflexes.—All that has been said about the depression by hunger of antagonistic religious reflexes is applicable, with the corresponding modifications, to legal reflexes when the latter are incompatible with food taxis acts.

The typical example in this respect is the act of violating rights of property under the influence of starvation. The social reflex of property consists of abstaining from taking and using, or dispossessing the owner of, things or objects belonging to someone else.

When there is no other way in which it can be satisfied, hunger seeks to disrupt these "hindering" reflexes, and very often it is quite successful. An accurate picture of a fight between food taxis reflexes and those of private property is represented by Hamsun in *Hunger*. The hero, who normally had very stable reflexes in support of private property, decided under the influence of hunger to sell a blanket which he had borrowed from a friend. After a long struggle and continuous starvation, a number of the reflexes of legal rights were suppressed. Thus, an objective picture of the struggle between determinants of hunger and incompatible reflexes of private property are represented in the form of subjective experiences. Hunger wins.[111]

Mass verification of this phenomenon may be seen in statistics of thefts and other offenses against private property. *Ceteris paribus*, the number of crimes against private property increases as mass starvation becomes more intense. Substantiations are seen in two ways: an established positive correlation between a rise in the price of bread and an increase in crimes against private property, and seasonal variations of the curves of theft and other crimes against private property, which reach their peak during winter, when it is more difficult to procure food, and drop to a minimum during summer and in September.[112]

Likewise, crimes against private property grew to enormous proportions in Russia during our years of famine. People were stealing, deceiving, and robbing almost constantly. The same behavior was also observed among children. In 1918–20 in children's colonies and asylums, crimes by children quadrupled and 70 per cent of them were against private property.

The second verification of hunger's victory over the reflexes favoring private property consists of the fact that sometimes the law is obliged to yield to starvation. Faced with the futility of the struggle against the influence of hunger, the law resorts to a specific solution. By this I mean it establishes the criminal-legal institution of extreme necessity, which is common to almost all nations, and which takes the form either of token penalty for theft in times of famine or the abolition of punishment entirely.

Such thefts have been and remain the most common types of crimes in the legislation of many peoples, such as primitive tribes, the ancient Peruvians, the Tahitians, and the ancient Chinese; the same is true in the laws of ancient Greece and Rome, Mohammedan Laws,[113] canonical law, Carolinian laws, and Russian laws—the Ulozhenie Alexeya Mikhailovicha, Voinskii Articul, and Ukazy. The same is true of law codes of contemporary Western European countries, and even in the corresponding ideologies of jurists, phi-

111. See other illustrations in *The Tramp* by Jack London and *Les Misérables* by Victor Hugo.

112. See figures in Gernet, *Crime and the Fight against It*, pp. 386–90 (in Russian); Zhizhilenko, *Crime and Its Factors* (Petrograd, 1922) (in Russian).

113. See Westermarck, *The Origin and Development of Moral Ideas*, 1:286–88, 2:14–15.

losophers, and moralists. "Theft under the condition of starvation" was everywhere either unpunishable, or carried only a small punishment.[114] The same is applicable to the other crimes against property such as robbery, burglary, and the various misdemeanors and crimes against persons. Because of "hunger," "need," or "dire necessity," the commission of these crimes leads everywhere either to a softening of the penalty, or to the complete annulment of punishment. Therefore, this all means a voluntary retreat of the law when it is confronted by starvation.

These facts are sufficient to show that hunger depresses some of the reflexes connected with the laws of property. The same is applicable to other conflicting reflexes embodied in laws. Under the increased pressure of starvation all the reflexes of law which are antagonistic to the satisfaction of hunger are either decreased gradually, or even are completely eliminated. As a result, the human being performs a number of acts which he would not have done, were he not starved, and vice versa, he does not perform some acts which he would have done had it not been for hunger.

If they are to withstand the attack of hunger, these reflexes must possess a force, which is no weaker than that of hunger, or they must receive an acceleration of force sufficient to counterbalance the increase of hunger. Otherwise, all these reflexes are broken. Later we shall discuss the measurement of the force of these reflexes. Here it is enough to note that hunger may serve as a good reagent for testing the solidity of the legal and other conditioned social reflexes of human beings that are opposed to it. *Ceteris paribus*, those who are unable to resist the attack of hunger exhibit the weakness of their counteracting reflexes, while those who do resist demonstrate the strength of theirs.

When legal reflexes which inhibit the acts of burglary and robbery hinder the satisfaction of hunger, the latter may crush or subdue them. Persons who are not robbers and burglars under normal conditions become such when driven by hunger. The Russian population during the famine of 1918–20 is an illustration of this.

Most people do not kill others when they have enough to eat. Murder is impossible—such is their conviction. During a period of

114. Rosin, op. cit., pp. 61–64; Oetker, "Notwehr und Notstand," 2:328–95; Belogrits-Kotlyarevsky, *On Theft According to the Russian Law* (in Russian); A. Hold von Ferneck, *Die Rechtswidrigkeit*, vol. 2 (1905).

starvation this legal reflex often loses force and sometimes it is incapable of preventing starving people from killing to obtain food. Such cases were discussed in the chapter on the depression of group self-preservation.

The great famines of antiquity and the Middle Ages, those of the sixteenth through the nineteenth centuries, are all noted for such events. Bands of brigands who robbed and killed multiplied rapidly. They robbed and killed not only strangers, but also their own relatives, parents, children, brothers, and sisters. In Russia, at the present time [1918–20] hundreds of bands are stopping trains, robbing everyone they meet, pillaging hamlets, villages, and small towns, etc. The causes of the appearance of such bands are not political—what are politics to the average peasant boy or man? The cause is mostly hunger and the possibility of surviving in a time of famine. This conduct indicates that hunger has overcome a number of moral and legal reflexes in the masses of the population, turning them into moral and legal "nihilists." At the present time in Russia such acts take place before our eyes, and the history of famine is acquiring a huge collection of new facts.

Hunger first conquers the less stable moral and legal reflexes. I mention here a few examples, and the reader himself can supply hundreds and thousands of additional observations.[115]

When the supply of food is adequate, most people do not misbehave. They do not engage in swindling and speculation, or put forward plausible but unscrupulous schemes to defraud others. But when they are starving they are apt to succumb to these sins. The corresponding legal reflexes which prevent the perpetration of such crimes become depressed. Scores of speculators, swindlers, and manipulators, both "legal thieves" and "honest scoundrels," are represented in the examples found daily in our present life in Russia [1918–20].

Many honest women when driven by hunger became· prostitutes, harlots, or "kept women." Thus, in addition to the depression of the sexual reflexes, their moral reflexes also are suppressed by hunger.

Let us consider some other moral-legal reflexes. When they have enough to eat, parents do not sell their children into slavery. Such acts are inhibited by the reflexes of self-preservation, and also by the moral-legal reflexes. When starvation is great such inhibitions

115. The reference is to the Russian reader of that period. E.S.

weaken, as indicated above, and the parents sell or give away their children into slavery, or "for export."

Man possesses a number of complex reflexes, which pertain to himself, and which are called "self-respect," "primogenital rights," "honor," "haughtiness," etc. These terms usually designate a number of definite experiences and certain forms of behavior. When food supply is adequate, many people are "proud," "behave with dignity," "keep their honor," "do not sacrifice their rights of honor and consciousness." Hunger often depresses these reflexes. Under its influence "honor," "consciousness," and "dignity" often disappear, i.e., the acts which correspond to these terms cease to be performed and are substituted for by the opposite actions. As a symbol of such behavior mention may be made of the biblical story of Esau who, under the influence of starvation, sold his birthright for a pottage of lentils, to his sly speculator brother, Jacob, thus abdicating his rights as firstborn. Esau is the prototype of the hundreds of thousands of people who have sold and are still selling verbally for the "pottage of lentils" (such as a loaf of bread, or a half pound of sugar) their birthrights and many other rights. How many people when driven by hunger have lost their dignity, and gone begging for jobs to those whom they despised? How many "specialists," intellectuals, and workers have sold their inalienable rights in a way similar to Esau selling his birthright? (Please, do not take these words as a condemnation. I do not judge or condemn anyone. I just investigate the causal relationships of these phenomena.) Such behavior indicates that the moral-legal reflexes of various kinds did not endure the "test" of starvation and were broken down.

During the famines of ancient times the people sold themselves into slavery. During the Middle Ages hunger forced poor people to enter voluntarily the ranks of slaves.[116] Such behavior is testimony to depression by hunger of a number of moral-legal reflexes and those of "freedom." The same occurred in Russia also, during the famines of 1128 and 1446.[117] During the travels of Moorcrost in the Himalayas in 1812, a simple man asked that he be accepted as a slave for life in order to get his daily food.[118] How do these "effects" of hunger

116. Roscher, op. cit., p. 60; Curschmann, op. cit., p. 55.

117. Ermolov, "Famines in Russia," in *On Famines in Russia and Western Europe* (Kiev, 1892), 1:9, 415 (in Russian).

118. Roscher, op. cit., p. 60.

differ from the contemporary cases of those who sell themselves into
slavery for the sake of a single food ration? Who could ever imagine
that human honor, consciousness, and dignity would cost less than
one pound and a half of very poor bread!

There also are examples of the depression, by hunger, of a number of social reflexes, commonly called proprieties of conduct, etiquette, conventional requirements of good behavior, etc. Only a few
years ago some of our citizens would have considered it shameful or
impossible for them to go to the black market and sell all sorts of
junk. But starvation came and formerly proud people (dignified
ladies, sweet girls, and solid gentlemen) now stand in rows in the
Sennoi or Andreevskii markets and sell old shirts, trousers, coffee
pots, lamps, etc. The corresponding reflexes of etiquette and pro-
priety have disappeared.

Depression by hunger of the aesthetical reflexes.—In the absence
of hunger most people have a sense of the beautiful. Some of them
are aesthetes "to the tips of their fingers." They "just love" beauty,
art, and comfort. Their lives consist mostly of conversation about
beauty, visits to exhibits, theaters, concerts, the purchase of objects of
art, vases, pictures and utensils, the establishment of comfortable
and beautiful homes, and beautifying themselves by manicures and
cosmetics. People spend money for perfume and face powders, spend
hours in arranging their hair, etc. (a whole series of conditioned reflexes). But when faced by starvation these reflexes become incompatible with the food taxis acts. A conflict arises, and the reflexes involved pass away.

The person who previously went ardently to the theater now
ceases to go there at all. There is work that must be done during the
daytime, and afterwards one must stand in the food lines. Then the
meal must be cooked on a slow "burzhuika" (a small sheet iron stove)
and so there is no time for the theater. The exquisite and comfortable
furniture goes in exchange for a few pounds of flour and potatoes; a
beautiful dress goes for a pound of butter; rare art objects go to the
junk dealer; and musical instruments, pictures, vases, utensils, etc.,
all go to the villages in exchange for flour. As for cosmetics, per-
fumes, face powders, and beautiful coiffures, ladies have ceased even
to think about them. Who among us does not know such persons?
How many people are found in Petrograd and Moscow who, when
faced with starvation, did not get rid of most of their valuable possessions in exchange for a little food? These vivid pictures of con-

temporary Russia have their counterparts in the past in the history of Europe. For example, the wealthy inhabitants of Prague, when confronted with hunger, sold all their treasures for food.[119] These facts demonstrate the depression of a number of so-called aesthetical reflexes by hunger.

The changes by hunger of the mimical reflexes.—It is unnecessary to dwell at length on the facts that under the influence of hunger the "expression" of the face and the unconditioned, and particularly the conditioned, mimical reflexes are changed. Who does not know that the expression on a person's face is quite different when he is starving than when he is not? The mimical reflexes of a starving person are different compared with those of the well-fed individual. For example, the reflexes of a smile after a funny event do not occur when a person is starving. In a satiated state the attention of the people is not concentrated on food objects as much as it is when they are starving. It is possible to observe cinematographically the changes in the facial expressions of starving peoples when they are shown food, particularly the ways in which they stretch their lips, and their attempts to produce serious, unconcerned facial expressions. During these years of starvation frequently I have observed such phenomena during scientific meetings, literary gatherings, and just social meetings of the intellectuals.[120]

Depression by hunger of other conflicting reflexes.—Finally, hunger depresses and deforms all the acts of human behavior which hinder its satisfaction. The whole behavior of man changes under its influence, which means that many acts cease to occur which would have taken place before, and, contrariwise, the individual begins to do things which previously he would not have done. The scientist, poet, painter, artist cease to function in their vocations if it does not

119. Curschmann, op. cit., p. 56.
120. Perhaps I should add here some of my personal recollections. One evening in February 1919 a friend came to visit us. He was a brilliant professor of the University of Petrograd, most erudite, and a very interesting conversationalist. We had greatly enjoyed his visits in the past, and usually we spent hours in animated discussions on various topics. This time he was quite thin, emaciated, and his facial expression was a mask devoid of any animation. When I offered him a dish of "pottage of millet" (pshennaya kasha) he ate it with such intense concentration on the food as if nothing in the world existed anymore. Truly, this was an example of complete degradation of a brilliant human personality. E.S.

bring food, and begin to do things which they would not think of doing in the absence of starvation. Now they have to spend hours standing in food lines in order to get a loaf of bread, looking for pieces of wood in order to cook food, running to find the speculators to exchange something for food, etc. Their own work, which they still may love, is now forgotten. Hundreds of scientists, artists, poets, and writers during these years went in the capacity of "specialists" to work for the administration, the defense commissariat, and other governmental propaganda advertisements, etc., disseminating science, lecturers, artists, readers of cinematographic scripts, painters of governmental propaganda advertisements, etc., vulgarizing science, literature, and the arts. The same can be said about other groups of population. During periods of starvation the food taxis acts—pure or mixed—occupy almost the entire budget of time.

Changes of man's speech reflexes under the influence of hunger. —Since hunger suppresses certain acts and induces others, i.e., it modifies radically our reflexes, it is therefore quite logical to expect that our speech reflexes, or the acts of verbal reaction to various phenomena, are also changed. The words which we pronounce, or our speech, represent a special form of reflexes by which we react to certain stimuli. Here it is easy to detect the deforming role of starvation. One and the same stimulus in the form of a certain phenomenon, object, or event often causes us to produce quite different "speech reflexes," depending upon whether or not we are starving.

Not so long ago upon seeing very bad bread, most of us would say, "I do not want it, one cannot eat such awful bread." Now we say, "not so bad." As the Russian proverb says, "It is not bad when the bread is replaced with a substitute, but it is very bad when there is neither bread, nor a substitute for it." We used to say about horse meat, "Oh, what a dreadul thing, I cannot eat it, it nauseates me," "This is sin!" Now, we hear seldom such words, but on the contrary we hear others such as "horse meat, a wonderful food, I enjoy it in the form of a pot roast." The food regime, which was called "half-starvation" or "pauper's fare" in the years of plenty, now is considered "excellent." "Oh, he has a wonderful diet, he receives 40 pounds of bread, 5 pounds of meat, 2 pounds of butter, 1½ pounds of sugar, and 10 pounds of gruel per month." Food which was considered unappetizing in former years under conditions of starvation becomes very tasteful and appetizing. "Hm . . . very tasty," commented Mikkelsen and his companions after eating the bitter liver of a dog.[121] Under normal conditions their reaction would have been quite different.

Such examples of deformation of speech reflexes are well known. However, the problem here is far more complicated. The changes are far deeper and wider and are spread over all the phenomena which are directly or indirectly connected with nutrition. Consider some examples.

From the facts presented, we know that when he is well fed a man may say, "it is sin to eat meat on fast days," while when he is starving the same man will say, "it is not a sin to eat meat during times of starvation." Furthermore, when satiated he will remark, "one should respect the property of other people," and when starving he will say, "go to hell. I am not going to die for the sake of your property." Or the well-fed man might say Ivan Ivanovich is a scoundrel and a villain, while when faced with starvation his conclusions may be, "Ivan Ivanovich is a wonderful man, he succeeded in getting me a job with good food ration." Or, to take a wider view, "The Soviet system is very destructive, we cannot live that way any longer" (one says before obtaining a good job with food rations). After receiving a job with five rations, the same individual proclaims, "Is it not correct that the economy and life are improving? True, it is a very hard experiment, but healthful and inevitable! This is a great creative epoch! A new society is created the like of which the world has never seen." I presume that every careful observer of our times has noticed thousands of similar facts in the behavior of people around him, as well as in his own behavior.

Changes in the sub-vocal reflexes (convictions, "ideologies") of a man under the influence of hunger.—So far we have depicted the external changes in man that are caused by starvation. We have been dealing with objective phenomena which are localized within coordinates of time and space and thus are susceptible to observation. The "speech" reflexes have not been excluded because, as a symbolic complex of sounds, they also have physical existence. Now, let us consider the "soul" of the people and try to determine the perturbations in the sphere of mental experiences which are caused by starvation.

121. Mikkelsen, *Lost in the Arctic*, p. 285.

In the second chapter of this book we indicated a number of deformations in this field which are caused by hunger. However, we discussed only the external changes of form, and not the content of mental experiences (such as changes in feelings, in perceptions, in the content and course of notions and ideas, in memory and attention, in sensations and emotions, and in volition and vital perceptibility).

Now we direct attention to the content itself of the mental representation and ideas, convictions and beliefs, aesthetical and moral evaluations and volition (sub-vocal and inhibited reflexes), and to everything which is called "ideology" or "outlook on life" (the Russian term "mirovozrenie"—E.S.). A question is raised: To what extent do these non-material phenomena depend upon the strictly material, such as a loaf of bread or a pork chop?

From all the evidence presented, and especially from the materials in the paragraph on deformation of "speech reflexes," we may deduce that all of these things follow from starvation. Moreover, a considerable part of the ideology which is related directly or indirectly to hunger often serves as a veil which is waved by the wind of hunger but which conceals this wind. Strictly speaking this dependence is such that, *ceteris paribus*, starvation tends to weaken and destroy, directly or indirectly, and by means of either a tactful or a blunt diplomacy, or without it, all the convictions and beliefs, tastes and obligations which prevent satisfaction of hunger. Conversely, it supports and enforces those which facilitate its satisfaction. In other words, starvation tends to alter our ideology and our outlook on life according to its own ends. It removes or obliterates everything with which it is in conflict, and fosters everything that is favorable to it.

The statement that the human soul is dark and complex and that its fanciful fluctuations and accords are very mysterious is often heard, and it is correct, but not completely true in all cases and under all circumstances. Sometimes the human soul is simple, like a geometric figure, and its processes are clearly understood, much as in the case of the motion of a simple mechanism. One pound more produces one accord, one pound less results in a different one. The symphony is simple and it has been repeated so often since the time of Adam that it has become fairly monotonous, stereotyped, and common; it leaves a bad taste in the mouth.

Let us consider first "convictions," "moral evaluations," and "beliefs" as the subjective experiences of man; and let us depict, somewhat superficially, on the scene of life, the tragic comedy of the "life of a man" which already has been played millions of times. Act one: We have a well-fed man. He is convinced that "it is sinful to eat meat during a period of fasting." He may or may not mention this fact. Act two: We have a man who for the past thirty-six hours has not consumed a single calorie, before whom a well-prepared beefsteak is placed. Then an interesting picture begins to develop on the scene of his "soul." He desires to eat, but it would be "sinful," "his consciousness does not permit it." Quite unseen by us a "devil" appears from somewhere and begins to whisper, "well, is it really sinful?" "The prohibition is only for well-nourished people, not for the hungry." "God does not want us to die." "Even the saints permitted some exceptions." "Christ ate heads of grain on the Sabbath." "Is it not absurd from a logical point of view?"

Hundreds of devils begin to emerge from the depths of the consciousness and intellect, and undermine the conviction. In this manner the process continues until "the monolith of convictions" is broken and the motivation and justification of the action is created: "it is possible to eat meat on fast days, because of such and such circumstances." Everything seems to be in order, hunger is satisfied, and the violation of the norm is justified.

Another example: "The characteristic feature of children of our time [1919–20] is their moral instability, which is manifested in small thefts of food, in taking bits of food away from the weaker children, lying to the adults, etc. They may express verbal morality, show feelings of repentance and regret for their wrong-doings, but because of the weakness of their psychological inhibition, they cannot withstand their lower impulses." [122] Such is the beginning stage and later on similar acts are repeated. The conviction becomes weaker and finally it is annihilated. Sometimes it is even replaced by an exactly opposite conviction.

The picture presented here may have, of course, other concrete forms (depending upon the man), but its essence remains the same: we are performing almost daily a similar tragic comedy called forth by hunger and other essential determinants. "Consciousness" and "reason" here play the roles of lackeys or prostitutes which are in the service of hunger (and other basic determinants) and work accord-

122. Aronovich, op. cit., p. 31.

ing to the demands of the latter. They always are ready to prove and
justify everything, one thing at the moment, and just the opposite
after a few hours have elapsed.

The process described is even simpler when the consciousness is
not a product of the actions due to reflexes. In such cases the consciousness seldom sees the contradiction. When satiated, a man believes it is a sin to eat meat on fast days, and when he is hungry
he believes that it is not sinful. That is all. Here the "convictions"
are just changing without any motives, justifications, etc.

Several variations are possible in each case. In some instances
hunger is powerless to annihilate immediately the incompatible conviction. Man violates the conviction, performs the forbidden act, but
realizes that he "acted wrongly, or against his convictions." However,
as the frequency of such violations increases, his convictions become
weaker and weaker. They begin to be "excluded" from his field of
consciousness, finally fade away, and are even replaced by directly
opposite convictions. It is difficult to steal or to kill a man for the
first or second time; but when one has stolen and killed tenfold,
nothing is left of the convictions "do not steal" or "do not kill." Sometimes they are replaced by the opposite convictions: "private property
is a theft" and "murder is a good thing." Thus, hunger gradually
disrupts the beliefs and convictions which hinder its aims.[123] There
are three typical ways in which hunger weakens and annihilates
convictions contrary to its satisfaction and creates and strengthens
those favorable to it: by means of the diplomatic twisting of the intellect; by a combination of the controversial arguments not induced
by the reflexes; and by weakening the convictions through the rico-
chet influence of the contradictory acts.

By these three means, hunger often changes the intrinsic nature
of our consciousness, our convictions and beliefs, moral evaluations
and aesthetical tastes, our sympathies and antipathies, our ideologies,
and our outlook on life.

The problem here is not limited to such trifles as the norm "it
is sinful to eat meat on a fast day." To hunger, nothing is sacred. It
is blind, and it crushes with an equal force everything large or small,
convictions and norms, when they are opposed to its satisfaction.
When satiated we preach "the sanctity of property," but when starv-

123. See details in P. Sorokin, *System of Sociololgy* (Petrograd, Kolos,
1920), 1:176–93. Cf. William James, *Psychology* (1916), chap. 24.

ing we can steal without the smallest hesitation. When satiated we are convinced of the impossibility that we will kill, rob, rape, deceive, defraud, engage in prostitution, etc. When starving we can perform these acts. We may even think that to "kill a blood-thirsty money bag" is a permissible act.

During the famine of 1918–20 in Russia the so-called intelligentsia sometimes showed examples of such activities. At the beginning of the October revolution it was considered shameful to go to work for the government and to receive "gifts" from its "bloody hands." But when starvation faced them on one side, and there were wonderful rations on the other, the intellectuals, professors, journalists, physicians, writers, artists, poets, lawyers, and engineers "went to Canossa" one by one, cautiously at first, and then openly. "The breaking point" arrived, and the same intellectuals who had deplored working for the communists now began to seek appointments to high positions and to praise highly their honest and sacred work. In other words they started by condemning and finished by singing "Hosannas."

This process showed up still more clearly in the behavior and convictions of specific individuals. Compare their convictions with the source of their food supply. When their well-being came from monarchism and nationalism, they bowed to Kolchak, Denikin, and the Tsar, and they kissed the hands of the princesses and countesses; but when their food supply began to come from the international sources and communism, they then became ardent "internationalists," or "national-internationalists." If the food had come from the Pope of Rome, they would have become papists.

Conclusions and Résumé

1. The fluctuation of the curve of quantity and quality of food, and particularly the degree of starvation, sharply shapes all human behavior.

2. The phenomenon of food taxis and the increase in our budget of the food taxis acts, on the one side, and the conversion of our whole organism into an apparatus dedicated to nutrition, on the other, represent the main character of these deformations.

3. Accordingly, hunger tends to depress all unconditioned and conditioned reflexes which hinder it and are incompatible with the

food taxis. It tends to change the "speech reflexes," "ideologies," and mental experiences of people, to remove everything which is in its way and to create and facilitate the conditions favorable to it.

4. The behavior of the population indicates that hunger frequently achieves such tasks.

Part II

4

THE BASIC EFFECTS OF
MASS STARVATION:
NUTRITION AS A DETERMINANT
AND ITS SOCIAL EFFECTS
AND THEIR FORMS

Because fluctuations in the quantity and quality of food change the behavior of people, they must, therefore, also be reflected in the processes of social life. The many changes in the behavior of people, as a result of these fluctuations, call forth changes in the social processes of a society whose members are starving. The social effects of nutrition as a determinant are extremely numerous and varied.

They can be subdivided, first of all, into two forms: permanent forms, called forth by the normal exchange of materials in any aggregate, and sporadic forms, or those that occur only during exceptionally sharp fluctuation in quantity and quality of food taken in by the organism. Each of these effects is further subdivided into direct, or primary, functions of the determinant (nutrition), which occur directly as its result, and indirect (secondary, tertiary, etc.), which are the results of the primary functions.

Not all these forms are included in the present investigation. Only the primary sporadic social functions which occur as a result of a sharp increase in deficiency and comparative mass starvation are investigated here.

As to the permanent functions of nutrition as a determinant, I shall restrict myself to a short general review. The secondary and the tertiary functions I shall mention after concluding the investigations of the sporadic primary effects.

The Permanent Social Function of Nutrition
as a Determinant

The metabolic exchange of substances takes place in every society, as well as in every organism. It represents a complex mechanism which absorbs the energy in food from the outside and expends it for its life activity. It lives, works, and creates by utilization of this energy. Because the expenditure of energy by the society in its "creative" or "uncreative" forms occurs incessantly, a source of food energy must be a permanent requirement.

It follows that, in any living aggregate, inevitably there must exist a permanently functioning "system of nutrition" of the society and its organs, as long as the society continues to survive. The existence of this system and of its organs is the permanent function of the determinant nutrition. The first is brought to life by the latter. If it were not for the latter, the first would not exist. Correspondingly, in every living aggregate we find such a system of the organs of nutrition, which occupies a principal place in the general structure of the society. This system consists of three elements: establishments and institutions for the procurement and processing of essential foods; organs for the exchange and distribution of the latter among members of the aggregates; and organs for consumption of these essentials.

Examples of organs for procurement and processing of essential foods are institutions of hunting, fishing, animal husbandry, agriculture, and those involved in the processing of foods. Each of these institutions represents a group of people who are performing definite functions by means of simple or complex tools (shovels, sticks, harrows, plows, nets, boats, machines, and factories, as well as fields, gardens, cattle, etc.), and resembling in its totality a pump, by means of which a society gathers the necessary food energy from the cosmos. All these together represent the system of social organs which procure food and they represent the permanent social function of the factor of nutrition. Admittedly, a number of the aggregates may not exhibit this in a direct way. This only signifies that they have the functions in a modified form, or that they obtain energy by means of some other aggregates (e.g., the industrial aggregates, agriculture, the parasitic-military exploitation, etc.), for which they must have an apparatus either in the form of a military apparatus, which makes requisitions of food by force, or by an industrial complex which produces goods that are exchangeable for food products.

A system of organs for distributing food among members of society exists alongside the system of food production. Markets, fairs, storehouses, stores, stock exchanges, and the whole merchandising apparatus engaged in the sale of essential foods perform the functions of distributing food energy among members of the society. Thousands of diversified activities are involved in this: vehicles, roads, market-places, buildings, stores, stock exchanges, various offices, money, ration cards, budgets, charge accounts, etc. All of this taken together forms the "blood system" of the aggregate, which includes the organs for distribution of nutrition.

Finally, every society has a system of organs for food consumption. Again, this system consists of groups of people, their definite activities and "material means of trade" which serve this function: the bonfire, hearth, kitchen, saloon, dining room, café, restaurant, knives, forks, pots and pans, stoves, samovars, teapots, spoons, cups, plates, napkins, bottles, etc.

In one form or another, all these organs, which together form a system for the nutrition of society, may be found always in any aggregate; and they represent one of the principal systems of the social organism. This is a permanent function of the factor of nutrition.

The numerous ways of producing, distributing, and consuming essential foods, which go on incessantly in any society, and which represent one of the principal forms of its life activity, are the permanent features of the factor of nutrition. They are the acts of hunting, fishing, animal husbandry, tilling the soil, working in gardens, fields, vineyards, plantations, working in food factories and shops, in bakeries and laboratories, in dining halls, in the preparation of ways and means of producing the essentials of nutrition, etc.

Society is always expending energy, and therefore it requires means of distributing and consuming the nutrients. The totality of such kinds of activity forms the nutritional process of the society, and this goes on incessantly.

From this characterization it becomes obvious that the phenomena studied by political economy are mainly those involved in the constant function of the factor of nutrition.

Along with these permanent social functions of the factor of nutrition which are of a material nature, all spheres of social life exhibit also many other permanent functions, which are directly connected with the former.

If we were to take the entire mental baggage of a society, the complex of knowledge which it possesses, it would be evident that much of it consists of our knowledge relating to the phenomena of nutrition, and all that may be called forth by the latter. This includes knowledge of ways of procuring or preparing necessary tools, the methods of their use, and their distribution. In a primitive society they are transmitted from generation to generation by tradition, imitation, and instruction. In more modern societies they have been developed into a system of theoretical and applied disciplines, such as the dozens of agricultural disciplines, or hundreds of the branches of applied science which deal with this problem in schools, learning institutions, and laboratories, and which are distributed by means of books, pamphlets, newspapers, journals, etc. In any society the rearing, education, and equipping for life of younger generations consists, first of all, in providing them with knowledge of how to procure food and how to use it. The same occurs in reference to the religious life of the society. A number of practices, prayers, services, testaments, and prescriptions, beginning with the religious customs of primitive peoples for "increasing the food supplies," including the petition "give us our daily bread" of any religion, and ending with the practice of "communion" (eating), and the prescriptions of what it is permissible and what it is forbidden to eat—all of this is called forth by the factor of nutrition, and exists and occupies a considerable place in the area of religious phenomena. All of these represent a complex, direct, and peculiarly flexed function of the nutritional factor. Thus, the problems of nutrition and of the corresponding topics have always occupied, and continue to occupy, a very large place in the field of knowledge and of beliefs.

The same is true of morals and laws of any society. When we consider the totality of the moral and legal norms, prescriptions and testaments of any aggregate, we find a large number of rules that are devoted to the regulation of relationships which occur in the field of nutrition, and which are connected with it. Or, in other words, they are the rules which determine the behavior of members of the society in the areas of procurement, exchange, distribution, and consumption of essential foods. In a large part the "politics" of any society always has been and continues to be, first of all, a "bread politics," i.e., a set of measures which are called forth by the nutrition' determinant and which are directed toward solving the problem "of the knife and fork." Similar conditions face administrators and rulers in general. The same can be said about the social struggle. It always has been first of all a struggle among the members and classes of the society for their shares of essential foods. Similar problems also are encountered in art. The "nutritional" subjects, pictures, epithets, comparisons, metaphors, etc., are and always will be the most popular and constantly employed themes of literature, paintings, sculpture, architecture, theatrical art, and special forms of song and music. Hundreds and thousands of novels, romances, and objects are devoted to these themes directly or indirectly (e.g., *Hunger* by Hamsun, *Les Misérables* by Victor Hugo, "Vagabonds" by de Maupassant, *Naked Year* by Pilnyak, the comedies of Aristophanes, *Weavers* by Hauptmann, etc.).

As far as human ethics and rules of the society are concerned ("do not eat with the knife," "dress for the dinner," behave in a certain way at the table, etc.), it is not necessary even to mention them. Therefore, no matter what area of social life, and particularly of spiritual life, of the society we might take, in every aggregate, and at any moment of its existence, we find evidence of the presence of the nutrition determinant. If this determinant did not exist, we would not have these permanent functions of it. With this I conclude the observations on the permanent functions of hunger, and proceed with the consideration of its sporadic social functions.

The Problem and a Summary of the Primary Functions of Mass Starvation

Suppose that in a given aggregate the quantity and quality of food consumed by the majority of its members is changed from normal to deficient (i.e., deficiency starvation has begun), or has declined sharply, and that the difference between the diets of the upper and lower classes has increased (i.e., comparative starvation has increased). What will be the social effects of this increase in deficiency and comparative starvation?

At the present, the cause of the increase in starvation of each type is of no consequence. I use it simply as an "independent variable," and am concerned only with its presence or absence. Its cause or causes (the shortage of crops, war, economic crisis, revolution, growth of the population, floods, etc.) are of no concern to me at present. My aim is to determine the social functions of mass starvation; and it is even more important to me if it has been caused by a variety of phenómena and occurs during different sets of conditions. Under such circumstances it is easier to isolate the specific functions of mass starvation by making it possible to distinguish that which is common to all starvation, from the diversified complex of accompanying phenomena which are caused by factors subsidiary to hunger.

Such is the principal nature and task of the problem. True, this problem cannot be solved in an absolute form. It is difficult to take into consideration the endless effects which mass starvation may produce. However, it is sufficient if we can outline some of the principal functions of this "independent variable." Because the phenomena are very complex, because the necessary materials and exact numerical data for determination of the curve of the nutrition of a given population often are lacking, and because the only source of information is the statements of the historians who describe in general terms the worsening or improvement of nutrition, an investigator may make serious mistakes in this field. But the problem is extremely important from both the theoretical and the practical viewpoints, and it is impossible to ignore it. No one is guaranteed against mistakes, but any that are made should help future investigators to avoid them.

In the behavior of an individual the result of deficiency (or comparative) starvation is expressed in the "desire" or "urge" for food, or its equivalents (e.g., money) which present the means of obtaining food. What is true about an individual is also correct for a number of persons.

With the advent of deficiency or comparative starvation, members of a given aggregate should show a corresponding increase in food taxis. This is manifested in the behavior of these people in the way outlined in the preceding chapter, i.e., the development of a tendency to lower and to depress all reflexes which prevent the satisfaction of hunger, and to strengthen and reinforce those favorable to the procurement of food. Members of a society who are starving either deficiently or comparatively will seek to satisfy their hunger and to return either to the pre-starvation state, or at a minimum to obtain a norm above complete deficiency starvation. What are the ways in which this may be achieved? There are six of these and they, in turn, may be divided into a number of forms.

1. Invention of new or improvement of available sources of food;

2. Acquisition (by peaceful means) of necessary foods from other groups;

3. Emigration, peaceful or military, of the population from the region of famine to one where there is food;

4. War and the forceful requisition of supplies from the well-fed groups by the starving people;

5. Redistribution of essential foods and of the riches which are found within the group by means of: (a) unsystematic acquisition in criminal ways from the well-fed people by the hungry; (b) massive, and to some extent organized, attacks by the hungry people upon the satiated who are seen as the holders of "food storages" and the equivalents (by way of revolts, insurrections, and revolutions); (c) interference by the authorities of a given group, which conducts the redistribution from above, and consequent changes of the economic-nutritional organization of the society; and (d) voluntary contributions by the satiated people of a part of the nutritive essentials to the hungry, either as gifts or for corresponding services (charity, private agreement between the satiated and the hungry on certain conditions, which often lead to the enslavement of the latter); and

6. Finally, if none of these ways are successful, there remains an old and "safe" way to satisfy hunger—the way of death, or "changing the natural movement of the population." This way is always present and available.

There are no other ways.

If it is true that mass starvation produces a mass food taxis, and if it also is correct that hunger may be satisfied exclusively in one of the ways mentioned, then it follows that in the presence of mass starvation in a social aggregate (the population of a village, town, region, state, or an entire continent) we must inevitably find one or more, or even all, of the indicated ways for the satisfaction of hunger.[1] This follows deductively from all that is said above. As we shall see later on, it also is confirmed inductively.

At first, the connections between these ways and hunger are not always clear. In social life the connection often is obscured in thousands of ways: by high-sounding "speech reflexes," which deaden rumblings of the stomach; by refined ideologies and beautiful ideals

---

1. I do not imply here that all such cases are caused exclusively by hunger, and that they cannot be produced by other causes. I say only that if there is starvation, the phenomena mentioned occur in this or that condition.

which are accompanied by the unaesthetic demands of the stomach; and by hundreds of comical and tragical scenes of history, which, at first glance, have no relationship to hunger. However, careful examination of the "film" of history indicates that hunger is often at the center of the "social drama." "The man becomes excited, but hunger directs him," is the famous expression of Jacques Bossuet [2] to describe such circumstances. As has been indicated, the starving masses of the population in a given social aggregate must inevitably cause either one, several, or all of these symptoms.

In concrete reality, deficiency (and partially comparative) mass starvations frequently are accompanied by several of them. But in a given society, one or another of the features become more sharply apparent, e.g., emigration, or the large-scale importation of food, while the other features, although present, are relegated to the background. In another society where the people are starving, the first place may be occupied by other of the sequences, e.g., increase in crime; in a third society, still other features may predominate, etc.

The exact symptoms from the indicated social effects of hunger, and the combination in which they will occur in every given case of mass starvation, are not accidental; but they represent a fact which is determined on one hand by a large number of conditions, among them the location of the aggregate, and on the other, by the mutual interrelationships among the effects of hunger.

Let me try to explain my thought. Suppose that the starving aggregate is quite wealthy and can import (from the county, state, other states, or even other countries) a sufficient amount of foodstuffs to provide the needed calories. If such imports are made, and hunger is satisfied, food taxis disappears and, therefore, the other effects of hunger are not felt. However, if the importation of the necessary food is impossible or is insufficient (if there is no money to pay for the food, or if a blockade makes it impossible to import, etc.), and the deficiency of calories is not met, then some other functions of mass starvation such as mass emigration certainly should be expected (if the nutrient mountain does not go to Mahomet, then, because of food taxis, Mahomet himself goes to the mountain). When emigration is possible (if there are ways of communication, freedom of exit and entry, availability of employment in the country having food, etc.), or when there are possibilities of inventions, beginning with the dis-

2. A French bishop and writer. E.S.

covery of food substitutes and ending with the intensification of the ways of production of nutrients, then hunger is satisfied and its other consequences do not take place.

However, suppose that the deficit is not covered (because neither importation nor emigration is possible, and inventions are insufficient); then we can forecast with great probability the occurrence of other effects of starvation, such as armed attacks by the famine-stricken upon well-supplied regions, or a whole series of perturbations within aggregates, that is, the starving people. Which of these takes place is not entirely accidental. If, for example, there is no sharp proprietal differentiation among members of a starving society, there is nothing to share, or nobody to rob. Similar would be the case if the rich are well organized and capable of resisting attack. However, if the neighboring aggregates are rich but poorly armed, and the force of the starving aggregate is tremendous, there is a high probability of an armed attack by the hungry society on the well-supplied one, of attempts by the former to subjugate the latter, of robbery, and of exploitation. If, on the contrary, the well-supplied societies are armed to the teeth, and their conquest is hopeless, while in the starving aggregate the differences in wealth are great, if near the people who are starving there are those who are well fed but who are poorly organized and armed (so that there is something to divide, and someone to rob), in such cases we may expect crime to flourish, disturbances to mount, even revolution, and various reforms of the nutritive structure of the society, at both top and bottom.

In this case the starving social aggregate resembles an organism supplied with a considerable storage of fats. When the food intake from the outside ceases, the starving organism begins to utilize its stores of fats and tissues. When all means of procuring food to the starving society from outside sources are closed or forbidden, and within the society the food supplies and the riches are concentrated in "the fatty tissues," the "hungry cells" obviously begin to be attracted toward these food supplies in order to secure them. In such cases the "power field" of the society, the food taxis attraction, begins to be emitted only from the inner storage facilities of the aggregate, or their equivalents. As a result there are within the society peaceful or bloody redistributions of the food essentials and their equivalents, seizures, disturbances, revolutions, crimes, voluntary distribution of their surplus by the rich, reforms from above, etc., up to the development of state socialism and communism.

Finally, it may occur also that the deficiency of calories is not covered by all of these measures. Then comes the *ultima ratio* of history—the constant surgeon of all complex social tumors—death. This is the final function of hunger: the extinction of the society itself with all its satellites of diseases, epidemics, and other phenomena connected with the "natural movement of the population."

The above paragraph explains why in every given case of social starvation, first place is occupied by one specific function of hunger, and not by another. It shows that the order of occurrence and distribution depends upon many conditions which affect the given aggregate. In certain cases the events would proceed in the way described here, while in other cases, because of the unavailability of ways to satisfy hunger, starvation would cause only an increased mortality, and its consequences would commence and terminate without involving the other social functions. In order to understand why during starvation one of the indicated effects would occur and not another, and also in order to be able to predict exactly what effect would take place during the starvation of the aggregate, it is essential to know the conditions under which a given society lives.

While varying in their combinations and in the order of their appearances these functions represent consequences of mass starvation—of the single cause $A;$ and in all of them there is the same element B—drive toward the food—which is caused by hunger, and which is only disguised by different "clothing."

When A appears in combination with the additional conditions a and b $(A + a + b)$, its consequence B would appear with the additional a' and b', or would assume the formula $(B + a' + b')$; when the combination is $A + c + d$, then the consequence would be $B + c' + d';$ when A is bound with c and f, its consequence would be $B + c' + f'$, etc. In other words the concrete difference of functions of one and the same cause—hunger—does not conflict with the principle that a given cause produces a given result, but becomes a direct application and verification of it.

Such in brief are the primary and basic social functions of mass starvation and of food taxis. Later we shall see that each of these functions contains very rich material, and most of them are divided further into very important social phenomena.

But even in this enlarged presentation not all of the social functions of starvation are included. Each primary function, moreover, calls into existence a number of social functions of the secondary, tertiary, etc., orders because "every action, every word thrown into an ever-living, and ever-creating world, is a seed which cannot die." [3] Hunger calls forth an emigration but the emigration itself gives rise to a whole complex of social phenomena; these, in turn, bring about new events, etc., so that the complex tragical comedy of human history proceeds *ad infinitum*.

I shall describe only the primary social functions of hunger. The secondary and the other functions require a special monograph. I mention their existence here only to remind the reader of the complexity of the problem, and that the effects of starvation continue to exist even after hunger has been satisfied.

3. Thomas Carlyle, *Sartor Resartus* (Moscow, 1902), p. 41 (in Russian).

5

HUNGER AND THE DEVELOPMENT AND IMPROVEMENT OF METHODS OF PRODUCING FOOD

When mass starvation appears in a social aggregate, and when the facilities for relieving it are insignificant, or lacking, then food taxis forces people to "strain their minds" in order to get, in one way or another, essential foods. Here hunger serves as a whip, to lash the lazy human brain to work on certain things. Under such conditions hunger presents an ultimatum to the starving group, the language of which is familiar both to the sage and the fool: "either find or discover and improve the production of the means of nourishment, or die."

Such ultimatums have been presented to mankind throughout the whole course of history, and are being presented now. In some cases the starving groups accepted the challenge and made certain improvements; in other cases, probably even more frequently, they just passed away, not that they liked such an end, but because inventions and especially the important ones cannot be made to order.

Let us define, on one hand, the exact role of hunger in this direction, and indicate, on the other, the extent to which it is possible to end starvation by inventions made during a famine.

In most cases the latter was inconsequential. Personally, I am not aware of a single case in which mass starvation was terminated instantaneously by means of new nutritional inventions. The inventions stimulated by the ravages of hunger almost never have been "strong action medicines," which would cure this disease of humanity. The reason is readily comprehensible: inventions are very capricious; in the past as at present they cannot be forced to appear by special decrees of *Sovnarkom* and *Sovnarkhos* (Soviet People's Commissariat and Soviet People's Department of Agriculture).

Out of all the suggestions which are freely offered by inventors of new sources of food, probably only the long-known products reappear on the table, i.e., such inventions as the use of Irish moss for food, a thing which has been known almost from the time of Adam. There are other causes, in addition to this capriciousness, which explain why inventions are not the cure for starvation. Great hunger weakens the energy of the brain and, consequently, decreases the chances for successful solution of the problem of invention, which is a realistic problem and not a metaphysical one. In the latter field the peculiar paroxysms of the brain in a starving body sometimes may produce interesting religious, philosophical, and aesthetic thoughts.

It is not surprising, therefore, that during a period of intense starvation most inventions are limited to the introduction of substitutes for food and other palliatives, anything to fill the hungry stomachs of the people.

A mere listing of the subrogates which have been "discovered" and consumed during famines gives a clear idea about them. Thus, the people have been brought to eating dogs, cats, donkeys, horses, wolves, frogs, snakes, carrion, special Haferbrot, all sorts of roots, grass, hay, bark, earth with a small addition of flour, clay, and even human flesh.[1] In addition, we find bread made of chestnuts, chopped straw and kindling wood.[2] This happened in Western Europe during the Middle Ages, in the fifteenth and eighteenth centuries, the same we now see it in Russia. They ate birch bark, moss, bark from pine, leaves of linden trees, hay, straw, mice and other unclean things. In 1734–35 in Nizhegorodskaya province, people ate rotten oak logs, acorns, pigweeds, and chaff, and in 1822 they ate bread made from clay, bulrushes, and pigweeds.[3] Similar conditions were observed among the starving Eskimos, Samoyeds, and other peoples.

1. F. Curschmann, *Hungersnöte im Mittelalter*, pp. 57–59.

2. Tsitovich, *On Famines in Western Europe and Russia*, pp. 4–6 (in Russian).

3. A. V. Romanovich-Slavatinsky, "Famines in Russia," pp. 35, 55, in Tsitovich, *On Famines in Western Europe and Russia*; A. Issaev, *Crop Failure and Starvation* (St. Petersburg, 1892), p. 12 (in Russian); Ermolov, "Famines in Russia," 1:7, 10, 17–23 (in Russian).

The list of substitutes for food presented has varied from time to time, but there have been no significant changes. Practically everything mentioned in it has also been used for food in our time. Thus, in Germany during the First World War, when starvation of the German people was considerable, new sources of food were not produced. There was an increase in the production of replacements; the use in bread of the blood of animals; use of so-called mineral yeast as a source of proteins in replacement of real yeast; a mixture of plant proteins and fat instead of eggs; utilization of the fish waste, bones, carrion, and fecal matter; and ways of getting vegetable fat from fruit; and that practically was all.[4]

The palliatives have consisted mainly of mere propaganda and the promotion of use of these subrogates by the government, by society, and by private individuals. As an example we can cite the propaganda in our newspapers about the use of Irish moss and other replacements for food. Similarly in 1833 the government was teaching how to make bread from the waste of winemaking, from potatoes, or with the pulp of sugar beets, etc.[5] Similar "inventions" are numerous but they lack variety. There is no need to discuss them further.

Thus, we can conclude that during periods of great starvation, inventions and discoveries of new means of nutrition are quite insignificant. Rarely has the deficiency in calories been delivered to a group by these means.

Does it mean, however, that the role of hunger in stimulating the discovery of new sources of foods is always insignificant, and that it is limited to various pseudo-inventions? The answer to these questions is no.

Hunger's role is considerable; but it is manifest not as much during a famine as after it ends. It consists not so much in the discovery of fast-acting remedies, which would decrease starvation immediately, as in the discovery and development of means for preventing the reoccurrence of famine, for decreasing the changes produced by starvation, and for gradually intensifying the production of essential foods and improving their distribution.

Starvation experienced once, or many times, has made human

4. O. Nicolai, *Die Biologie des Krieges* (Zurich, 1919), pp. 206–7.
5. Romanovich-Slavatinsky, op. cit., pp. 35–36; cf. *Izvestia*, Commissariat of Health, Petrograd Commune, 1919, nos. 5–6 and passim.

beings use their brains to devise ways of avoiding it in the future. It is difficult to conceive of a more active force in inducing a lazy person to work or a slothful one to use his brain, and in causing all humanity to make supreme efforts to improve its material and closely related spiritual culture. Humanity hardly could exhibit intense energy in the matter of "conquering the world," and go so far "in the way of progress" without this teacher. I am afraid that without hunger we would have neither animal husbandry nor agriculture, nor the tremendous field of "food" industry, nor even the great development of the arts and sciences.

This was especially significant during the early stages of human existence. What forced man to go wandering through the forests, to spend hours catching fish, to perform the monotonous work of collecting fruits and seeds, to dig in the ground day and night, to uproot the stumps, to till the earth, etc.? "The necessity of development" (in the terminology of P. L. Lavrov)? No, the latter did not exist at that time. The instinct for hunting and the passion for fishing? No. Were it not for hunger, man would not spend most of his energy and time, suffer great need and scarcity, and endure bitter cold and intense heat, fatigue and sleeplessness, in his endeavor to get food. Had it not been for starvation, primitive man would have been lazy and sluggish, and would not have developed his muscles and his brain capacity.

Bücher [6] asks why the native should force himself, when he feels no hunger? Westermarck concludes that primitive people are lazy or diligent according to how easy or difficult it is for them to obtain the means of existence. He states that they prefer to be lazy as long as they can force other people to work for them in the capacity of slaves or servants. [7] The numerous facts brought up by him and a number of other investigators confirm his observations. Native peoples who live in fertile regions, where little work is required in order to exist, are lazy and little developed. Natives who live in surroundings requiring constant labor are energetic and full of initiative. The same groups of natives (Polynesians, Samoans, Tahitians, the natives of the Sandwich [Hawaiian] Islands, New Zealanders, etc.) work

6. K. Bücher, *Industrial Revolution* (Russian translation), 1:19; cf. 2:11–12, 16, 18, 27, 40, passim.

7. Westermarck, *The Origin and Development of Moral Ideas*, 2:268–69.

hard when nature does not favor them, and are quite lazy under favorable conditions.[8]

We see somewhat the same thing now on the part of some representatives of the "leisure class," for whom "food and housing" are always available. Do not some of them lead empty and parasitic lives? Do they not become fat and degraded both physically and mentally? [9] Just observe the behavior of the people around us. What forces them to get up at 8 A.M. and to perform tedious and heavy work? What forces many professional people to engage in mental work "to turn their brains"? (This is a Russian idiomatic expression. E.S.) Hunger, in the first place. A considerable proportion of my contemporaries would have stopped work both physically and mentally without this whip. The social struggle for power, for privileges, for shortening the working day is to a considerable extent a struggle for the right to leisure. The privileged classes are fighting against any shortening of the workmen's day, while the working people are fighting for it. If such condition exists at the present time, the more probable its existence in the past. From this point of view the "fosterer" of human progress should sing praise to the great teacher of humanity—hunger.

Stimulated ceaselessly by hunger, primitive man worked, made discoveries (which grew, accumulated and were passed on from one generation to the next, and from one group to another), and, consequently, made the greatest discoveries of antiquity, which were the foundation of animal husbandry, agriculture, and industry proper.

All the main steps of further improvements during later stages of history were to a considerable degree a function of hunger. It never ceased giving its ultimatum, forcing people to be inventive. Nicolai indicates correctly that hunger and the need for food called forth numerous inventions. They led people to practice agriculture, to domesticate animals, to invent the plow and other agricultural implements, and they stimulated them to hunt and fish, and to develop weapons and arms.[10]

It is true that other hypotheses have been advanced to explain

8. See facts and literature justifying this induction in Westermarck, ibid., p. 269, and the whole chapter on "Industry."
9. See Thorstein Veblen, *Theory of the Leisure Class* (New York, 1899).
10. Nicolai, op. cit., p. 197.

this progress. One of these is "The greater or lesser density of the population conditions the change of the economy. Libich had already calculated the size of the space required to maintain a hunting family. With the growth of the density of the population . . . there is no possibility to avoid the transition towards more intensive forms of the economy" (agriculture, winemaking, horticulture, animal husbandry, etc.).[11]

This statement is correct, but the growth of population plays such a role only because the population must eat, i.e., if the amount of food produced is stable this growth itself means the increase of hunger and, therefore, an increase in its coercive role. In the absence of hunger and of the concern about food, the population could grow indefinitely without the development of agriculture and horticulture. Furthermore, its growth properly is possible only in the presence of the means of subsistence. Each time that growth of population reaches a maximum, hunger issues an ultimatum: either invent, or die. Some groups have invented, others have perished. This story has repeated itself during the whole course of history, and it is continuing now.

From this point of view the theory of M. M. Kovalevsky is a variation of my own thesis. The history of the development of economies, particularly of agriculture, confirms this point. Not only the technique of tilling the soil is connected with the growth of density of the population, and consequently with an increase in the pressure of hunger, but also the changes of the ways of using the soil result from it. The investigations of Kovalevsky, Kocharovsky, Kaufman, Oganovsky, and others on the history of Russian Obshchina [12] show this connection quite clearly. The same can be said about any industry. In order to secure food, the nonagricultural countries must have an equivalent of "exchangeable goods." This means that the development of their industry is conditioned by hunger. This thought is well illustrated by Plutarch, when he speaks about Athens: "Noticing that the population of the town is increasing, and seeing that this region shall never produce good crops, and is known for its poor soil, meanwhile the sailors, as a rule, do not bring anything to the place where they do not get something for exchange, Solon made his citizens to

11. M. M. Kovalevsky, *Economic Growth of Europe*, 3 vols. (1898–1903), vol. 1, chaps. 8–9 (in Russian).
12. The Obshchina is an agricultural community. E.S.

learn trade, by issuing a law, according to which the son can refuse food to his father, if the latter did not teach him some industry." [13]

This dependence of development of industry upon hunger, or the threat of the latter, was known before Solon, during his time, and after it. It is not surprising, therefore, that some industrialists who previously did not understand this dependence made these efforts.

Several examples from the history of Russia also may be mentioned. The culture of wheat, millet, and of several vegetables was introduced in Russia after the famines of the eleventh century. We see the proof of this at the beginning of the next century when the chronicles mention wheat, millet, and many vegetables along with rye, which up to that time had been the sole crop. In addition to this, "the growth of the population forced people to drain marshes and fell forests, turning them into meadows, fields and vegetable gardens." [14] Later on, or exactly after periods of famine, efforts were intensified to increase acreage, to improve methods of agriculture, and to develop industries related to farming, as well as to improve hunting and fishing.

During the reign of Alexei Mikhailovich, there were decrees to subordinate officials such as, "you must direct them how to plow and sow their lands . . . and if they resist your advice, by punishment you must force them to do so." [15]

During the famines in the time of Peter the Great, there again

13. Plutarch, *Solon*, p. 24. The same thing is seen at present. Before my own eyes a number of cooperative groups are organizing laboratories and shops for the production of implements, such as fire lighters, agricultural tools, chemicals, etc., with the sole purpose of getting goods for trade with villages. The same cause forces laborers to work overtime in order to get a share of the products of industry to exchange for food, and the government to issue decrees ordering peasants to give bread to laborers in exchange for nails, plows, etc. The laborers in turn are told that they will get bread and that a regular exchange of goods will be established. It has been known for a long time in industrial countries, e.g., in England, that during periods of prosperity, when profits are high and the exchange of goods is easy, industrialists take very little interest in the improvement of their businesses. When the price falls and the enterprises show losses, they begin to use all the inventions which have been lying unused for many years. See Tugan-Baranovsky, *Industrial Crises in Contemporary England* (St. Petersburg, 1891), pp. 182–83 (in Russian).

14. Leshkoff, *The Russian People and the State*, p. 489.

15. Novombergsky, *Description of the Internal Governmental Policies in Russia in the XVII Century*, vol. 1 (Tomsk, 1914) (in Russian).

were orders to intensify agriculture and diversify crops.[16] After crop failures during the reign of Catherine II, work began on introducing potatoes into Russia. A decree of 1765 indicates that all possible effort should be made to introduce potatoes, because, in the absence of bread, they make a good substitute. During this period recommendations also were made for the introduction of cultivated lily plants (*Lilium martagon*) and the mulberry, for the keeping of bees, and the construction of milk separators, flour mills, etc. The same occurred after the famines of 1833 and 1840–41.[17]

Similar intensive measures also were undertaken later. Following the famine during the regime of Tsar Paul, a School of Agriculture was established for peasants who lived on small farms (*udel'nye*).[18] It was specified that they were to put into practice their knowledge of agriculture and to establish five-field rotating systems in their villages. In 1834, following the famine of 1833, the first agricultural journal was founded, scientific investigations were encouraged, and many reforms designed to increase the food supply were introduced. Measures of different nature were introduced after severe famines, especially that of 1891–92. Similar endeavors are now underway. From sowing campaigns to "nutritional institutions" the measures are plentiful. Scientific investigations, the growth of agricultural education, the establishment of all kinds of agronomical institutions, stations for artificial selection, experimental fields, "food institutes," courses on vegetable growing, introduction of new cultures, enlarging the field of activity of the organs of agriculture, etc., all are directly connected with the threat of hunger, and express a desire to prevent or to diminish its grave results.

In countries which have learned well the "lessons from hunger" similar methods of the rationalization and improvement of methods of securing food are carried on constantly. In backward countries (e.g., Russia and India) the curve of improvements rises sharply after periods of starvation, and falls off during long periods of prosperity.

This role of hunger is to be observed not only in connection with production of food essentials and sources of nutrients, but also in in-

16. Ermolov, op. cit., 1:16.
17. Ibid., 1:29.
18. In Central Russia the majority of peasants were still under servitude at that time and lived in communities called *Mir*. E.S.

stitutions of exchange, distribution, and consumption. The existence
of these and their improvement are dependent upon the great teacher
—hunger.

Such, therefore, is the fundamental relationship between hunger
and the improvement of the organization of food supply for a group.

However, it is possible to raise a question: because hunger has
played such role in the past, does it necessarily follow that the countries which have experienced the greatest famines also are the ones
most advanced in these respects, and vice versa? Actually we see just
the opposite. Therefore, is the opposite conclusion perhaps more correct? Answer: If the growth of inventions and improvements were
the function of hunger alone, this expression would be fully valid. But
I do not think this is the case. The capability for inventions depends
on a large number of factors, beginning with the racial qualities
of the population and a number of social conditions. The starving
Hottentot and the starving Anglo-Saxon of the tenth through the
twelfth centuries developed this capacity to different degrees. Therefore, under equal conditions of starvation the coefficient of inventiveness may be quite different. However, had it not been for the famines
in England and other European countries or in Japan (and, according to Walford, from the eleventh century on there were about 57
great famines in England, and no less than 160 in other European
countries),[19] and had it not been for the constant threat of hunger,
we would not have expected the intensive work that has been done
to improve methods of securing food for the population.

I do not maintain that starvation alone increases the "capability
of invention." On the contrary, as indicated, during acute starvation,
although hunger may promote the need for inventiveness, it at the
same time decreases the possibility of its realization because it weakens the mental capacity of people. That is why, when famines occur
too frequently, the population usually perishes and does not invent
means of salvation.

Furthermore, as has been indicated, invention and improvement
are only two of the ways of satisfying the people's hunger. These ways
are solid and safe, but do not work quickly and do not reduce the
hunger that already has been experienced. There also are some other
ways which are simple and available, and are more effective in satisfying any given hunger. Many people prefer to take that which is

19. Mulhall, *Dictionary of Statistics*, p. 256.

available, either through honest trade or by sly compulsions, and still others prefer to migrate to regions where food is available instead of working for new inventions, work which is difficult and which seldom brings reward to the inventor. That is why the countries with frequent famines may not lead in the field of inventions, but often become military, show considerable emigration, and have high rates of crime. The existence of such "escapes" provides the possibility of not perishing completely during great famines even when inventiveness is lacking. To this is added a series of other considerations. The density of population of a given nation, which has a specific economy, may have reached its maximum, and if its people have no "escape" means, they must invent in order not to perish. Other population groups, such as in India or in Russia, which possess large unpopulated spaces for expansion may find an answer to their problem not so much through the intensification of the means of producing food, as simply by extending the cultivated area. Under such circumstances inventions are not necessary.

Groups which live in a densely populated area do not have this means of escape. For them inventiveness becomes a dire necessity. It is obvious that the necessity for intensification of means of production of food and other means of existence is quite different in countries where the density of the population per square mile varies as follows: England, 341.6 (1901); Germany, 290.4 (1905); Holland, 406.4; Belgium, 588.7; France, 189.6; Japan, 316.9; Russia, 1.2; Turkey, 32; and the native states of India, 92.[20] Certain peoples may allow themselves the luxury of existing like Adam, but others cannot. Such circumstances explain why the mentioned objection to my thesis does not contradict it, but even supports it.

Conclusions

1. The invention of new means of procuring food for the population and improvement of old methods have been, and still remain, as functions of the independent variable—hunger, or the threat of it.

2. All social institutions of production of food—direct, or indirect (equivalents for the exchange for food)—and the apparatus for distribution, exchange, and consumption of it have evolved and developed under the pressure of hunger or the threat of it.

20. Webb, op. cit., pp. 467–68.

3. This role of hunger has been manifested and still is manifested not so much during the periods of starvation proper, but rather after the famine is over. During the periods of actual starvation its role is rather negative.

4. New inventions and improvements seldom cover the deficiency of calories in the struggle with existing starvation. Their roles in this respect have been insignificant, therefore, during the times of famines. The population rarely has tried to obtain salvation by this means, and has searched for other ways.

5. Once inventions become a fact, they change essentially the whole life and behavior of people, and the change appears stronger when the invention is important. They have been, and remain, the principal and almost the sole methods for the liberation of humanity and for improvement in the lives of people.

6

HUNGER AND THE EXPORTATION AND IMPORTATION OF FOOD PRODUCTS

Importation and prohibition of exportation of food are the simplest and most readily available methods of supplying necessary calories to a given population. In such cases the mass food taxis occurs as a behavior complex which has its purpose to deliver the "food mountain" to Mahomet, by some means, either peaceful or military. Provided there are no obstacles (and these often occur in the form of lack of money, or its equivalents, lack of roads, presence of blockades, etc.), these methods are used when a human aggregate has no adequate production of food regardless of whether the aggregate is a village, town, state, region, an entire country, or even a whole continent.

From this we may conclude, *ceteris paribus*, that in the absence of any obstacles, (1) the consuming groups inevitably must be importers either by peaceful trade or by military ravages; (2) importation into such countries must increase as deficiency of calories becomes greater after a crop failure, and vice versa; (3) the quality of imported food products must be in inverse proportion to the amount the group can produce (limited by the minimal quantities of the essential necessities). In real life this is not always the case, and the problem may be affected by the lack of credit or its equivalents, by means of communication, by a state of war, by blockade, by irregular distribution, etc. These facts, however, do not mean that the theory is wrong, but that there are other subsidiary determinants which weaken, or even annul, the effects of mass food taxis. Hence, I want to emphasize that the conditions are quite correct for a society which

175

satisfactorily balances its food requirements. In contrasting cases, when the food requirements of the society are not balanced, and the deficit is not covered, other social effects of the mass taxis (emigration, etc.), or an increase of the death rate with all of its accompanying features, may occur. When the lack of a nutritional balance becomes chronic in a given society, the resulting difficulties also become chronic.

Let us consider some of the facts. It is well known that groups which do not produce a sufficient number of calories, but which still have adequate food supplies, are those that import essential foods. They may be towns, entire regions, or whole countries. The nutritive essentials move toward them, not away from them. In the final balance their food imports are higher than their exports, even in cases when they perform an intermediary function.

The big cities of antiquity (Babylon, Memphis, Thebes, Athens, Rome), of the Middle Ages, and of the present time, with large populations, were in the past and remain at present as centers which did not produce, and do not produce now, sufficient quantities of nutrients. Hence the necessity of a constant importation of foods from the country. In the past and also at present this importation took place partially by peaceful trade and partially by the military plunder of the rural population through the collection of unlawful taxes and the requisitioning of crops for the towns.[1] When the food taxis deficit is covered by such means, other effects of starvation may not appear. However, when it is not covered, as is often the case, we almost inevitably see the other functions (an increase of mortality, flight of people from the starving towns, revolts, revolutions, etc.).

The "consuming" countries and regions constitute the second series of examples. When their food balances are satisfactory, their importation of nutrients is greater than their exportation. The greater the difference, the larger the deficiency in calories in the country. England is a typical example of countries which in recent decades balanced their food budgets by importations. From the study of consumption, production, and importation of food products, we see how importation increases with growth of population and decrease of production of food essentials.[2]

1. See K. Bücher, *The Development of Agriculture* (St. Petersburg, 1907), vol. 2 (in Russian). Cf. A. Böckh, *Die Staatshaushaltung der Athener* (Berlin, 1851), 1:47, 55, 115.

2. This importation rose from 16 million to over 36 million quarters in the period 1841–1911: Webb, *The New Dictionary of Statistics*, p. 477. Edi-

Years	Number of quarters of grain harvested in England and Wales	Imported wheat (in quarters)
1839–40	4,022,000	1,782,482
1840–41	3,870,648	1,925,211
1841–42	3,628,173	2,985,123
1842–43	5,078,989	2,405,217
1843–44	5,213,454	1,606,912
1844–45	6,894,368	478,190
1845–46	5,699,868	2,732,134
1846–47	5,363,196	2,458,000

These data show the inverse relationship between amounts of imports and quantity of grain produced in England; as the insufficiency of the latter becomes more pronounced, the former increases. Variations in the size of the importation of edibles is seen still better from the following material. The better the crops in a country, the smaller the amounts of food products imported; conversely, the fewer the number of calories produced, the more of them imported.

"The years 1833 to 1836 were remarkable in the history of English agriculture because of production of extremely good crops." "The harvests were so plentiful, that for several years England hardly needed to import bread at all." Therefore, imports of the latter decreased considerably. This is shown in the following figures. In comparison with the yearly average amount of wheat imported during the preceding four years, the imports of wheat during the years of abundant crops were equal to, in 1833, only 7 per cent (of the yearly average imports of wheat during the preceding years of deficient crops); in 1834, 5 per cent; in 1835 and 1836, 2 per cent. Because of two big crop failures in 1837 and 1838, the amount of breadstuffs imported into the United Kingdom for the purpose of domestic consumption increased considerably and reached an unprecedented figure of 10.5 million pounds. In 1836 the value of imported breadstuffs was equal to about 0.1 per cent of the total exports of goods from the United Kingdom, and in 1839 it reached 20 per cent.[3] Likewise, we

tor, "War and Population," *The Edinburgh Review* (July 1920), p. 199. [Note: the quarter is equal to eight bushels and once was considered the equivalent of one-fourth of a ton. T.L.S.]

3. Tugan-Baranovsky, *The Periods of Industrial Crises* (St. Petersburg, 1894), pp. 118, 132 (in Russian).

observe a high rise in imports in 1846 and 1847 when there were crop failures. During 1847, the total amount of different breadstuffs imported into the United Kingdom for domestic consumption was equal to 29 million pounds, which was unprecedented in the entire history of agriculture in England. The imports of breadstuffs were equal to 50 per cent of the total value of all the exports of goods from the United Kingdom, while in 1845 they were only 3 per cent.[4]

The absolute and relative growth in imports of food products which were called forth by growth of the population, by industrialization, by decreases in the acreage of agricultural lands, etc., indicate the same trend. They made the food produced in England increasingly insufficient and accordingly caused the increase in importation of foodstuffs.[5]

This is illustrated by the following table, which shows the quantity of the food products imported by the United Kingdom per unit of population.

Food products (in pounds)	Average per person per year					
	1866–75	1876–85	1886–95	1896–1905	1906–1907	
Grain and flour (wheat, oats, corn, and others)	295	424	462	526	504	505
Rice	18	12	17	18	22	21
Potatoes	10	19	8	17	10	21
Meat	7.6	19.1	26.8	44	47.3	47.6
Butter, oleo, and cheese	8.7	12.4	15.7	19.8	20.7	18.9
Eggs (units)	17	24	34	49	52	51

4. Vigor, "The Increased Yield per Acre of Wheat in England Considered in Relation to Reduction of Area," *Journal of the Royal Statistical Society* (1910), pp. 398–99.

5. Great Britain, *Agricultural Statistics: 1907*, part 3 (London, 1908); Webb, op. cit., pp. 281, 247, passim; Mulhall, *Dictionary of Statistics*, pp. 7, 135, 287, 715, 718, passim; Crawford, "Notes on the Food Supply of the United Kingdom," *Journal of the Royal Statistical Society* (1899), p. 598 and passim. F. Rutter, *Cereal Production of Europe*, U.S. Department of Agriculture Bulletin no. 68 (Washington, 1908), gives the figures on exports and imports of food products for other countries.

Thus we observe that the population rose from 28,927,000 in 1861 to 41,459,000 in 1901, which led to a greater deficiency of calories not covered by production of essential foods by the country, and which, in turn, required an increase in imports.

Were it not for various handicaps, food deficits always would have been resolved satisfactorily. Suppose a group requiring 5 billion calories a year, and producing these calories within the aggregate, would suddenly be able to produce only half a billion per year. In such a case, imports of edible goods would have to rise to 4.5 billion. The imports would be near this figure, if there were no obstacles. The latter, however, may be present and quite often they are very powerful and not to be overcome. Therefore, the amount of imports deviates from this "ideal" norm, and under these circumstances other effects of the mass food taxis may occur. However, in this or that form, importation is always taking place as a result of mass starvation of a given group. It always has represented and continues to represent the most easily available means to cover the food deficit of a group during a period of intense starvation, varying only in its magnitude.

During the famine of 1024 the inhabitants of Suzdal (Russia) went down the Volga River and "bought bread from the Bolgars," according to an early chronicle. During the famine of 1230–31, the salvation of the people of Novgorod was achieved by arrival of Germans with wheat from "beyond the sea." Similarly, in 1279, bread was imported from the "yatvyagi" (or "jotvingiai," ancient Lithuania. E.S.). One of the most important actions during the reign of Boris Godunov was the importation of bread reserves from other provinces where it had been accumulated in preceding years.[6] The authorities and private people often appropriated sums of money to help the starving population by purchasing breadstuffs and importing them from other provinces. Before, during, and after the reign of Peter the Great, such subsidies from the government were quite frequent. In 1812, 2.5 million rubles were appropriated for the "purchase and distribution of bread" to the starving population of the province of Moscow. In 1813 the provinces of Kaluga and Smolensk were granted 6 million rubles; in 1833 the subsidy increased to 29,768,212 rubles; in 1839–40, to 25,414,185 rubles; in 1844–46, to 11 million rubles; in 1880–91, to 11,518,170 rubles; in 1890–91, to 174,992,802

6. Leshkoff, *The Russian People and the State*, pp. 476, 487; Ermolov, "Famines in Russia," 1:20, passim.

rubles; in 1905–6, to 77,570,398 rubles, etc.[7] Similar conditions are found in other countries during periods of starvation.

During the famines in the Middle Ages "the first concern of Charles the Great during such periods was the preservation and the importation of food into the country."[8] The same took place in the history of other countries. In the Italian republics of the eleventh century and the ones that followed, in cases of crop failure, which were quite frequent, the *officiales bladi* or *abudantiae* (the magistrates of plenty, similar to the authorities of Comprod, or Petrocommune of our time) got in touch with various towns and secured from them the permission to purchase and export bread from their provinces.[9]

Studies of trade in breadstuffs in eighteenth-century France indicate that during every crop failure a considerable increase in imports of breadstuffs from abroad took place, together with prohibition of exports from starving regions. For example, during the famine of 1768, "it was necessary to import foreign breadstuffs in a considerable quantity." The same took place during 1740 and 1750, when up to 200,000 kentals were imported from abroad, and this was repeated in 1775.[10]

In India, a considerable increase in the imports of food occurred during years of famine, particularly during recent decades. This can be seen in the subsidies for the relief of starvation by the government, which reached tens of millions of rupees.[11]

In the absence of obstacles, therefore, importation of nutritive products into a starving country must increase in proportion to the

7. Afanasiev, *Historical and Economic Articles* (1909), 1:379–83, 409, passim (in Russian).

8. Curschmann, *Hungersnöte im Mittelalter*, pp. 74–75.

9. M. Kovalevsky, "The Measures Employed by the Italian Republics in Their Fight against Starvation," in *Relief of Starving People* (Moscow, 1892), pp. 352–70 (in Russian).

10. G. E. Afanasiev, *The Conditions of the Food Trade in 18th-Century France* (Odessa, 1892), pp. 167–68 (in Russian).

11. See the figures in Digby, *The Famine Campaign in Southern India*, vols. 1 and 2; see especially Appendix H, 2:490–91; see other details in the *Reports* of the Indian Famine Commission (London, 1880–85), part 1; in addition, for the years 1898 and 1901, see the *Statistical Atlas of India 1895*. In the past "the government forbade the export of grain, and tried to import it and fix the price": *Imperial Gazetteer of India* (1907), 3:484.

development of starvation. A theoretical scholar may visualize pictures of increased movement of food products into similar regions. However, the realistic observer writes, "On the road . . . we often passed loaded wagons. Without any interruption they followed each other in front of us and behind, forming an endless ribbon, which disappeared in the distance." [12] "Long trains loaded with grain were seen in front," writes Kipling in describing the famine in India; "the cars were waiting on the side tracks to be later attached to the train." [13]

Whether the starving aggregate succeeds in increasing importation of food up to required norm or not, the activity and structure of the society are reconstructed so as to make this importation possible. Accordingly, the usual import duties on the foreign breadstuffs are removed (provided they existed before), various premiums are offered to increase imports,[14] a number of measures are accepted to decrease importation of other goods in favor of nutrients,[15] export of edible produce from the starving regions is hindered, and all efforts are directed to keeping the imported products.

The phenomena mentioned represent the manifestation of transformation of the structure and of social life of a society which was called forth by the increase of the food taxis.

Such is the relationship between mass starvation and the curve of importation and exportation of nutrient products. This relationship

12. Korolenko, *During the Year of Famine*, in *Collected Works* (Moscow), 5:17 (in Russian).

13. Kipling, *During the Famine* (St. Petersburg) (in Russian); Sorokin, *System of Sociology*, p. 93 (in Russian).

14. This was seen during the Middle Ages, and can be observed now. For example, in England in the year 1795, a very large premium was introduced for wheat when it was imported in quantities of from 400 to 500 million quarters. Similar premiums were offered in 1800. During the Middle Ages in France during the famines of the sixteenth through the eighteenth centuries, in Germany in 1846–48, and in some other countries it was quite customary to abolish import duties on bread products. See Roscher, *Traité d'économie politique rurale*, pp. 95–97; Afanasiev, op. cit.; Curschmann, op. cit., pp. 71–75.

15. In Athens, where, according to Böckh (op. cit., 1:116–20, 123, passim) bread was always in short supply (a deficit of 1 million medimni) and during the crop failures almost half of it had to be imported, "export was entirely forbidden," and importation was greatly encouraged. Similar conditions existed in Rome. See the references in O. Hirschfeld, *Die kaiserlichen Verwaltungsbeamten, von Augustus bis auf Diocletian* (1905), p. 116, passim.

is direct. In the absence of obstacles, the growth of a food deficit increases importation and decreases exportation of nutrient products from the starving country.

However, this "function of hunger of the first order" does not cover the entire problem. A whole series of events may appear (secondary functions) as a result of the effect of the primary functions. For example, in order that importation, and particularly an increase in it, may be realized, the group must have either things of equivalent value to trade, or the military force needed to requisition or seize the food from the other groups. Consequently, the food taxis induces the development of industries and other forms of activity which supply products suitable for exchange and trade with the producers of breadstuffs, and also creates a strengthening of the military organizations necessary for making the requisitions, which can attack and carry away the food from the other groups. Once the industries are instituted or the military organization is formed, this fact in itself calls forth a number of other consequences.

The same can be applied to the other functions of the "secondary order." For example, because of the limited credit available even in well-to-do societies, increased importation of food products inevitably causes a corresponding decrease in importation of other products, and is followed by the flow of gold abroad, etc. This limitation and outflow inevitably affect a whole number of processes in the life of the society, and the change in each of these in turn will be reflected in a number of other phenomena connected with them.[16]

Conclusions

1. With a fast and sharp decrease of the food supply necessary for a given group, efforts are made to cover the deficit by increasing imports of nutrient products, or by decreasing exports of the same.

2. Correspondingly, in the absence of other obstacles, the "consuming" groups must import constantly.

3. When there are no obstacles, *ceteris paribus*, this importation increases in direct proportion to the food deficit.

16. See, e.g., the social, financial, and industrial effects caused by the crop failures of 1834–38 and 1846–47 in England; Tugan-Baranovsky, op. cit., pp. 118–22, 137–40, passim.

4. The nutritional deficit is often covered in this way, but sometimes these means are insufficient.

5. The satisfactory attainment of the food balance of the former groups eliminates other effects of mass starvation; however, for the latter groups, these effects become inevitable and new means have to be found to cover the deficit.

6. As a result of these "primary" functions, a number of secondary, tertiary, etc., functions are developed, in the creation of which hunger represents one of the independent variables.

7

HUNGER AND PEACEFUL EMIGRATION

When the food mountain does not go to Mahomet, then the hungry Mahomet is attracted to the food mountain, because of the food taxis. An insufficient quantity of calories in a given group and the abundance of food in another forces people to leave their homes and go to the regions where they can obtain food. Hence the phenomenon of emigration is a function of hunger and of the food taxis. During a famine people from the starving regions are attracted toward regions of plenty by the "food magnet," and they become settled or are "polarized" there.

This phenomenon of migration essentially is not very different from daily migrations to places where food is obtainable (dining hall, restaurant, tavern, kitchen, delicatessen, etc.). We migrate daily, even two or three times a day, to such places (breakfast, dinner, or supper). The difference between these daily migrations and migrations in the narrower sense consists in distance which people travel. When the food is found in the dining hall, the journey is very short. However, when there is no food in the home of one person and none of it can be obtained in the homes of other people, or even in a whole town, then the food taxis forces the individual to "run" tens, hundreds, and even thousands of miles in search of food.

In the absence of obstacles, and other conditions being equal, (1) the number of emigrants from the starving country is in direct proportion to the number of starving individuals at certain stages of hunger; and (2) the number of starving people indicates the intensity of the famine. These are, first of all, conditions which affect intensity of emigration. However, the problem is not limited by these conditions. A number of other factors change concretely the ideal coefficient of intensity of emigration induced by hunger. They are the physical possibility of emigration proper, which, however, is often absent (right now in the USSR the authorities prohibit emigration, and other countries do not accept the emigrants); the presence or the absence of a plentifully supplied country to which it would be possible to emigrate; its distance from the country affected by famine; availability of transportation; chances of finding employment in the new country; presence or absence of supplies among the rich groups of one's own country; etc. All of these conditions influence the intensity of emigration produced by hunger, and they produce variations between the size of its coefficient and the coefficient of the number of starving people and that of the degree of their starvation.

The intensity of emigration as a result of food taxis depends upon the degree to which the hunger can be satisfied and is being satisfied by some other means. If these other means can cover the deficit of food, then emigration may not take place at all. Generally speaking, (3) when other conditions are equal in a starving aggregate, or in one which is threatened by starvation, the size of the emigration due to food taxis is higher, to the degree that imports, inventions, and other methods of covering the deficit are unavailable. When the deficit is entirely covered by some of these means, then emigration due to food taxis is reduced to zero. The importance of each of these methods of covering the deficit, in the sense of its distribution and size, is in reverse proportion to that of each of the others. The more one of these methods contributes to the elimination of starvation, the less necessary the other methods become, and accordingly, their size diminishes.

Such, briefly, is the direct connection between deficiency in and, partially, the comparative lowering of the nutritional curve and that of the growth and movement of the curve of emigration due to food taxis.[1] Let us substantiate this connection.

1. The migratory primitive peoples form the first category. It is well known that they remain at a definite place as long as that place provides sufficient food. When it becomes exhausted, as, for example,

---

1. By this I do not want to say that every emigration is a function of hunger. There are other forms of emigration which are called forth by other determinants. However, these are not included in this treatise.

when the game has been killed or frightened away, the fruits and seeds have been consumed, and the fish no longer can be caught, when the natural pastures for the cattle are exhausted, and when the place no longer provides sufficient nutrients, the group starts moving to new places where the nutritional possibilities are more adequate. When the new place does not fulfill expectations, the group moves farther away. Sometimes it divides into subgroups to facilitate the search for food.

2. The history of the peopling of earth by human beings and variations in the density of population in different regions is partially explained by, and partially serves as a proof of, this connection. It is known that the early settled regions were those which provided the opportunity of the group to be well fed in accordance with the given level of its "productive forces." The "hungry" regions, lacking edible animals, fish, plants, fruits, and those with unfertile and barren soil were inhabited much later in history, and sometimes even now remain uninhabited (deserts such as the Sahara and the Gobi, and the polar regions).[2]

Mayer writes that the influence of the natural factor of greater fertility of soil is demonstrated in a higher density of population, and vice versa. Such a relationship between density of population and quality of soil in the basins of separate rivers becomes particularly clear when the influences of industrial development are weak, thus indicating concrete cases of attraction of population by fertile lands.[3] Mayo-Smith says that people tend to live in valleys because the land is usually fertile.[4] By comparing the density of the population of different regions of the earth, even at the present time, it is possible to

2. Cf. Mayer, *Statistics and Social Studies* (St. Petersburg, 1901), 2:71, passim (in Russian); Richmond Mayo-Smith, *Statistics and Sociology* (New York, 1900), pp. 270, 366–67; E. Levasseur, "La répartition de la race humaine," *Bulletin de l'Institut International de Statistique* (1909), 18:48–63; Levasseur et Bodio, "Statistique de la superficie et de la population des contrées de la terre," *Bulletin de l'Institut International de Statistique* 12:1–110; Sorokin, *System of Sociology*, 1:254, passim; L. Mechnikov, *Civilization and the Great Historical Rivers* (1899), pp. 74–76 (in Russian); Jean Brunhes, *La géografie humaine* (1912); C. Vallaux, *La géografie social* (1911); E. C. Semple, *Influences of Geographic Environment* (New York, 1911); and particularly Ellsworth Huntington, *Civilization and Climate* (New Haven: Yale University Press, 1916).

3. Mayer, op. cit., 2:71.

4. Mayo-Smith, op. cit., pp. 366–67.

observe the relationship between density of population and ease with which food may be procured.

Such settlement in regions having an abundant food supply indicates the same food taxis tension.

3. Almost the whole of human history, beginning with historical migrations of population and ending with present-day emigration, testifies that the latter is a function of hunger. Only a few examples are mentioned here, and the details can be obtained in the literature mentioned.

The breaking up of groups of primitive people and the emigration of the separated parts often have resulted from hunger. With the increase in size of the horde of Asiatic nomads, hunger forced them to divide into parts which proceeded in different directions in search of food. This was known to take place among the Fijians, the inhabitants of the Andaman Islands, the African Bushmen, etc.[5] Similar reasons are indicated in the biblical story for the division of the tribes of Abraham and Lot.

What was the main cause of emigration of the ancient Greeks from their native land, their scattering, and their colonies? Food taxis. With the production techniques of the period, the growing population could not maintain itself in the small space of Attica. Therefore, the danger of the overpopulation, i.e., of hunger, became evident. The solution was in emigration and the conquest and colonization of new countries. "The surplus of the ever growing population had to be provided with new tracts of soil, which could be found only outside the limits of the country." ("I am going towards the undivided land, says the Tsar Polydor.") Hence follows the peaceful and military colonial activity of the Greeks, "the powerful sweep of the Greeks towards the areas outside their country, which had become too overcrowded." [6] Did not the same cause initiate expansion and military colonization by Rome? [7] Was not relative overpopulation (and therefore increased difficulties of procuring food) the main reason for other

5. E. A. Ross, *The Principles of Sociology* (New York, 1920), p. 86, passim.

6. R. Pöhlmann, *Essays on Greek History and the Study of Sources* (St. Petersburg, 1908), pp. 44, 33–34, 183 (in Russian); E. Meyer, *Die Wirtschaftliche Entwicklung des Altertums* (1893), 2:138.

7. W. Roscher indicates correctly that overpopulation and lack of food were some principal causes of the colonization. Cf. W. Roscher and Iannasch, *Kolonieen, Kolonialpolitik und Auswanderung*, 3d ed. (1885).

colonization ventures at later dates, including our own? [8] However, we now leave the general facts in which growth of mass food taxis develops rather slowly, and therefore at first glance appears to be ineffective, and turn to the closer correlation between fluctuations in the curve of nutrition and that of emigration. Different times, peoples, and countries are considered; because "the same cause calls forth similar consequences," if there are no disturbing conditions, they also must be similar in this case. Consider the facts.

"When prices rose the mass deportation of foreigners from Rome was the favored method of eliminating nutritional difficulties." [9] Curschmann indicates that during the Middle Ages the important consequence of any period of starvation was the fact that people were forced to leave their homes. After small reserves of food were exhausted, peasants had no recourse except to leave their homes and yards to try and find salvation elsewhere. The appearance of innumerable paupers who wandered about asking for alms everywhere presents a typical picture of periods of starvation. Charlemagne mentions this phenomenon in one of his writings, indicating that the paupers wandered between the burgs and the towns and often died of starvation. Other similar examples are mentioned in Curschmann's treatise. [10]

Pursued by hunger, large masses of people often crossed great distances (for those times), e.g., from France to Leipzig, from Bohemia to Tubingen and other parts of Germany, from Krakow to Russia and Hungary, from Hungary to the River Don in Russia, etc. In regions of starvation, loss of population was considerable. The dimensions of such desolation are described by Cont. Aquienctina in 1196: "Such a great number left the country, that paupers who remained behind could exist more or less adequately." Entire villages, towns, and monasteries were abandoned.

Also connected with hunger during the Middle Ages is the colonization movement to the east. Hungry people from the Netherlands colonized Holstein, from west to east. During the eleventh century

8. See Ernst Hasse, "Kolonieen und Kolonialpolitik," *Handwörterbuch der Staatswissenschaft*, 2d ed., 5:135–247; and Philippovich, "Auswanderung," ibid., 3d ed., 2:260–61, 273–74.

9. L. Friedlander, *Scenes from the Living History of Rome* (St. Petersburg, 1914), pp. 27, 28 (in Russian); J. P. Waltzing, *Étude historique sur les corporations professionelles chez les Romains* (Louvain, 1896), 2:102.

10. Curschmann, *Hungersnöte im Mittelalter*, pp. 62–68.

France had more than eleven big famines and connected with them
are such migrations as the Crusades. In 1095 Belgium experienced
a great famine, and during the next year an unusually large con-
tingent of Crusaders came from that region. Similarly in 1145–47,
just before the Second Crusade, there was a very severe famine. During such years the appeal to participate in the conquest of the Holy
Land and the promise of absolution from sins fell upon particularly
favorable soil. Many contemporaries emphasize this connection between starvation and the Crusades.[11]

The picture given shows that during the Middle Ages starvation
caused (1) emigration from regions of hunger and settlement in
better supplied places; (2) considerable distances traveled in emigrating; (3) depopulation of the regions of famine, and increase of
population in the regions where food was to be obtained; (4) a large
number of extremely important historical events, including the colonization of the east and the Crusades, in which one of the most important roles was played by hunger. Similar conditions were observed
during the famines in Byzantium, where the population fled from the
regions of hunger.[12]

We see the same picture later on. For example, in 1570 in Germany, "many peasants left their homesteads because of starvation and
went to foreign lands in search of work." Similar happenings occurred
in 1634, 1649, 1719, and 1736.[13] During the years of famine in
France in the eighteenth century, "big crowds of five, ten, twenty
thousand people were loitering along the main roads in almost every
province. A figure of one million paupers was officially established
in 1777. The peasants left their homes in great masses in hopes of
finding better conditions elsewhere." [14]

Similar conditions prevailed during famines in Russia and India.
Ancient chronicles relate that during the starvation years of 1127–
28 in Novgorod "many died, others left to go to foreign lands."
The same was true in 1214–15, and in 1228. In 1419 and 1421
many people migrated to Lithuania, and in 1436 "many left to go to

11. Ibid., pp. 51–55.
12. Scabalanovich, *Byzantine State and Church*, pp. 250–51 (in Russian).
13. Hazzi, *Betrachtungen über Theuerung und Noth der Gegenwart und
Vergangenheit*, pp. 11–21.
14. Kropotkin, *The Great French Revolution* (Moscow, 1919), p. 16
(in Russian); cf. H. Taine, *Les origines de la France contemporaine. L'ancien
régime* (Paris, 1899), 2:206.

Lithuania, to the Germans, to unbelievers, to Jews." "Whole regions became desolate, as the population left." In 1601 "The tsar's charity brought into Moscow a great number of people." [15]

During the reign of Peter the Great, recorded petitions and appeals often depict conditions existing during the years of famine; "from the year 1711 and up to the year 1716 in many counties the peasants lost everything, crops and cattle, and either died or went away." [16]

In 1725 Yaguzhinsky wrote: "the masses of people just ran away into Poland; in Vologodsky region alone, 13,000 souls disappeared." The same happened in 1735. [17] During the famine of 1733 inhabitants of regions afflicted by hunger moved towards Yaik, in the way similar to our times. Tens of thousands of hungry peasants went there, and also still further on into Siberia. [18] In 1732–36 from the domain of Prince Cherkassky in Nizhegorod county (where the famine was particularly severe) out of the 3,024 souls in his domain, 1,008 fled because of poverty and crop failure. In addition, many others left their homes with their wives and children and wandered from place to place asking alms. "From Paninsky county which listed 3,927 souls, 1,016 souls ran away." "In the county of Belgorod the famine of 1749 attracted masses of population to the town of Belgorod, where the food was dispensed; the authorities were obliged to put up tents for the people." During the crop failure of 1833 "thousands of peasants (not less than 38,000) were pressed by starvation to leave their native villages, and migrated to Caucasus; there they suffered a terrible period of starvation in 1833, and moved back." [19]

During the starvation years of 1891–92 because of the lack of bread a huge wave of emigrants from the provinces and regions afflicted by hunger swept into Siberia. [20] The study of statistics of migration to Siberia indicates clearly that the major proportion of the

15. Leshkoff, *The Russian People and the State*, pp. 460–66 (in Russian); Soloviev, *The History of Russia*, pp. 741–42 (in Russian).

16. Klochkov, *The Population of Russia during the Reign of Peter the Great* (1911), pp. 218–19 (in Russian).

17. Soloviev, op. cit., pp. 876–77.

18. Ermolov, "Famines in Europe," in *Famines in Russia and Western Europe*, 1:8, 17.

19. Romanovich-Slavatinsky, op. cit., pp. 42, 52–53.

20. Ermolov, op. cit., 1:103.

emigrants came exactly from the provinces afflicted by crop failures and hunger.

During the famine of 1807 in India "the large numbers of rural people moved to towns in search of help." The same was repeated in 1833 and 1837. In 1860 "hunger forced half a million people to migrate from the afflicted region." In 1867–68 "a considerable proportion of the rural inhabitants was obliged to leave the afflicted region and to flee with their cattle from their native land, some of them south, and some to the north. Up to a million people migrated at that time." [21] The people migrated in colossal numbers with their belongings and their cattle. From the total population of 1.5 million in the province of Marwar 1 million migrated.[22]

Here are some of the details. During the terrible famine of 1876–79, out of Indapure's population of 67,000, and of 44,200 head of cattle, "57,500 people and 33,000 head of cattle emigrated en masse." In Acola, of 815 inhabitants and 780 head of cattle, there remained only 76 people and 20 head of cattle; in Pimple, of 228 men and 153 cattle, only 9 men and 3 cattle remained; and in Bhatawad, of 346 people and 340 head of cattle, 77 and 22 remained. In other places "more than 50 percent of the population left their homes." During three months in 1877, 207,763 human beings migrated from the province of Madras.[23]

Figures on transoceanic and inter-European emigration show a somewhat similar picture. It has been observed frequently that in agricultural countries the number of emigrants from a given country is high during years of crop failure and immediately thereafter; this is also true of strong industrial crises in industrial countries, and generally during years of economic disorganization, all of which lead to deficiency and comparative starvation for the majority of the population. This interrelationship occurred clearly during severe famines and strong crises in the past, when the world economy was not highly developed, when isolation of various countries was greater, and when industrial crises were more acute in comparison with depressions of

21. Ibid., 2:97–100.

22. *The Imperial Gazeteer of India*, 3:487.

23. Digby, *The Famine Campaign in Southern India*, 1:288–93, 10, 13, 247, 265–66, 271; 2:349, 333–50, 385–94, passim. Cf. *The Imperial Gazeteer of India*, 1:467–71; 3:484.

later years. The same connection was observed also in countries receiving immigrants: the number of immigrants rose during the years of economic prosperity and fell during years of economic depression.

"In the accounts of the prefects and syndics, poverty is the most frequently mentioned cause of emigration." [24] And Philippovich sees in worsening economic conditions the force that produces most migrations.[25] Of the plentiful data which corroborate this statement, I mention only a few cases, and refer the reader to the literature cited. According to the theory of the interrelationship between hunger and emigration we should expect, *ceteris paribus*, a rise in emigration from agricultural countries during years of severe crop failures and one from industrial countries during years of strong industrial crises.

First I take Ireland as an agricultural country. In the 1840s the number of emigrants from Ireland was: in 1845, 686; in 1846, 109,624; in 1847, 217,512; in 1848, 187,803.[26] The marked increase in the number of emigrants in 1846 and 1847 coincides with crop failure and severe famine during those years.[27] To this total number of emigrants from Ireland should be added the number of Irish migrants to England and Scotland (ca. 500,000 men).

For another agricultural country, Russia, the number of Russian immigrants to the United States was:[28]

1890	35,598
1891	47,426]
	Famine, 1891–92.
1892	81,511]
1893	42,310
1894	39,278
1895	35,907
1896	51,445

24. Bodio, *Emigration from Italy*, in *Population* (Moscow, 1897), p. 307 (in Russian).

25. Philippovich, "Auswanderung," in *Handwörtenbuch der Staatswissenschaft*, 3d ed., 2:273–74.

26. Philippovich, "Emigration from Various European Countries of Europe," in *Population*, p. 284 (in Russian); and Philippovich, "Auswanderung," p. 291.

27. Mulhall, *Dictionary of Statistics*, p. 257; and the *Commissioner's Report* gives even larger figures for Irish emigrants (equal to 1,079,000).

28. These figures are taken from Philippovich, "Emigration," p. 284; Ermolov, op. cit., pp. 102, 153, 232, 261–63; Tugan-Baranovsky, *The Periods of Industrial Crises*, p. 165 (in Russian).

1897	25,816
1898	29,828] Crop failure, 1898.
1899	60, 982
1900	90,787] Industrial crisis, 1900.
1901	85,257] Big crop failure, 1901.
1902	107,347] Crop failure in eastern and southeastern provinces, 1902.
1903	136,093] Crop failure, 1903.
1904	145,141
1905	184,897] Crop failure and war, 1905.

From an examination of these figures, as from a consideration of a number of other factors which worsened the material conditions of the masses (such as the crop failures, the industrial crises of 1900–1902, and the war of 1904–5), we see a definite connection between the number of people who immigrated to the United States from Russia, and the degree of deficiency and comparative starvation of the masses.

Notwithstanding the fact that emigration, as indicated, is a result of many causes, the relationship between the rise of deficiency and comparative starvation and the condition of crops, and that between industry and unemployment, also may be seen in the movement of the curve of emigration in other countries.

Emigration from Belgium is taken here as an example of that from a partially agricultural and partially industrial country. Considering the curve of emigration and the corresponding figures, we see that the number of emigrants increased sharply during the years 1844–47, 1854–56, 1863–66, and 1885–89. These were either the years of great crop failures or of industrial crises, or even of both.[29]

German emigration to the United States during a number of years had somewhat similar causes. The number of these emigrants increased sharply during 1825–26 (crisis of 1825); 1845–54 ('the years of great crop failures and agrarian crisis in the second half of the 1840s and the beginning of the 1850s. There also was an industrial crisis connected with the industrial change during the late 1840s revolution. In addition, and at the opposite pole, the discovery of gold in California attracted immigrants from all parts of the world,

29. H. Denis, "Le mouvement de la population et ses conditions économiques," *Memoires Courants*, Belgian Royal Academy (1900), 59:1–16.

including the Germans); 1866–69 (the agrarian credit crisis; the wars of 1864 and 1866). During the years 1874–79 the number of the emigrants did not exceed 47,671. This period is known as the blossoming of Germany. Another increase took place in 1880–85 (years of an agrarian crisis and industrial depression), and again in 1891–92 (resulting from the crisis of 1890–91). From then to 1906 the figures for emigration are low, varying between 20,000 and 30,000. This was a period of great economic development in Germany.[30]

The emigration from the United Kingdom prior to the 1880s showed somewhat similar trends. The rise of the curve of emigration was noticeable in 1816–19 (crisis of 1815–16), 1825–26 (crisis of 1825), 1836–37 (crisis of 1836–37; crop failure in 1837), 1840–42 (depression), 1846–54 (famine of 1846–47; crisis 1847; economic stagnation of the following years; discovery of gold in California and Australia), 1862–66 (crisis of 1862–66; lack of cotton), 1873 (crisis of 1873).[31]

With the further softening of the crises and with the change towards less pronounced and longer periods of prosperity and depression, which did not show any noticeable worsening of the condition of the workers, the indicated relationship became less prominent.[32]

The statistics of immigration into the United States show a similar trend. The table shows the number of immigrants during years of prosperity and those of depression.[33]

Because of the famine in Ireland and the sociopolitical conditions in continental Europe, the number of immigrants into the United

30. The data on the number of the emigrants are taken from Philippovich. Those on the crises are from Herkner, "Krisen," *Handwörterbuch der Staatswissenschaft*, 2d ed., 5:427–33.

31. For the migratory movements of the laborers in England during these years, see Tugan-Baranovsky, op. cit., chaps. 7, 8 of part 2, and chaps. 4, 5 of part 3.

32. See the statistical tables related to emigration and immigration from and into the United Kingdom, in Philippovich, "Emigration from Various Countries of Europe," p. 28, passim; Herkner, op. cit.; Tugan-Baranovsky, op. cit.; Welby, "The Progress of the United Kingdom from the War of the French Revolution to 1913," *Journal of the Royal Statistical Society* (1915); and Schou, "The Statistics of the World's Foreign Commerce," *Journal of the Royal Statistical Society* (1900), pp. 329–30.

33. Philippovich, "Auswanderung," p. 244.

Years (ending June 1)		Number of immigrants	Imports (in millions of pounds)	Economic condition
1873		459,803	642	Thriving
1879	(1878)	177,826	437	Depression
1882		788,992	725	Thriving
1886	(1885)	334,203	578	Depression
1893		439,370	866	Thriving
1897	(1898)	230,832	616	Depression
1906		1,100,735	1,226	Thriving

States became very large beginning in the 1840s. It fell during the Civil War, but rose rapidly concomitantly with industrial expansion, up to the crisis of 1873. Under the influence of industrial depression, it fell sharply after that date, and only in 1880 was the depression overcome. In 1882 the volume of immigration reached an unprecedented size, but the depression of 1885–86 cut the number of immigrants in half. After that there was another rise until the great economic crisis of 1893 which greatly lowered the number of immigrants to a figure of only 229,229 persons in 1898. Another rise took place in 1907, when the figure reached 1,285,349. After the crisis of 1907 it again declined sharply.[34]

These figures indicate plainly that during the years of depression, the desire of people to immigrate declines, and that during those of prosperity it rises. Thus, we have confirmation of the theory of a direct connection between variations in hunger and food taxis, and movement from the regions where food is lacking to those where it is plentiful.

Finally, all these statements are well illustrated by migrations of people within Russia during the famine years of 1917–22. Here we have observed mass migration of people from towns, villages, and regions where starvation prevailed to places where food was to be found.

In 1920, and also in 1921–22, peasants from provinces along the Volga River, afflicted by crop failures, left their villages en masse, and in a way similar to medieval migrations, with no preconceived

34. Sartorius von Waltershausen, "Einwanderung," in *Handwörterbuch der Staatswissenschaft*, 3d ed., 3:769–70.

plan, migrated from regions of famine to those where food was available. Hunger forced them to leave their homes, and, along with their old people and children, to travel from place to place in the search of food, thus forming great disorganized hordes. The same phenomenon also was exhibited by the flow of population from the "hungry" regions toward the better supplied. For example, in 1918–19, the movement was to the Ukraine, the Don, and the Kuban regions. This outflow was expressed in different forms: by voluntary spontaneous migration with the permission of the authorities, by escape abroad to other countries, by planned movement of people despite prohibition by the authorities, and by planned transfer of workers to the Don region, which was considered to be counterrevolutionary and where there was plenty of food. The latter was done for the purpose of implanting there a "Red population" loyal to the government. In addition, various specialists in the service of the government, Red Army soldiers, nurses, doctors, etc., were eager to leave their famine-stricken northern provinces and migrate to the southern and southeastern provinces, which were rich in breadstuffs and other foods.

The trend of population between 1916 and 1921 in the cities where starvation prevailed also indicated the same tendency. I take for examples the populations of Moscow and of Petrograd, which decreased conspicuously from 1917 to 1920.[35] The figures show a colossal decrease of the population in our cities during these years. Even in 1918 it decreased by 40 per cent in Moscow regardless of the fact that the government moved there, while in Petrograd it decreased 50 per cent. This decrease was produced not only by mortality (from

Years	Population of Moscow	Population of Petrograd
1915	1,617,700	2,314,500
1916		2,415,700
1917 (February)	2,017,173	2,420,000
1917 (September 17)	1,854,426	
1918 (April 21)	1,716,022	1,469,000
1919		900,000
1920 (August 3)	1,023,000	740,000

35. *Krasnaya Moskva*, 1917–20, *Moscow Soviet Workers and Peasants Deputies*, p. 54, *Materials on the Statistics of Petrograd*, 1920 and 1921, Issue 1, no. 10; Issue 3, pp. 3–4; Issue 5, paper by S. A. Novoselsky (in Russian).

1917 to July 1920, only 226,417 people died in Petrograd, whereas the population decreased by 1,670,000), but mainly by migration of population due to lack of food.

During the famine of 1921,[36] migration of the population assumed tremendous dimensions. "The inhabitants of the regions along the Volga River are fleeing; they descend like an avalanche," we read in the papers even before the time of the great crop failure.[37] "A catastrophic migration of the starving population takes place. Whole villages move away from their homes."[38] "The hungry migration continues. They sell almost for nothing their belongings and go to the Ukraine, or to Siberia. Many villages become completely depopulated."[39]

The fact of emigration or immigration has a tremendous sociological importance in the development of the social processes within a starving group, as well as outside it. Emigration of population caused by hunger carries further a number of "secondary functions" which change the course of social life, the structure of the group, and the composition of the population. Some of these are listed.

1. Changes in the composition of the population of the group: the size of the group decreases with the increase of emigration. Hence, growth of the number of members of the group either weakens, or ceases.[40]

2. The age, sex, occupational, and economic compositions of the

36. This famine of 1921 and the plight of peasants of the afflicted districts of Samara and Saratov provinces (Volga region) were powerfully described by Pitirim Sorokin in his first book published in the United States, *Leaves from a Russian Diary* (New York: E. P. Dutton and Company, 1924). It has been reprinted by Kraus Reprint Co. (New York, 1970). Because I observed personally all these events, the only bright recollection of the period remains the help which the Hoover American Relief Administration brought to the millions of starving people. This help shall never be effaced from the memory of the Russians. E.S.

37. *Makhovik*, July 7, 1921.

38. *Krasnaya Gazeta*, July 7, 1921.

39. *Makhovik*, July 27, 1921.

40. See details in E. C. Hayes, *Introduction to the Study of Sociology* (1921), p. 267, passim; Ross, *The Principles of Sociology*, p. 10, passim; H. P. Fairchild, *Immigration;* Philippovich, *Auswanderung*, pp. 275–78; Fed. Chessa, "Le fenomeno dell'emigrazione in Italia," *Revista Italiana di sociologia* (1913), pp. 61–71.

population change more to the disadvantage of the group. Since more men emigrate than women, the people who are capable of working, more than the incapable (those under 15 and those over 60), the more energetic and enterprising people leave, rather than the opposite.

3. All of this affects the military capacity of the group, its productive energy in the area of economics, and also the intellectual and moral life, etc.

4. Emigration also is reflected in the biological composition of the group. During emigration the superior parts of the population leave, and those remaining become the progenitors of a future "second-class" generation.

5. The wealth of the country also is changed. When emigrants carry away with them their savings, do not send back their earnings, and do not return, the country obviously becomes poorer. The reverse takes place in the cases in which they do send back their earnings.

6. When emigrants return from foreign lands, they bring back new customs, new ideas, and new ways of thinking. Foreign elements of cultural and social life infiltrate the group, and this can produce either a positive or negative effect upon it, depending upon the "school of life" through which the emigrants have passed. Therefore, a "mixture of cultures, tribes, languages, and wealth" occurs. Often these effects cannot be observed immediately, but they become apparent when food taxis emigration from the group is frequent and considerable.

7. Emigrants also frequently cause a whole series of changes in the group to which they migrate. Changes take place in the composition of the population—age, sex, occupational, and economic (by an increase of available labor, growth of production, competition, import and export of wealth, etc.). Immigration leads to a mixture of customs, ideas, and blood in the population. It changes the military capacity of the country, populates new regions, and forms little islands of immigrants in the country receiving them, like Little Italy, or the German America. The famished immigrants, particularly, sometimes become disseminators of disease and epidemics; hence, they may produce a rise in mortality in the countries receiving immigrants, and a number of other phenomena.

Each of these secondary functions of starvation calls forth still other new functions.

Summary

1. When starvation becomes more intense and it is impossible to terminate it by some other means, emigration from regions afflicted by famine to regions where food is more plentiful becomes a general function of mass starvation.

2. Emigration, *ceteris paribus*, becomes larger the greater the number of starving people, the more intense the degree of starvation, the more prosperous the regions receiving immigration and the easier it is there to obtain means of subsistence, the shorter the distance spanned, and the less available are other means of covering the food deficit.

3. Hunger causes the occurrence of a series of other secondary functions. These include changes in the composition of the population and its qualities, natural mobility, the organization of society, and its anatomy and physiology.

8

HUNGER AND WAR

When peaceful emigration is for any reason impossible and is resisted by the population of the country to which the emigrants might go (as presently is true for the population of Russia), and when the deficit of food cannot be met by any other means, peaceful emigration is replaced by forced emigration-immigration, and war becomes a function of mass starvation. The hungry masses, attracted by the prosperity and the abundant food supplies of other countries, attempt to crash the barrier forcibly by war and pillage.

Ceteris paribus, this attempt is stronger the larger the starving group and the nearer it is to the apex of the curve of intensity of food taxis, the richer the population of the country they are invading, the shorter the distance involved, and the stronger the military power of the hungry group in comparison with that of the well-fed group.

As the consequence of such military immigration, or the threat of one, the following three events may occur: a preventive attack by the country that is well fed upon the one suffering from famine in order to impede the danger of invasion from the latter; counteraction by the well-supplied country against the wave of invasion from the hungry country, which results either in a bloody social struggle in the starving country, or in its "quiet expiration"; victory by the starving population and its conquest of the satiated country. This can be expressed in several different forms: the well-fed population, pursued by the hungry group, may retreat and press upon its other neighbors, who in turn may press further upon their neighbors, and as a result of this "a mass migration of peoples" may occur (indeed, such migrations took place many times in the history of Europe, Asia, and Africa);

oppressed on both sides, the well-fed group may be annihilated; and, finally, the well-fed group may become conquered by the hungry group.

In the last case, the well-fed group becomes the exploited one, whereas the starving group assumes the role of exploiter. (The Roman conquerers, and the peoples conquered by them, the Athenians and their victims, Islam and the people conquered by it are examples of this.) All this may occur in the form of aristocratic conquerors, who settle in the conquered country and become its rulers (the military colonies of Rome, Greece, the Aryans in India, etc.). Or it may take the form of conquerors who live outside the limits of the conquered country but who collect taxes from it and levy requisitions of food from it. (The history of the wars and the conquests in Persia, China, Islam, India, Rome, Greece, and Byzantium, those by the Turks, Mongols, and those in European countries is filled with such examples.) Finally, it may be expressed in the form of periodic raids to pillage and plunder the possessions of the well-fed countries.

Such are the most typical outbreaks of compulsory emigration due to food taxis. They are presented here in a somewhat schematized form, but they existed in the history of mankind, and they still exist at present.

We see that a simple "deficiency of calories" or "the deficient food metabolism" may cause the greatest social catastrophes. The invisible director hunger may stage on the scene of history the greatest tragedies, call forth torrents of blood, bring into action tanks, cannons, boomerangs, and spears, and create conquerors and conquered, exploiters and exploited, masters and slaves.

Hunger, or the threat of it, gives rise to war, when there are no other means of satisfying it, and war, in turn, gives rise to more hunger. These twins almost always are inseparable and they travel together all over the world.

Let us now consider in more detail this functional relationship. The numerous wars, from the days of Adam and up to our own times, which were caused either by actual hunger or the threat of it, or by the foresight of wise leaders who were considering future supplies of food for their people, all serve as a general proof of this relationship.

It is almost impossible to find in the entire history of mankind wars which directly or indirectly did not have the motivations mentioned. It is true that some causes other than hunger also have been involved in wars, but this does not rule out the important role of hunger. Furthermore, in almost all wars, and particularly in those of ancient times, hunger and the threat of it and the procurement of food for the population have played and still play the major role.

We can conclude, therefore, that in all the wars there is, on one side, the attempt to grab possessions, land, cattle, riches, industry, and other spoils from the enemy, and, on the other, the endeavor to protect one's own possessions from intruders. War is inseparable from annexations, imposts and levies, all sorts of plunder, and usually terminates with them. M. I. Rostovtzeff correctly reminds us that "the wars of antiquity" and particularly those connected with conquests had not so much a political purpose, but a commercial purpose of enriching all participants. The acquisition of the enemy's goods and the protection of one's own possessions were the main stimuli of war, and plunder its military action.[1] Such were the conditions in the past, and so they remain at present, except that at present the stimulus is veiled by highly "enlightened speech reactions" (about human rights, the preservation of culture, liberty, and justice, etc.). Even now we speak of "the war of liberation," but in reality we are faced in the Versailles treaty with the plunder of the conquered enemy and even of an ally—Russia.

All this is questionable. Truly, it may be said that possession and acquisition are not limited to food products or their equivalents. I do not deny this. But, looking at it from another point of view, we must keep in mind figures of income and expense. Even now 50 to 80 per cent of the income of the masses is spent for food and nutrient products. Therefore, 50 to 80 per cent of every acquisition through war or every defense of their own possessions is acquisition for nutrition, or the defense of the "right to be satiated." This has great significance during the present period of starvation, and was especially significant in the past when produce in the form of cattle and food supplies, cultivated fields, meadows, forests, rivers, etc., were the principal and almost sole forms of wealth.

This is why a thesis which attempts to prove the "commercial" character of every war simultaneously is proving another thesis, i.e., that war most frequently is the direct or indirect function of food taxis.

Thus, the wars of "primitive peoples," directly or indirectly, oc-

1. M. I. Rostovtzeff, *The Origin of the Roman Empire* (St. Petersburg, 1918), 2:11 (in Russian). See also Nicolai, *Biologie des Krieges*, pp. 34–35.

cur most frequently on the basis of food taxis, although the subjective ideology very often obscures the reality. Such are the encounters between groups of hunters resulting from violation of the limits of the hunting territory of one group by a group of invaders who have exhausted the game on their land and move in on that of their neighbors. M. M. Kovalevsky writes, "we find among the primitive people the factual defense of their regions from any intrusion from without. When the intrusion took the aspect of forceful appropriation of this region by the neighboring tribe, the counteraction took the form of an open war." [2] The constant wars which characterize hunting tribes were caused at the beginning by an increase in membership of the group, and by the food deficiency connected with it. According to the ancient rules of warfare, the conqueror acquires the right to all of the possessions of the enemy, regardless of the nature of the property and its location.[3] The Roman rule *Omnia in victoria lege belli licuerunt* always was and still remains a general rule.

The pastoral peoples showed the same tendencies. Here, the lack of means of subsistence led to the necessity to find new pastures for multiplying herds. These pastures could be obtained only by force through war and the subjugation of neighboring tribes.[4] Among pastoral peoples, raids on cattle were frequent. Not only disputes over pastures, but also cattle stealing often were reasons for hostile encounters, as we now can observe it among South American tribes, and as took place on the borders of Scotland a few generations ago. We learn also from the ancient books of the East that these things were the causes of their constant wars.[5] Similar conditions prevailed in ancient Germany, among the Incas of Peru, etc., where this tragedy and its variations took place earlier. The same can be said about the wars by white colonizers upon natives whom they deprived of land, cattle, and other sources of procuring food.[6] To this period, also, according to Tacitus, belong the wars for specific food products such as the terrible wars of the Germans for salt.

Let us leave the hunters and pastoral groups and consider the

2. M. M. Kovalevsky, *Sociology*, 2:138–39 (in Russian).

3. Herbert Spencer, *The Principles of Sociology* (New York: D. Appleton and Co., 1893), 2:547.

4. Westermarck, *The Origin and Development of Moral Ideas*, 2:26.

5. Kovalevsky, *Economic Growth of Europe*, vols. 1, 9 (in Russian).

6. See details in Steinmetz, *The Philosophy of War* (St. Petersburg: Ed. Obrazovanie, 1915) (in Russian).

so-called historical peoples. Here again we see pictures of endless wars, which took place from the days of Adam up to present times, the endless number of forced migrations, intrusions, and encounters. Who was their director? What were the causes? First of all, let us consider the deficiency and comparative deficiency types of starvation of the groups involved.

In ancient Egypt we note constant raids by nomadic Bedouins, who lived in barren lands, upon the settled agriculturists. We also see endless wars of the Egyptians with the Nubians and the Lydians, the stormy intrusion of the Hyksos (*ca.* 1800–1600 b.c.), the tremendous forced migration of the Assyro-Babylonians, which took place about 4000 b.c., those of the Canaanite-Amorites, of the Arameans, Arabs, etc. What caused all these invasions? Directly or indirectly, they were results of food taxis. Ancient documents prove that. In the first place, speaking about invading Lydians, ancient documents state that "they come to the land of Egypt because of food, they pass through the country fighting in order to fill their stomachs daily." [7] These sayings may serve as epigraphs to all Egyptian wars. The military spoils of the conquerors signify the same. Snofru boasted that he returned from Nubia with 7,000 prisoners of war and 200,000 head of cattle; Nar-Mer boasted of 142,000 small cattle and 400,000 oxen.[8] Furthermore, the Lagashi forced Ennagali "to pay the war levies in bread" and generally, "by the products of agriculture, particularly by the bread made of grain levied from the conquered neighbors." These facts indicate the real cause of the wars. Indirectly the same reason is indicated in the numerous wars "for the blossoming valleys, essential to Egypt" for the preservation and protection of the system of irrigation and the mines, which produce the equivalents for the acquisition of food. And what were the causes of the huge migrations? The ever increasing population of Arabia was always looking for a movement of its population to regions which were capable of maintaining them. From time to time this was expressed in large migrations which contributed the Semitic population to the neighboring northern and southern countries.[9] And what did

7. A work by Waitz is cited.
8. J. H. Breasted, *A History of the Ancient Egyptians*, 2d ed. (London, 1909).
9. Turaev, *History of the Ancient East* (St. Petersburg, 1913), 1:66, passim (in Russian).

the Hyksos do after they had conquered the country? They ruled the population with an iron fist, and forced the people to feed them. And in general how do wars terminate? By levies, by seizure of the possessions of the conquered, and by forcing the vanquished population to provide "food" or its equivalent.

Similar pictures are seen in the history of Assyro-Babylonia, Persia, Rome, and Greece. *The Iliad* and *The Odyssey* tell us that the main purpose of the raids and wars was seizure of cattle.[10] Thucydides relates that as soon as the Greeks learned navigation, they became pirates in order to obtain riches and bounty, i.e., directly, or indirectly, food. The colonization by the Greeks of Asia Minor, and also of other territories, which usually led to wars and was accompanied by them, was the function of a "relative overpopulation," of food deficiency. Sparta was an agricultural and inland kingdom and its leadership depended upon military superiority alone.[11] Because the economic basis of the ruling military class was landed property exclusively, the surplus of an increasing population had to be provided with new pieces of land (otherwise there would be starvation), and these tracts of land were outside the country. Hence follows "the mighty trend of the Greeks to migrate from their native land, which became too crowded for them." This was followed inevitably by conflicts and wars, e.g., the subjugation of fertile Messenia by Sparta, etc., which was followed by military "distribution of the population and the partition of the territory." [12] Conditions in Athens were similar. According to J. Beloch,[13] during the times of Pericles the density of population was equal to 89 persons per square kilometer, which surpasses the density of France today (73 persons) and that of a number of other European countries. The population could not be self-sustaining with the productive facilities existing in the country at

10. *The Iliad* (Gnedich, translator), 11:670–86; 18:525, passim (in Russian); *The Odyssey* (Zhukovsky, translator), 11:288–91, 400–402; 22:7–10; 24:110–12 (in Russian).

11. M. I. Rostovtzeff, *A History of the Ancient World* (Oxford: Clarendon Press, 1926), 1:263. (The Russian version was published in 1909. E.S.)

12. R. Pöhlmann, *Essays on Greek History and the Study of Sources* (St. Petersburg, 1908), pp. 33–34, 44, 183 (translation from Russian); R. Pöhlmann, *Geschichte der Sozialen Frage und des Sozialismus der antiken Welt*, vols. 1, 2 (1912); and Meyer, *Die Wirtschaft Entwicklung des Altertums*, 2:138, passim.

13. J. Beloch, *Griechische Geschichte*, 2d ed. (1912).

that time. (According to Levasseur, the density of the agricultural population, but not of the industrial, varies from 10 to 40 persons per square kilometer and any surplus population must either die, emigrate, or fight.) In Attica, therefore, 49 persons per kilometer were in excess of the norm, hence the necessity of either peaceful or military emigration, seizure of land, or war. "The country sustained only a limited number of people, and its history consisted in the continuous outflow of the population" as long as peaceful emigration existed.

During the later history of Athens, growth of population and weakening of peaceful emigration caused greater food deficits and, connected with this, an increase in the number of wars. The maximum density of population in Attica was reached in the fifth and fourth centuries B.C. During the same centuries Athens witnessed endless wars. The deficit produced by the wars was easily made up by "the fast-growing number of slaves, who restricted still further the means of subsistence for the free population." This resulted in the strong wave of the emigration to Asia beginning with the period of Alexander. The conquests of Alexander were the direct functions of food deficiency. The density of the population had decreased in the third and second centuries B.C. During the time of Polybius the towns became empty because of low birth rates and scarcity of people. "The Roman rule, which began in 197 B.C. brought back peace and economic well-being." And what do we see? There were no wars, at least none of long duration and significance. The pressure of food taxis had decreased, and concomitantly there was a fall in the frequency curve of wars. This connection is expressed more clearly in an inscription [14] on the founding "of one of the colonies on the shore of the Adriatic Sea in 325 B.C. The inscription mentions that the Athenians desire to have their own Adriatic Sea and places from where they could receive their own bread." [15] The concern about food was the primary purpose here. To secure the safety of the ship transporting bread it was accompanied by warships and the harbor was fortified. When six warships of Sparta were lying to at Keos, Aegina, and Andros,

14. E. Meyer, *The Population of Antiquity*, in the Narodonaselenie Collection (Moscow, 1897), pp. 50–53 (in Russian); B. Niese, *Geschichte der Griechischen und Makedonischen Staaten* (Gotha, 1903), pt. 3, pp. 9–11; Levasseur, "La répartition de la race humaine," pp. 61–63.

15. Novosadsky, "The Struggle against High Prices in Ancient Greece," *Journal of the Ministry of Public Education* (Petrograd, 1917) (in Russian).

Chabrias gave battle to them in order that the food products could be delivered to Epirus.[16]

The endless wars with the barbarians, with the Persians, the struggle between Sparta and Athens for hegemony—were they not connected to a great extent with the struggle for booty and food, for the "right" to seize the belongings of other people, to subjugate populations and to force them to feed the conquerors? This was done by the 20,000 Athenians, who exploited many groups and peoples, and who turned the whole state into a simple business enterprise. Some of these wars were caused directly by the food crises, and others were caused partially and indirectly by them, but there was hardly any war in which this "independent variable" did not figure.[17]

Similar conditions existed during the Roman colonizations and in connection with most of Rome's foreign and civil wars. Lack of food forced the citizens of the "eternal city" to emigrate, to colonize, and to invade more and more new regions; it forced Rome to conquer Sicily, Egypt, and other countries with food reserves. The same cause led it to the conflicts with enemies, be they Carthage or the Mithridates of Pontus. The Roman army was a plundering, requisitioning organization; the Roman war leaders were mercenary *condottieres*. The soldiers were attracted by booty in the form of property of the conquered enemy, in the form of secure rations from the government, in the form of land distributed to both soldiers and citizens. The methods used to get enlistments by Marius, Sulla, Anthony, Caesar, Pompey, Octavian, etc., were very characteristic and typical. During the procedure very definite promises were made in respect to the booty, to the prizes, and to the increases in pay (*emerita stipendia*). These promises always insured the success of the call. The soldiers and the legionnaires shifted to the highest bidder.[18]

Simple calculations of the population of Italy and Rome and of the space they occupied indicates that hunger gave its ultimatum early and quite clearly: either die, or fight, or colonize. According to the census of Servius Tullius, Italy had 80,000 citizens. In A.D. 225 the

16. Böckh, *Die Staatshaushaltung der Athener*, 1:115–16.

17. W. Drumann, *Die Arbeiter und Communisten in Grieschenland und Rom* (Königsberg, 1860), pp. 50–53.

18. Wipper, *The History of the Roman Empire* (Moscow, 1908), pp. 10–18, 20, 36–37, 78 (in Russian); G. Ferrero, *Greatness and Decline of Rome* (Moscow, 1916), 3:115–16, 130, 137, 141–43, 155, 179 (in Russian).

census showed that the free population of Rome was 900,000 people, and that of Italy 2.7 million (slaves and unfree people excluded). Rome occupied at that time 22,700 square kilometers, and the area of all Italy was 198,700 square kilometers. Therefore, for each free person in Rome there was 0.025 square kilometer, and for all of Italy about 0.07 square kilometer. According to the computations of Levasseur, the maximum population during the agricultural epoch fluctuated between 0.1 and 0.025 square kilometer per person. Because of the low state of technology and productivity in Italy and Rome, they were already overpopulated at that time. In addition, if one takes into consideration 1.5 million slaves, then the overpopulation becomes indisputable. Hence, the increased deficiency of food demanded colonization, wars, and seizures. Later on in Roman history this necessity became more acute. Such is the main key for the understanding of the military growth of the Roman Empire.[19]

On the eve of the Middle Ages we encounter a great migration of the population. Where did it come from? "The cause of it was the drought, which even now still continues to be the main reason of emigration [hunger followed this and thus resulted in the necessity of migration. P.S.]. When the inhabitants of North West Mongolia and of Eastern Turkestan saw that the water was leaving them, they had no choice, but to descend to the lower plains and to drive to the East the inhabitants of those regions." [20] The emigrating population caused further migration by the former inhabitants of the region into which they moved, etc. Thus a historical "square dance" of migrating nations took place in the history of Europe and caused serious disruption of the states and organizations for the next two or three centuries.

In the later history of Europe it is difficult to find a war in which the necessities of *boire et manger* did not play a role. Be it the invasion of the Normans, or the conquest of England by William the Conqueror (the stimuli of the former were pillage and plunder, and the same is true even of the latter, as is obvious from the seizure and division of land by the conquerors immediately after the conquest), or the Crusades (which, as we have seen, took place at a time of

19. E. Meyer, op. cit., pp. 53–64; Pöhlmann, *Die Uberbevölkerung der Antiken Grosstädte* (1884).

20. Levasseur, " La répartition de la race humaine," pp. 61–62; E. Meyer, "Bevölkerung des Altertums," *Handwörterbuch der Staatswissenschaft*, 3d ed., 2:905–9.

unprecedented starvation in the countries afflicted by famine and which participated in plunder and robbery).[21]

The stormy conquests of the Islamic movement during and after the time of Mahomet were directly connected with the overpopulation of the plateau terrain of the Arabian peninsula. In Medina the needs of the followers of Mahomet increased steadily, so that it became very difficult to feed them. Under such conditions one Arab would steal from a neighbor anything he lacked. Hence followed Mahomet's first robberies of the caravans. Rich booty (which usually was divided among the participants) served as an attraction which could not be resisted. This was one of the reasons for the occurrence and success of the Islamic wars. "Because plentiful booty was always provided, the community of Mahomet was easily reconciled to the idea of war." [22]

Even during the religious wars, which were carried on under the banner *ad majorem gloriam Dei*, property and possessions of the enemy were confiscated at once. During the colonization of the territory east of the Elba River by the Germans, who came from provinces afflicted by hunger, the old method of securing soldiers was the same: they were promised the conquered land. In almost any of the subsequent endless series of wars we can recognize the presence of our invisible director—fluctuations in and lowering of nutritional levels of the masses, and its consequence in the form of forced emigration and war.[23]

Let us turn now to the history of Russia and observe the raids by people of one region upon those of another. What for? For plunder and booty. The Vikings robbed the Slavs, one tribe of Slavs robbed another, the inhabitants of Novgorod robbed the northern people, the Polovets and the Pechenegs robbed the Slavs and vice versa, the Tartars invaded and collected taxes from the Slavs, and so on. All of

21. During the Middle Ages "war was a very profitable occupation." In the Holy Land knights appeared who were in search of wealth, and merchants who were looking for profit. The Crusades owed their success to these people. Laviss and Rambo, *The Epoch of the Crusades* (Moscow, 1914), 1:53, 324 (in Russian).

22. A. Muller, *The History of Islam* (St. Petersburg, 1895), 1:8, 19, 119, 121, 138, 162, 310, passim (in Russian); Bartold, *Islam* (1918), p. 30 (in Russian); Hammer, *Über die Länderverwaltung unter der Chalifate* (1835), p. 96, passim.

23. Curschmann, *Hungersnöte im Mittelalter*, pp. 51–55, 62–68.

these wars depict in almost pure form the role of actual hunger or the threat of it. Irrespective of the labels attached to the cause of war, such as "religious causes," "in the name of the socialism or communism," "in the name of the dynasties," etc., the disturbance of the food metabolism of any social group which participates in such a "noble" military enterprise plays almost a dominant role in all wars of this kind. In certain cases this determinant has represented the main cause of the war, in other cases it was only one of many causes.[24] The object of wars and of the struggle for existence is nutrition, and therefore, the struggle for existence can be called the struggle for food.[25]

The recent world war [the First World War. E.S.] and the Russian civil war are no exceptions. According to the "speech reactions" the causes of this world war were far removed from deficiency or comparative-deficiency starvation. True, in their speeches the Germans frequently mentioned "the necessity to find a place under the sun" as the basis for the war, thus indicating the necessity to increase their food and, correspondingly, their colonies; while some other nations were mentioning everything but hunger or the threat of it as the cause of the war. Here the speeches were concerned mostly with the fight for freedom, the right of self-determination, liberation of the oppressed, etc.

The treaty of Versailles dissipated all these wordy illusions and showed the actual cause of the war. All high-sounding words were forgotten; as we know now, Germany would have acted in a similar way if it had been victorious.

Such is the unquestionable evidence which indicates that the real cause of the war was the problem of *boire et manger*, and not the fancy words about freedom and equal rights. We come to the same conclusions if we consider the problem from a different point of view.

It is well known that during the nineteenth century the population of Europe, and of some other countries of the world, increased very fast. The population of Europe almost doubled in 60–70 years,

24. Otlet considered that out of 286 major wars from the time of Constantine, 124 had economic causes: P. Otlet, *Les problemes internationaux et la guerre* (Genève, Paris, 1916), pp. 31–33. These figures are questionable, but even they indicate the high percentage of wars caused by food factors.

25. See more details in Nicolai, *Biologie des Krieges*, pp. 171–213.

Increase in Number of Inhabitants per Square Kilometer,
1820–1903 [26]

Country	1820	1840	1860	1880	1890	1900	1903
Germany	49.1	61.2	70.4	83.7	96.5	104.2	112.1
Austria	47.0	56.0	61.0	73.7	79.6	87.2	—
France	56.5	63.2	67.8	71.2	72.5	72.6	73.2
Italy	64.9	80.5	91.2	96.0	—	113.3	—
England, Wales	79.9	105.3	132.8	71.1	192.0	215.3	—
Sweden	5.7	6.9	8.5	10.1	10.6	11.5	—
Belgium	—	138.3	151.3	187.4	206.0	227.3	—
Switzerland	—	—	60.6	69.0	73.3	80.5	—
Netherlands	—	87.8	100.8	121.6	138.7	154.3	—

and in certain countries it tripled. The table of increases in density of population may give some idea.

The populations of other countries also increased. The question arises, did the production of foodstuffs in Europe increase correspondingly? Certainly not! Most European countries (with the exception of Russia, Hungary, Roumania, Bulgaria, and Serbia) import nutritive products because they do not produce them in sufficient quantity.[27] Even when European countries export foodstuffs, it is usually connected with the decrease of the nutritional norms of the population. Europe generally is not self-sufficient in nutritive products and must import food from non-European countries and colonies.

Prior to the war was the amount of food which was produced sufficient for the world as a whole? According to the calculations of Hardy and Yves Guyot, if the total world food production was equally distributed, the ration of proteins available for each individual would be short by one-third of the standard recognized as sufficient to produce efficiency.[28]

Yves Guyot also studied the size of the population of the earth

26. H. Rauchberg, "Bevölkerungsstatistik," *Handwörterbuch der Staatswissenschaft*, 3d ed., 2:880.

27. See figures in Webb, *A New Dictionary of Statistics;* N. Kondratiev and Nikitin, eds., *World Agriculture* (Moscow, 1922) (in Russian).

28. J. O. Bland, "Population and Food Supply," *Edinburgh Review*, vol. 227, no. 464 (April 1918), p. 247.

in 1902–4 and the amount of food produced. He came to the conclusion that notwithstanding the progress of agriculture, there is not a sufficient amount of food produced on the earth as a whole. He considered as a norm the ration of the French soldier, which was equal to about 1 kilogram of bread and 300 grams of meat per day. Instead of 300 grams of meat, only 133 grams per person were available, and thus there was a deficit of 167 grams. With respect to wheat, only 91.6 kilograms per year could be made available per adult, only one-fourth of the normal ration of a French soldier.[29]

Similar findings are given by Crooks and some others who investigated the increase of the cost of living before the war.[30] Europe, as a whole, was not self-sufficient in nutritive products: it did not produce, and it is not now producing, enough bread or meat. The deficits have been covered by imports from other parts of the world, the Americas, Asia, etc. Hence, the importance of having colonies on other continents becomes paramount for a number of European countries. These colonies serve not only as markets, but also as the source of food products, without which the European countries cannot exist. This explains why countries like Great Britain and Germany are interested in colonies, and why the struggle for colonies was one of the main reasons for the world war.

Furthermore, if we were to take the world production of all principal foodstuffs before the war and consider that they were equally distributed, we would not be able to indicate a surplus of food. An average yearly production of the principal food products for the whole earth for the years 1908–12 is shown in millions of tons:[31] barley, 33; rye, 57; oats, 65; rice, 85; wheat, 106; corn, 128; potatoes, 161.

29. Yves Guyot, "The Bread and Meat of the World," *Quarterly Publication of the American Statistical Association* 9 (September–December 1904): 79–119.

30. V. Crooks, *The Bread Question* (Moscow, 1909) (in Russian); Glier, "Die Preiskurve und das Teuerungsproblem," *Zeithschrift fur Socialwissenschaft*, nos. 7, 8 (1914); Zalts, "The Increase in the Price of Bread on the World Market," *New Ideas in Economics*, no. 4, pp. 123–25 (in Russian). According to Zalts, 858 million double tsentners of wheat were consumed whereas only 839 were produced in 1905; 482 million of rye were consumed and only 382 million produced. The deficit was covered by use of supplies stored in 1904, stores accumulated as a result of starvation of some populations.

31. The reference to the sources is defective, and it is impossible to verify them. E.S.

Thus, the total amount of all bread grains was equal to 474 million tons, and of potatoes to 161 million tons. If we were to exclude the use of these products for other industrial and agricultural purposes (beer and wine making, cattle feed, etc., which require a considerable proportion of the total) and, furthermore, consider the total global population as equal to 1.6 billion, we get the figure of approximately 18 pud [32] per person in the form of bread, cereals, gruels, etc., and about 6 pud of potatoes. In Europe the average consumption of bread in 1901–5 was 20.7 pud per person. [33] The per capita figures decreased still more by 1907–11, and they indicate beyond doubt that before the war the population of the world was not self-sufficient in nutritive products.

Europe was more or less well fed, so that the nutritional deficit must have been covered by some other countries. A number of non-European countries exported breadstuffs to Europe, not because they had surpluses, but because of the undernourishment of their own populations. The same can be said about European countries such as Russia, Serbia, and Bulgaria, which exported breadstuffs. Under such circumstances the struggle for edibles has to increase. Still greater were the deficiencies of meat, sugar, fats, etc., the more delicate food products. As I have already said, the struggle for colonies and its intensification were directly or indirectly connected with nutrition.

Neither importation nor emigration could help overcome the deficiency of food in the world as a whole, since importation from and emigration to other planets in space are not available as yet. The rate of inventions and of making improvements in the means for procuring essential foods were still slower than the rate of population growth. The only help available was a decrease in the number of people. And this inevitability would occur either through extinction by starvation, by epidemics, by bloody wars, or a combination of all of these. Thus we see the inevitability of war and a quite sufficient reason for it. There were definite signs indicating its approach, one of which was the increase in the cost of living. Thoughtful observers pointed out already several years before the war the increasing pressure of the population upon their means of nutrition, indicating also the re-

32. A pud is equal to 40 pounds. E.S.
33. Computed according to the figures by Pervushin, "Consumption," in Grant's *Encyclopedia*, 33:161–62 (in Russian).

tardation of the growth of agricultural efficiency, regardless of the capital and labor which were introduced. Agricultural productivity did not increase in proportion to the increase of labor, hence, the continuous rise in the cost of agricultural products during the last years before the war.[34]

Bland is correct in saying that the cause of such increase in the cost of nutritive products depends upon the fact that the demand exceeds the supply. The growth of the world price is conditioned by the growth of the density of population, higher standards of living, and by the relative decrease in size and productivity of agriculture.[35]

Hence follow high density and relative overpopulation, the "need for a place under the sun," and war. It matters not for history who fights whom, because history is concerned with the final result of bringing into equilibrium the disturbed balance of food consumption by the population. A decrease of population is the most logical way of achieving this. Indeed history has accomplished this by means of wars, revolutions, epidemics, famines, decreases in birth rate, and increases in death rate. The invisible director, hunger, has done his duty, and still continues to perform it. War is created by him, if not exclusively, then predominately.[36] Malthus must triumph, not in the details of his theory, but in its essentials.

"Imperialism," "the struggle for the straits," "for colonies," "for mines," "for freedom of the seas," for "annexation and contributions" —all these realistic reasons for wars are partial manifestations of their fundamental cause, namely, the deficiency of nutritive products and the struggle for food.

The same reason forced the 76 million people of Japan, pressed into small islands and without a secure food supply, to expand their "place under the sun" without which they were threatened with annihilation. Hence followed the attacks against China, Russia, and the spheres of influence of the United States of America and its "imperialism." There is no doubt that in the future this overpopulation

34. Bland, op. cit., pp. 246–47. The increase in the cost of nutritive products during the last decade was experienced all over the world. The price of grain rises in all parts of the world; the high prices are general. See Glier, op. cit., p. 521.

35. Bland, op. cit., p. 247.

36. See the editorial "War and Population," *The Edinburgh Review* (July 1920).

will cause new wars, as it already has caused the 1905 conflict with Russia.

In the light of these statements many problems of the Russian civil war become clarified.

All that was said above substantiates this thesis: in the absence of other means for covering a nutritional deficit, if emigration is impossible, and if there are well-fed groups near to a population that is starving, the most frequent function of hunger is war in one form or another.

Let us now investigate this problem from a somewhat different point of view. Instead of using governments as a frame of reference, we now consider the aggregates of population as the units. On one side are the aggregates which do not produce food, or produce it only in a minimal quantity, and on the other are those which are mainly occupied in the production of food. To the first group belong the populations of the large towns; to the second group belong the populations of villages and farms.

The question arises as to the ways in which populations of towns have secured delivery of food. For contemporary towns, which are not only centers of consumption but manufacturing centers as well, the problem has been solved in a simple way by importing food in exchange for the industrial products of the town. The development and convenience of means of transportation under normal conditions makes this quite a simple task. This applied also in part to the towns of the Middle Ages which were small (from 2,000 to 25,000) and in which the artisans produced sufficient goods to exchange for imported food products.[37]

When the city does not produce any equivalents and is solely a consuming center, then entirely different effects become apparent. Its population must eat, and there is nothing to exchange with the village. So what happens? Since other ways are almost completely lacking, war, plunder, and the exploitation by the town of the rural agricultural population begins in the form of raids by city detachments, in the form of subjugation and imposition of levies, in the form of various measures and laws to exploit the rural population and secure the

37. See Bücher, *The Development of Agriculture*, vol. 2, chaps. 10–12; Inama-Sternegg, "Bevölkerung der Mitterlalters," *Handwörterbuch der Staatswissenschaft*, 3d ed., 2:882–98.

delivery of food to the city. These conditions existed in the past and they exist now when the towns experience the described needs. So it was in the ancient East, Egypt, Assyro-Babylonia, Greece, Rome, during several centuries of history, and at the present time in the USSR.

As Bücher indicates, the typical ancient town was despotic. The burdensome duty which was imposed on the conquered tribes filled the storehouses of the potentate and fed the court retainers and the lesser people attached to them who were numbered in the thousands. From time to time new campaigns brought additional revenue. From the economic point of view such a town was strictly consuming. The leader of such a tribe subjugated many other tribes and became the ruler over them. Such a town became the center of exploitation, and had the army as its power. Its method of supplying the people with the necessary nutrient deficit was by plundering the conquered rural population, and by endless oppression.[38]

Similar conditions prevailed in Athens and in a number of other Greek cities. Neither Attica nor Athens was self-sufficient in bread and other products of agriculture. The deficit was covered partially by emigration, importations, and exchange for the equivalents, but mainly by plunderings, seizures, wars, and compulsory diplomatic ways. The existence of such multitudes of people was possible only because the Athenians had transferred their leadership in the Athenian league into a hegemony over hundreds of towns and islands which were obliged to pay duty (i.e., to feed them. P.S.). The Athenian population thus became the owner of a huge estate, and over 20,000 people received their maintenance from this source, i.e., from the conquered and exploited population.[39]

Rome also was not self-sufficient, especially during half of the period of the republics. The population of Rome had no independent incomes. There was nothing to use in payment for food, but they had to live. Hence, Rome's wars of conquest became a necessity. The population of Rome made good use of their position as leaders; the rich made their fortunes utilizing their positions, and from the state the poor received "bread and entertainment" (and many other things— P.S.). More than two-thirds of the inhabitants of the cities received free bread. Rome and, later on, Constantinople founded their econo-

38. Bücher, *Agriculture*, pp. 122–23 and chap. 10.
39. Ibid., p. 128; see also details in Böckh, op. cit., passim.

mies on the natural collection of duty from the provinces (which had either been conquered or pacified). "This was a communistic-imperial economy, the like of which the world had not seen" (but we see it now). "The productive labor of half the world was put at the disposal of the capital city." The same took place in other provincial towns of the Roman Empire.[40]

Thus, we see that Mr. Hunger also had created here continuous wars, oppression, and exploitation.

The situation was somewhat similar with the medieval feudal lords who by armed might collected into their storehouses that which they did not sow or harvest.

In the medieval Italian city-states conditions were somewhat similar. The interests of the rural population, who were obliged by the law of the republic to deliver to the town all the bread they produced, were certainly sacrificed in favor of the urban population.[41]

In France, in the eighteenth century and earlier, the regulation of the trade in bread was a sequence of the "relationship between the town and the country. The people of the towns considered the peasants as a hostile force, and tried by all means to disarm them and to take things away from them once the peasants reached the town walls. Such is the meaning of all the regulations which require the peasants to sell their produce cheaply on the town market." [42]

Since under equal conditions similar causes produce similar consequences, the cities of the USSR in our time ceased to be centers of production and became solely centers of consumption. In 1918–21 they had nothing to give in exchange for produce. We ourselves may confirm almost daily the connection between hunger and the struggle which it produces. Who has not witnessed the numerous quarrels, fights, and conflicts during the irregular distribution of the food rations? Who does not know the hatred for the people with "privileged rations"? And the numerous guerrilla bands (Zelionykh) who plunder villages and farms, trains and transports, to obtain bread, do not they represent the fact that hunger motivates war? The answer is "yes."

The preceding facts explain to us the mechanism of the functional

40. Bücher, *Agriculture*, pp. 189–90.

41. M. Kovalevsky, "The Measures Employed by the Italian Republics in Their Fight against Starvation," p. 368 (in Russian).

42. Afanasiev, *The Conditions of the Food Trade in 18th-Century France*, p. 445, passim.

relationship between hunger and war. We have seen that during starvation some conflicting determinants of behavior and their reflexes are weakened, but those which help to satisfy hunger are either formed or strengthened. "Peaceful behavior," which leads to starvation, prevents satisfaction, *ergo*, it must be suppressed. Food taxis leads the person toward the food stored by another person, and the corresponding reflexes increase accordingly. As a result the most peaceful individual may become a fighter-oppressor because the well-fed people do not willingly give him a share of the food. When there are no other ways to cover the food deficit, the same phenomenon, taken in a larger scale, produces war, plundering, seizures, and other sharp forms of conflict between larger or smaller aggregates, in the manner similar to individual conflicts.

Since under indicated conditions mass starvation initiates wars, the latter in turn call forth a series of further important social events, which represent the social functions of hunger of the secondary, tertiary, etc., degrees. These functions are very important: (1) changes in the composition of the population, in its character, and in the natural mobility called forth by "the military selection"; (2) changes in the organization of the society; (3) changes in the social processes.

With regard to the first of these, the principal effects of war are as follows. War decreases population by eliminating from life the best elements of the society in preference to the worst. These groups are the first to be called to arms: population aged 18 to 48, those most capable of working, while old people and children remain; the healthiest biologically, since the cripples, the blind, the deaf, and the sick are not drafted; the people who are best in the moral and social sense, since criminals and anti-social elements are not drafted, and cowards and people without social responsibility evade the draft; men but not women; the most gifted, talented, and energetic, those people who are considered by the enemy as dangerous.

War produces a reverse selection, by eliminating the best elements and encouraging the worst. "Give us the best" was the war cry of the Romans. Truly, war takes and kills the first-rate material, the best blood of the country. It does not produce, but it "carries away the heroes," leaving behind human material of second- and third-rate qualities.[43]

43. See P. A. Sorokin, "The Effects of War on the Composition of the Population and on Social Organization," *The Economist*, vol. 1 (1921) (in

The human material of the warring community is degraded and worsened. The "worst people" who would have been in the background in the competition with the "best" under normal conditions are now pushed forward, survive, and come to occupy the top places. In this respect war is somewhat similar to a farmer who pulls out the useful plants and leaves the weeds to grow. Furthermore, according to the laws of heredity, the worst elements not only survive but also become progenitors of the future generations. Thus, not only the best elements themselves, but also their progeny perish. According to a correct observation of Franklin, the real payment for the war comes after the war, one or two generations after, in the form of the progeny of the "worst" elements.

The more warlike a society, the more it is degenerating, and the noble features of humanity are pushed out by the weeds, who are less healthy, of shorter stature, weaker, more criminal, less gifted and energetic, and possessed of less will.[44]

In the last analysis, those people who fight often and very hard decline and weaken much faster than those who, contrary to general belief, do not fight, or fight very little: they live longer, and become stronger even in the military sense. The original racial stock of the Romans and Greeks was splendid. Hence the colossal energy exhibited by these people during the early history of Greece and Rome, their miracles of bravery, of duty, of ingenuity, of brain power, and their colossal achievements in the fields of science, arts, techniques, politics, etc., which until the present time have not been attained by many nations. But the more they fought, the more their best elements perished, leaving the worst to inherit the upper positions and to become masters of the situation. As a result decadence was inevitable. We see that Greece began to decline after the Persian and Peloponnesian wars, and the same happened to Rome after the Carthaginian and the civil wars. From the end of the republic Rome increased its possessions very little and began to be more on the defense; but the wars continued, deteriorating the remainder of the "best blood" and the star of Rome began to decline.[45]

Russian); Novikov, *Les luttes entre société humain* (Paris, 1901), p. 15; and Nicolai, op. cit.

44. L. Darwin, "On the Statistical Inquiries Needed after the War in Connection with Eugenics," *The Eugenics Review*, 12:159–89.

45. Rostovtzeff, *Origin of the Roman Empire*, pp. 28–29, 38–41, 42, 104, passim (in Russian). (M. I. Rostovtzeff, *A History of the Ancient World*,

The vigorous Arabian race, which blossomed for two centuries, later exhausted itself rapidly because of continuing wars. In 1905 Japan defeated Russia not because it had warred much before, but because for about 250 years it had had no big wars and was in the period called the "big peace," while the Russians were continuously occupied with wars. The United States also developed fast its potential powers, because it did not have too many wars. At the present time the most powerful states are those which have fought the least (Japan, the United States, England, which was always concerned about its own human material, and sent to war mostly other nations, the allies, and the population of the colonies). The world war and the wars of the revolution completely degraded Russia. Despite the large population, Russia now is so weak that even Poland can defeat it.

Furthermore, war, being the opposite of peaceful life, changes the quality and the reflexes of the surviving nations. During peaceful times the reflexes of murder, oppression, bestiality, robbery, swindling, and destruction are inhibited, while war tends to develop them, considering such qualities as heroic. Peace develops initiative, personal freedom, productive work, and war calls forth unquestioning subordination and discipline, limits initiative, detracts labor from productive work, and encourages destructive activities; the former also strengthens the moral and legal reflexes, respect for the individuals, their rights and property, whereas the latter stimulates the opposite characteristics. Therefore, impoverishment, bestiality, etc., are the common correlates of war.[46]

Some naïve people think that the acts which we perform pass away without leaving a trace. This is wrong. They are changing our whole being, and particularly so the acts which are induced by war. Hence it would be a real miracle if the murderer and beast of war-

---

vol. 2, chap. 24, "The decline of ancient civilization," pp. 351–66 [Oxford: Clarendon Press, 1926]. This edition in English contains the earlier material of the Russian edition. E.S.) O. Seeck, *Geschichte des Unterganges der antiken Welt;* Fahlbeck, "La décadence et la chute des peuples," *Bulletin Institut International de Statistique*, vol. 15, nos. 1–2, pp. 367–89; C. Gini, *Fattori demografici dell'evoluzione della nazioni* (1912); Vassilief, *The Problem of the Fall of the Eastern Roman Empire* (1921) (in Russian).

46. See the economic consequences of the late war in N. Kondratiev, "Changes of the World's Agricultural Economies during the War," *Vestnik Selskogo Khoziaistwa*, nos. 6–7 (1922) (in Russian).

time should not remain the same after the war is over. Indeed, it would be a miracle if the denial of man's life, values, rights, property, and possessions, which are encouraged by war, would not appear after the war. It would be strange if raw force, destructive instincts, and ignoring of moral and legal rights did not appear after the war. Therefore, if after the big wars we encounter a rise in the curve of criminality, numerous bands of pillagers, monstrous destructive acts by the masses, the weakening and deterioration of rights, decrease of peaceful labor, speculation and deceit, riots, seizures, lack of respect for private property, and general bestiality, we have to look for one of their causes, namely, war.

In the field of social life war changes "the normal mobility of the population" of the countries involved in the war by lowering marriage and birth rates and increasing the death rate.[47]

Such are the functions of war in respect to the composition of population, its qualities, and its natural mobility.

The functions of war are equally impressive in the field of social organization. Once the composition and quality of the population has changed, inevitably the structure of society and its social organization also must change. A society of devils is different from one of angels. The principal effect of the war in this respect is that, *ceteris paribus*, it centralizes, militarizes, and makes social organization uncontrollable by law, thus converting the entire society into a camp or military barracks, into one military commune under absolute dictatorial power and with the population devoid of any rights. The barracks and the military organization are schools for absolute obedience. The soldier does not have his own will; he must perform his orders blindly and without any hesitation. He is merely a tool which is being operated

---

47. See J. W. Nixon, "War and National Vital Statistics with Special Reference to the Franco-Prussian War," *Journal of the Royal Statistical Society* 79 (July 1916):418–44; J. Athelstane Baines, "The Recent Trend of Population in England and Wales," *Journal of the Royal Statistical Society* 79 (July 1916):399–418; Döring, "World War I and the Natural Mobility of the Population," *Vestnik Statistiki* (1920), nos. 5–8 (in Russian); N. A. Novoselsky, "The War and the Natural Mobility of the Population," *Obshchestvennyi Vrach* (January 1915) (in Russian); Novoselsky, "The Influence of War on the Natural Mobility of Population," ibid.; and A. B. Wolfe, "Economic Conditions and the Birth Rate after the War," *Journal of Political Economy* 25 (June 1917):521, passim.

by the power above; he has no initiative, and he does not control his own life.

War inflicts all these features on the whole social organization. The rights and dimensions of power (Romanovs, Frederick the Second, Cromwell, Napoleon, Peter the Great, "The Committee of Salvation," or "The Secret Council" are all the same; these are only the signs) become tremendously enlarged. They begin to interfere in everything. The population becomes, in the hands of this power, a body deprived of rights. Freedom is eliminated, protests are suppressed, and self-determination is denied. A real military "communization" of society, in the sense of its centralization, of despotism, makes a colossal leap upward, and increases further with the continuation of the war.[48]

Thus, centralism, despotism, and forced state control are the inevitable functions of war. Those who work for war work to facilitate these things. The actual great creators of military socialism have been the great warriors, the militarists, and the conquerors.

Finally, the change in the composition of the population and in its organization leads, naturally, toward colossal changes in all of the social processes, in all fields—economic, genetico-reproductive, political, moral, legal, religious, aesthetic, intellectual, and scientific. I am not going to describe these changes in detail, and shall restrict myself to stating that all the "physiology and psychology" of the social organism is changing. All of its processes begin to function in a different manner, and in a way that is far from being beneficial for the society from the biological and psycho-social point of view. If the war lasts for a long time and is exhaustive, society is stricken with a grave disease which brings it to its doom.

Such are in brief the social functions of hunger of the "secondary order." They give rise to war, and war, in turn, promotes them. Furthermore, each of the latter functions, also in turn, gives rise to other new functions. Here again we see how hunger may cause ripples in the sea of social events, not unlike the great circles produced by a stone that is thrown into the clear mirror of the ocean of history.

48. See the excellent theory of Herbert Spencer, *Principles of Sociology*, 2:547–82; P. Sorokin, *A System of Sociology*, 2:135–37 (in Russian); and P. Sorokin, "The War and Military Socialism," *Artel'noe Delo* (1922) (in Russian).

Conclusions

1. During a period of starvation or the threat of it, in a society, and if it is impossible to cover the food deficit by some other means, and also if there are neighboring groups that are well supplied, the main result of hunger, or the threat of it, is war. This war occurs as a result of the forced emigration of the starving people, and from their attempts by force to colonize the country and to seize supplies of food (produce, cattle, land, pastures, etc.) or their equivalents to the detriment of the well-fed groups.

2. The phenomena of war are more likely to occur, the greater the number of people who are starving, the nearer in degree that starvation is to the maximum, the less are other means available of covering the deficit, the greater the contrasts between the group and its neighbors in wealth and food supply, and the stronger the military force of the starving aggregate.

3. Wars may have different forms (sporadic raids, pitched battles, permanent wars) and terminations: annihilation of well-fed groups, and other groups as well, their expulsion from a given habitat, their dying out, their subjugation, and exploitation; vice versa, the same may occur to the starving groups, if they are weak militarily.

4. This is substantiated by the history of wars in general which were caused mainly by hunger and by the necessity of procuring food along with some other factors; by the rise in the number of wars during periods of increasing scarcity of food and the decrease in them as the emergency decreases; by the history of the relationship of the unproductive towns to the villages, beginning in the days of Adam and coming down to the present time; by the absolute deficiency in the world's food supply, which makes war inevitable; by the multitude of repeated small events in the struggles between peoples that are caused by deficiency of food.

5. The starvation which initiates the war calls forth other "special functions" of the "secondary order," which are reflected in the composition of the population, dimensions of the "physiological mobility," in the area of social organization, and in the realm of society's "physiology" or processes.

6. The changes called forth by war in these respects are colossal and catastrophic. The greatest historical cataclysms and tragedies are the functions of many independent variables, among which prob-

ably the first place belongs to disturbances due to the deficient food metabolism of the social aggregates and of the social organisms.

7. As long as such disturbances exist, as long as the size of the population of the world, as a whole, or that of parts of the world is not adjusted to the food supply, war will not disappear.

8. The amount of the food on earth at present apparently is not sufficient to feed the total population. Hence the conclusion: either the food supply has to be increased, or the population must decrease.

9

HUNGER AND THE MOVEMENT
OF CRIMINALITY

If we were to assume that all the ways we have described (inventions, imports, emigration, wars, and seizures) are insufficient to cover a deficit of food, and the group continues to starve, then we would be faced with this question: what will happen to the group?

Once the food taxis of hungry people cannot be satisfied by receipts from outside the group, or by emigration of its population, it will find satisfaction within the group itself.

Something similar to that which takes place during starvation of an organism happens to society. In such cases the former begins to live, not by the regular metabolism of food, but by utilizing its stored reserves of fat and other tissues. In the social aggregate, likewise, the hungry cells, if deprived of the means of obtaining nutrition from outside, tend to procure it from their "fat reserves" in the form of the stored food of the aggregate itself, by trying to seize and take possession of it.

However, since the reserves belong to and are guarded by some definite cells, the result of such attempts will be intensification of the social struggle for food within the social aggregate. As we have seen, hunger tends to weaken and suppress all the reflexes which are contrary to its satisfaction. The "brakes" become loose and they cease preventing people from performing various acts which they would not resort to if they were not starving. This phenomenon belongs to the so-called legal and moral reflexes. Those reflexes which prevent satisfaction of hunger by prohibiting this or that act are subjected to attacks by hunger, and in many instances they cannot resist it. As a

225

result of this, rules are broken and crime appears and gradually increases. Starving people, who are no longer held back by inhibiting reflexes, unable to satisfy their hunger, now, under the influence of food taxis, begin to obtain food within the limits of the group itself, either secretly (by theft), openly (by plunder or robbery), or by deceit (misdemeanors). If such attempts to obtain food encounter obstacles, either from the satiated cells, or the groups within the society, from the organs of power, or anyone else, the desire to obtain the means of satisfying their hunger may lead to felony, to murder and bodily injuries—to crimes against the person.

Thus, under conditions when the food deficit cannot be covered by other means, the principal result of starvation is to increase, first, crimes against property, and afterward crimes against persons, which represent the specific case of intensification of the social struggle within a society. All that is needed for this is the presence in the aggregate of the "fatty cells" next to the hungry ones or, broadly speaking, other means of nutrition (food, money, valuables, and other equivalents) found in the possession of some members of the group, even in quantities which are not very large.

Here, too, we can indicate a series of more or less detailed theorems, which determine the degree of increase in the rate of criminality. Other conditions being equal, the curve of criminality becomes higher (1) the greater the number of starving people, and the degree of their starvation, in other words, the less it is covered by means of securing food; (2) the stronger the contrasts in property held by the hungry and the well-fed; (3) the less the satiated people give up voluntarily to the hungry; (4) the weaker and less well organized the apparatus for safeguarding possessions of the well-fed (police, secret agents, searching parties, courts, punishments, etc.); (5) the less the power of the aggregate does to procure food for the hungry.

One may say that, in reality, curves of criminality do not always follow this course because of the existence of chronically hungry societies in which criminality does not vary greatly. This is true, but it exists only because of inequality of other social conditions. In certain cases there is an increase in imports; in others, a heavy emigration; and in a third, the opposing reflexes remain very strong. Furthermore, these exceptions to the proposition may be caused by several factors: (1) such great uniformity within the group that nobody can be robbed and there is no one to steal from; (2) an increase of the inhibiting factors, e.g., terror, strengthening of police force and guards, locking of doors, instituting guard duties at the gates of apartment houses (as is the case now in the USSR), and colossal increases in punishment, repression, etc.; (3) legalization of the acts through which the criminals carry on their theft, robbery, plunder, murder, etc., through governmental ordinances and decrees. Why should one rob anyone and plunder, when the robber and thief can obtain an order from the authorities and "legally" go wherever they wish and take anything they desire? Such acts naturally would not be included in the government's statistics of crime. It is not strange that under such circumstances figures of criminal statistics deviate from the aforementioned theorems.

All these, and also some other phenomena, may deflect the curve of criminality from its ideal norm, or they may obscure it by some "legalizations," but the theorems do not lose their significance because of this. Regardless of all the deviations mentioned here, reality confirms the main proposition, as we shall now demonstrate, that an increase of amount and intensity of starvation (up to its maximum) causes a rise in the curve of criminality, and sharpens the social struggle within the aggregate.

Confirmation

1. As the first confirmation of this functional relationship, it suffices to indicate the nature of the social medium which produces the mass of those who commit crimes against private property. These criminals are mostly from the poor social classes. The proprietary class produces a much smaller percentage of crimes of this kind. This fact is definitely established by the research of Wassermann, Lindenau, Tarnovsky, Vsesviatski, and others. For example, in Austria, for every 100,000 laborers, 480 people were found guilty of theft, while for capitalists and retired people living on pensions the corresponding figure is only 45. "The typical crimes of the working class are expropriation of the property of others and bodily injuries. Among all artisans convicted, 52 per cent were accused of theft, and for factory workers the comparable proportion was 42 per cent."[1]

1. Gernet, *Crime and the Fight against It*, pp. 391–92, 396 (in Russian). In Italy, in 1889, of the total number of crimes, 77.8 per cent were from the poorer classes, 13.3 per cent from those who had a minimum of the es-

It is obvious, without any further elaboration, that the poor (i.e., those who are most likely to starve) show a higher level of theft than well-to-do people.

2. The so-called calendar of criminals serves as the second confirmation of the thesis presented. "In France crimes against property reach their maximum during December and January, the months when the poor suffer most from deprivation and need." [2] As indicated by a number of investigators (Lavasseur, Meyer, Foinitsky, Ettingen, Tarnovsky, and Gernet) the same is true for some other countries, e.g., Germany, Russia, Bulgaria, Serbia, and Belgium, in which year after year the maximum crimes against property occur during winter months, when food is difficult to procure, and the minimum during summer and fall.

3. Increase in crimes against property in agricultural countries during years of crop failure and high costs of living represent the third category of facts illustrating clearly the thesis under discussion. This occurs when imports or other means do not make up for the effects of the food deficit. The same also occurs during economic crises in industrial countries.

These phenomena are firmly established by vital statistics. Studying the movement of crime in France from 1838 to 1886, Levasseur said, "The crops had a considerable influence on the movement of crimes, particularly when the countries were poorer and the imports did not change the rise in the crime rate." Law-breaking increased during periods of crop failure, when the lack of food forced people to commit thefts. This was particularly evident from 1847 to 1854 during the severe crop failures.[3] After comparing the yearly fluctuations in price of bread and the number of crimes in Bavaria from 1836 to 1861, Mayr came to the same conclusions.[4] Similar figures are re-

---

sentials, 6.1 per cent were from the well-to-do classes, and 2.8 per cent from the rich. In Austria, in 1896, the economically insecure people produced 86.7 per cent of the criminals, those having medium security 13 per cent, and completely secure people 0.3 per cent. In Switzerland, insecure people made up 81.8 per cent, secure people 5 per cent. In Prussia, in 1905, the poor classes produced 77 per cent of all criminals. Zhizhilenko, *Criminality and Its Factors* (Petrograd, 1922), p. 62 (in Russian).

2. Levasseur, *La Population française*, 2:456–57.

3. Ibid., p. 442.

4. George Von Mayr, *Statistik und Gesellschaftslehere* (Berlin, 1917), vol. 3.

corded for all Germany (1882–92) by Berg, for Serbia by Wadler, for Italy by Fornasari di Verchi, for England by Tugan-Baranovsky, and for Russia by Gernet, Tarnovsky, and others.

Thus, for the province of Kaluga (an agricultural and consuming province), "the years of high prices of bread (1881, 1892, and 1907), and also the years of low prices (1883, 1888, 1894–95, 1900–1901) always were accompanied by corresponding changes in crime, either during the same year, or the year after. In the province of Kaluga the number of people condemned for thefts varies with the price of the bread and the amount of bread required for satisfying the local needs. Robberies and plunder follow the same course." [5] A similar relationship was established by Tarnovsky for the province of Petrograd.

In industrial countries the worsening of nutrition of the population and the rise in crimes against property, and partially against persons, both take place during years of economic crises when unemployment increases and incomes fall.

The industrial regions of England may serve as an example. The studies of Tugan-Baranovsky indicate that during years of satisfactory conditions of existence, crime declines, and, conversely, it rises during years of crises. The industrial stagnation of the 1840s produced a considerable increase in the crime rate. The same was observed during the years 1825, 1826, and 1827 (crises), and in 1847–48 (crises and stagnation). Later, peaks of criminality were observed in 1851, 1857, and 1863; the first two of these were years of general crises, and during the third the scarcity of cotton reached its maximum. Further peaks in the crime rate were observed in the second half of the 1870s, which were years of industrial depression.[6]

4. Finally, the thesis is confirmed by the fact that during years of mass starvations the curve of criminality rises very sharply. Such years, *ceteris paribus*, appear particularly "criminal," i.e., as the years during which hunger depresses all inhibiting moral and legal conditioned reflexes, and as a result people break laws. The numbers of thefts and robberies increase, and whole bands of robbers and plunderers are formed which attack all who have food and money.

This was observed early in the history of man, in the ancient

5. Gernet, op. cit., pp. 386–87.

6. Tugan-Baranovsky, *Les crises industrielles en Angleterre*, chaps. 4, 6, and 9.

world, during the Middle Ages, and up to our own times during the famines of 1919–21 in Russia.

The years of starvation in contemporary Russia (1922) deserve special attention. It is possible to say without exaggeration that during these years, almost the entire population, regardless of sex, age, status, or profession, became "criminal." In one way or another all became thieves, and swindlers, and a considerable number were subjected to bribery, robberies, and murder. I am afraid that my contemporaries will be offended by such a designation. Nonetheless, during these years of starvation Russia became a real criminal country. In regions of starvation it was extremely difficult to find a person who, in one way or in another, was not involved in some crime connected with nutrition; in theft, large or small; in a small or large swindle; or in deceit connected with ration cards, or with rations. Here are some examples. In Petrograd in 1918, the discrepancy between the figures of the population as recorded in the census and the number of the food ration cards issued was equal to 327,000, i.e., 22 per cent of the population.[7]

In the legal language of normal times this means that 327,000 people were thieves who were robbing the public domain. In Moscow, in May 1918, the number of the food cards issued was equal to 2,213,000, i.e., 530,000, or 31.5 per cent, more than the actual number of the population, and by June the number of extra cards rose to 1,100,000, i.e., to 65 per cent of the total population.[8] Thus, 65 per cent of the population became thieves who plundered public property and deprived hungry people of some portions of available food. The same took place in other towns in regions of famine. During normal times such acts would have caused indignation on the part of the population, but during a period of starvation people accepted them permissively. Hunger inhibited any contrary convictions.

Another illustration may be obtained from a comparison of the criminality of people in Moscow in 1918 with that in 1914. If we were to take the rate of crime in 1914 as equal to 100, then the corresponding indexes for types of crimes in 1918 would be as follows:[9]

7. *Materials on the Statistics of Petrograd*, issue 3 (1921) (in Russian).
8. *Krasnaya Moskva* (1917–20), vol. 53 (in Russian).
9. Ibid. See also the article on the tremendous growth of criminality in Petrograd in 1921 in *Pravda*, January 5, 1922.

theft, 315; armed burglary, 28,500; prostitution, 800; attempted murder, 1,600; murder, 1,060; misdemeanor, 170; swindling, 370.

Furthermore, in 1920, according to the figures of the People's Commissariat of Transportation, 17,000 pieces of luggage were misappropriated and 1,098,000 pud of cargo contained in 100 railway cars of one-half-ton capacity were stolen every month. During seven months of 1921, in one warehouse at a station on the Moscow-Kursk railroad, 2,200 pieces of luggage disappeared. Before the war the amount of luggage handled was 15 times as great, and an average of only 225 thefts occurred for the same period.[10]

To this had to be added speculation with ration cards (receipt of two to four extra rations per person, which is a crime from a moral and legal standpoint), fabrication of fraudulent imitations of orders, unlawful receipt of food under the pretext of sickness, massive speculation with "natural premiums," which often resulted in the illegal sale of all the contents of a factory, enormous bribery perpetrated under lawful and unlawful forms,[11] thefts from governmental warehouses by officials who sold the goods on the black markets.[12]

To this must be added the tens of thousands of illegal "requisitions and nationalizations" in which the acquired goods became the private property of corresponding authorities, hundreds of "legal" murders and shootings for the acquisition of valuables, and the requisition without any ceremony of cattle, clothing, or food during punitive expeditions. Furthermore, the massive robberies of trains, villages, and warehouses, the tremendous increase of bandits who robbed everyone, whether they were "red" or "white," thefts from fields, gardens, and homes, perpetrated by ordinary people, the general beastliness which was widespread throughout Russia during these years when respect for human life declined to zero (vanished), when a "murder" became just "an insignificant event"—all this confirms the thesis that during these years of famine almost the entire population of Russia became criminal. If it were possible for moral statistics to

---

10. *Isvestia*, October 2, 1921.

11. "We have briberies at every step," authoritatively concludes Lenin in *Moskovskaya Pravda* on October 22, 1921, Lenin's address. Nowadays we have reached such a state that expense for bribery is even included in official budgets and accounts.

12. *Krasnaya Gazeta*, April 15, 16, 1921.

Number of Criminal Cases

Province	1920	1921
Astrakhan	10,800	11,520
Ufa	13,000	18,000
Saratov	25,000	27,000
Samara	37,000	39,000
Simbirsk	30,500	31,200

record all these facts, the curve of criminality certainly would have shown an unprecedented rise. The following citations from Soviet publications of the period attest to the same thesis.

The advent of famine in the provinces along the Volga River coincided with a considerable increase of criminality (*Makhovik*, July 21, 1921). With the increase in starvation in the Don River region in 1922 came a tremendous increase in thefts, burglaries, and murders, both on farms and in villages. The bandits take away the cattle, slaughter them immediately, divide the meat, and eat it at once without any concern about being apprehended. If they are caught and brought to justice, their only explanation is that they were hungry. They are put in jail, and when the term expires and they are freed, they continue the same kind of burglaries (*Isvestia*, February 18, 1922). Thus, during the years of famine of 1921 and 1922, crime increased even in comparison with the 1920 figures.[13] All this occurred despite a decrease in population due to emigration and mortality. The real figures are perhaps even higher. Such is the situation with the adult population.

Not much different is the plight of children. In the regions of famine they also became thieves, burglars, robbers, speculators. The limited statistical material indicates also that the increases in their crimes are connected with the food problem. In 1918–20, the criminality of children in Petrograd had a very specific character. First of all it increased. The Commission for Minors in 1918 handled 6,000 cases, 8,000 in 1919, and in 1920 even more, although the population decreased by one-half (from 1,469,000 to 706,841). Of all crimes 79 per cent were those against property, and of these 49 per cent were thefts of food from members of households, and 30 per

13. Vasilevsky, *Starvation*, p. 17 (in Russian).

cent were swindles connected with the items of first necessity (fraudulent orders, etc.). In 1910 in Petrograd the index for criminality of children was equal to 3.68 per cent; in 1920 it rose to 26.97 per cent, which means that criminality of children for these ten years increased 7.4 times.[14] The same is true in other towns in Russia.

Conclusions

1. During massive starvation and inadequate coverage of the food deficit by other means, the main function of food taxis is to direct the "hungry cells" of a society toward the "well-fed." This involves breaking the moral and legal reflexes and the growth first of all crimes against property and within the aggregate.

2. *Ceteris paribus*, the growth is greater: (a) the larger the number of starving people and the degree of starvation; (b) the greater the differences between the hungry and satiated in the society; (c) the less the well-to-do voluntarily give to the poor; (d) the less the government provides for the poor; and (e) the weaker the police protective apparatus of the aggregate.

3. From this primary function of massive starvation, there follow a series of functions of the secondary order, which together disorganize the entire social life of the group and lead to its decline.

14. Aronovich, "Children's Criminality," *Psikhopatia, Nevrologia*, issue 1, pp. 38, 102 (in Russian).

10

HUNGER, RIOTS, INSURRECTIONS, AND REVOLUTIONS

When increasing starvation pinches the nutritional reflexes of a population, and when there are no other means to satisfy their hunger, starving people commit crime. They are attracted by the storehouses of food found within the country, and they attempt to get it by struggling and fighting either with the owners of the goods or with the organized police and legal apparatus of the government. When such phenomena are on a massive scale, and the acts of seizure and appropriation become a collective action, then we do not speak of an increase in the rate of crime, but we are faced with the phenomena of riots, revolts, and revolutions.

When a single unit acts against the proprietal rights of another person, we call it "a crime." But when similar actions are committed by a mass of people, by a whole stratum of a society (massive seizures of land, estates, movable and unmovable property), then it is called revolution, with the adjective "social." When, to achieve their aims, persons violate norms of the law and kill individuals or resist the agents of power, we call it crime. But when similar actions are perpetrated by a large group, when the breaking of law assumes a massive dimension, the struggle with rulers becomes collective, and murders and seizures are on a large scale, then it is called insurrection, social uprising, and revolution.

Some may say that a social uprising always takes place in the name of high ideals and great mottoes, while crimes lack an ideology. This is very naïve! The "ideology," the high-sounding "speech reactions" ("freedom," "fraternity," "the land and will," etc.) are only a

234

cover for the real issues (land, riches, increase of income, decrease of labor, etc.) without which mass movements and revolutions cannot be stirred up. Furthermore, a number of social movements, such as the Jacquerie of the French Revolution, had more prosaic slogans, and nobody calls them criminal movements.

The insignificant role of these "high-sounding slogans," by means of which the crimes are differentiated from social movements, follows from the fact that not a single movement expressing one of the guiding principles ever achieved its aim. "Liberty, equality, and fraternity," "progress," "The Kingdom of God," etc., are still unattainable.

The people are apt to explain many of their actions by a "beautiful ideology" which ennobles them and justifies their actions. A man seldom grabs another by the throat without a reason. Often he does it in the name of "God," "goodness," "beauty," "progress," "the happiness of mankind," "socialism," "in the interests of the revolution," "the salvation of the country," etc. When he is robbing, assaulting, or killing, these actions in most cases are explained by "noble words and motives." People who do not amuse themselves, or other people, by such ideologies are comparatively rare. Hence, they are identified as cynics. Most people hypnotize themselves, as well as other people, with such "illusions" which give a beautiful color to acts that are atrocious. Almost all people in this respect are Tartuffes, whose subvocal (convictions) and speech reactions do not agree with their actions.

In a larger degree the same occurs during the extensive social movements. Here are some examples. In China, Persia, Turkey, Egypt, Greece (fifth century B.C. to fifth century A.D.), and Rome (after the end of the republic), the revolutions were carried on under high-sounding slogans, none of which was ever fulfilled. Christianity made its entrance on the scene with the ideology of equality, fraternity, and communism, and objectively it fulfilled none of these promises. The Great French Revolution went under the mottoes of "human rights," "liberty," "equality," and "fraternity"; and in reality there never was a time of less freedom, equality, and fraternity (just recall the tens of thousands of "brothers" beheaded by the guillotine, the despotism of the Convention, etc.) than during the years of the Revolution and those of Napoleon.

The same happened with the mottoes of the great Russian Revolution. Rather than the achievement of "equality," "bread," "peace," "communism," "destruction of capitalism and the government," etc., people received NEP (New Economic Policy), gambling houses, starvation for some and luxury for others, the crudest type of capitalism, and the all-protecting government.

Single crimes due to hunger occur when only a few people are starving. When the masses starve, they are attracted to stores of food and attempt to get them. The inevitable struggle then begins between the hungry and the well-fed, between the poor and the rich, and the latter are helped by the protective powers of the government. These phenomena constitute that which, depending upon the severity of the struggle, are called disturbances, riots, insurrections, and revolutions.

Such is the mechanistic interpretation of the relationship between hunger, or the pinching of the nutritional reflexes, and society.

The conditions under which hunger causes these phenomena are as follows.

1. The presence of a considerable degree of comparative or deficiency starvation of the masses.

(a) Not only is the decrease of the nutrition of the masses from adequate to inadequate important, but also every considerable lowering of the food regime from a high standard to a lower one is significant, even when that lower state is not actually deficient nutrition.

(b) The speed and abruptness of the decrease also have great significance in worsening the nutrition of the masses. Therefore, the faster the decrease, the stronger the pinching of nutritional reflexes and the probability of social disturbances. Both psychologically and physiologically, the reaction of the organism may be quite violent.

(c) There is a third condition, which derives from the two preceding. "The pinching" of the reflexes has its own limit, and after that is passed, it leads toward complete apathy of the individual and away from a struggle for life.

Therefore, *ceteris paribus*, we must expect to have the strongest reactions from the starving masses at the time when hunger is great but not excessive.

During absolute starvation the hours of maximum activity are the first three days. During comparative and deficiency starvation, such hours occur when conditions worsen suddenly, and they last up to the moment when the deficit becomes so great that the organism loses the energy essential for performing activities. Then the organism becomes a living corpse.[1]

1. "After losing a considerable part of itself the organism does not think about active measures to improve its existence. Hunger acts like a narcosis,

Such is the first condition with its relevant circumstances.

2. The second necessary condition for the outbreak of disturbances is the presence of proprietorial differentiation in a given society, the presence of a stratum of wealthy people who possess food reserves, or their equivalents in the form of various kinds of wealth. When such differentiation is lacking, when everybody is poor, when there are no food reserves or their equivalents within the limits of the starving district, food attraction is absent, and there is nobody to attack or from whom to take.

Conversely, the stronger the proprietorial differentiation, and the greater the reserves that are concentrated in the hands of certain people, the stronger the magnet, the more intense its attraction of the hungry human masses, and the greater the attempts to seize the possessions of the rich.

3. The third self-explanatory condition is the *incapability, or the great difficulty, of covering the nutritional deficit of the hungry by any other means.*

Such are the essential basic conditions necessary for an outbreak of disturbances, insurrections, revolts, and revolutions to result from hunger.

Some other circumstances may provide additional conditions that lead to the occurrence of disturbances. They are: (1) *the degree and the size of the voluntary help to the poor given by the rich people, or by the government* (the more help, the less the chance of revolt, and vice versa); and (2) *the nature and the stability of the conditioned reflexes of the population.* When for a number of generations the conditioned reflexes frequently have led to violation of proprietorial and personal rights, and the corresponding ideologies permit and approve of them, then under the stimulus of hunger the disturbances may readily occur. Conversely, when the reflexes show regard for the private property of others, when they are opposed to the breaking of proprietorial and personal laws with respect to other people, the hunger first must overcome the force of the resistance of such convictions; only after they are suppressed can it cause disturbances.

---

when after some preliminary excitability and violent reaction of the organism, there follows a period of depression, paralysis and apathy." Such emaciated, hungry people are not only indecisive, but they produce great astonishment by "their humility, acceptance of their lot, begging for favors and flattery." Waldman, "On the Problem of Clinical Starvation," in *Jubilee Collection in Honor of I. Grekov,* p. 441 (in Russian).

The question arises whether massive starvation always leads to disturbances when indicated secondary conditions also are present, namely, the lack of voluntary help from the rich and the powerful, and the presence of reflexes favorable to the protest, etc. *The answer is yes, except in those cases in which the pressure of hunger is neutralized by other equally powerful determinants.*

I have experimented with hungry dogs by putting a piece of bread or meat in front of their noses. The dog usually grabbed the piece greedily. After this I put another piece before him, but this time I had a stick and forbade the dog to touch the food. If the dog did not obey, it received a strong blow; and after two or three such "lessons," the dog did not touch the piece while I held the stick. The same thing happens to a man. If we were to place a juicy beefsteak in front of a hungry person he would eat it. But if at the same time we were to put a revolver at his head, the discharge of which could kill him, then naturally he would not touch the meat. The same may happen to the masses of the hungry.

Regardless of the severity of hunger, social disturbances may be inhibited if a pistol is held to the head in the form of introduction of martial law, or if people are shot on the spot at the slightest indication of a riot. In this way the effect of hunger may be neutralized by other strong, active forces.

This is the reason why during the greatest famines in India, Russia, and in Western countries in earlier periods, social disturbances were insignificant, although the conditions necessary for their existence were present.[2]

M. Kovalevsky indicates correctly that a strong deficiency starvation, which results in extreme emaciation of the people, is not accompanied by disturbances and revolutions. However, as I have indicated, his contention that "the revolutionary movements arise at the moment of a comparative improvement of the well-being of the masses," or, in other words, at the time of an improvement of their nutrition, is very questionable and would be extremely difficult to prove.

A number of facts observed every day, as well as those of historical events, indicate that large social movements start exactly at the time of a worsening of the existing level of nutrition of the masses, and not when there is an improvement of it.

2. Kovalevsky, *Economic Growth of Europe*, 2:525–26 (in Russian).

Such are in brief the conditions under which the lowering of nutrition of the masses (comparative and deficiency starvation) leads toward disturbances and revolutions. Now let us try to substantiate the existence of a relationship between hunger and social disturbances.

The first indication of the existence of this relationship is seen in *the manifestation of dissatisfaction, beginning with mutterings and complaints, and ending with "riots" among small aggregates of people* (in dormitories, dining halls, food lines, among people eating at a certain place, in restaurants, in pubs, among soldiers, workers, and other people who receive definite rations, etc.), which almost always coincide with a worsening of their nutrition. Contrary to the opinion of M. Kovalevsky, I know of no facts indicating that such groups react by muttering, swearing, cursing, breaking dishes, beating up personnel, etc., forms of "riot," when their rations or meals are being improved. Every increase in quality and quantity of their food usually calls forth expressions of "pleasure," "satisfaction," "gratitude," etc.

Conversely, after a decrease in quality and quantity of food, reactions of "dissatisfaction," "protest," and "indignation" are quite common. Who has not heard about food riots in schools (student dining halls, dormitories), factories, armies, asylums, and old folks' homes, which were caused by the worsening of their nutrition? Hundreds of such riots occurred during recent years in the Russian "governmental dining halls," when food that was bad to start with became even worse, or during the distribution of rations that had been decreased.[3] The lowering of quality and quantity of food received by the corresponding group has always caused small riots, disturbances, sometimes even revolutions, which frequently resulted in dismissal of existing nutritional authorities, and in breaking dishes, destroying buildings, and often beating up real or supposed culprits.

These facts indicate clearly the stated relationship between the lowering of nutritional standards and the occurrence of disturbances and revolutions.

Is it necessary to mention here that these phenomena are small copies of the similar large social disturbances? Suppose that instead

3. Personally, I observed hundreds of such protests in 1921 when rations were decreased in "Dom Uchenykh" (an organization of nutritional help to scholars. E.S.), or in the dining halls of the university, etc.

of 50 people there are 500,000 whose nutritional levels are decreased, then, instead of "a tempest in the teapot" (in an asylum, old folks' homes, etc.), there is a great storm, which acquires the characteristics of a social event (in the form of a tremendous meeting, or a mass demonstration with slogans of "bread," or in the form of plundering food stores, markets, food depots, etc., which disturb the peaceful life of the large aggregate). The mere mention of these facts is sufficient to be considered as proof of the mentioned postulate.

The second category of facts which confirm this theorem is found in a historical comparison of times and places of great social uprisings with times of great variations in the curve of public nutrition. Contrary to the general opinion of historians, the historical proofs are not completely accurate, as there usually are many unknowns in the accounts, and the older they are, the more mistakes they may contain. Nonetheless, for the verification of fundamental processes, they can be used. If, e.g., on the basis of available material, it is impossible to decide the number of calories involved in the decrease in nutrition of English laborers in 1840, or of French peasants and city people in 1788–89, it still is possible to decide whether the nutrition improved or worsened, i.e., whether "pinching" of food reflexes decreased or increased.

Confirmation of Our Proposition

The Ancient East.—Although the history of the Ancient East has not been well studied, there are descriptions of the occurrence of disturbances as a result of food shortages. In Egypt, according to Maspero, small riots occurred frequently and they always were caused by need and hunger. Remuneration for work consisted mostly of bread, millet, oil, and allotments of food which the supervisors of the works usually distributed at the first of each month. During the first days of a month the family ate well, but about the middle of it, rations decreased and discontent began. Near the end of the month starvation often took place, manifesting itself in worsening of work. Official notations of scribes who made their records at the places of work indicate that general strikes occurred at the end of every month, and that they were caused by hunger and general weakness of the workers.[4] It would be very interesting to follow in the history of Egypt the

4. G. Maspero, *L'histoire ancienne des peuples de l'Orient classique*, 6th ed. (1904); Turaev, *Ancient Egypt* (1922), pp. 120–121 (in Russian).

fluctuations showing the relationship between poverty and the disturbances, but unfortunately there are no quantitative data for doing so. However, it can be stated that various periods of disturbances and riots coincided with the periods of impoverishment of the country. Thus, the period after the Twelfth Dynasty was one of the worst in the history of Egypt, and during this time "the country declined very fast economically." [5] The general unstable condition of the country undermined agriculture and industry.[6] The same period is characterized by great social revolutions and riots, about which ancient documents of Ipuwer ("Admonitions") give some idea.

Very similar events occurred during different periods in Egypt, as for example after the death of Ikhnaton, or after the end of the dynasty, during the time of Ramses III, after him, and also during the Twenty-first and Twenty-fourth dynasties.

Greece.—Beginning with the seventh to the sixth centuries B.C., Greece witnessed the unification of the country and worsening of the food supply, and this was accompanied by a rise in disturbances and revolutions. This period is known for its agrarian revolution which deprived the peasants of land, which lowered the general well-being of the masses, and which saw the emergence of wealthy groups and of different economic strata. Social revolutions with all their cruelties and oppressions also originated during this period. Exploitation of the peasants became enormous. In Athens, e.g., they had to be satisfied with one-sixth part of the crop, delivering five-sixths of it to owners of the land. It was impossible for peasants to exist on one-sixth of the income. The masses were doomed to a hungry, or semi-hungry, existence.

Revolutions began exactly at this time. A proletarian party of the "fists" (in the terminology of the time) made its appearance and an excruciating struggle began between rich and poor. The realization of hopeless social poverty had to give way to other moods. All social classes, with the exception of the privileged, were involved in the revolutionary movement. Terrible passions and criminal instincts flared up.[7] Then came the insurrection of Megara (*ca.* 640 B.C.) which, according to contemporaries, was ruled by the dictum seek first for food; and do good deeds, after you already have the essentials

5. Turaev, *Ancient Egypt*, p. 70.

6. Breasted, *History of Egypt.*

7. Pöhlmann, *Geschichte der Sozialen Frage und des Sozialismus der antiken Welt*, vols. 1, 2.

for life. The poor people attacked the rich, rabid emotionalism began to rage, and adversaries yearned to "devour each other alive." [8] During later history, with some interruptions, the poverty of the masses and inequality of wealth did not decrease, but rather increased. Democracy did not annihilate poverty, but merely made it more sensitive. The number of the poor grew *steadily*. Disturbances increased, the struggle of the parties became more acute and cruel, and overturnings of regimes became more frequent.[9]

Even in democratic Athens the common person was dressed no better than the slave. The masses had a very low level of living. Daily wages were not sufficient to feed a family, even with low requirements of the southerners. Later the wages increased, but the cost of the products increased proportionately. The situation was worsened by the war, which lasted for fifty-five years.[10]

It is not surprising that in such a social aggregate with its deficient metabolism, social convulsions occurred very often and became almost a permanent feature of the society. Poverty creates a civil war and crime, says Aristotle, in summarizing his observations on contemporary affairs.[11] "The proletarian of these centuries was an inborn revolutionary." "Poverty and proprietorial inequality become stimulating agents for continuous revolutions." [12] The social struggle, according to Thucydides, was born of a desire to get rid of poverty, which the people had to endure for a long time, and also of an insatiable greed for other people's property. Thus, revolutions followed one another, with confiscation of property of the rich, seizures of lands, and endless murders and oppressions.

The same relationship may be studied in greater detail in Athens. The economic situation in Athens after the Persian wars and the thirty years of peace was quite good, and we do not read of any revolutions or disturbances during this period. Desolation and poverty came with the advent of the Peloponnesian wars. Then governmental subsidies decreased, and the masses experienced extreme want.[13]

8. R. Pöhlmann, *History of Ancient Communism and Socialism* (St. Petersburg, 1910), pp. 358–59 (in Russian).

9. Ibid., pp. 397–99, and chap. 12.

10. Ibid., pp. 371–72, 375, 376.

11. Aristotle, *Politics*, 2:3, 7.

12. Pöhlmann, *History of Ancient Communism and Socialism*, pp. 451, 452, 548–49, 702, passim.

13. G. Buzold, *Griechische Geschichte* (Gotha, 1904), 3:1402–3, passim.

Toward the end of the war, food supplies disappeared completely as a result of blockade, and people began to die from hunger. With the increase of poverty and hunger, convulsions in Athenian society took place. The internal struggles increased and one overthrow followed another. Such were the revolutions of the years 411 and 409. These were followed by social revolutions which were directed by Critias and the Thirty Tyrants, who in turn were soon overthrown. In brief, the social aggregate began to shake almost incessantly in the strongest of revolutionary convulsions, blood flowed continuously, and cruelty reached unprecedented dimensions.

In Sparta acute poverty and increases in proprietorial differentiation occurred in the middle of the third century. By that time most citizens had become poor and wealth was concentrated in the hands of the few (not more than one hundred). The most acute social revolutions, and uprisings with colossal terror and confiscations, belong to this period. Agis IV (ca. 245 B.C.) and Cleomenes III (ca. 235–20 B.C.) carried through radical programs of social reforms and confiscations.[14]

During the later history of Sparta, wars worsened conditions still more. Many citizens came out of the war impoverished instead of enriched, and this was the cause of subsequent struggles and overthrows of regimes. Social revolution became a permanent occurrence. Under Nabis (end of the third and beginning of the second century) the old story was repeated again; "many outstanding and well-to-do citizens were murdered, or exiled, their property given to the poor by the tyrant, and their wives to his friends and soldiers," etc. Later on, the situation worsened, and concomitantly social cataclysms continued almost without interruption, which led Sparta to downfall and perdition.[15]

It is true that the correlation between revolutions and impoverishment and starvation of the masses is presented here in general terms, with many desirable details lacking. Nonetheless, it indicates roughly the relationship. Revolutions began at the time of impoverishment of the masses and growth of differences in wealth; they increased steadily until the subjugation of Greece by Rome, when a terrific depopulation and peace brought material security.

14. B. Niese, *Geschichte der Griechischen und Makedonischen Staaten* (1899), Teil 2, p. 296, passim.
15. Ibid., p. 563, passim.

Rome.—Very similar conditions we find in the history of Rome. During the early period when "a completely conservative peasantry, which was holding strongly to the land, dominated the forum, there was no mention made either of sharp class differences, of deep class conflicts, or of attacks upon the ruling groups." [16]

Later on, the peasantry were deprived of their land, and as the proletarians increased, the curves of poverty and hunger accompanied a rise in the curve of disturbances. At one stage poverty became enormous. "The army of the paupers grew tremendously. It was made up of the city's proletariat, the poor country proletariat, and the army of slaves." A large mass of these elements, which could be classed as the lower stratum of pauperism, concentrated in Rome.

Outside of Rome the conditions were no better. Near the end of the republic the general conditions of the masses continued to decline, and the differences in wealth to increase. "In an entire Roman state there would not be found 2,000 people who would own property, as the tribune L. Philipp declared in the year 104 B.C." [17]

"Even the animals in the woods have their lairs" says Gracchus Tiberius in his speech, "while the citizens who fought for the honor and glory of their country do not know where to lay their heads. Nothing is left to them, except the light and the air."

As a result there was a series of revolutionary convulsions which followed each other with small interruptions, such as those of Gracchus, Catiline, Dolabella, Spartacus, Saturnius, on the one side, civil wars on another, and *on the third*, a rise in criminality.

Pauperism had now become a powerful and destructive force; it survived the republic, and it did not cease worrying the system of the Caesars.

Next to these "permanent revolutions," which were concentrated around the end of the republic in the second century B.C., Italy was plagued by an enormous number of bands of robbers. Dionysius said that "it never happened before that the poor would break into the homes of the rich in the hope of finding food, or attempt to seize bread which was delivered to the market. Now everything became a

16. Pöhlmann, *History of Ancient Communism and Socialism*, pp. 546–48.

17. E. Meyer, an article in the collection "Narodonacelenie" (in Russian); cf. Niese, *Grundriss der Römischen Geschichte* (Munich, 1906), p. 146, passim.

norm." Revolts of the slaves appeared with great frequency. Civil war covered the entire country. "War to the palaces and peace to the hovels" became the motto.

The whole social organism was suffering convulsions. Lacking sufficient food, the cells of the organism began to destroy each other. The peaceful existence of the aggregate had completely disappeared. That the "question of the stomach" had the principal role in all of this is substantiated by the fact that, directly or indirectly, the principal requirements of all the rebels always were connected with the problems of bread, e.g., the demands to subdivide governmental lands of Cassius, the agrarian and grain laws of the Gracchi, the law lowering bread prices by Marius, the slogans of "expropriation from the rich" during a number of other revolutions, the agrarian demands of Saturnius and Drusus, etc. Even the purely political demands had the purpose of obtaining economic and nutritional advantages. Thus, the slogans requiring transfer of all power to the people's assembly were for the purpose of getting free bread later on. Or, speaking realistically, the bread was paid for by subordinates and dependencies of Rome, or by the proprietorial classes toward whom all means of compulsion were permitted.[18]

As for Rome itself, a city of almost a million people, at the end of the republic it experienced chronic starvation, and consequently uninterrupted disturbances. It was necessary to pacify the masses constantly and this pacification was frankly admitted to be the motive which forced the Caesars to accept the right of the masses to bread and entertainment. But quiet pacification was not always achieved. Violent gatherings of riotous masses of people and various oppressions were typical scenes in the history of this city. The indignation of the masses usually was caused by their difficult economic situation, complaints about high prices of food, and exasperation against the culprits, real or imaginary, responsible for the high prices. The Roman plebs were always ready for riots whenever there was a delay in the delivery of bread from across the sea.[19]

18. Rostovtzeff, *The Origin of the Roman Empire* (in Russian). (For a selected translation of this, see Rostovtzeff, *A History of the Ancient World*, vol. 2. E.S.)

19. Friedlander, *Scenes from the Living History of Rome* (St. Petersburg, 1914), pp. 27–28 (in Russian); and Pöhlmann, *History of Ancient Communism and Socialism*, pp. 555–56.

Soon after the agreement at Brundisium [in 40 B.C. E.S.] Pompey's fleet cut Italy off from grain supplies and starvation began; with it came a resumption of the civil war.[20] Because of the high price of bread there was almost a riot in the year 32 B.C. The crop failures of A.D. 5–8 were accompanied by disturbances and riots, and the same was true in the year A.D. 19. In the year A.D. 52 in Rome, there was enough grain on hand for only fifteen days; a riot took place, and Claudius barely escaped the people's fury. Similar events occurred in the year A.D. 68, and subsequently.[21]

In the first and the second centuries A.D. the economic situation in Rome was more or less stable, and this period was characterized by a comparative quietness. Sharply worsening conditions began during the third century. Due to a number of causes, poverty and hunger increased on one hand, and on the other, the concentration of wealth and proprietorial differentiation also increased. During this period land began to produce very little, starvation became a constant threat, and industry decreased. There were no new conquests and booty, the inflow of slaves ceased, and pressures by the barbarians increased. In other words a colossal impoverishment of the masses and an intensification of their starvation took place.[22]

As is well known, starting in this period there were rises in the curves of anarchy, riots, banditry, disturbances, and revolutions, which, with short interruptions, continued up to the fall of the Western Roman Empire.[23] During this period and afterward we find similar pictures prevailing in the Roman provinces which had not yet been overrun by the barbarians. Constant disturbances, proletarian social revolutions (such as the revolution of African peasants), anarchy, tremendous bands of robbers and plunderers—all these were typical of the period. Hungry soldiers collected about themselves hungry civilians and vagabonds of different nations, and formed hosts which gave battle to the regular army and made treaties with the Roman commanders on equal terms.[24] A contemporary remarks that "everybody took up arms for the sake of mutual destruction." In brief, the

20. Rostovtzeff, *A History of the Ancient World.*
21. Waltzing, *Étude historique sur les corporations professionelles chez les romains*, 2:20.
22. Duruy, *L'histoire des Romains* (1885), vol. 6, chap. 95; cf. Niese, *Grundriss der Romanischen Geschichte*, for the fifth and sixth centuries.
23. Duruy, op. cit.
24. Tierri, *Récite de l'histoire Romain au V siècle* (1860), pp. 141–71.

connection here between hunger and disturbances is quite clear. The deficient metabolism of the Roman aggregate brought bloody convulsions and struggles.

Byzantium.—In the history of Byzantium after Justinian (and partially during his reign), there were abundant disturbances, insurrections, and large and small revolutions. From the tenth century on they became almost permanent. It would not be a mistake to assume that deficient metabolism was one of the principal causes of such social "fever." The rural population, which was not very secure economically, was further ruined by endless requisitions, robberies, and taxes, and therefore they started the disturbances and riots. Even in the time of Justinian "the provinces were involved in war" almost incessantly.[25] Living conditions of the population were very difficult. Catastrophes and famines occurred quite frequently, particularly in the tenth, eleventh, and twelfth centuries, and revolutions were increasing. Emperors were constantly changing; they were elevated and overthrown almost every year. "No sovereign was secure in his exalted position. Among those who occupied the throne fully half were murdered." [26]

According to the computations by Holmes, at that time population was equal to about one third of the population of contemporary England. Considering the low state of the productivity of that period, such density of population was excessive, and it resulted in starvation for a considerable part of the people; this in turn created disturbances and riots.

The Middle Ages.—Small disturbances, plundering of stores, breaking into homes of the wealthy, and murder were quite frequent during the famines of the Middle Ages. For example in Prague, in Magdeburg, and in Strasburg, in a number of monasteries the abbots were overthrown, and new people were elevated to their positions.[27] If similar disturbances did not happen very often during that time, it should be remembered that, on one hand, the famines were exhaustive and deadly, and that, on the other, their results were obscured by the various happenings during the Middle Ages. These

25. W. Holmes, *The Age of Justinian and Theodora* (London, 1907), pp. 450–52.

26. Skabalanovich, *Byzantine State and Church*, pp. 252–53, and chaps. 1, 3 (in Russian).

27. Curschmann, *Hungersnöte im Mittelalter*, pp. 53–54.

were manifested in permanent struggles, robberies, plunderings, wars, movements against the heretics and unbelievers, and communistic uprisings, and ended with crusades against the heretics and unbelievers—all of which shook the aggregates of the Middle Ages with permanent fevers and convulsions.

If we concern ourselves with their causes, we can hardly agree with those historians who consider them either a result of certain religious beliefs [28] (i.e., conditioned stimuli, which are always weaker than the unconditioned) or a result of "some spirit of freedom," which suddenly would enlighten the community, or to the role of ignorance, or conversely, to that of knowledge, etc.

The complex of conditioned reflexes which were caused by conditioned stimuli, called religion, would not be able to set in motion hundreds of thousands of people and force them to move to the Holy Land, or to the South of France, to risk their lives, to suffer, and to perish. The lack of content and the poor basis for the hypothesis of "the spirit of freedom" in the communal movements was indicated recently.[29] It is still less confirmed by the facts of robberies of the rich, by plunderings, by grabbing jewels from rich ladies, etc., which usually came during the communal revolutions.[30] All these religious and other conditioned stimuli have their own limited significance; but the more serious motives are to be found deeper—in the realm of the unconditioned stimuli, and, particularly, in the famished condition of the masses.

During the Middle Ages the latter was an everyday phenomenon. "The population at that time was poor, but fertile." Because of the unbelievable poverty and oppression, the masses of the population starved perpetually.[31] As indicated, catastrophic famines were frequent also. The instability of the psychology of the masses was very typical for such a period. The extreme sensationalism and abnormally illusionary character of the populace made possible the

28. Pareto correctly says that to see in the wars, such as the Albigensian crusade, only the religious purposes is to be entirely unrealistic. *Trattato di sociologia generale*, 1:804–5.

29. See Ottokar, *Studies on the History of French Towns during the Middle Ages* (Perm, 1919) (in Russian).

30. See Laviss and Rambo, *The Epoch of the Crusades*, 1:403–4 (in Russian).

31. Charles Lea, *The History of the Inquisition* (St. Petersburg, 1911), 1:388 (in Russian).

existence of mediaeval epidemics, psychoses, mass hypnoses, and insanity with all their beliefs and ideologies of that time (witchcraft, sorcery, self-flagellation, naked women running through the streets, children's crusades, inquisitions, etc.).[32] As indicated below, this psychology and behavior are typical in a starving aggregate.

Experiencing a food deficit the social organism suffered convulsions, war was considered to be a normal occurrence, disturbances were carried on under different pretexts, "individual members of the population were frequently fighting each other" (Dante), and there was no peace or stability, as there could not be under such conditions. The specific slogans used in the different movements were quite varied, oftentimes ridiculously stupid. For example, in 1220 a dispute over a dog arose between the ambassadors from Florence and Pisa, which resulted in a war. It would be rather naïve however, to consider that such an occurrence was the real cause of the war. Had it not been for the dog, the war or insurrection might have occurred over a cat. Or if the movement for liberation of the Holy Land had not taken place, some other slogan would have appeared once the social organism was sick; the symptoms of the disease could appear in this or that form.

From this point of view we next consider a number of important social movements in the histories of England, France, Germany, and Russia. The correlation between these movements and the worsening of the economic status of the masses, and therefore of their nutrition (since 50 to 80 per cent of the budget of poor people goes for nutrition), is clear: the movements erupt when nutrition is worsened. They are particularly abundant during economically difficult years.

England.—During the period immediately preceding the Barons' War, social conditions in England went from bad to worse. Dissatisfaction increased as a result of famine (in 1257–58) and surpassed all limits.[33] According to Lingard, the great uprising of barons, which was of great importance in the history of the English constitution, apparently was accelerated by the high cost of living in 1257–58.[34]

The beginning of the fourteenth century (after the death of Edward I in 1307 and during the rule of Edward II from 1307 to

32. Ibid., pp. 38, 94.
33. J. R. Green, *A Short History of the English People* (Moscow, 1897), 1:185 (in Russian).
34. G. Roscher, *Traité d'économie politique rurale*, pp. 60–61.

1327) was a very turbulent period of the history of England. This was the time of the rule of the fist, of the overthrow and murder of the king, of great disturbances, anarchy, and mutual annihilation by the members of disputing parties. These were also years of starvation and sharp increase in the price of bread.[35]

According to Rogers,[36] average prices of a ton of grain (in marks) were as follows: 1271–80, 84.50; 1281–90, 75.71; 1291–1300, 90.73; 1301–10, 79.64; 1311–20, it increased suddenly to 111.79; 1321–30, 99.90; later on it decreased to 67.75.

Due to a number of conditions the nominal movement of prices is not a satisfactory criterion for judging the variations in the economic level of social groups (and for this reason I do not present the entire table); however, in some cases it has some validity, especially when supplemented by other evidence, and may serve to indicate an increase or decrease in the curve of nutrition for a given population.

The lowering of the economic level, and consequently of nutrition, took place before and during the "Peasant's Revolt" of 1381. The increase of level of nutrition in the 1370s from the previous low in 1349, after the "Black Death," was followed by another decrease in the 1380s. The country underwent the final stages of a destructive war, which had been ruining it for ten years, the burden of which fell upon the peasantry. To this was added the infamous poll tax of 1380, "the heavy burden of which fell on the poorest population." The number of landless peasants rose, and in towns formed pauper groups of unskilled laborers, who never were far from starvation. At the same time very rich people appeared, so that social differentiation took place. Contemporaries described life in the following terms: "the wealthy are rejoicing, the paupers crying, the people can't stand it any longer, and the country is being depopulated." Fruassar emphasized that these conditions were particularly acute in Kent, Sussex, and Bedford where the revolts began. In the end, social convulsions in the form of revolts spread widely throughout the country,

35. The last six years (of the second decade of the fourteenth century) belong to the darkest period in the history of England. A number of terrible famines increased the disaster. Green, op. cit., 1:248.

36. J. E. T. Rogers, *A History of Agriculture and Prices in England* (Oxford, 1887).

and, as always in such cases, ideologically they were ascribed to noble motives.[37]

The period during the reign of the Tudors (at the end of the fifteenth and during the sixteenth century) was one of comparative plenty, of low prices for grain (54 to 30 marks per ton), and internally of stability and the absence of social disturbances.

The years preceding the revolution of 1649–50 witnessed a considerable lowering of economic level, and a consequent lowering of nutrition of the masses. During these years signs of impoverishment could be seen everywhere. The poor crops of 1646 and 1647 brought increases in the price of a quarter of wheat from 30 mills to over 58 mills. Prices of oats, buckwheat, and peas increased proportionately. Meat doubled in price. Wages also rose, but far less rapidly than the cost of food.[38]

To the crop failures of 1646–47 must be added the colossal growth of population (by that time it had reached 4 million people, while half a century earlier it was only 2.5 million, according to Rogers), increased scarcity of land, cancellation of leases of tenants (during the reign of Charles I), thus depriving them of bread. "They are ruining us in order to procure pastures for Essex calves, everything has dried up and all that remains for us is to die," said the peasant rebels. Accompanying this process was the enrichment of some other groups, thus producing sharp differences in wealth. As a result, social convulsions appeared, locally at first (in Lincolnshire in 1642), then spreading to other places, and in 1649 general revolution took place.[39]

With respect to internal disturbances, the next stormy period in the history of England began at the end of the eighteenth century and continued through almost the entire first half of the nineteenth

37. Ch. Oman, *The Great Peasant's Revolt in England*, ed. Mir, pp. 6–7, 9–16, 18, 25–26 (in Russian); M. Kovalevsky, *A History of the Ancient World*, 2:589, 600; Petrushevsky, *Nat Tyler's Revolt* (Moscow, 1915) (in Russian).

38. M. Kovalevsky, *From Direct Rule by the People to Representative Government*, 2:178 (in Russian); cf. Rogers, op. cit., 5:205, 623; 6:54, 286, passim; G. Roscher, op. cit., p. 61; Tooke and Newmarch, *Die Geschichte der Bestimmung der Preise* (1858), 2:797–99.

39. Kovalevsky, *Economic Growth of Europe*, pp. 360, 367, 369; Rogers, op. cit., 2:174.

century. Except for occasional respites, this period was one of the most turbulent in England's history. It was characterized by impoverishment of the masses, the high cost of living (which exceeded the income of the people), increased differences in wealth, and low real wages. The following facts are indicative of the prevailing conditions. In England, 1795 was one of the most turbulent years. Crops were poor, war had destroyed industries, the masses were reduced to pauperism, and concomitantly they had developed a tendency toward disorders. Mass meetings were held in the open air, one of which was attended by 150,000 people. The mottos of the time were "peace" and "give us bread." There even was an attack upon the royal coach.

In brief, during this period, impoverishment of the masses, and consequently the worsening of their nutrition, are beyond question. As a result of this we see that the English social aggregate remained in a state of permanent disturbances, revolutions, convulsions which became less severe at times, but which did not disappear entirely until the end of the 1840s.[40]

During the second half of the nineteenth century there was steady improvement in the material conditions of the masses of England, as well as of their nutrition.[41] This period is characterized by comparative stability, internal peace, and tranquility. The revolutionary tendencies of English labor moderated and disappeared,

40. Thus we learn of revolts of agricultural laborers, numerous burnings of food storehouses and of mills, riots in towns, tremendous meetings of protestors and strikers, various plots, formation of powerful unions, murders, unprecedented agitation, an extreme development of vagabondage and theft, struggles over parliament, reforms of the 1820s and those of 1832, fights against bread laws, Chartism, etc. The most violent struggles here also appeared during the years after the crop failures of 1837–40 and 1845–47. In addition to the works cited, see F. Rosenblatt, *The Chartist Movement in Its Social and Economic Aspects*, Columbia University studies 73, no. 1 (New York, 1916); P. W. Slosson, *The Decline of the Chartist Movement*, Columbia University studies 73, no. 9 (1916).

41. The following index numbers of real wages of laborers from 1850 to 1900 gives an idea of the improvement. Using the real wages in 1850 as equal to 100 we get the following values: 1850, 100; 1860, 103; 1870, 118; 1880, 134; 1890, 166; 1900, 183. G. H. Wood, "Real Wages and the Standard of Comfort since 1850," *Journal of the Royal Statistical Society* (March 1909), pp. 102–3. Other figures are given in Kareev, *The History of Western Europe* (St. Petersburg, 1913) (in Russian); Tooke and Newmarch, op. cit., pp. 797–99; Levasseur, *Le prix du blé*.

classes became more bourgeois, and liberalism and reformism replaced revolutionism. From time to time there were some disturbances, but they never assumed large proportions and they occurred mostly in times of unemployment and worsening of conditions, i.e., with the increase of comparative or deficiency starvation. Such, e.g., were the disturbances in 1862 which were caused by unemployment, which in turn resulted from "cotton hunger," and the fall of the working class to the level of pauperism in the 1870s, particularly in Lancashire in 1878, and the disturbances of 1885–86 in London, which even reached the point of the plundering of shops and stores. Also there were strikes, meetings, the growth of ideas of anarchism and of communism in 1890–93. These years were exactly those of crises and unemployment.[42]

But these small disturbances were just a ripple, which did not disturb sharply the internal peace of England. It lasted until 1917–21, when the economic level of English labor declined, when the army of the unemployed grew steadily, along with a rise in prices, i.e., when impoverishment and a worsening food supply took hold. At the same time differentiation in wealth and income increased. The rate of unemployment of members of the trade unions increased as follows: 1916, 0.5 per cent; 1917, 0.5; 1918, 0.9; 1919, 2.1; 1920, 1.1; and in 1921, 6.9 in January, 8.5 in February, 10.0 in March, 17.0 in April, and 22.2 in May. The total number of unemployed in April 1921 was 1,615,000, and 897,000 others worked part time only.[43] These figures indicate clearly the growth of comparative, if not of deficiency, starvation of the masses—starvation to a degree that for a long period had not been experienced in England. Accompanying this growth we see an increase of disturbances and of revolutionary convulsions of the *labor class* to an extent that had long been unknown in the history of England.[44] The number of strikers were: 1914, 327,005; 1915, 401,980; 1916, 284,396; 1917, 860,-727; 1918, 1,096,000; 1919, 2,581,000. The labor movement became "leftist"; disturbances increased; demonstrations, meetings, seizures of establishments, plunderings of food stores and shops took

42. See details in Tugan-Baranovsky, *Les crises industrielles en Angleterre*, 3d ed., pp. 413, 425, 427–28, 433–35, 438–40, 452–53.

43. Bogolepov, *Europe after the War* (1921) (in Russian). See also *The Economist*, vol. 4, no. 5, p. 293.

44. *Statistical Information on the Contemporary Economic Conditions of the Foreign Nations* [a collection] (Moscow, 1922), p. 32 (in Russian).

place from time to time; the Communist Party was organized; and the left wing of the labor party was strengthened. In other words, as starvation increased, the social organism of England became less placid and began to writhe in convulsions of disturbances. Hundreds of telegrams received by Russian newspapers indicated the connections among these phenomena. An example of these is as follows (London, April 20): "In the coal mines of Lancashire the striking miners plundered food stores, bakeries, and fish markets. Many products were thrown on the street, where women and children picked them up to take home. The damages amount to several million pounds." [45] In Norwich unemployed demonstrators entered the city hall and made threatening demands for food. "We must have something to eat, or we shall rebel. We cannot die from starvation." [46] Many similar disturbances forced the government to mobilize military forces and to take severe measures, especially during the tremendous strike by miners in March and May of 1921.

Truly, similar causes under similar conditions produce similar results. To paraphrase a saying of Bossuet, [47] "the people revolt and the number and the quality of the calories guide them."

France.—The worsening of the economic condition of the French peasantry before 1358 is well known. In the thirteenth century and at the beginning of the fourteenth their material situation was comparatively satisfactory. D'Avenel even finds that in the thirteenth century real incomes of peasants and workers were very high. [48] However, beginning with the second half of the fourteenth century their conditions worsened considerably. "The period from 1351 to 1375 was the most costly: the average price of bread increased by 9 francs per hecto-liter. These 25 years during the reigns of John II (the Good Fellow) and Charles V (the Wise) were also those when the purchasing power of money became very low, and when the cost of living was very high." [49]

The price of bread made a sharp jump exactly at this time. A ton of wheat cost an average of 71.99 marks in the years 1276—

45. *Rul*, April 21, 1921. (*Rul* was a daily newspaper in Petrograd. E.S.)

46. *Pravda*, Petrograd, February 1, 1921.

47. Jacques Benigne Bossuet (1627–1704) was a French bishop and writer. E.S.

48. D'Avenel, *Paysans et ouvriers* (Paris, 1899), pp. 11–18, 28.

49. Ibid., p. 152; D'Avenel, *La fortune privée* (1895), p. 37.

1300, 96.00 in 1301–25, 75.04 in 1325–50, and 100.80 in 1351–75.[50] These conditions were worsened by plunder of the population and by two consecutive years of crop failures preceding 1358. The hopeless condition of the peasantry led it to a bloody confrontation with the class of landowners. After the defeat at Poitiers the army "lived by robbing the population systematically, and therefore the peasants ceased cultivating the land for about two years prior to the rebellion." In 1358, when the Jacquerie made their first appearance, "the grapes were not collected at all, the fields were not plowed or seeded, and there were no cows in the pastures. The eye could not rest upon green meadows or ripening fields. Extreme poverty prevailed everywhere, particularly among the rural population, because the nobles increased the suffering of the people by taking away from them all the necessities of life." [51] Since great differences in wealth and income also prevailed at that time, tremendous convulsions of the social aggregate, as is well known, shook the country.

Under the influence of the same factor, and simultaneous with the peasants' revolt, Paris also experienced a revolution (Estates-General, a movement led by É Marcel). During the disturbances in the second decade of the fifteenth century, during the civil war between the Armagnacs and the Burgundians, and during the Cabochien revolt of 1412–13, this relationship is demonstrated still more clearly. This period was very dark in all respects. The misfortunes of the Hundred Years' War, the unruly government, the madness of the king, etc., entirely destroyed the economy of the country and worsened the living conditions of the people.[52]

The span of years between the 1440s and the middle of the sixteenth century was characterized by increasing prosperity, low bread prices, and high wages,[53] and during it there were no large disturbances or revolts.

50. O. Schmitz, *Die Bewegung der Warenpreise in Deutschland von 1851 bis 1902* (Berlin, 1913), pp. 434–35.

51. Kovalevsky, *Economic Growth of Europe*, 2:543.

52. The price of bread increased again during this period, and starvation was uninterrupted. The hungry Armagnacs moved on Paris where they and the Burgundians poured each other's blood upon the streets. D'Avenel, *Paysans et ouvriers*, pp. 152–53; and Coville, *Les cabochiens et l'ordonnance de 1413* (1890).

53. D'Avenel, *Paysans et ouvriers*, p. 154.

The next turbulent period in the history of France is the second half of the sixteenth century, which witnessed the Religious Wars, the Massacre of St. Bartholomew, numerous insurrections in towns and villages, the Holy League, the revolution of Paris, and the change of dynasty from Valois to Bourbon.

A question arises: is this increase in disturbances functionally connected with the qualitative and quantitative decrease of nutrition?

This question must be answered positively. This is proved first of all by the concrete causes of separate disturbances. Thus, the revolt in 1548 in Guienne was because of a tax on salt, that of 1586 in Normandy was caused by the plunder of civilians by the military, and by high taxes. Similar causes were responsible for the revolts of 1593–94.[54] Still more important is the fact that during this time the cost of bread and other produce made a sharp and unprecedented jump upward. The cost of a ton of wheat averaged 44.80 marks in 1476–1500, 44.80 in 1501–25, and 74.80 in 1526–50. Then it more than doubled or tripled in 1550–75, and jumped to 134.40, then to 224.00, in 1576–1600. Afterward it fell somewhat, to 159.00 in 1601–25. The price of bread during the period 1576–1600 remained the highest for the whole period from the fifteenth to the middle of the eighteenth century.[55] "It is quite obvious that this extraordinary increase in the cost of food caused tremendous poverty."[56]

This increase in pauperism becomes still more evident if we consider that the purchasing power of money was decreasing steadily. In comparison with the nineteenth century its coefficients were as follows: 1451–1500 = 6; 1501–25 = 5; 1526–50 = 4; 1551–75 = 3; and 1576–1600 = 2.5.[57] The nominal wages of agricultural workers and industrial laborers also decreased considerably. "A daily worker" who earned 3 francs and 60 sou during the time of Charles VIII (1483–98) received no more than 1 franc 95 sou dur-

54. *The Forerunners of Modern Socialism*, vol. 2, article by Hugo, pp. 315–21 (in Russian).

55. O. Schmitz, op. cit., pp. 434–36. In Paris, according to Levasseur, the price for a ton of wheat (in marks) rose as follows: 1520–29, 80.30; 1530–39, 87.70; 1540–49, 88.59; 1550–59, 96.77; 1560–69, 145.38; 1570–79, 183.01; 1580–89, 195.58.

56. D'Avenel, *Paysans et ouvriers*, pp. 156–57.

57. D'Avenel, *La fortune privée*, p. 7.

ing that of Henry IV. Thus at the end of the sixteenth century a laborer had for his living expense only half as much as his grandfather had had a hundred years earlier.[58] As for artisans, the fall in the wages of masters, as well as of the less-skilled workers, began early in the sixteenth century. Thus, daily wages fell from 4 francs 80 sou in the time of Louis XII to 2 francs 85 sou in that of Charles IX (1560–74). By the end of that century they had dropped even more.

Thus, the price of food was increasing and wages and purchasing power were decreasing. Consequently, nutrition worsened and starvation became more acute. With his annual income a laborer could buy 46 hecto-liters of grain in 1451–1525, only 25 as early as 1526–50, only 15 in 1551–75, and finally only 9.75 in 1575–1600. Such was nutrition during these times.

The next period of disturbances took place during the second half of the eighteenth century, culminating in the French Revolution of 1789. Small bread riots occurred intermittently between the epochs of the great upheavals (e.g., in 1699 in Pontoise during the famine, etc.), but we shall not consider them here.

The eighteenth century was characterized by *a decrease in the purchasing power of money, a lowering of the wages of workers and peasants, rising prices of bread and produce, crop failures,* and *unprecedented luxury of the privileged classes,* i.e., by a series of phenomena which indicate objectively the increase of starvation, impoverishment of the masses, or lowering of their nutrition, on the one hand, and a number of conditions which favored the revolts, on the other. Moreover, these conditions became more and more intensified toward the end of the century. Thus the disturbances increased steadily parallel with the worsening of nutrition, and they culminated in the cataclysm of the Revolution.

Let us confirm briefly these statements. The coefficients of the purchasing power of money were as follows:[59] 1701–25, 2.75; 1726–50, 3.00; 1751–75, 2.33; 1776–90, 2.00.

The wages of agricultural laborers, servants, casual workers, artisans, and laborers were extremely low, and they became still lower during the reign of Louis XVI. If the daily wage of a worker was equal to 3–5 francs per day during preceding centuries, then

---

58. D'Avenel, *Paysans et ouvriers,* pp. 28–29.
59. D'Avenel, *La fortune privée,* p. 17. See the details there.

during the period 1751–75 it was no more than 1 franc 75 sou; under the rule of Louis XVI it fell to 1 franc 64 sou.[60] The daily wage
of a master fluctuated in the seventeenth century from 3 francs in
the times of Henry IV, to 2 francs .30 during those of Colbert, and
the comparable daily wages of the workers for the same periods
ranged from 2 francs .20 to 1 franc .70. In the next century the
master earned 2 francs daily during Fleury's administration and
2 francs .30 at the time of the outbreak of the Revolution; the comparable wages of the workers were 2 francs .10 and 1 franc.[61] "The
France of 1789 was rich, but its laborer and peasant were poor; the
France of 1475 obviously was poor, while its proletariat was rich.
This seems to be a phenomenon which is worth remembering." [62]

The price of wheat per ton (marks) shows the rise in the price
of bread during the eighteenth century:[63] 1726–50, 123.20; 1751–
75, 148.40; 1776–1800, 214.52.

In addition, the eighteenth century was constantly plagued with
crop failures. In the course of eighty years Paris experienced twelve
periods of highly increased cost of living, and famines in the provinces occurred constantly. This resulted in the economic impoverishment of the masses and increased starvation. According to the *Cahiers
of 1789* the nutrition of the masses is depicted in the following way:
"the food of the daily worker consists of bread which was dunked
in salt water. Meat was eaten only during the last day of the carnival,
on Easter, and on birthdays." The workers lived almost exclusively
on bread and water, slept on straw, and dwelled in hovels. Their
living conditions were worse than those of the American Indians.[64]
"The impoverished peasant looked much like a savage. His clothing
and habitation were terrible. Food was very scarce." [65]

With the worsening of the economic situation of the masses, and
particularly of their nutrition, during the second half of the eighteenth century disturbances began to increase. "The crop failure of
1739 caused three rebellions in the provinces." Because of the lack

60. D'Avenel, *Paysans et ouvriers*, pp. 66–67.
61. Ibid., pp. 120–21.
62. Ibid., p. 135. Cf. Tocqueville, *L'ancien régime et la revolution*
(1877), p. 179, passim.
63. Schmitz, op. cit., pp. 434–36.
64. D'Avenel, *Paysans et ouvriers*, vol. 1; cf. Taine, *Les origines de la
France contemporaine*.
65. Afanasiev, *Historical and Economic Articles*, 1:65 (in Russian).

of grain, the people revolted in Lille in 1740. In 1740 considerable disturbances occurred in Toulouse, again because of the lack of grain, and for the same reason they took place in Bern in 1750. In 1752 rebellions in Rouen, Dauphiné, and L'Auvergne lasted for three days. "In Normandy disturbances caused by the lack of bread were recorded in 1725, 1737, 1739, 1752, 1764, 1765, 1767, and 1768." "There were disorders in Reims in 1770; in Dijon, Versailles, St. Germain and Paris in 1775; and in Paris and all over France in 1788–89. The crop failure of 1752 caused many disturbances." Moreover, beginning in 1765 there was noticeable worsening of the crops, which steadily continued year after year and became very serious in 1768–70. During these years the disorders in Limoges and L'Auvergne became real catastrophes. The rise in the bread prices caused disturbances in Nantes and Rouen and in other towns of Champagne, Normandy, Ile-de-France, and Burgundy. The aroused population attacked the bread storehouses, the markets, and they even plundered the granaries of the peasants.[66] The crops of 1774 and 1775 were very poor. The disorders during the spring of 1775 were very extensive, and came to be known as the "flour war." This rebellion was suppressed by 25,000 soldiers.

Beginning at this time proclamations against the king and his ministers appeared on the wall at Versailles. These rebellions were suppressed, but they left deep scars.[67] From 1777 to 1783 crops were good, and riots were comparatively few. In 1784 a new series of crop failures began, and concomitant with this the disorders increased. In 1785, 1786, and 1787 a number of disturbances and riots took place in Lyons, Sèvres, Vivarais, and other places.

At the end of the eighteenth century France came to resemble a volcano with uninterrupted rumblings, tremblings of the earth, and small but frequent eruptions. Simultaneous with the increase of disturbances the numbers of paupers, vagabonds, bandits, robbers, and thieves also increased, thus making up the army of the Revolution.[68] Because the hunger of the people was continuing, while the privileged classes were enriching themselves, these convulsions of the social aggregate finally had to end in a catastrophe. This catastrophe was accelerated by a complete crop failure in 1788. "And

66. H. Taine, op. cit., pp. 200–213.
67. Kropotkin, *The Great French Revolution*, p. 23 (in Russian).
68. H. Taine, op. cit., pp. 280–98.

suddenly the riots assumed wide, and threatening dimensions. . . . The foremost cause of the disturbances was the problem of the price of bread." [69]

Industrial crisis and unemployment were added to the crop failure. Unemployment and the high cost of living were the two whips from which the population of Paris suffered in 1789. The industrial crisis was already quite obvious in 1787, and at the end of 1788 France had 200,000 unemployed. Everywhere consumption had decreased. The winter of 1788–89 was particularly hard on industry and trade; production had decreased. In addition the year of hunger had forced masses of the unemployed people to come to Paris, and this incendiary material caused great concern to many of its inhabitants. This was the ground on which the stormy eruption took place; it characterized the extreme excitability of the needy urban mass in 1789, and its readiness for unmotivated and decisive reaction toward the most insignificant external causes. The first eruption occurred in Paris before the opening of the Estates-General (in April 1789); it led to the plunder of the houses of the industrialists Revellion and Arno. The course of these riots was motivated exclusively by hunger, unemployment, high cost of living, and lack of bread. [70]

Conditions became much worse as hunger raged throughout Paris; even very poor yellow scorched flour was not sufficient (by July 27 and afterward). In a number of places there were attempts to cut the unripe grain. [71] Starvation continued to increase and so did disturbances, both in Paris and in the provinces. On July 8 there was a riot of the unemployed; on the tenth the burning of the gates of Paris; on the twelfth Demoulain issued a call to arms; on the thirteenth the mobs went where there was some bread, namely to the monastery of St. Lazar, and seized it with the shouts of "bread," "bread"; and on the fourteenth the Bastille was stormed. In September the harvest was finished, but still there was no bread. Great lines were formed at the doors of the bakeries, and after long hours of waiting the people went home without bread. The outbreak of the mob on October 5 was caused by hunger and demand for bread.

Thus, hunger grew crescendo in 1789 and 1790, and the Revo-

69. Kropotkin, op. cit., pp. 39–41.

70. Tarle, *The Labor Class of France during the Epoch of the Revolution* (St. Petersburg, 1909), 1:17–18, 2:51 (in Russian).

71. Kropotkin, op. cit., pp. 46, 61–72.

lution also developed crescendo. But in 1790–91 "the deepening" and "broadening" of the Revolution assumed a slower pace. The question is why: because the years 1790 and 1791 were more favorable economically than the year 1789. In 1790 and particularly in 1791 the economic crisis lessened; the crops of these years were good, industry began to revive, and unemployment decreased.[72] The deepening of the Revolution slowed down considerably. A weak hope appeared of being able to guide the storm into proper channels. But, alas! In 1792 this temporary improvement disappeared, especially after the beginning of the war with the First Coalition, and France plunged into a new lengthy crisis.[73] The curve of revolution rose sharply; as famine and starvation intensified, the fury of the Revolution reached a maximum and France was flooded with running blood.

"With the coming of the winter of 1792–93 hunger assumed an even more sinister character. The municipalities tried desperately to obtain bread, even as little as ¼ lb. per person." Simultaneously the people's discontent with the rich ruling class, the Girondists, rose, and the rebellion against the latter broke out on May 31, 1793. But the National Convention did not produce any food, so that revolts against it also took place the same year of 1793. Since hunger did not diminish with the dictatorship of the Peak, it had to fall. Thermidor was inevitable.[74] During all these years of starvation the revolts due to hunger continued. On the twenty-first of Germinal there was a revolt in Avre, where for a week only two pounds of flour were distributed, on the fourteenth and fifteenth of Prairial one in Dieppe, on the ninth of Prairial in Vervins and on the fourth of Messidor one in Lille. Two revolts caused by the lowering of the bread ration from one pound to three-quarters of a pound occurred in Paris, in Germinal and Prairial of year III. These revolts continued even after Thermidor and sometimes they assumed great dimensions.[75]

Napoleon succeeded in giving an outlet to the revolts through the war of conquest. Because of revolutionary terror and war, the density of the population had decreased; due to this condition, along with

72. Tarle, op. cit., pp. 116 ff.
73. Ibid., p. 122.
74. Kropotkin, op. cit., pp. 327, 394, 495, passim.
75. Taine, op. cit., 3:529–32 ff.

some others, *the epoch of the restoration was comparatively favorable for the well-being of the masses.*[76]

Worsening conditions and the stagnation of industry began during the 1820s.[77] The disorders reappeared in the form of the Revolution of 1830, and in a number of insurrections, like that in Lyons which had as its motto *"vivre en travaillant ou mourir en combattant."* A vicious circle was created in which unemployment caused the rebellion, and the latter brought even worse economic conditions. Hence, the years 1831–32 were ones of "permanent revolts" of the laborers with the mottoes of "work or bread." [78]

The revolution of February 1848 and the rebellion of June 1847 were also connected with hunger. The crops in 1847 were very bad and in addition there were industrial crises in 1847 and 1848. Living conditions of the peasants, and especially those of workers, worsened considerably. The studies by Levasseur indicate that wages of workers fell to levels even lower than those prevailing at the beginning of the nineteenth century. The crisis of 1848 affected practically all labor. In many industries the decrease was tremendous. Meanwhile the cost of living in Paris increased twofold. While in 1730 an income of 3,000 francs was adequate, in 1848 it required 6,000 to maintain a comparable level of living. During periods of crisis and crop failures, poverty was particularly great in the industrial and commercial departments of France.[79]

Thus, the February revolution of 1848 was the social function of this determinant.[80] But, as happens in all revolutions, it did not improve conditions; the number of calories did not increase. There were more than 100,000 unemployed in Paris, and the industrial provinces were also in the same sad situation. The workers were in hopeless condition after the closing of the national shops. Their closing, on June 22, created hunger and the threat of it that caused the insurrection of June 23.[81]

76. Kareev, op. cit., 4:590.

77. L. Blan says that in 1830–31 wages of workers decreased from an average of 4–6 francs per day to 18–25 sou: *L'histoire de dix ans*, 3:48. Levasseur, *L'histoire des classes ouvrières* (1904), 3:6 ff.

78. Levasseur, *L'histoire*, 3:10 ff.

79. Ibid., pp. 259, 262–63, 281, 285 ff.

80. Karl Marx, *The Class Struggle in France 1848–55* (St. Petersburg), ed. Prosveshchenie, pp. 32–33 (in Russian).

81. Levasseur, *L'histoire*, 2:382–87.

Finally, *the connection between revolution and the commune of 1871 and hunger and starvation is a well-known fact.* The worsening of living conditions of the workers and the increase in strikes connected with it began with the crisis of 1866. It was augmented by the war and the siege.[82] The revolution occurred in the besieged city where the populace was experiencing acute deficiency starvation, and where there was no possibility of covering the deficit in any other way. At the same time there were in the city huge differences in wealth and income of the people.

A comparable relationship appeared later in other places, as in Belgium during the crisis of 1884–86, when the demand for working hands decreased sharply. This was particularly evident in 1886, which also was a year marked by tremendous bloody strikes.[83]

Similar conditions were observed in 1919–21. At this time the following also were evident: the high cost of living, an economic crisis,[84] a fall of the wages of workers, a rise in unemployment, or, in brief, the worsening of the economic conditions of France's workers which caused them to "turn to the left" politically. This period was characterized also by the growth of the Communist Party and of its adherence to the Third International, by the development of the ideas of "direct action" and "social revolution," and by the increase of strikes, disturbances, and bloody confrontations.[85] We see again and again that the same cause under similar conditions produces similar results.

Germany.—It would be possible to confirm our postulate by reviewing the entire history of Germany. However, I shall not do it at this time, but shall consider only a few of the revolutionary movements in her history.

The years at the end of the fifteenth century and the first thirty-

---

82. N. Lukin (Antonov), *The Paris Commune* (1922), p. 55 (in Russian).

83. H. Denis, "Le mouvement de la population et ses conditions économiques," 59:8.

84. Bogolepov, op. cit., p. 28. Considering the price level of 1901–10 as 100, prices during the years of the war increased and reached their maximum in September 1920, when the index was 607.5. Then it fell and was 411.9 in March 1921. This was the year revolts were most numerous.

85. The number of laborers on strike was 160,566 in 1914, and 651,702 in 1919. *Statistical Information on the Contemporary Economic Conditions of the Foreign Nations*, p. 82 (in Russian).

five years of the sixteenth were ones of very stormy insurrections of the peasants, communal movements, and struggles between paupers and wealthy in the towns (in addition to being ones of rebellions by the knights, religious confrontations, and wars).

As the investigations of Rogers, Sommerland, and Kaser have shown, during these periods there were sharp increases in the price of food, falling incomes of the working masses, heavy burdens of taxation, increased pauperism, and connected with all of these a worsening of nutrition. In Saxony the prices of grains rose sharply.[86]

Year	Rye	Wheat	Barley	Oats
1455–80	10.02	13.90	10.69	5.47
1521–30	22.50			
1531–40	29.44	29.80	22.89	12.51

During the period income did not rise, but rather it fell, and there were crop failures during several years. Nutrition of the peasants was poor. It was particularly bad during the wars, because the military forces had to provide nutrition for themselves by plundering the populace. To this must be added the pillaging "rides" of the king and the unbearably high taxes. Starvation of the population was beyond question.[87]

The rise of disturbances at the end of the fifteenth and beginning of the sixteenth centuries was a direct consequence of the conditions described. In 1476 there was an insurrection in Begeim, in 1493 one in Swabia, in 1514–15 that of "poor Konrad," and in 1525 there was the "great peasants' revolt," as well as others in Osnabrück, Paderborn, Münster, and the Rhineland, in 1530–32.[88]

The relationship under study appears still clearer during the disturbances in the 1840s in Germany, and in the revolution of 1848, the soaring prices, industrial upheaval, rise in unemployment, falling incomes, and high cost of living, along with the crop failures of

86. A work of Sommerland is cited.

87. Kulisher, *Economic History and the Mode of Living* (St. Petersburg, 1918), pp. 98–105 (in Russian).

88. See details in Kaser, *Politische und sociale Bewegungen im deutschen Burgertum zu Beginnen der 16 Jahrhunderts* (1899).

1847–48. The workers could hardly pay for the salt in their porridge.[89]

Finally, a perfect exposition of the relationship studied is to be found in the revolution of 1918–19 and in the subsequent disturbances led by the Communists, the laborers, etc.

At the end of the war the nutrition of the German populace was very poor. Notwithstanding substitutes, proteins and fats were lacking, and connected with this was a rise in mortality. Accompanying the rise in the cost of living and increased starvation, there were increases of disturbances, strikes, "leftist" tendencies, etc. The hungry social aggregate of the "nonrevolutionary" German populace began to writhe in the convulsions.

The stormy disorders of the second half of 1923 confirm still further the indicated relationship.[90] We all remember the catastrophic fall in the price of the mark in July and the months following in 1922–23. Every visitor to Germany at that time could see the deficiency in the nutrition of the urban population. As a result disturbances took place in various German cities and in some of them it reached great proportions.

Russia.—The relationship between hunger and disturbances appears just as clearly in the history of Russia. The method of "concomitant changes" easily outlines and confirms it.

The ancient chronicler (letopisets) wrote, "in 1024 in the region of Suzdal the populace was dying from hunger, was rioting and revolting." [91] Similar occurrences were reported in the years 1070, 1230–31, 1279, 1291, and 1314.[92] Thus, an independent variable, hunger, is followed by its function, the disturbances.

Similar conditions occurred later in Russia's history. At the end of the sixteenth century the economic situation of the masses worsened considerably. In central Russia a peasant with a little land, after paying all the taxes and obligations, had a deficit of 14 deneg and

89. Bloss, *History of the German Revolution of 1848* (St. Petersburg, 1907) (in Russian); and Hartmann, *Die Volkserhebung der Jahre 1848–49 in Deutschland* (1900).

90. This paragraph was written by P.S. in longhand on the page of the proof from which the translation was made. E.S.

91. Leshkoff, *The Russian People and the State*, p. 453 (in Russian).

92. The corresponding citations of the events described by the chronicler are in Old Slavic and are difficult to translate. E.S.

could not make ends meet. Only the wealthier peasant had some surplus. The peasants of the older regions became poorer and were ruined, while the tax burden was unbearable.[93] This condition favored eruptions and convulsions and only a stimulus was required to start them. This stimulus was supplied by catastrophic crop failures in 1601–2, and by "unbelievable starvation." [94] The disturbances arose as a direct result of this. To save themselves from death by starvation, the populace organized bands of robbers which roamed all over Russia. One band near Moscow was suppressed with difficulty by a large military force. In 1601 a rumor about a false Dmitri appeared and the Time of Troubles began.[95] The starving aggregate of Russia fell into convulsions, its members began to annihilate one another, one ruler was changed for another, who in turn was rejected because he could not feed the populace. Thus the country was impoverished and the density of the population diminished.[96]

The reign of Tsar Alexis was filled with disturbances and revolts. The patriarch Nikon in a letter to the Tsar in 1661 described the general condition and nutrition of the people as follows: "You advocate for all to fast, but now, because of the absence of bread, everybody is fasting, in some places fasting to the death, as there is nothing to eat. All have to pay tremendous duties on everything; everyone is crying and lamenting, and nobody is joyful." In a letter in 1665 he added: "they conscript the people into service, they take away bread and money unmercifully, the entire Christian world is burdened by taxation, twice, three times and even more, and everything is futile." [97]

It is, therefore, not surprising that the entire reign of Tsar Alexis abounded in revolts and disturbances. Many large disturbances occurred along with small riots. In 1648 there were riots in Moscow, Ustyug, Kozlov, Solvychegodsk, Tomsk, and other towns; in 1649 a riot was put down in Moscow, and rebellions suppressed in Nov-

93. Rozhkov, "Economics of Muscovitic Russia during the Second Half of the XVI Century," *Dela i Dni*, 1:78–79 (in Russian).

94. Firsov, "Hunger before the Time of Troubles," in *The Historical Characteristics* (Kazan, 1922) (in Russian).

95. Platonov, "The Famine in Moscow, Russia in 1601–1603," *Artelnoe Delo*, nos. 9–16 (1921–22) (in Russian).

96. Leshkoff, *Russian People*, p. 484.

97. Klyuchevsky, *Russian History* (1913), 3:307–8 (in Russian).

gorod and Pskov. In 1662 a new rebellion broke out in Moscow, and finally in 1670–71 the great peasant revolt led by Stephen Razin erupted in the Southeast.[98]

Many of these riots, e.g., those in Novgorod and Pskov, arose directly as a result of hunger.[99] Similar causes stimulated the riots of 1648 which were also against the high price of salt. Rodes, who was serving as the ambassador of Sweden, wrote in his reports: "It is obvious that the disturbances are spreading. As soon as the fire is extinguished in one place, it starts in another; under apparently cold ashes the fire is burning."

Platonov and Soloviev point out correctly that the revolt of Razin had also some nutritional foundation. "Because of the difficult economic situation" the populace was fleeing to the Ukraine and to the Don River. The number of people in the Don region increased, while the food supply decreased. "Many fugitives concentrated in the Don region and starvation was tremendous." Thus we see that deficiency of calories had played its role.[100]

During the reign of Catherine II serious crop failures occurred in 1766, 1772, 1774, 1776, 1783, 1784, 1785, 1787 and 1788 and they were accompanied by a great increase in the exploitation of the populace and by riots, such as the potato riot of 1765, the Moscow "plague" riot, which also was caused by starvation, and, finally, by the insurrection of Pugachev (1773–74).[101] Here again the connection between hunger and the disturbances is obvious. "Several investigators consider that Pugachev's rebellion was connected with the crop failures which occurred in the Eastern regions of Russia. The peak of the riot occurred during the fall months of the famine year 1774." [102]

A number of comparatively small disturbances occurred after crop failures in 1867–68, 1873, 1880, and 1891–92; but at these times the government and the society took some precautions in the

98. Ibid., p. 303.

99. B. Kurts, *The Condition of Russia in 1650–55, as Recorded in the Reports of Rodes* (Moscow, 1915), pp. 23–24 (in Russian).

100. Platonov, *Lectures*, p. 364 (in Russian); Soloviev, *History of Russia*, 3:291 ff.

101. Firsov, "The Peasant Riots until the Nineteenth Century," in *The Great Reform*, 2:4 (in Russian).

102. Ermolov, "Famines in Russia," 1:22 (in Russian).

form of resettlement of population and some other measures, and in these ways overcame the effects of starvation.

Later, *beginning in 1905 Russia again entered a period of crop failures*. That of 1905 was enormous. It embraced a large area of land in European Russia including many of the most important agricultural regions (the Chernozem, the middle-Volga, and the trans-Volga districts), the fields of which make up 43 per cent of all arable land in Russia. In comparison with the average for five previous years the shortage of grain in some provinces was as follows: Penza, 65.3 per cent; Riazan, 53.3 per cent; Voronezh, 51.3 per cent; Tula, 49.5 per cent; Saratov, 48 per cent; Tambov, 42 per cent; and Simbirsk, 40 per cent.[103]

The disturbances began with the plundering of estates of the nobility and of food storehouses, and fights in which local officials and landowners were killed by crowds. This agrarian movement, which was caused by starvation, coincided with general insurrections in the towns, which were caused by some other determinants; and as a result, all of this was known as the Revolution of 1905. One of the principal causes of this was the lowering of the number of calories below levels essential for nutrition of peasants and workers.

The crop failures of 1906 were also quite extensive, and the area they covered was large. The extremely severe winter of 1906–7 added to the discomfort of the populace. Prices rose sharply, from 20 to 100 per cent, in comparison with the fall months. Thus, the revolution of 1906–7 continued.

Finally, *the factor of hunger was also at the base of the 1917 revolution*. Beginning with the year 1916 we began to experience personally the worsening of nutrition (particularly in the cities). At the end of 1916 and at the beginning of 1917, the populations of the towns began to starve. As a result of this, we witnessed occasionally a sacking of the stores and markets, and growth of discontent and agitation. Because of the weakness of the government, and of a whole series of contributing conditions, bread riots involving men, women, and children occurred in January and February 1917. They started with the stopping and overturning of streetcars, and continued with the overthrow of the more solid items, such as the throne, and the government. The monarchy was ended, but hunger

103. Ibid., 1:276–78.

grew worse.[104] The revolution began to "deepen" further. The Provisional Government was overthrown in October and the "bourgeois class began to be socialized."

Because starvation was increasing, and because there was something to "socialize," the revolution deepened, and power came into the hands of those who encouraged this socialization. However, as soon as there was nothing more to nationalize, a break occurred. Hunger was not satisfied, and the peasants had to give away more than they received. Thus, in 1919, when everything had been divided, when the need increased in towns and in the consuming provinces, and when in the productive provinces all surpluses, even the seed for the next year's crop, were subject to requisition, then the revolts against the Soviet Government began and they soon assumed wide dimensions.

This phenomenon is again sharply demonstrated by the events in February and March 1921. All of the extraordinary rations were terminated, and the ordinary rations were cut by more than one-half. As a result the workers demonstrated on the streets on February 24–27. Strikes, disturbances, and armed confrontations followed. The government applied its brakes: a military situation was introduced on February 25, and on March 2 it was changed to the state-of-siege condition. The disturbances reached Kronstadt [a military fortress near Petrograd. E. S.], and the war was on in full fury! The government took extraordinary precautions to control the revolt and to enforce delivery of food supplies to workers. The latter were promised special trains to bring food supplies and also the distribu-

104. For example, in Petrograd a worker of the first category received:

Year	Month	Calories	Year	Month	Calories
1917	July	1698	1918	January	698
1917	August	1657	1918	February	554
1917	September	1584	1918	March	954
1917	October	1393	1918	April	992
1917	November	1167	1918	May	480
1917	December	1038			

The median for 1918 equals 617 calories (plus what was bought on the black market). The median for 1919 equals 1,394 calories (less was bought on the market). The median for 1920 equals 1,577 calories. Slovtsov, "Governmental Nutrition of the Foremost Group of Labor (Udarniki) for 1917–20," *Bulletin*, Division of Labor Statistics, no. 32 (in Russian).

tion among them of the last remnants of the food in the storehouses. These radical measures helped to curb the disturbances and rebellious Kronstadt fell.

The role of hunger as a factor in the strikes is clearly demonstrated by the demands made by the strikers. For example, the railroad workers demanded the right to bring food supplies in freely, and other workers the right to bring in 2 puds of grain (a pud is 40 pounds). Thus, all strikes in Petrograd were connected with nutrition. The political demands were insignificant.[105]

These detailed materials make the stated relationship still more obvious and its validity beyond all doubt. And even at present such phenomena occur almost daily. The wire services of almost all the newspapers include similar items. Thus, demonstrations, strikes, and disturbances took place during these years in France, England, Germany, Austria, Poland, and Italy. Afterward the gradual improvement of nutritional conditions in Europe was accompanied by "pacification" of the revolutionary labor movement, making it turn more to the "right" politically. Abolishment of bread cards when bread became available was far more efficient in pacifying the disorders and controlling the counterrevolution than all the proclamations against them and the introduction of a state-of-siege.

However, I do not maintain that revolutions are caused exclusively by "pinching the nutritional reflexes," and that other factors play no important roles. Of course they do. But it has been important to show by the example of one of the fundamental reflexes the significance of its "pinching" in the emergence of disturbances. This is why I concentrated my research on the problem of hunger.

Every concrete historical event represents a result of many determinants, which work with the one studied, either by weakening or strengthening its effects. For example, the speech reflexes of the enlightened philosophy of the eighteenth century or the ideas of liberty of Russia's liberal socialist intelligentsia impeded many conditioned reflexes (religious, or legal, in the form of respect and subordination to the nobility, king, tsar, capital, bourgeois, etc.) which hindered the development of the revolution. And conversely they encouraged the indicated philosophy and ideology, and revolutionary,

105. Novoselsky, "The Strike Movement in Petrograd's Industries," *Bulletin*, Division of Labor Statistics, no. 8 (November 15, 1919), pp. 3–7 (in Russian).

atheistic, nihilistic, and democratic reflexes (Rousseau, Voltaire, the Encyclopedists). All of this assisted hunger to induce revolutions and disturbances by enhancing its effect.[106] But from this it does not follow that the indicated disturbances are the function principally of "ideological" determinants. Among the disturbances mentioned, e.g., during the Times of Trouble, the disturbances during the reign of Tsar Alexis, Pugachev's revolt, and the Jacquerie, the preparatory ideologies were entirely lacking, but the disturbances took place; conversely, the revolutionary ideology may exist, when disturbances are lacking. The latter simply do not take place during a satiated state of the aggregate. We shall see also that the degree of acceptance of a revolutionary ideology has a definite connection with fluctuations in the curve of nutrition of the masses. Therefore, the disturbances which have been discussed above cannot be considered primarily as functions of the "ideological variables." They are secondary factors in the disturbances, but not the decisive ones.

If we designate the disturbances by the letter y and their independent variables by letters a (hunger), b, c, d, . . . n (the remaining determinants), then the validity of a would be in these cases considerably higher than of any of the other factors. If, furthermore, we were to designate the influence of all the factors by the figure 100, we have to give a much higher coefficient of validity to a than to any of the remaining, e.g. ($y = a_{50} + b_{10} + c_5 + d_{10}$ . . . n_{25}).[107]

The secondary function of hunger.—The disturbances and revolutions which represent the primary functions of hunger, in turn, are the cause of a whole series of secondary functions of hunger, which deform the composition of the population, the structure of society, and the courses of social processes.

If we consider large disturbances in the form of deep and serious revolutions with shedding of blood, assaults, and war—and real revolutions involve these—then we see that the social sequences pro-

106. "The socialistic ideas which deny private property, the teachings of Tolstoy, Marx and others, played a tremendous role in the events of October 17, 1905 and the subsequent years." Vitte, *Memoires*, 2:4.

107. I again emphasize here that the series of disturbances discussed in this investigation do not include all of the disturbances which have occurred during the course of history. In some of the other disturbances the role of hunger was minimal, and those of the wars, of ideological factors or of the sex factor far more important. But at present I am not dealing with those cases.

duced by them closely resemble the results of wars in general. Why? Because serious revolutions which assume the form of civil war actually are wars.

1. As far as the *composition of the population* is concerned, revolutions call forth a tremendous decrease of the population (through war, hunger, epidemics), and qualitative selection in "reverse," i.e., the loss of the best elements: (a) those capable of working, and the healthy stratum of the population (for the same reason as in the war); (b) more males than females; (c) the most gifted, energetic, and outstanding personalities of both factions (the rank and file of the monarchists and Jacobins survived while Robespierre, Danton, Condorcet, Hébert, and important royalists perished); (d) the most qualified intellectually; and (e) the most honest. Add to this the facts of emigration and significance of heredity, and we may say that a *bloody revolution is a powerful instrument of selection, which kills first-rate material and lets the human seed of the second-rate live and multiply.*

2. In the area of *natural movement of population*, deep, prolonged revolutions cause a fall in the birth rate and a rise in the death rate.

3. The change in the behavior of the people calls forth fundamental *changes of the structure of the social aggregate and of the social organization.* Among the principal changes are that the most important social groups and social strata (racial, language, proprietary, religious, professional, and legal) [108] become intermixed and partially abolished. Confusion and uncertainties result. It seems as if the kingdom of equality is reached, and all social inequalities are destroyed forever. But very quickly "the perennial illusion" disappears and stratification reappears, in a new form and with changes in the composition of each stratum. Former occupants of the "upper stories" are thrown into the basement, while many of those who occupied the latter begin to live in the upper stories; rich become poor, and many poor become rich; those who lacked any rights become the privileged rulers, and former rulers and aristocrats lose all their rights and privileges; laborers become ministers, and ministers become laborers, etc. Very soon afterward the destroyed structure is rebuilt but its inhabitants have changed positions. "The perennial illusion" is destroyed, and everything becomes what it was before. A revolu-

108. See P. A. Sorokin, *System of Sociology*, vol. 2 (in Russian).

tion, similar to a war, calls forth centralization, despotism, and absolutism in the entire political and social organization. The degrees and dimensions of interference of those in power in the lives of the citizens broaden tremendously, and the rights and privileges of the latter shrink to a minimum. Here power is a dictator, and the populace a mere puppet. All life begins to be controlled from the top.[109]

Truly a joker was he who invented the idea that the epochs of revolutions are those of freedom, and of rule by the majority. Freedom (above all, that of the masses) and revolution are incompatible. Dictatorship and rule by the majority are opposites. Never has a despot had such despotical powers as those of the revolutionary dictatorship. Every slave of the former has had more rights than those of the citizens of the revolution, the peasants and workers (with the exception of agents of the revolution). Freedom of speech, press, and assembly, and personal liberty, are all annihilated by either a red or by a white revolution. Power interferes with everything. People are slaughtered en masse *ad majorem gloriam* of the revolution, or the counterrevolution. There is neither justice nor guarantees. There is no one to whom to appeal. The citizen becomes merely a snail which at any moment may be crushed beneath the heel of the commissar. That is why the paradoxical statement says that the greatest periods of reaction are the periods of revolution, and the greatest despots are the greatest revolutionary dictators.[110] The so-called counterrevolutionary pacifiers are only another version of the revolutionary dictatorship. When, in the course of time, following a revolution, the period of restoration of human liberties, of their energy and labor, begins, it comes not because of the revolution, but rather in spite of it, and it comes several years after the termination of the revolution.

4. *All processes of social life are changed.* Productivity falls, economies are destroyed, and peaceful labor becomes weaker. Poverty, hunger, epidemics, and death arrive. Creativity in all fields of culture comes to a halt: in science, art, social life, etc., everything except in ways of annihilating people, the techniques of the firing squad and of the guillotine. This is caused by hunger and the ten-

---

109. Lebon said, "Social revolution has a consequence . . . of putting the society into a strait jacket." G. Lebon, *The Psychology of Socialism* (St. Petersburg, 1908), p. 536 (in Russian).

110. N. Webster, *A Study in Democracy* (London, 1919).

sions to which creative people are subjected. However, in the field
of speech reactions (fraternity, equality, freedom, etc.) the revolution exhibits great productivity. High-sounding slogans are poured
out like waterfalls, but, alas, they remain mere slogans, and not
facts. I know of no revolution I have studied which paid its obligations and promises and survived. A revolution is a great tempest.
Under contemporary conditions inevitably it occurs from time to
time, like an inevitable disease of the organism. Such diseases are indications of poor living conditions and of the poor constitution of the
organism. Healthy organisms can live without them. The same applies to revolutions. Bad diseases either make the organism weak, or
lead it to death, either weaken society, or put it away in the archives
of history and revolution.[111]

111. All of these statements will be proved in my forthcoming book *The
Sociology of Revolution*. (The book was published in 1925 by J. B. Lippincott,
New York. It is now available in reprinted edition by H. Fertig [New York,
1967]. E.S.)

11

The changes in the whole social organization of a starving aggregate which occur after the imposition of additional conditions (to be indicated) represent an additional social function of hunger. The changes are referred to here under the designation of compulsory statism.

The Concepts of Compulsory Statism and Anarchist Society and the Connection between the Former and Hunger

By ideal or completely compulsory statism I mean such an aggregate in which the centralized power of society regulates all aspects of the behavior of its subjects, beginning with the religious, juridical, and moral interrelationships, and ending with the economic. In other words, under complete compulsory statism, society is characterized by *unlimited interference in safeguarding and regulating life, behavior, and mutual relationships among the citizens, complete lack of autonomy and self-determination,* and *frequently egalitarian despotism.* This is a society in which the power and its agents regulate absolutely the entire behavior of the citizen: what he must do, which profession to select and how to practice it, whether or not to marry and under what conditions, what to eat, what clothes to wear and when, what to believe, how to think, what to study, what to read, what to write, whether or not to have children, to live or to die, i.e., every sphere of behavior and interaction of the subjects. In legal

275

terms the *private-legal relationship is completely absent, and all relationships are public-legal and are regulated and determined from above*. The principal features characteristic of such society are as follows.

1. *The power of such a state is absolute and unlimited*. A man or citizen has no rights which the central power may not abrogate. There is no sphere in the behavior of the citizen into which the state's power may not reach. "State power here is higher than the law," since "what the state power wants becomes a law." The subjects, like soldiers in an army, must obey it without any reservations.

2. *Such a society is centralized in every respect*. There is no private initiative; there is no room in it for individual enterprise (and if it occurs occasionally, it must be according to the will of the central power). (a) *All economic relationships are regulated by the centralized power. All arms, means of production, and utilities belong to it. Private property does not exist, and there is no private ownership of the means of production*. The state and its top officials determine what to produce, how much to produce, and how to distribute and use the products. This is an organized society, which has neither anarchy in production nor competition between private industrialists.[1] (b) *The central power also determines all the other relationships of subordinates from cradle to grave*. (c) *The central power regiments individuals in both positive and negative directions. It tells the individual what he can and what he cannot do*.

3. Accordingly, such a society is characterized by an *egalitarian despotism, where all are slaves, deprived of all legal rights and power*.

4. In a private-capitalistic society the accrued interest becomes the property of those who own the means of production, i.e., the capitalists. In a compulsory-statism society the group which acquires the accrued interest is the central power and its agents.

Such are the principal characteristics of completely compulsory statism. Its opposite form is the completely individualistic-anarchistic society, without god and without a central power, in which people have full autonomy in their behavior, and where all relationships are private-legal and have no regulation from above. Neither type of society has ever existed in its ideal form. All forms of social organization represent intermediary types between the two pure ones at the

1. Bukharin and Preobrazhenskii, *The ABC's of Communism* (1920), pp. 51–52 (in Russian).

extremes. Some aggregates are nearer to compulsory statism, while others resemble more the anarchistic type. History swings to and fro between them, sometimes approximating one, sometimes the other of the types of societies it has created. The costumes change; the actors vary, as do the scenery, the decorations, the space and time; but the types of the society indicated are perennial.

If in various ways we dilute, trim, or soften completely statist society, we would obtain these societies: the primeval societies of ancient times, the kingdom of the Incas, the despotisms of the East (Egypt, Assyria, Babylonia, Persia, China, Japan) and during certain periods of history, those of Sparta, Athens, Rome (in the third and fourth centuries), the realm of Mahomet (in a number of the caliphates), some of the medieval aggregates and communes (Tabor, the New Jerusalem of I. Leiden, the commune of Munster), and some societies during their periods of wars and revolutions (Austria in the period of Franz Joseph, Prussia in that of Frederick the Great, Russia under Peter I, France under Napoleon, and the USSR during the period of the military communism and state capitalism).

The same *mutatis mutandis* refers to the pure individual-anarchistic type, some diluted forms of which also have existed in the past (although not as often as the first type). At present, in the time of capitalism and individualism, they appear quite frequently, as, for example, most of the aggregates of Europe and America, and particularly England and the United States in the modern period. This type, therefore, is more characteristic of modern times in Europe and America, while the other type prevailed more in earlier periods; hence compulsory-statism societies of the anarchistic type also existed in the past. Also the transformation of the latter into statism takes place even now.[2]

Various kinds of socialistic and communistic societies (with the exception of purely voluntary socialism—which is another designation for anarchistic society) are diluted versions of statism. The main characteristics of the latter are the nationalization of all the means and instruments of production (and some of the doctrines also include

2. The proposed classification of societies, which was outlined earlier by Spencer, is far more essential, well founded, and important than the division of societies into republics and monarchies, autocracies and democracies, capitalistic and socialistic states, etc.; the latter classification does not deal with the most essential characteristics of such societies.

consumption); elimination of private property; replacement of the "anarchy of private volitions" by an economy planned by the government or the society; regulation of exchange, distribution, and consumption (in the name of equality); equal public education for all (regulated from the top); communization of the family and marriage, the regulation of births, etc. This also represents statism, only in a different version and proportions. To accomplish this mission most ideologists favor "dictatorship" with the application of force. Very old things are offered to us as the greatest salvation. True, those who approve of such constructions inform us that their societies would not know class distinction, inequality, exploitation, war, poverty, struggle, and that the state would have no power! However, it is important to know not what they promise, but what the actual reality has to offer.

Facts indicate that, among all the numerous attempts to realize such a society, there is not a single one in which these illusions were fulfilled. Diametrically opposite results occurred in all cases, with no exceptions, i.e., exploitation, inequality, struggle, war, despotic use of power, poverty, etc., not only failed to decrease, but indeed increased. When a scientist performs an experiment in the laboratory one, two, five, ten, twenty-five times, and the results are opposite to ones he expected, then he must admit that his hypothesis is faulty, and that the opposite is correct. Social life is a laboratory. The events of history are the experiments. When numerous attempts to realize the statist type of the society have failed to achieve the wonderful results, then one must be either a fool, or a scoundrel, to insist that the indicated beneficial properties exist in such a society. In the natural sciences, experimenters of this kind are dismissed, but in the social sciences they still flourish.

Under some definite conditions, massive starvation calls forth changes in the social organization in the direction of compulsory statism, at least in the area of the nutritional mechanism, and through it in some other aspects of social life. This deformation is expressed in an increase in governmental regulation and interference; restriction of autonomy and self-determination in the behavior of the citizen; as the result of the latter, limitations of the rights of ownership and other proprietorial rights, all of which lead to taxation, monopoly, requisition, redistribution, nationalization, and often to complete communism in consumption; the growth of centralization and regulation from above of the economics of the society (industry, trade, distribution of food). All of this is at the cost of the decentralized "anarchistic" self-regulation of the citizens, or in other words is the *growth of compulsory (state) economy at the cost of free enterprise.* This is easy to understand. *When the supply of any kind of goods is plentiful, everyone can consume as much as he wishes. The regulation of consumption is unnecessary, and all limitations of the freedom of the citizen are needless.* From this it is evident why, to date, there has been no regulation of consumption of air and water. In the past, when land was plentiful, everyone could claim as much as was desired. The same is true about every valuable product, particularly bread and other foods. The picture changes rapidly when there is a deficiency. Increased density of population causes a number of regulations and limitations upon land, its use, ownership, and distribution; the same happens to water, where the supply is limited, and the same occurs with respect to food. *There is complete freedom in consumption of that which is in abundant supply, and limitation of consumption when the amount available has to be taken into account.*[3]

Therefore, statism is an absolute necessity for the society that is experiencing deficiencies and hunger. It takes place in three instances: *when the society is unable to satisfy its hunger by some other means* (importation, etc.); *when there is great proprietary differentiation:* stored food supplies, and wealth inside the country (without which there would be nothing to divide, to regulate, or to attract the hungry); and *under some supplementary conditions.* These include: (1) *the extent of power of the rich and the poor* (when the rich are all-powerful, they repel the attacks of the poor and statism occurs as a result of the oppression of the latter who become dependents; conversely, when the poor are strong, their ruling group wields the power, and then statism favors them); (2) *the strength of the central power and the direction of its politics,* which, however, cannot prevent statism, but can only direct it to the advantage of those in power (depriving the hungry of the last piece of bread in favor of their clients and supporters), or in favor of the wealthy (enslavement of the lower classes), or in favor of the poor (expropriation of the wealth of the exploiters, nationalization of the property of the bourgeois class, etc.); (3) *the character of the reflexes of the*

3. Barnish, *The Principles of Positive Politics According to Solvay* (Brussels), p. 34.

population (e.g., if the reflexes of private property and respect toward other people's property are strong, this will inhibit the development of statism, but if they are weak this will encourage it).

When lack of food cannot be overcome by some other means, food taxis will push the hungry to seize the food reserves and wealth which are found in the country. This task can be accomplished in three principal ways: *by the direct action of the hungry masses*, expressed in disturbances, revolutions, and "nationalization"; *by the pressure on the central power*, forcing it to feed the hungry at the cost of the well fed; and *by the voluntary gifts by the rich and satiated* of parts of their possessions and food to the hungry, either free or for different services or obligations (this does not occur on a large scale). The last phenomenon occurs when the degree of the resistance of the rich is great and is sufficient to withstand the "direct actions" of the hungry. In this case a type of statism develops which favors the wealthy through the enslavement of the hungry and the increase of inequality. The first two cases lead directly, or indirectly, to the growth of statism.

When a revolution is successful, after the overthrow of the former power by direct action, the hungry form their own dictatorship, which expropriates and nationalizes everything, or, in other words, limits the autonomy of the people. The history of "successful" revolutions confirms this. When food taxis of the starving does not lead them to a great revolution, it may, nevertheless, exert pressure upon those in power in other ways to force them to feed the hungry at the cost of the satiated. Because the central power does not produce the food itself, but only collects it, it can perform this task only by interfering with the economy of the society by taxes, requisitions of supplies, monopoly of distribution, etc., or, in other words, by statism. In such cases the growth of statism is inevitable.[4]

4. Here are some examples: In Vienna at the end of 1921 the food situation was very bad, and the luxury of the wealthy was extreme. "The workers demanded the introduction of governmental control over the operations of the stock exchange, a prohibition of the importation of objects of luxury, the requisition of the property of the church, of gold, and the confiscation of large fortunes and gains" (*Krasnaya Gazeta*, December 16, 1921). "Vienna. A resolution was adopted by the unemployed during their meeting in Vienna which demanded the organization of public works, enlargement of the governmental subsidies, insurance for the workers, and compulsory hiring" (*Krasnaya Gazeta*, February 18, 1922). With some variations similar phenomena happened in the USSR.

Finally, even in the cases when revolution is unsuccessful and it is suppressed by the rulers, some increase of statism is inevitable. Why? Because, in order to suppress disturbances there must be an army, supporters, and praetorians. These have to be fed, and the food has to be obtained within the country itself, as we have excluded all other means of procurement. This means, in turn, an increase in the requisitions of supplies, in interference, in control, in centralization, and in governmental monopoly. Otherwise, without food the praetorians will disperse, and there will be an end to government. In times of starvation the central power is forced to requisition from the population not only surplus supplies, but also the last of the grain, not only from the wealthy, but also from the poor, and again not only to feed the hungry, but to feed its supporters. The combination of compulsory measures and brakes, by means of which the central power takes away the last "crumbs" from the populace, keeps the starving under control and lets them die in peace. Thus, the curve of statism rises to the maximum because the central power has to concentrate in one place all possible supplies of food. Terror, despotism, and oppression become enormous and therefore the growth of statism in all these cases is more or less inevitable.

Hunger leads to the same result in still another way, i.e., by means of war and revolution. We see that centralization, militarization, and military communization, or the same compulsory statism, are the direct consequences of war and revolution. During periods of frequent wars, changes in the social organization in the direction of "military communism" are called for in the name of self-preservation, or in the interest of group survival, since the group which is transformed into a military camp has a better chance of survival than the unmilitarized one. The same determinant of self-preservation in the interest of the preservation of the group requires statism in the society that is starving or deficient in nutrition, because in the absence of statism the perennial struggle between hungry and well-fed individuals would continue. Such a struggle would weaken the group and would diminish its chances for success in confrontations with other groups.

Because of the struggle for preservation of the group, and with no other purpose intended, a regime of statism must be established which would be suitable for the existing conditions. From this it is obvious that in analyzing causes of the occurrence of statism in a given aggregate, it often is difficult to determine how much is caused

by war (as a determinant of group preservation) and how much by
hunger.

The general guiding principle in such cases is this rule: *In the
area of economic and nutritional relationships, statism is primarily
a function of hunger; statism in other fields is primarily a function
of the determinant of self-preservation. Thus, statism is a function
of both variables working simultaneously, plus other, less important
determinants.*

These facts explain the mechanism of the relationship between
statism and hunger, and indicate that the increase of hunger is not
the only independent variable in the development of statism.

The Basic Propositions and Their Verification

If the main hypothesis of relationship between mass starvation and
statism is correct, then from it follow further propositions, the verified proofs of which may attest to the validity of the principal
theorem.

*The first proposition: Under equal conditions in the insecure ag-
gregates, which are subject to a constant threat of starvation, and
in which proprietorial differentiation prevails, statism exists in the
field of economic-nutritional relations (and through them in some
other fields, especially if the society is militaristic); i.e., statism prevails in the aggregates where the amount of interference and the
regulatory functions of the central power are extensive and development is centralized, while the economic autonomy of private individuals is very limited. In the aggregates where nutrients are more
secure, statism must be less developed, while the economic autonomy
of the citizen is considerably broader.*

The second proposition: Ceteris paribus, *in one and the same
aggregate the curve of statism in the economic-nutritional field must
rise under these conditions: starvation of the masses increases (or nutrition worsens), the proprietorial differentiation increases, or the
two conditions exist simultaneously, i.e., nutrition of the masses
worsens and proprietorial differences increase. Conversely, the curve
of compulsory statism must fall when nutrition of the masses im-
proves (deficiency and comparative deficiency starvation decrease),
proprietorial differentiation decreases, or both conditions are present. Finally, the curve of statism may remain constant, when the
worsening of nutrition of the masses coincides with a decrease in pro-*

prietorial differentiation, or the improvement of the former is accompanied by the growth of the latter.

To prove these propositions according to the principle that "similar causes under similar circumstances call forth similar consequences," we must secure *models of the groups* which will satisfy the conditions indicated, and must see if the facts support the propositions. History provides numerous such models.[5]

We shall consider first *the constantly repeated facts*, and, second, *the histories of different people.*

The substantiation of the propositions by means of constantly repeated facts.—In social life we often observe a number of aggregates in the position of being threatened by hunger. Such groups of people are found in besieged fortresses, on wrecked ships and trains, among explorers at certain moments during their expeditions (e.g., Przhevalsky, Stanley, Scott, Mikkelsen, etc.), and also in certain families and other larger groups. In observing them, we see that as soon as the threat of starvation appears, statism arises in one form or another: all available food is taken into account (in towns, fortresses, ships, expeditions, families); the right of individuals to dispose of any of it is limited at once; and the entire supply becomes the property of the aggregate. Rationing, the portions to be given out, is established, as well as a public regulation of distribution and consumption, or, in other words, statism in its pure form. The more severe the starvation, the stronger the force of statism. Everyone has observed that in many families where the food supply is limited, members are not allowed to eat as much as they wish, and food is portioned out. In place of autonomous free will, a planned distribution occurs in accordance with the dictates of the head of the group, or of all its members. As soon as food becomes plentiful, such statism disappears. These processes are repeated constantly; on a small scale they show what takes place in larger aggregates under similar conditions. These phenomena may be observed, and they serve as proofs of both propositions.

The historical verification of the first proposition.—To confirm

5. The method of models, which I have used before, is a major method of the Anglo-American physicists. In sociology, unfortunately, so far we have been unable to construct the models ourselves and must take them from history. However, the method of models does not suffer from this. See Dugem, *Physical Theory: Its Purpose and Structure* (St. Petersburg, 1910) (in Russian).

the validity of this proposition we shall take as models, first, the aggregates with insecure food supplies which are constantly threatened by hunger, and, second, the ones with plentiful supplies.

The following aggregates may serve as models of those which are constantly threatened by starvation and that frequently actually are starving: many "primitive societies," the large cities and many regions of the ancient East, Egypt, China, Persia, Japan, some of the states of ancient Greece, Rome (during certain periods of its history), Byzantium, some Islamic states, many medieval aggregates, and some poorly supplied societies of modern times. The majority of the most advanced states of Europe and North America in the nineteenth and twentieth centuries may serve as models of the comparatively satiated aggregates in which mass deficiency starvation came to be unknown.

The primitive societies. Because these were aggregates of hunters, fishermen, and collectors of wild tubers, seeds, and fruits, they did not develop ways or possibilities (due in part to the absence of salt) for preserving food. They lived from day to day with no care for the morrow. Dependent upon the elements, fishing, hunting, they either overindulged in food, or, more often, "suffered bitter need, and their only garment—the belt—served as a means by which they could reduce the pangs of hunger by compressing their stomachs." [6] Therefore, both the threat of hunger and actual starvation were always present. There were some exceptions to this, but they were comparatively few.[7]

6. K. Bücher, *Die Entstenung der Volkswirtschaft* (Leipzig, 1893), 1:37, 2:13, 40–46.

7. See Herbert Spencer, *Principles of Sociology*, 1:26–30, 2:557–58; E. Westermarck, *The Development of Moral Ideas*, 2:269–71; Vierkandt, *Naturvölker und Kulturvölker* (1896), pp. 20 ff.; Steinmetz, *Rechtsverhältnisse von Eingeborenen Völkern in Afrika und Ozeanien* (Berlin, 1903); Spencer and Gillen, *The Northern Tribes of Central Australia;* and *The Native Tribes of Central Australia* (London, 1899), chaps. on nutrition and the mode of living; Bücher, op. cit., vol. 1, chap. 1; L. T. Hobhouse, G. C. Wheeler, and M. Ginsberg, *The Material Culture and Social Institutions of the Simpler Peoples: An Essay in Correlation* (London, 1915); E. Grosse, *Die Formen der Familie und die Formen der Wirtschaft* (Freiburg, 1896); M. Kovalevsky, *The Origin of Family and of Property: Lectures on Primitive Culture and Ethnography* (in Russian). It is true that the ownership of property is on a very small scale in these societies, but it exists to some extent, and the threat of starvation is tremendous.

In such aggregates, accordingly, we should expect to find highly developed communism in consumption, broad dimensions in the power of the group [8] in the area of regulating food, absence of or very limited private property, little individual autonomy with respect to food as well as in other aspects of behavior, very tight control over the whole group, which is manifested in strong repression of every deviation from the established norms, etc.

This situation exists in the primitive groups which have no especially favorable conditions of life. Among most primitive peoples all food secured is *the common property of the whole group*, except for the part of it that is consumed on the spot (by hunters, etc.). The rest is placed at the disposal of the group as a whole, is divided among its members according to certain rules, or is consumed during special festivals, either by the group or by one of its subdivisions. The individual's rights of ownership, use, and distribution are negligible. The power of the group (through its chief, medicine man, leader, elders of the assembly, etc.) is absolute. Thus, the reality confirms our proposition.[9]

In a still greater degree, similar conditions refer to the *main factors in the production of foodstuffs*—land, water and herds.

Finally, among primitive peoples the full and complete control of the individual and the regulation of his behavior and of his ways of living by the power of the group is obvious and needs no further proof. The autonomy of the individual is absolutely negligible.[10]

---

8. It is immaterial whether the power is wielded by one person or many, or whether the chieftains are elected or appointed; the important thing is that the group's power, either willingly or unwillingly, binds all the members of the group and restricts their actions and autonomy.

9. There is some dispute about whether we are dealing here with "communal ownership" or with "communal use." To me this problem is insignificant. The important thing is to know whether the people themselves distribute it autonomously, or whether it is done by the power of the group.

10. If the "primitive communism" of primitive groups is the function of hunger and nutritional insecurity, then total control and regulation of the life of the members is the function of a number of other independent variables, among which an important role is played by the determinant of group protection and group self-preservation. This determinant may necessitate wars for the survival of the group. Together with hunger it produces the all-inclusive statism of primitive peoples. In these societies both of these independent variables are working concomitantly. Were it not for the communism in consumption, the chances of perishing from hunger would be high: without help

Thus, the primitive communism and complete submergence of personality in the group (statism) among primitive peoples are functions of constant wars (determinant of group self-protection) and of the permanent threat of hunger. This model, therefore, confirms the connection between hunger and statism.

Ancient Egypt. The nutrition of Egypt, particularly in towns, was built on the shaky foundation of plunder by the military. As can be learned from the ancient records, famine was frequent and the threat of it was constant. The condition of the masses was lamentable.[11] Wars were frequent, and, therefore, throughout almost all the ancient period essentially a *state economy* prevailed. The autonomy of individuals was negligible. The people were absolutely at the mercy of the king and his officials. In the political life of the country they had no share whatsoever; they had no right to private property, especially in land. Their lives, their goods, and their labor were in the king's hands, and he might dispose of them as he thought fit. He decreed which fields were to be sown in any year, what seed should be sown, and who should sow it; he indicated what share of the harvest the husbandman had to surrender to the government. He named the individuals to perform public services, dig canals, build dikes, erect temples, make tombs, construct palaces, quarry stone, hunt wild animals, and mine for salt or metals. Education was the monopoly of the state, and foreign trade as well. The state prescribed religion, profession, nutrition, and habitations. In brief, it regulated and controlled all economic and spiritual life. The pharaoh was believed to be the son of a god, and himself to be divine; his power was unlimited, and everything was centralized.[12]

The state made regular accountings of all the population and their possessions. It controlled all agriculture and industry, and was

---

from other members, an unsuccessful hunt for several days by some individuals could bring them to their deaths. Furthermore, because of food taxis, some starving members of the group attack the well-fed persons, thus producing perennial struggle within the group. Either phenomenon could weaken the group and decrease chances of survival. Therefore primitive communism of consumption, dictated by hunger, increased chances of survival, and the problem of survival itself led to the communism of consumption.

11. J. H. Breasted, *Ancient Records of Egypt* (Chicago, 1906–7), vol. 1.

12. J. H. Breasted, *A History of the Ancient Egyptians;* Turaev, *Ancient Egypt,* pp. 42–45 (in Russian).

the principal agent for exchange and distribution. It determined rations for workers and payments to agents and officials; it was in charge of the work of all the enslaved population, their nutrition, their clothing, and their habitations.[13]

The feudal period of Egypt's history was a time of trouble and disorder. This state of things was deplored with pathetic eloquence and profound pessimism by Ipuwer in his "Admonitions." [14]

Ancient (and in part modern) China. Famine occurred frequently in China in ancient times and in modern times also. The nutrition of the masses was very poor and general poverty was extreme.[15]

China already was overpopulated in its early history. Periodically the population was reduced by tens of millions of people, by epidemics, famines, wars, and revolutions. The figures on the density of population are given by Parker and Smith. For example, in A.D. 723 the population was 45.5 million; in A.D. 755, 53 million; and in A.D. 781, only 20 million (after anarchy, war, and famine). Later, the rebellion of Taiping reduced the population from 334 million to 260 million people.[16]

Under such conditions (plus wars and civil struggles), the level of statism had to be very high. And, indeed, high it was. The behavior of the people was very uniform. It was conditioned by the perennial guide of Confucianism, which regimented all the details of life, except a few minor ones. The rights of the governing power

---

13. Breasted, *Ancient Records of Egypt*, 1:84–95. The food ration was not very bad at certain times; during the reign of Pharaoh Seti a mason received four pounds of bread per day, two bunches of vegetables, and a piece of fried meat; twice a month he received new garments. In the towns the people lived in barracks, which belonged to the state. Occupations and professions were hereditary. Rights and privileges did not exist. Private initiative was insignificant. In brief, the most complete form of statism existed in Egypt.

14. M. Rostovtzeff, *A History of the Ancient World* (Oxford, 1936), vol. 1; cf. G. Maspero, *Historical Readings* (St. Petersburg, 1905), chaps. 1–4, 12 (in Russian), and G. Maspero, *L'histoire ancienne des peuples de l'Orient classique.*

15. See Parker, *China: Past and Present* (London, 1903); see also Arthur H. Smith, *Village Life in China* (New York, 1899): "Poverty, poverty, poverty, always, and evermore poverty" (p. 310).

16. Parker, op. cit., pp. 28–29; on famine as a "perpetual possibility," see Smith, p. 317.

were absolute. The emperor was the son of the heavens. The economic functions of the central power were very extensive (taxation, state monopolies of agriculture and industry, etc.).[17]

Thus, throughout the long history of China the degree of statism fluctuated somewhat, but it was always comparatively high and it remains so up to the present time. In other words the Chinese example corroborates the proposed theorem.

Ancient Japan. Because of the existence of similar causes, such as unceasing wars and frequent famines and constant threats of them, the old pre-reform Japan was similarly regimented. Accordingly, the whole social regime was marked by the stamp of a strong military-starvation statism.[18]

Ancient Greece: government of the Lipari Islands (sixth century, B.C.). Living on an island, the population of Lipari produced nothing for themselves and lived by military plunder.[19] Militarism and the constant threat of hunger called forth a complete statism, the communism of Lipari. Land and booty belonged to the group; nutrition was communal, and centralization and regulation of the lives of the citizens were absolute.

Sparta. Like most other large towns and states of ancient Greece, Sparta was not self-sufficient in food. Here, as well as in some other centers, the economy of the society depended upon trade and industry, as the products of local agriculture were insufficient

17. Beginning with the ancient periods of history, the land was considered as the property of the central power. Private property did not exist, but the subjects were assigned tracts of land to cultivate, and they were required to deliver part of the crop to the government in payment. In the past (and to some extent now) strong religious rules regulated the everyday life of the subjects, as well as that of the authorities. These rules kept the governmental organism intact during several centuries. Hardly any act of the government, or of public life, could be executed without a prescribed ceremony. These rules prescribed how to dress, what to say, and what the general deportment of people should be in private as well as in public life. Occupations and professions were regulated, and often they were inherited. See Hirth, *The Ancient History of China* (1908), pp. 109–15, 204, 297–98.

18. See details on the poverty of the population during federal and monarchist (pre-reform) Japan, caused by wars, civil disorders, earthquakes, crop failures, etc., in S. Gulick, *Evolution of the Japanese*, pp. 47, 52, 277.

19. R. Pöhlmann, *Geschichte der Sozialen Frage und des Sozialismus der antiken Welt*, 1:2–6, 26–27.

to satisfy requirements for food. Hence, every economic crisis, every interruption of contact with countries supplying provisions, every delay in delivery of goods was reflected in fluctuations in the economic life of the town. *Under such circumstances, supervision over industries and distribution of goods and radical interference with the lives of citizens were not only the right but also the obligation of all the town officials.*[20]

It would have been miraculous if, under such constant threats of hunger, a tight statism had not developed there, particularly in the field of nutrition. Interference in and regulation of economic life by the central power were absolute and included the trade in bread, prohibitive measures against speculators and against the high cost of living, bans on exportation of agricultural products and raw materials, strict control of export and import of merchandise, restriction on transportation of wares, interference with the exchange of money, governmental monopolies, etc. In other words, there was "complete economic tyranny."[21] In addition to hunger, wars contributed to the development of an all-embracing, unlimited, "compulsory statism," with all its characteristic features. From the moment of birth, all matters of life and death were decided by the government. If the decision favored preservation of life, it was only so that the government could take control of the education and upbringing of the individual, a guardianship which only death could terminate. The state determined all activities for everyone and kept the individual under control day and night. It determined the time to marry. The citizens could not leave their place of residence. They were the property of the state.[22] Therefore, the all embracing, compulsory statism of Sparta was the function of an insecure food supply and the accompanying danger of hunger, as well as of militarism. This "model," as well as the preceding ones, confirms the proposed theorem.

Athens. Similar conditions were observed in Athens. According to Böckh, "Attica consumed 3,400,000 medimni of bread per year, but could produce an average of only 2,400,000 medimni. Therefore it had to import at least one half of the total requirement

20. Ibid., pp. 334–35.
21. Ibid., pp. 334–37.
22. Ibid., pp. 32–33. See the description of Spartan statism by Xenophon, *Republica Lacedaemonium*, pp. 1–10, and Plutarch's *Lycurgus*.

any year in which there was a small crop failure." [23] Under such
conditions, had it not been for certain measures and appropriate institutions, great need could have arisen at any moment. This is why
the safeguarding of nutrition was Athens' main task.[24] Aristotle also
testified to this. Ten times a year a question was put before the population "about the bread and the safety of the country." [25] Notwithstanding all the measures taken by the Athenians, hunger often prevailed.

This insecurity and the extremely great danger which threatened
the state in case trouble should arise in securing the necessary
amount of food for the populace forced even the most progressive
communities to accept a system of governmental regulation.[26] This
regulation was expressed in a hundred different measures. The government regulated import and export of nutritive goods. Exportation
was absolutely prohibited; two-thirds of the food products imported
by Attica had to be sold to the Athenians, and only one-third could
be sold to others. The central power restricted private commerce.
Sale or purchase of amounts above those prescribed was punishable
by death.[27] The government controlled the price of bread. It took
strict measures against high prices and against speculators. All exchange of foodstuffs was regulated and controlled by a special department of the government. The government itself operated many
enterprises and industries; it bought up breadstuffs at places where
the crops were good and sold them to the citizens at low prices.[28]
There was an agency for the free distribution of bread, fish, salt,
and fuel, which during the time of Pericles had become the norm.
The poor were supported by the government. There were also
"bread marks" (ration cards), as is shown by an inscription found
in Elevsis. In brief, almost all the food supply was a monopoly
centralized in the hands of the government. Concomitantly, guardianship and regulation by the central power was spread over the whole
economy, and even into other fields of the citizens' behavior and pub-

23. Böckh, *Die Staatshaushaltung der Athener*, 1:125.
24. Ibid., p. 115.
25. Pöhlmann, *Geschichte der Sozialen Frage*, p. 430; cf. Novosadsky,
"The Struggle against High Prices in Ancient Greece," *Journal of the Ministry
of Public Education* (1917), pp. 78–80 (in Russian).
26. Novosadsky, pp. 235–36.
27. Böckh, *Die Staatshaushaltung der Athener*, p. 17.
28. Plutarch, *Pericles*, 2:12; Aristotle, *Republica Athen*, pp. 47–54.

lic life. The same also was true in other Greek towns.[29] Thus, the principal features of the developed statism are present also in this "model," which again confirms the proposition being tested.

Rome. From the moment of its expansion and the decline of agriculture in Italy, Rome was a city constantly threatened by starvation and frequently visited by it. After the Second Punic War agriculture in Italy declined, and even the most fertile provinces of Sicily and Sardinia, and later Africa as well, could not meet the ever increasing demands for bread. Bad management, wars, civil strife, and speculation during the last century of the republic made the living conditions of the population of Rome intolerable, and the apparition of hunger frequently arose.[30]

This ever increasing danger of hunger, which could not be prevented or overcome by other measures, according to our theorem, had to bring the growth of "compulsory statism" in the field of public nutrition. The reality confirms completely this postulate. Only the government, through its energetic initiative, could produce substantial improvement, and this conviction *began* to develop gradually even during the republican period.[31] Even earlier in its history, in cases of famine, agents bought bread in Etruria, Umbria, and Sicily, and resold it at a low price to the populace.[32] But with the growth of nutritional crises, the screws of "governmental socialism" began to tighten more and more. This was manifested in several ways. The grain laws of Gaius Gracchus (123 B.C.) were passed, which gave every citizen the right to receive from the governmental stores a certain amount of unground grain per month (about 5 modii at 6.5 asses per modium).[33] Commissars, having complete power in the struggle to prevent hunger, were established in 104 B.C. They were

29. Böckh, op. cit., pp. 117, 119–24, 125, 301; Novosadsky, op. cit., pp. 79–80, 82–85, 90, passim; Pöhlmann, *Geschichte der Sozialen Frage*, pp. 430, 591; Francotte, "Le pain à bon marché et le pain gratuit dans les cités grecques," in *Mélanges du droit publique grecque* (Paris, 1910), p. 291, passim.

30. O. Hirschfeld, *Die kaiserlichen Verwaltungsbeamsten, von Augustus bis auf Diocletian*, p. 231. There were famines in the years 22 and 18 B.C., and in A.D. 19, 32, 41, 52, 68–69, and later on as well.

31. Ibid.

32. J. P. Waltzing, *Étude historique sur les corporations professionelles chez les Romains* (Louvain, 1896), vols. 1–4 (1895–1900).

33. M. Rostovtzeff, "The frumentarii and the frumentary laws," *Encyclopedia of Brockhaus-Effron*, 72:826–30 (in Russian).

reorganized into a permanent institution under Caesar and their number was increased. Later on the membership of the Roman "prodkom" was increased even more, and after a long famine in 22 B.C., Augustus himself became its head, as *curaturannonae*. In 18 B.C. four *praefecto frumenti dandi* were established.

The principal functions of these institutions were to collect or buy food supplies and transport, store, and distribute them. At first private contractors handled the business, but later the government took the entire operation into its hands. This required an enormous administrative machinery, which included detachments to requisition bread in the provinces, transport agents, carriers, weighers, keepers of granaries, guardians of supplies, boatmen on the Tiber, divers, etc. Thus, the government had monopolized almost all enterprises related to nutrition. Each year the prefect sent orders to the provincial authorities indicating how much bread, wine, pork, iron, cloth, horses, etc., each one of them had to get from the population and where to deliver and store it. The governmental agencies supervised the quality of the produce, baked the bread, and distributed it to the needy people.[34]

The competition of private tradesmen played little part in Roman life. Governmental control was complete even in fields such as trade which were not subject to regulations and norms.[35] Furthermore, at the beginning of the period of Caesar in Rome the government increased free distribution of bread, so that the number of people and their families who received it rose to 600,000. Caesar later cut this number to 150,000 by banishing the others to the provinces, but Augustus raised the number to 200,000. From then on, the emperors never dared to touch this privilege of "plebs the king." Their policy in Rome was to feed and amuse the plebs, who were called "the bread-plebs" because they cared for nothing but food and shows. This was their price for freedom. However, when the delivery of grain from overseas was late, they were ready to rebel. Later in history grain was given in place of bread, and in the North vegetable oil was also dispensed. During the time of Aurelianus pork and lard were added to the rations. Along with these regular

34. Waltzing, op. cit., pp. 26–103.
35. Hirschfeld, op. cit., p. 231; L. Friedlander, *Town Life in Ancient Italy* (New York, 1902), p. 26.

gifts of food, there were also some extraordinary gifts to the people (*condiaria*) of money, wine, salt, clothing, snacks, tickets to the theater, etc., including "stamps for the prostitutes" (*tesserae missiles*, e.g., *tessera vinaria*), which gave the right to buy wine, drink it, and have sexual intercourse with one of the many prostitutes in Rome.[36]

The actual techniques of distribution varied from time to time. At first "rations" of grain were given out monthly. Still later, instead of grain, bread was distributed daily. At first there were merely special lists of eligible people; later on a card system was introduced.

Thus, compulsory statism began to permeate the whole economy of Rome, and later on it even controlled almost all the behavior of its citizens. In Bücher's words, as a result of this "we have before us a fully developed communistic-imperialistic economy." [37] It is evident from the material presented here that this model of the aggregate suffering starvation, or the threat of starvation exactly at the moment of the appearance of the danger, showed the inevitable consequence—a highly developed form of compulsory statism. Thus, our proposition has still another confirmation.

Byzantium. Because of constant famines and wars, the conditions were not different from those in Rome. As a matter of fact Byzantium was a copy of the latter. The amount of governmental interference in the lives of the citizens was tremendous, particularly in economic and nutritional fields.[38]

Byzantium was an empire of monopoly, privileges, and protectionism. The government interfered in everything, controlled and

36. M. Rostovtzeff, *The Roman Leaden Tesserae* (St. Petersburg, 1903), pp. 111–13 (in Russian). Also see the details in the works cited above of Hirschfeld, Friedlander, Rostovtzeff, Waltzing, and Pöhlmann.

37. Bücher, op. cit., 2:189–90; Kühn, *Die stadtistische und burgerlische Verfassung des Romanischen Reichs.* See also the above-mentioned works of Waltzing, 2:19–115; Hirschfeld, op. cit., pp. 230–46; Rostovtzeff, *Roman Leaden Tesserae;* and S. Dill, *Roman Society from Nero to Marcus Aurelius* (1905).

38. The basis of Byzantine statesmanship was the idea of authority, of complete subordination of personality to the state, of the private to the common. The application of this idea was manifest by extreme centralization and despotism.

regulated everything. The eparch was in charge of the industrial institutions, as well as of the corporations of artisans. Everyone was assigned a definite occupation. Under threat of corporal punishment and confiscation of property, everyone was forbidden to have more than one specialty. To enter a corporation of the artisans, a permit from the eparch was required. Trade and industry were under careful surveillance by the police.[39]

The well-developed state economy—with all the monopolies, complete regulation of all economic life, taxes and requisitions, concentration of all trade in the hands of the government, regulation of the behavior of the population with respect to professions, occupations, beliefs, etc.—was typical of Byzantium. Personal rights were insignificant, and private property existed only on paper, because the central power violated it incessantly. In the interest of perpetuating their own control, the authorities organized from time to time bloody riots against the rich, and nationalized the property of the wealthy.[40]

As indicated, in Byzantium poverty was great and famines were extremely frequent. Even during the outwardly brilliant reign of Justinian I the condition of the masses was terrible. There was no peace with other powers, and no prosperity internally. The brilliance of Sophia and the *corpus juris* were just surface decorations, beneath which poverty and lawlessness were hiding. After Justinian I the picture became still worse. Incidentally, as in all similar societies the institution of espionage was highly developed, and scholars were given a number of privileges and encouragements. This is true for the USSR at present, and in the past it was true of China, Japan, Byzantium, Greece, Persia, Egypt, the world of Islam, the despotism of Tamerlane, etc. And they say that history does not repeat itself!

The Islamic world. Now let us consider an entirely different region. The origin of the community of Mahomet was militaristic. It was made up of paupers. Its economic foundation rested almost entirely on the unsound basis of military spoils. This militarism and the constant threat of hunger gave to the organization of the community of Mahomet and to the first caliphates the stamp of a strongly

39. Bezobrazov, *The Byzantine Culture* (1919), pp. 96–104 (in Russian).

40. Holmes, op. cit., pp. 144, 149–51, 158–62, 190–96, 297, 433, 754.

expressed statism (communism).[41] All that has been said about the community of Mahomet and the caliphates is applicable also to other hungry militaristic societies, like the kingdoms of the first Turkish rulers, of Genghis Khan, Tamerlane, the Mamelukes, etc.[42] Strict military-statism prevailed in these.

The ancient kingdom of Peru. Let us now consider still another world—the ancient kingdom of the Incas. For the same reasons as were discussed for the preceding models, military statism flourished.[43]

Europe in the Middle Ages. We consider next several models of aggregates which were threatened by starvation during the Middle Ages. Generally speaking, almost all of medieval Europe consisted of territory which was either constantly threatened by starvation, or in which frequently the population actually was suffering starvation. Larger towns, and even entire regions, were particularly afflicted because they were not self-sufficient with respect to food, and also because the deliveries of the supplies from the rural districts, or from other sources, were either inadequate or frequently interrupted. There was no common market, and the towns were isolated like

41. The power of Mahomet, as well as that of the first caliphs, was absolute and unlimited. Centralization was complete. The subordination and the discipline of members were ironclad and rigid. See Müller, *History of Islam*, 1:109, 124, 186, 238, passim (in Russian). All behavior of the people was regulated to the utmost. Personal rights did not exist, and there was no private property. Complete communism reigned: everything seized in the raids was divided among the members, except for the small part given to God and the paupers. Every deviation from the established norm was punished mercilessly. Unbelievers were destroyed. Statism was also established in all of the subjugated countries. The conquered land was confiscated and was leased to those who worked it. Life and death, rights and possessions, all became subject to the capricious wills of the rulers.

42. Hammer, *L'histoire de l'empire Ottoman*, 2:6, passim; Müller, op. cit., vol. 3; Howorth, *History of the Mongols* (London, 1878).

43. The army, and the entire population as well, were subjected to complete regimentation. In the villages officials supervised plowing, sowing, and reaping. The government rationed water during droughts, regulated food, clothing, education, beliefs, marriages, etc. There was no private property, and the people lived in assigned places: "Peruvians had no money; they did not sell clothing, houses, or estates; and their whole trade consisted in exchange of consumers' goods": H. Spencer, *Foundations of Sociology*, 2:435–36 (in Russian); see also Martens, *Un grand état socialiste au XV siècle* (Paris, 1910).

islands in the sea.[44] In addition the proprietary differentiation of the population also was slight.[45]

According to our hypothesis, these causes had to lead to highly developed governmental regulations, interferences, and "statism" in the area of nutrition and in general economic relationships. The extent of the power of the authorities (towns, regions, states), therefore, had to be very great. *Indeed, almost all of medieval Europe represented an epoch of great regimentation and interference of the central power in the fields of nutrition, trade, and industry. Autonomy of the citizens did not exist.* All public relationships were regulated by numerous authorities of the medieval aggregates, and individuals were entirely deprived of any roles. Towns and states regulated purchase and acquisition of bread, its distribution to the populace at a low price, establishment of regulations upon bread and beer, levying of taxes on foodstuffs, regulations upon imports and exports, determination of time and place for sales, etc. All these phenomena were typical of the whole of medieval Europe to a greater or lesser extent.[46]

Insecurity of the food supply and the constant threat of hunger occupied major places among the causes which produced this strong development of compulsory statism. This proposition, as indicated below, follows from the fact that the "regulations" themselves were called forth by hunger. They were established either during or immediately after years of famine, so that once more the curve of regulations increased exactly during the famines.

Thus, medieval times, taken as a whole, also exhibit the correlation between hunger and "statism." However, this picture is too

44. Bücher, op. cit., vol. 2, article 11, p. 145, passim. The extensive agriculture of the period was incapable of supporting even the insignificant populations of medieval towns. Large numbers of people perished every two or three years from plagues, hunger, wars, and sieges. Sometimes in the course of a summer, one-tenth, one-sixth, or even a quarter of the population would die. From 1326 to 1400 there were thirty-two epidemics of plague, and from 1400 to 1500 about forty. Ibid., pp. 145–46.

45. Kulisher, *Economic History and the Mode of Living*, pp. 118–21 (in Russian).

46. Kovalevsky, *Economic Growth of Europe*, 2:670–71, 3:1–85, passim; Ashley, *The Economic History of England* (Moscow, 1897) (in Russian); Kulisher, op. cit., pp. 106–8.

general, and it is preferable to study the details in specific medieval aggregates, and thus confirm the theorem.

The Italian republics of the twelfth to fourteenth centuries. These aggregates also are suitable for study as "models" of societies which are constantly threatened by hunger. Because of their small foreign trade, frequent wars with their neighbors, and the insignificance of the territory controlled by the towns, governments of the small Italian republics were obliged to direct all their efforts to securing food for their populations. Not only were the years of crop failures disastrous for them, but if a neighbor destroyed the growing crops by a "raid" or if fugitive emigrants cut contact between town and surrounding villages, the population would have died from hunger if the public storehouses had not previously been filled with adequate quantities of rye, barley, and rice.[47]

Exactly what is understood to be the function of this "independent variable" (the danger of starvation)? It is that which we have called "compulsory statism" in the field of nutrition. The larger the threat of starvation for the population of a republic, the greater the governmental interference, monopoly, and regulation in this field. Strictly speaking, an absolute monopoly in the field of public nutrition existed in only a few communities, which were cut off from neighbors, by the sea, and which had relatively small stores of breadstuffs. The picture of nutritional communism in such countries is as follows: at the head of nutritional affairs was a special "magistrate of plenty," "Orson Michele" (which is equivalent to the Russian "prodkom"). His task was to secure bread, wine, vegetables, butter, eggs, etc., for the people. This official requisitioned and bought food, regulated exports and imports, set prices, levied taxes upon products, established norms for distribution, organized mills and bakeries, distributed the products, supervised weight and quality of goods, punished speculators, and, finally, regimented and controlled all exchange of goods. In brief, like our own "prodkom," he monopolized and nationalized almost all the nutritional affairs of the population.

The regulation was very detailed. For example, the villagers were forced to till the land (any defaulter was punished), they were forbidden to leave the estate to which they were attached, and they

47. M. Kovalevsky, "The Measures Employed by the Italian Republics in Their Fight against Starvation," pp. 355–61 (in Russian).

could not change occupations. All the work (such as plowing, sowing, weeding, reaping, and the delivery of crops to the towns) had to be done according to prescribed rules and set times. Except for seed for the following year, and minimum amounts for the family's use, all the grain had to be delivered into the town. Every purchase of grain was supervised by the authorities, and no one was permitted to buy more than four baskets of wheat in the course of a fortnight. Punitive detachments searched for and requisitioned goods from offenders.

With some minor variations, the same picture is encountered throughout medieval Europe, which never had a secure food supply, and where people were frequently starving and often dying from hunger.[48]

It is curious to note that during our era of impoverishment, in the ideology of guild socialism and syndicalism, we see attempts to return to and restore medievalism.

The people of the thirteenth and fourteenth centuries would have been unable to understand what we mean by the expression "free trade in breadstuffs," just as we cannot comprehend that in those centuries the tiller of the soil, the miller, and the baker were public servants, who were bound by oath to pursue their occupations for mutual benefit of the community, and to sacrifice their personal interests for the benefit of society. That medieval governments considered them as such is proved easily by reading any of their judiciary documents.[49] It was so in England where the statutes for bread and beer for the whole country started in 1202, were gradually broadened, and continued in effect without interruption during the whole medieval period.[50] So it was also in France where, beginning at the end of the thirteenth century, because of frequent famines, the central government and the municipalities felt that it was

48. Free trade, in our sense of the word, did not exist in these republics. It was restricted in different ways, such as the "just price." Activities of the middleman were restricted in great detail. The workers also were regimented in time, techniques, etc. The concept of freedom of labor was foreign to this economy. The fact of development of guilds, corporations, associations, which submerged the personality, is connected with our "independent variable."

49. Kovalevsky, "The Measures Employed," pp. 352–53.

50. Kovalevsky, *Economic Growth of Europe*, 2:670–71 (in Russian); Ashley, op. cit., pp. 20, 21, 27 (in Russian).

their duty to establish a maximum price for bread, to prohibit the export of grain, and to prevent the possibility of speculation by middlemen, by introducing strict measures of control.[51]

I shall limit my presentation here of the facts, which were taken from different times and locales. Other "models" of starving aggregates will be considered below in connection with the verification of our second proposition, which, in turn, also serves to substantiate the first.

"Models" of satiated aggregates.—Let us consider now the "models" of the satiated aggregates, those which rarely experienced massive starvation of the population. Are they really characterized by the lesser governmental regulation, guardianship, centralization, and interference in the sphere of nutritional relationships? Is the autonomy of persons more significant? What are the rights of people, personal and proprietary? Are freedom and self-determination restricted in any way?

Our task is comparatively simple. The Western European countries of England, France, and Germany, the United States, and nineteenth-century Japan after reform may serve as examples of such comparatively "satiated" societies. During the nineteenth century massive deficiency starvations were unknown in the histories of these countries. They were getting wealthy, the standard of living of their populations was rising, and their nutrition was improved in comparison with the preceding centuries.[52] The nineteenth century was an era of personal autonomy *par excellence*, of individualism, of unprecedented development of the individual initiative, private property, and free trade and industry. *Briefly, it was an era of sharp decline of governmental supervision, regimentation, and centralization, first, in the procurement of the food for the country, and, second, in the spheres of trade, general social organization, and industry.*

There was no more question of governmental monopoly of bread, or other products; price regulations were absent; the production, exchange, and distribution of foods was entirely in the hands of free

51. M. Kovalevsky, "The Measures Employed," p. 353.

52. E. Cauderlier, *L'évolution économique du XIX siècle* (Stuttgart, 1903), p. 73, passim. This author gives a résumé of the improved economic welfare of the populations of England, France, Belgium, and the United States in the nineteenth century. D'Avenel said that King Charles IV hardly had better food than the contemporary middle-class Parisian: D'Avenel, *Le mécanisme de la vie moderne*, 1st ser. (1908), pp. 158–59.

men; trade was free; in brief, the will and autonomy of the citizens took precedence over governmental regulations which in this sphere had declined to a minimum. These facts are all well known and require no proof.

If an increase of governmental interference occurred during the wars in the twentieth century, it was a rather unique case, and it took place exactly during the growth of militarism, the danger of famine, and when there was a decrease in the quantity and quality of the food. These few variations do not contradict our theorem, but rather strengthen it.

Furthermore, the richer and the more secure a country, the less likely to occur interference on the part of the government. Who does not know that the first place with respect to "individualism" and the minimal interference of the government in the behavior of the citizens is occupied by England and the United States? Who does not know that these countries are the most prosperous, have working classes with the highest standard of living, and are better fed than the rest? A remarkable coincidence? At first it may seem to be paradoxical, but I am inclined to see in this "individualism" of the Anglo-Saxons the function of many variables, among which the primary position is occupied by their great prosperity, and particularly by their plentiful food supply. In contrast, neither in the nineteenth nor in the twentieth century did Russia get out of the position of a "starving" aggregate. And does not Russia still remain a country in which the amount of governmental interference is the greatest, which continues to regulate the behavior of the people, in which there are no citizens but only subjects, in which the central power is still despotic, in which the autonomy of the personality and its inalienable rights have never existed, and still do not exist, or, in brief, in which statism ruled before, and in which it has increased still more particularly with the spread of famine and the war of 1914–21? In this case we have again a remarkable coincidence! The Russian statism (both the old pre-revolutionary, and that of the October Revolution, which resembles the former even in details) is the function of two causes: hunger and militarism.

Truly, I can be asked a number of questions: Are you forgetting that the nineteenth century was the era of socialism? Have you forgotten the growth in the role of government in the nineteenth century? Is it not a fact that in the nineteenth century the government began enlarging its role far beyond the limits of security of the country and interfering in economic matters more actively than ever before? Never before had a state such active industrial and trade policies.[53] And the safety of labor? And social insurance? And minimum wages? And the regulation of working hours, of hygiene and of safety? And governmental monopolies: telephone, telegraph, mail service, railroads, banks, savings institutions, etc.? What is all of this but the growth of the regulatory functions of the state? Do we have to repeat the Spencerianism which was comprehensive in its own time, but not now?

The answer to this is that, for the time being, we put aside the ideology of socialism and communism, because it is as old as the world itself, and represents no special feature of the nineteenth century.

Moreover, I am not interested in ideologies, but in stark reality, which in the nineteenth century did not correspond to ideology. Socialism and communism still continued to be ideologies, but the reality of the nineteenth century was individualistic-capitalistic. Furthermore, in a special section I shall consider in detail the rise and fall of socialistic-communistic ideology during the nineteenth century. This study will show that its course is explained by the point of view expressed here and is by no means contradictory to it.

Now a few remarks about Spencerianism. Like Spencer and other antistatists, I do not consider that functions of governments will die out in the future. Neither do I consider, like the statists, that they will continue to develop, and I do not foresee any "historical tendencies." The only thing I say is that, *ceteris paribus*, when hunger increases, compulsory statism grows, and when hunger decreases, the latter falls off. The aggregates mentioned here did not suffer from massive famines during the nineteenth century, so, according to the proposition, the curve of compulsory statism had to fall, and it did so. This is all. As to the future, my thesis says: Other things being equal if the satiety of the aggregates increases, statism and the role of the government in nutritional matters will decrease; contrarily, if adequacy of food supply decreases, and the danger of starvation increases (as was the case during the years of war), the growth of the regulatory functions of the government in the economic-nutritional field will increase. This position, obviously, is quite different from the "historical laws," either those of the statists or the antistatists.

53. Bourguin, *Les systèmes socialistes* (1917), pp. 275–76.

Whether in the future we shall have an increase in famines, or a plentitude of everything, I do not know and do not prophesy; but I know what results will follow in either case.

I turn now to more serious objections in respect to the comparative development of the regulatory power of the state in the nineteenth century. In the first place, in the area which interests me, nutritional matters, as had been stated above, the nineteenth century showed a sharp decrease of the economic-nutritional functions of government in certain aggregates, in contrast with the models of starving societies studied. Second, taken as a whole, the totality of the regulatory functions of the government in the nineteenth century in these countries was insignificant in comparison with these functions in the same countries in the past, when the population was threatened by famine. Did not the whole sphere of behavior of the citizens, which previously was regulated, cease to be in the sphere of influence of governmental regulation? Is it not true that during this century the liberty of the press, union, assembly, religion, were established, all of which were regimented in the past? In this period did not the personality acquire an autonomy which did not exist before? Were not guarantees of inalienable rights established in the nineteenth century, which put strict limits upon interference by the central power?

If the statists, socialists, and the militarists forgot these truisms, it is of little use to remind them. In the economic sphere things are not much different. Protection of labor, social hygiene, regulation of working hours, postal and telegraph systems, railroads, etc., are mentioned as indications of the growth of the role of government.

Oh, yes, now the government occasionally interferes in a dispute between labor and proprietors. But have those who raise objection forgotten that before the government not only interfered as a judge mediator, but owned the enterprises which supplied work for all its subjects and determined everybody's status, occupation, economic conditions, food, clothing, marriage, dwelling place, etc.? Were not the whole territory and its inhabitants the property of the government, which it controlled just as it wished? Just compare present-day France with that of Colbert, England of the nineteenth century with England of the fourteenth to seventeenth centuries, or Prussia under Frederick II with contemporary Germany. As to the comparison with the ancient states, I shall not even suggest it!

Oh, yes, now the government is concerned with health and sanitation. But did not the government of the aggregate in ancient times perform the same function according to the level of knowledge of that time, in the form of fights against epidemics, venereal diseases (prostitution), in the form of improvement of the sanitary conditions? Those who doubt this should read a number of religious and judicial treatises, beginning with the Veda, the Avesta, the Koran, the Laws of Manu, the Bible, the Laws of Hammurabi, and ending with the police regulations and municipal ordinances of the sixteenth, seventeenth, and eighteenth centuries. They will see that hygiene was regulated to such extent that it was specified whether the food should be hot or cold, whether to be eaten with the head covered or uncovered, whether to face the south or the north while eating, and when and where the men could urinate, facing the sun, with backs to the sun, into the ashes, against the wind, etc.[54]

The government of the nineteenth century, certainly, had a number of monopolies, but these monopolies, with the exception of the recently formed ones (telephones, telegraphs, which, however, were not monopolized in some of the countries) were even greater in the past, such as the monopolies of the central power (mail service, roads). But except for these, it had few monopolies. The critics also mention insurance and social security, but these also existed in the ancient world. In Athens all needy people were certain to receive 2 obols daily; in Rome, as we have seen, almost the entire population lived on the "states account." The same was true in Judea, in Europe during the Middle Ages, etc.[55]

The regulatory power of nineteenth-century governments was restricted to their direct function, but many other aspects of public life became autonomous. In this respect the size of the regulatory functions of government in contemporary England, the United States, France, and Germany is absolutely incomparable with those of the earlier militaristic and starving aggregates.

If even in the nineteenth century the governmental power in-

54. See the *Laws of Manu* (St. Petersburg, 1913), chap. 3, verses 236–44, chap. 4 verse 45, passim (Russian translation). See the police ordinances, especially of the old courts.

55. Uhlhorn-Münsterberg, "Geschichte der offentlichen Armenpflege," *Handwörterbuch der Staatswissenschaft*, Band 2 (1909), pp. 6–30.

creased in times of war and comparative starvation, it was caused exactly by the same factors which, according to our postulate, are the progenitors of "compulsory statism."

Moreover, if it did not disappear completely, that was because apart from the war and other reasons, during the nineteenth century the comparative starvation (unlike deficiency starvation) increased due to an increase in proprietary differentiation.[56] The existence of sharp differences in wealth and income, regardless of prosperity, increased the growth of the comparative food taxis, and, together with wars, which did not disappear, also led toward "statism."

If absurd statements about the growth of active functions of government during the nineteenth century were not so widespread, it would be unnecessary to reiterate the obvious facts. Thus, in the nineteenth century, prosperous countries showed the growth of individualism, of the autonomy of the personality, a decrease in governmental supervision and regulation, a weakening of centralization and absolutism in all fields of endeavor, particularly in the sphere of economic-nutritional relationships.

In the nineteenth century these countries ceased to be threatened by famine. These "models" of the prosperous (satiated) societies confirm the proposed theorem from the opposite point of view. Now let us consider the second theorem.

The historical verification of the second proposition.—According to this proposition, and if other things are equal, we should find in the history of a given people the rise of compulsory statism during these periods: a worsening of the nutrition of the masses (the growth of deficiency or comparative starvation); the growth of differences in wealth and income; and, particularly, the growth of both hunger and economic differentiation. Under the opposite conditions the degree of compulsory statism should fall. The improvement of nutrition of the masses, and at the same time the growth of economic differentiation (as well as worsening of the former and decrease of

56. Despite the degree of prosperity in contemporary society, the distribution of wealth is far from being equal, and in a civilized and prosperous society this difference is extreme, says Levasseur (*L'histoire des classes ouvrières,* 2:282–83). See data on the distribution of income in Kider, "Répartition sociale de revenu," *Bulletin International de Statistique,* vol. 17, no. 1, pp. 68–75; Einkommen, article in Meyer's *Handwörterbuch der Staatswissenschaft* (1909), pp. 3–13, 663–94; Sorokin, *The System of Sociology,* vol. 2 (in Russian).

the latter), may neutralize one another and leave the level of compulsory statism unchanged, or changed to a lesser degree, than it would have been without such neutralization. Let us consider the facts.

The history of ancient peoples of the East tells us of various cases of increase of compulsory statism during periods of hunger. The biblical story about Joseph is one of these examples. At the beginning of "seven thin and ill favoured kine" (seven years of famine), Joseph established an absolute governmental monopoly of breadstuffs. Taking advantage of the certain high prices in Egypt, Joseph not only bought all the land for the pharaoh, but made the free owners of the land into slaves of the king, increased compulsory organization of labor, established compulsory work on public projects, etc.[57] Similarly the increased centralization of power in nutritional matters during the years of famine, concentration of the supplies of food, enlargement of governmental works and of governmental control, free food for the people—all this is shown in the ancient documents.[58]

Similar occurrences took place in Babylonia.[59] In a number of cases, as we have seen, the process of an increase in statism (and of communism) was accomplished by means of social revolution, which nationalized everything and which brought the supervision by the central power up to the zenith. This, as has been indicated, occurred during the epochs of poverty and famine. Almost identical phenomena are seen in the history of China, where rises of the curve of statism took place in periods of poverty.

If we take into account the flourishing of the all-embracing statism-communism in Persia (where not only all the belongings of the people, but also all women were communized), which was ac-

---

57. Roscher, op. cit., p. 61; Genesis, chaps. 41, 42.

58. The following was inscribed on a monument of Egypt: "When the country experienced need, I supported the town with the help of a measure of grain and permitted the citizen to take grain for himself, his wife, and son. I cancelled all debts." We see on a second, "When hungry years arrived I plowed all the fields of Antilonia," etc. So spoke the pharaoh. Breasted, *A History of the Ancient Egyptians*, 1:168–69.

59. Such as, e.g., the building of huge granaries and the distribution of grain during times of famine. Furthermore, during the period of Hammurabi public works were organized, and bondage, as well as compulsory labor, increased.

complished by the leader of Mazdaism (Mazdak) in cooperation with King Kobad, we would see that this also was an epoch of economic disruption and increased hunger on the part of the population, which also explains the short existence of this reform.[60]

Under similar conditions the eruption of such movements occurred later in the history of the Islamic World and Turkey. Furthermore, starvation in India during the reign of Akbar forced nationalization of land and requisition of grain from the peasantry.

As we have already seen, statism was strongly developed in Athens. However, its screws were tightened, especially during the years of crop failures and famines. When, with the advent of hunger, prices for bread and for other necessary articles began to rise, and to reach extreme limits, the government took special measures to fight this. They organized a siton (grain) institute. They elected special representatives, the commission of sitons, who purchased bread at cost for the government, and sold it to the population at a low price. The establishment of the commission of sitons was not permanent in Athens, and it signified approaching famine and the beginning of poverty. The grain institutes apparently were widespread in ancient Greece, and we have indications of their presence in many communities.[61] Such is the general *evidence* of the correctness of our proposition. With the rise of hunger, interference of the central power in the life of the people increases, the autonomy of the personality decreases, compulsory regulation rises, proprietary rights decrease, and the tendencies towards egalitarian-despotic statism appear.

Considering the topic from a broader point of view, it is possible to safeguard the nutrition of the population not only by the distribution of food—this is an extraordinary measure—but also by procuring ways and means of production for the people. In agricultural countries the main means of production is land. Hence it follows that an egalitarian distribution of the land, according to our proposition, must occur during the periods of increasing poverty and hunger among the masses. It is true that in Sparta "we encounter for the first time in the history of Greece the demand for

60. "There is no private property in the world, only God is the proprietor. We cannot say: this is my property, my wife, my daughter, my son, etc." These were the commands of the leaders, and they were obeyed. See Malcolm, *The History of Persia*, 1:100, 104, passim.

61. Novosadsky, op. cit., pp. 80–82.

the division of the land during the hard times of the second Messenian war." [62] In the sixth century B.C., as is well known, the masses had become impoverished because they had lost their land holdings, and concomitant with this there was an increase of hunger. About the same time the demands of "land for the people" were first heard, and these were followed by a social revolution which ended in tyranny. During this the amount of interference by the central power in the life of the people increased beyond limit; not only was movable and unmovable property confiscated, but even wives and children of the rich were nationalized. Briefly, during this century of impoverishment and increased differences in wealth and income, the curve of statism rose sharply in all fields of social life.[63]

Later in the history of Athens, the period following the Peloponnesian Wars was one of severe impoverishment and increased hunger of the masses. From this time on, permanent social revolutions were underway (particularly during the years 411 to 409), when the conquerors increased to the maximum the interference of the central power, and everything was nationalized, guarded, and regulated; this was true of both the oligarchic and the tyrannic conquerors. Rights, autonomy, and private property became fictions, and compulsory statism reached its zenith.[64]

Similar conditions were encountered during the late history of Sparta, where great impoverishment of the masses and growth of differences in wealth and income occurred during the last half of the third century B.C. As a result of these processes social revolutions broke out in which the Spartan kings assumed leadership of the starving masses (Agis IV, Cleomenes III, Nabis). The private rights of citizens were greatly limited. Property, including wives and children of the rich, was confiscated and distributed among the partisans; interference of the central power assumed unprecedented dimensions; even the right to life was denied and people were put to death en masse. Briefly, an unlimited compulsory statism reigned.[65] The reverse process started only after the subjugation of both Athens

62. Pöhlmann, *Geschichte der Sozialen Frage*, p. 49.

63. Ibid., p. 360, passim.

64. Busolt, *Griechische Geschichte* (Gotha, 1904), Band 3, Teil 2, pp. 1402–3, 1456, 1614, 1623, passim; Böckh, op. cit., pp. 157–64.

65. B. Niese, *Geschichte der Griechischen und Makedonischen Staaten* (1899), Teil 2, p. 296, passim, Teil 3 (1903), p. 42, passim.

and Sparta by Rome, when a period of comparative prosperity began.

The same relationship may be clearly seen in the history of Rome. The sharp rise of compulsory statism was seen during the last two and a half centuries of the republican period (the second and first centuries B.C.). The following examples are evidence of this development: the agrarian and the grain laws of Gracchus, the distribution of bread by the government, the growing monopoly of the central power in nutritional-economic affairs, the gradual decline of autonomy and of the rights of private individuals, the limitation upon and factual abolishment of private property, the growth of the despotism of the central power, which finally led to dictatorships (Marius, Sulla, the Triumvirates, Caesar, Augustus) and to imperial power, etc. Various redistributions, confiscations, and nationalizations took place exactly during these periods. The central power ceased entirely to consider the personal and proprietary rights of citizens and interfered in everything, disregarding all laws which were not suited to its purpose.

These centuries were periods of severe impoverishment of the population of Italy, the increase of hunger and of differences in wealth and income. Later, during the first two centuries A.D. the economic condition of the masses improved very little, but neither did it worsen. Accordingly, the curve of statism did not fall significantly, but it did cease to rise.[66]

Another severe worsening of conditions occurred in the second half of the third century A.D., when victories were over, pillaging of conquered peoples ceased, and pressure by the barbarians increased. Roman trade fell off. The land became barren, agriculture declined, and so did industry. Imports of slaves ceased, and only the proletarian class increased steadily. Starvation threatened constantly. Briefly, a full economic crisis arrived, while the concentration of the wealth in a few hands became enormous.[67]

And what do we see? Beginning exactly in the third century

66. M. Rostovtzeff, *The Birth of the Roman Empire* (1918) (in Russian); [or see the English version, *Social and Economic History of the Roman Empire* (1926). E.S.]; cf. Wipper, *The History of the Roman Empire* (in Russian); G. Ferrero, *Greatness and Decline of Rome*, vols. 1–3 (1907); the corresponding chapters in Mommsen, *Roman History* (Moscow, 1887) (in Russian).

67. O. Seeck, *Geschichte des Unterganges der antiken Welt*, 1:318–68; Waltzing, op. cit., 2:263–64.

compulsory statism made a new colossal jump upwards. There were several manifestations of this. Central power became absolute and unlimited. The emperor assumed the role of a deity, who was above the law. Complete centralization and surveillance of all activities of the population followed. There was a complete loss of autonomy and freedom by the citizens. State-planned economics and the annihilation of private industry and trade prevailed. The monetary system was eliminated and replaced by taxes and duties. Different categories of rations were introduced. There was an enormous increase in the army of officials and clerks. Briefly, there was complete compulsory statism.

Waltzing gives a concrete picture of the situation during that period: "Watch is kept over the people and everything is controlled. To accomplish this a huge army of officials is created. They steal, plunder, and thus worsen the conditions. The state needs a tremendous income (for the court, for feeding the plebs, for the army, the officials, and the war). Furthermore, the work of the population and of the professional corporations, which were free before, now became obligatory and hereditary. *Corporati et collegiati* (the members of the professional unions) became the property of the state beginning with the third century. The government which intended to satisfy both private and public needs ended by enslaving even free labor. The artisan and the merchant had to devote themselves completely to their businesses, in a way similar to that of the peasant (*colonus*), who had to cultivate land. The empire was transformed into a huge workshop where, under the control of a large group of officials, everybody worked for the emperor, the state, and a few private individuals. Almost all industry was controlled by the state, which distributed the production unequally. All the inalienable rights of the citizens were abolished, and they were deprived of any freedom. The whole regime was based on compulsion; the hand of the government was everywhere, so was its tyranny, and private initiative and free labor did not exist." [68]

As a result of all this the Roman Empire perished. If we were to analyze in greater detail the above-mentioned relationship, we would see that during the years of famine (e.g., 20 and 18 B.C. and A.D. 5, 8, and 19, and also the year 58, during Trajan's reign) the curve of statism rose sharply.

68. Waltzing, op. cit., pp. 480–84.

Thus, the proposition under consideration is fully supported in the history of Rome. Several centuries later, a similar fate befell Byzantium where a regime of statism "killed all freedom and initiative in the great army of labor." [69]

The same proposition is also confirmed by the history of the Middle Ages. Once starvation appeared, the curve of statism also leaped upwards. A few facts may be mentioned briefly. Because of the famine of 792–93 Charles the Great introduced in the Frankish Synod the first taxation on prices.[70] During the famine of 805, imports and free trade were prohibited and strict regulation of prices was established. Since free prices generally were higher than the newly established ones, they had to be enforced by strict measures. Personal liberty was restricted completely, and compulsory statism developed in various forms.

Similarly during other periods of starvation in the medieval period, the regulation of prices, restrictions on free trade, and on imports and exports, cheap or free distribution of bread, the confiscation of the stores of rich people and their distribution among the poor, searches and requisitions, the establishment of maximum norms of what anyone could possess and the confiscation of the surplus, regulations on the planting of crops, specifications as to the size of a loaf of bread, etc.—all these forms of interference by the central powers, and the restriction of the autonomy of the people, were common during the famines. These phenomena occurred so often that it would be superfluous to list them. Therefore only a few cases are mentioned here. Others may be found in the literature cited.

During the great famine of 1201–2 in England, regulations for bread and beer were, for the first time, established for the entire country.[71] Further development of compulsory statism was manifested during the years 1483, 1512, 1521, and 1586.[72]

At the beginning of the seventeenth century, trade and England's dominance of the seas secured supplies of grain from the colonies, so that the menace of starvation, and with it the compulsory measures, disappeared. Free trade and self-regulation were established,

69. A work by Besobrazov is cited.
70. F. Curschmann, *Hungersnöte im Mittelalter*, p. 71.
71. Kovalevsky, *Economic Growth of Europe*, 3:22.
72. Ibid., pp. 287–91, 297–311, passim; Schanz, *Englische Handelspolitik gegen Ende des Mittelalters* (1881).

and the curve of statism fell. Later it fluctuated slightly, and then rose somewhat during the continental blockade and the Napoleonic wars.

Similar parallel movement of the curves of hunger and of compulsory statism also took place in the history of France. The principal edicts which regulated the economic-nutritional relationships also appeared there during the years of famine. Examples of these are the edicts of 1304–5, those of Francis I in 1565, the king's ordinances of 1567 and 1577, the orders in the Paris laws of 1391, 1591, and 1635, the decree of the Paris Parliament of 1662, and some other regulations in 1664, 1684, 1693, 1699, 1709, and other years.[73] As soon as hunger began to increase, compulsory interference also increased, and, conversely, when the former fell the latter did likewise.

When crops were good, the government was not concerned with feeding the population; bread was cheap and the rules of trade were relaxed. However, in times of famine the regulations were strictly enforced. Then searches and requisitions by special detachments became the norm. All the surplus of grain was seized and taken away. Trade, market, and prices all were regulated in every detail. Rationing and the sale of bread by the government at low prices were introduced. The land was plowed and sowed by a communal arrangement (as in the Russian kolkhoz), etc.[74]

Every rise in prices was considered suspicious by the government and the farmer was compelled to supply the market. During the famine of 1693 the amount of grain in the hands of the farmers was checked every month, and the person with any surplus was penalized. As soon as hunger diminished, the pressure of the central power also decreased. Whenever famine appeared, as for example, in 1708, all the regulations relating to bread were re-established.

The causal interdependence was manifested very sharply when the whole economic policy of the government was headed by persons ideologically opposed to governmental interference. Turgot may

73. Afanasiev, *The Conditions of the Food Trade in 18th-Century France*, p. 73 (in Russian); Araskhanianz, "Die Französische Getreidehandelpolitik zum Jahre 1789," *Staats und Socialwissenschaft Forschungen*, ed. Schmoller (1882), vol. 4, part 3, pp. 10–12.

74. See details in the works of Roscher, Ashley, Afanasiev, Schanz, Araskhanianz, Kovalevsky, and Tsitovich in *Hunger in the West* (1892) (in Russian); P. Clement, *La police sous Louis XIV* (1866).

serve as an example. In 1774 he issued an edict of free trade and tax reform. But the crop failure of 1774–75 quickly put an end to this freedom and forced Turgot himself to proclaim a number of regulatory measures. So the edict of 1774 remained only on paper. The same was repeated under Necker, Du Pont de Nemours, and in the period of the National Assembly. The latter issued a decree on free trade in 1789, but alas! Hunger increased during these years, and the law remained only on paper. Judicial decrees were annulled by the demands of necessity. During the first years of the Revolution no less than five similar edicts were issued; but, because of famine, they all remained inoperative. The severe famine of 1788–89 induced the growth of compulsory statism, which culminated, as is well known, in the maximum law of May 3, 1793, the law of September 29, 1793, and in the practices of the Jacobins who elevated compulsory statism to the maximum.

Under the dictatorship of the Jacobins (partially *de jure*, but mainly *de facto*), the amount of interference by the central power increased beyond limit. Personal as well as proprietary rights of the citizens were annulled, as was their autonomy; private property was factually annihilated. Confiscations, requisitions, and sequestrations became the rule, and communization and nationalization became the norm. Governmental power guarded and regulated everything. Even in the fields of thought, beliefs, marriage, esthetics, family, education, religion, morals, and the feelings of the individual, everything was sacrificed to the community. Such was the practical program of the Jacobins.[75]

Partially because everything had been equalized and nationalized and there was nothing more to plunder because proprietary differentiation had disappeared, but mainly because of continued famine, the maximum law was annulled on December 23, 1794. Nevertheless, government interference weakened very little.

We also see later on, during the Napoleonic period, a similar rise and decline of the degree of compulsory statism in connection with our independent variable. Because of starvation and wars, compulsory statism was extremely high during that period, one "charac-

---

75. H. Taine, *Les origines de la France contemporaine* (1885), 3:120–21; cf. pp. 370–72, 461–550, of this same volume; and Kropotkin, *The Great French Revolution*, pp. 434–42 (in Russian).

terized by the unlimited interference with the life of the country." [76]
All France became "a barracks."

Still later we see the rise of statism in 1812, 1817, 1837, 1848, and 1871, which were years of crop failures, crises, and the increase of famine.[77] Finally, the same phenomena were repeated in 1914 and 1918, when connected with the war and difficulties with food supplies.

A similar relationship can be observed in the history of Russia. During the years of increasing hunger (*ceteris paribus*) and in the presence of proprietary differentiation, compulsory statism occurred in a variety of forms. The following socioeconomic processes have served previously and are serving now as demonstrations of its rise.

1. *An increase of governmental regulation of the importation and exportation of foods.* An ancient chronicle stated that without the permission of the ruling prince the export of grain was prohibited in years of crop failure. So it was, for example, in Pskov, in 1279, 1452, and 1650, where the people were forbidden to sell rye grain abroad. During the reign of Peter I, permits to export were given only when the price of bread in Moscow was less than one ruble. When it was higher than that, "no permissions for overseas shipment were given." The same thing was repeated in the famine-stricken provinces during the time of Catherine II, and later in the years of 1789–1802, 1803–6, 1812, 1833–34, 1848, 1854–55, 1891–92, and 1905–6.[78] It also prevails during our era.

2. *Governmental regulation of the prices of bread and other foods.* During the famine of 1601 Tsar Boris fixed the prices of various grains (rye, oats, barley). Similar regulations were in force during the reigns of Alexei, Peter I, Catherine II, and later rulers.

3. *Various compulsory measures imposed by the government, such as compulsory declarations of the amount of foodstuffs available and limitations upon it; the establishment of the maximum norm; the obligation to deliver foodstuffs to the market; limits on the size of purchases; requisition of bread and other foods, as well as*

76. Kareev, *History of Western Europe*, 4:193, passim (in Russian).

77. Levasseur, *L'histoire des classes ouvrières*, 2:285–86, 337, passim.

78. Ermolov, *Our Crop Failures and the Problem of the Food Supply* (St. Petersburg, 1909), pt. 1, pp. 8, 14, 27, 55, 104–5, passim (in Russian); and Romanovitch-Slavatinsky, *Hunger in Russia* (Kiev, 1892), pp. 47–48, 56 (in Russian).

other limitations upon the rights of the ownership; searches; punishments for default; and other measures for interference by the central power in the regulation of nutritive and other economic conditions.

Such measures were in effect even before the famine of 1601–2. During those years, however, an inventory of the whole supply of grain was ordered, with requisitions from those who tried to hide it. "The clergy and the nobles were ordered to sell bread at a low price." Speculators were punished by whipping or imprisonment, and their stores were confiscated. The production of beer was entirely prohibited during the famine.[79] All of these practices were widely used during the reign of Alexei when a governmental monopoly on bread was declared. Similar conditions prevailed during the reign of Peter I. "Because many people die from starvation during the years of crop failures, it is necessary to have supplies to feed the poor. Therefore, investigate the amount of bread available, confiscate from the wealthy, leaving them just enough for their own nutrition, and distribute the remainder to the needy," proclaimed the Ukaz of 1723.[80] This system was adopted by the Ukaz of 1734, and it was further confirmed by the Ukaz of 1749–50. Under Biron a failure to disclose supplies was punishable by death. Similar measures were practiced during severe famines later in the history of both the central and the local governments. An inventory was made of the supply of bread in a number of regions during the famine of 1891–92. Owners were forbidden to sell foods without special permission, and local officials made thorough searches of the premises for undeclared supplies. The same also happened in 1918–21.

4. *The sale of food supplies by the government for a nominal price, or its free distribution to needy people.* This also is a very common feature during periods of starvation and it also shows the growth of compulsory statism. It took place during the famine of 1601–2 (the Tsar's charity), during Shuisky's rule, in 1674, 1682, etc. In the form of free loans, natural and monetary help, organization of free public dining halls, feeding stations, etc., the same thing was practiced later on, and even in our own times.

5. *The government-organized public work projects during the years of famine.* This was true in the past, as well as in the present.

79. Platonov, "The Moscow Famine of 1650–55," *Artelnoe Delo*, nos. 9–16 (1921) (in Russian).
80. Leshkoff, op. cit., pp. 494–95; Ermolov, *Crop Failures*, pp. 14–16.

6. *The government-organized special communal plowing and sowing of the land.* Thus, the ideas of "*sovkhoz*" and of "*kolkhoz*" are not new. Following a Ukaz of 1827 communal plowing of fields was organized with members of the "*mir*" sharing the work of growing and harvesting the crops under the supervision of special agents. In this way the influential originators of this project hoped to achieve miracles. During the famine year of 1834 the bureaucrats planned to put this scheme into practice. However, due to the negative report of experts from the institutes, it was rejected.

All these phenomena, which took place during severe famines and represented various expressions of compulsory statism, confirmed once more that similar causes under similar conditions produce similar consequences, and that an increase of hunger under definite conditions leads to an increase of compulsory statism.

If we examine in greater detail the measures which were indicated in the above paragraphs, the growth of compulsory statism becomes quite obvious. This can be accomplished by a study of a definite period of famine in our history, such as, for example, the reign of Alexei Mikhailovich.

This reign was characterized by prolonged periods of food shortages and starvation. The country had just emerged from the "troubled times," and war and the army completely emptied the stores of provisions, and in addition crop failures, speculation, bribery, etc., increased the catastrophe. Economic conditions were disastrous; people thought the "end of the world" was near and that "blood would be flowing up to their knees." Riots and disorders broke out, and as a result of all this, compulsory statism increased tremendously. This was expressed in several ways.

1. *A state monopoly of bread and other necessities.* According to the testimony of Ambassador Rodes the "bread belongs to His Majesty, and not a single person is permitted to sell it." [81] (Exactly the same happened in Russia in 1918–21.)

2. *The existence of a planned distribution of available supplies, with specification of the amounts of grain, cereals, etc., that should be delivered to the state by each region and province.* (Similar measures existed in 1918–22.)

81. Kurts, *The Condition of Russia in 1650–55, as Recorded in the Reports of Rodes,* p. 159 (in Russian).

3. *Compulsory requisitions of supplies when the orders of the planners were not fulfilled.* A report of an official of that period indicated that offenders were severely whipped. (In 1918–22 special detachments of "*pushkari*" [ruffians] roamed throughout the country.)

4. *The production of bread by the state.* Special fields were plowed, sowed, and harvested by governmental agents. (Similar to the Social Khoziaistva [Kolkhos] of 1918–22.)

5. *Compulsory measures regulating sowing and increasing the size of the fields.* The materials for the period were compiled by Novombergsky,[82] and they describe in great detail various punishments for failure to obey. (In 1918–22 the "sowing campaigns" were somewhat similar.)

6. *The storage of the grain that was collected and requisitioned and rigid governmental control and distribution: to whom to give, where-to send, how much to buy or sell, the price, etc.* (The same thing also occurred in 1918–22.)

7. *The issuance of governmental rations to employees.* (Exactly the same thing took place in 1918–22.)

8. *Fixed prices for bread.* (The same again in 1918–22.)

9. *Supplying bread on credit to those in need of it.*

Briefly, we see here a completely planned state economy in which private initiative had no place. Compulsory statism went still further by completely monopolizing the trade in salt, silks, furs, fish, tobacco, jewelry, etc., and by facilitating further enslavement of the population.

Finally, the events of the twentieth century also demonstrate the correctness of the proposition under consideration. Soon after the outbreak of war in 1914, the situation with respect to the food supply became critical in all of the countries involved. As the war continued these conditions became even worse. Keeping pace with the worsening of the problems of food supply, the curve of compulsory statism increased in all the belligerent countries, and later on it rose even in the neutral states. This rise was greatest in the countries which suffered most acutely from the shortage of food. Because of the threat of starvation (due to the decrease of imports), a Committee on the Food Supply was formed in England soon after the

82. Novombergsky, *Description of the Internal Governmental Policies in Russia in the XVII Century* (in Russian).

beginning of the war. Its functions were gradually increased and in 1916 it became the Royal Commission on the Wheat Supply. On December 26, 1916 a bill for governmental control of all food products was issued.

Thus, the industry and trade of all the beleaguered countries were subjected to governmental control to an extent unknown since medieval times. Even in England, which always had liberal traditions, a considerable proportion of economic activities gradually was subjected to governmental management, and a large number of businessmen ceased to be autonomous persons who were ready to sell and buy.[83] These tendencies were even more pronounced in Germany, France, and other countries, both belligerent and neutral.

As soon as the war ended and the food supply began to improve, the curve of statism declined. Economic crises prevented somewhat a further fall of statism, but as soon as these would be over, additional decline was expected.

The rise in the curve of compulsory statism was particularly sharp in Russia, where nutritional difficulties arose very soon after the beginning of the war and where they soon reached a critical stage.

The rise in the curve of compulsory statism was started, even before the October Revolution, by the Tsar's ministers, the Duma, and the Provisional Government—all adherents to an idea of freedom of industry and trade. In this respect the October Revolution added nothing new, except the introduction of special "class rations" and further centralization. Everything had already been done before October 25. The laws of necessity forced those who were far from idealizing compulsory statism themselves to perform that task, thus presenting an excellent example of verification of the proposed theorem.

The establishment of the "special council for unification of the governmental measures to supply food and feed," and further rules of October 25, 1915, which entitled the authorities to inventory the supplies of food in storage and in the markets, to investigate accounts and documents with the right to requisition and sequestration

83. Hilton, "Merchant Shipping and State Control," *Edinburgh Review* (April 1918), p. 359, passim; H. S. Early, "Phases of Food Control," *Edinburgh Review* (January 1918), pp. 108–30; Clynes, "Food Control in War and Peace," *The Economic Journal* (June 1920).

—all of these measures represented the Rubicon, the crossing of which started the tsarist government on the way of compulsory statism.

Further development was easy. The established Food Committee of the Soviets of Workers' and Peasants' Deputies, on May 5, 1917, had such great powers that the October Revolution could not add anything to them. Indeed, the decree regulating supplies led to a condition in which private and cooperative trade organizations were entirely eliminated, being replaced by governmental control. The same happened in the regulation of the distribution and consumption of food products. Here also ration cards and the norms of consumption were introduced before the Bolsheviks got power. Because of the civil war, the increase of famine, and proprietary differentiation, the October Revolution led only to the development of the final stages of communism and statism. The laws of necessity force people of entirely different ideologies to perform exactly the same works. In times of calamity the laws of necessity direct destiny.

Thus, by the year 1920 everything was equalized and communized. Poverty was universal, and there was nothing more to do to foster statism. The tremendous decrease in proprietary differentiation had to bring a decrease in compulsory statism, all the more because the equalization of wealth coincided with the end of the war, which itself is a factor opposed to statism. Conditions would have been favorable for a decrease in governmental control had it not been for the famine of 1921. Starvation hindered it, and, therefore, many discrepancies occurred between the decrees of the government and actual life.

From what has been said above, the following prognosis for the future can be established: Ceteris paribus, *with the increase of the wealth of a country and a decrease of famine, and if there is an average proprietary differentiation, the curve of compulsory statism will decrease under any power and form of the government, and vice versa.*

In conclusion we may accept three axioms: the validity of the principal theorem of a relationship between hunger and compulsory statism, as well as that of the two additional theorems, which determine in greater detail that relationship: the proposition that under similar conditions similar causes produce similar consequences, and the correctness of the statement that "nothing is new under the sun." That which many people think is unusual and absolutely new has occurred before many, many times. Only the actors, the stage settings, the costumes, the places, and the times are different; but the play itself is very old, repeated time after time in the history of mankind.

History presents very old things and ideas in new dresses. It is like an old writer, who has exhausted his creative ability and therefore repeats himself. Compulsory statism, which is considered by many as a new and higher form of social organization, is a very old form of power. It has existed for ages. Many people still promote the idea of "the socialist society," which in reality usually turns out to be nothing more than statism. It is quite understandable why the popularity of the ideology of socialism had risen during these years of war and impoverishment. But as this study indicates, it is false to assume, as many socialists do, that truly socialistic governments have not existed previously, and that nationalization has brought positive results. The experiences of Russia and other countries studied in this volume indicate just the opposite: namely, nationalization, communization, and the development of statism leads to poverty, not to prosperity, and by no means do they improve the social conditions of the masses.

Caveat consules!

Pitirim A. Sorokin
Professor of Sociology
University of Leningrad
1922